Urbanization and Growth

Commission on Growth and Development

Urbanization and Growth

Edited by Michael Spence, Patricia Clarke Annez,
and Robert M. Buckley

Contributions by
Michael Spence
Patricia Clarke Annez and Robert M. Buckley
Richard Arnott
Gilles Duranton
Dwight M. Jaffee
Sukkoo Kim
John M. Quigley
Anthony J. Venables

COMMISSION ON GROWTH AND DEVELOPMENT

1818 H Street NW
Washington, DC 20433
Telephone: 202-473-1000
Internet: www.worldbank.org
        www.growthcommission.org
E-mail: info@worldbank.org
        contactinfo@growthcommission.org

This volume is a product of the Commission on Growth and
Development, which is sponsored by the following organizations:

Australian Agency for International Development (AusAID)
Dutch Ministry of Foreign Affairs
Swedish International Development Cooperation Agency (SIDA)
U.K. Department of International Development (DFID)
The William and Flora Hewlett Foundation
The World Bank Group

ISBN: 978-0-8213-7573-0
eISBN: 978-0-8213-7574-7
DOI: 10.1596/978-0-8213-7573-0

Library of Congress Cataloging-in-Publication Data
Urbanization and growth / edited by Michael Spence, Patricia Clarke
Annez, and Robert M. Buckley.
    p. cm.
  Includes bibliographical references and index.
  ISBN 978-0-8213-7573-0 — ISBN 978-0-8213-7574-7 (electronic)
  1. Urban economics. 2. Urbanization—Economic aspects. 3. Cities and
towns—Growth. I. Spence, Michael. II. Annez, Patricia Clarke. III.
Buckley, Robert M.
  HT321.U338 2008
  330.9173'2—dc22

                                                        2008044060

Cover design: Naylor Design

Contents

Boxes

Figures

Tables

Preface

The Commission on Growth and Development was established in April 2006 as a response to two insights: we do not talk about growth enough, and when we do, we speak with too much confidence. Too often, people overlook economic growth when thinking about how to tackle the world's most pressing problems, such as poverty, illiteracy, income inequality, unemployment, and pollution. At the same time, our understanding of economic growth is less definitive than commonly thought—even though advice is often given to developing countries with great confidence. Consequently, the Commission's mandate is to "take stock of the state of theoretical and empirical knowledge on economic growth with a view to drawing implications for policy for the current and next generation of policy makers."

To help assess the state of knowledge, the Commission invited leading academics and policy makers from around the world to a series of 12 workshops, held in 2007 and 2008 in Washington, D.C., New York, and New Haven, and commissioned a series of thematic papers. These papers reviewed areas such as monetary and fiscal policy, climate change, inequality, growth, and urbanization—the subject of this volume. In addition, 25 case studies were commissioned to explore the dynamics of growth in specific countries. Each presentation benefited from comments by members of the Commission and other workshop participants from the worlds of policy, theory, and practice.

The workshops turned out to be intense and lively affairs, lasting up to three days. It became clear that experts do not always agree, even on issues that are central to growth. The Commission had no wish to disguise or gloss over these uncertainties and differences. It did not want to present a false confidence in its conclusions, beyond that justified by the evidence. Researchers do not always know the correct "model" that would explain the world they observe; and even if they know the factors that matter, they cannot always measure them convincingly.

While researchers will continue to improve our knowledge of the world, policy makers cannot wait for scholars to satisfy all of their doubts or resolve their differences. Decisions must be made with only partial knowledge of the world. One consequence is that most policy decisions, however well-informed, take on the character of experiments, which yield useful information about the way the world works, even if they do not always turn out the way policy makers hoped. It is as well to recognize this fact, if only so that policy makers can be quick to spot failures and learn from mistakes.

The workshops on cities and housing were held in March and May 2007. We were immensely fortunate to benefit from the wisdom and insights of outstanding researchers and experienced practitioners. We are grateful to all of the participants, who are listed below. The remainder of this preface is not an exhaustive summary of the workshops or the chapters in this volume. It instead replays some highlights of the discussion and presents some of the ideas that shaped the conclusions of the Commission's final report, *The Growth Report: Strategies for Sustained Growth and Inclusive Development.*

Productivity and Cities

Structural change is a key driver of rapid growth: countries diversify into new industries, firms learn new things, people move to new locations. Anything that slows this structural change is also likely to slow growth. Because urbanization is one of the most important enabling parallel processes in rapid growth, making it work well is critical.

Deciding whether urbanization causes growth or growth causes urbanization is very difficult, and largely beside the point. We know of no countries that either achieved high incomes or rapid growth without substantial urbanization, often quite rapid. There is a robust relationship between urbanization and per capita income: nearly all countries become at least 50 percent urbanized before reaching middle-income status, and all high-income countries are 70–80 percent urbanized. In all known cases of high and sustained growth, urban manufacturing and services led the process, while increases in agricultural productivity freed up the labor force that moved to the cities and manned the factories. In the high-growth cases that we examined in the Growth Commission, the average productivity of a worker in manufacturing or services is on the order of three to five times that of a worker in traditional sectors, and sometimes much more.

Urbanization deserves attention not to the detriment of improving agricultural productivity and rural livelihoods, but as a complement to such measures. Improving agricultural incomes is very important for reducing poverty among the large numbers of people living in the rural areas of poor countries today. Still, no amount of growth in the rural sector is going to match the productivity increase that is caused by people moving across that boundary into high-productivity employment.

Urbanization's contribution to growth comes from two sources: the difference between rural and urban productivity levels and more rapid productivity change in cities. In the early decades of development, when the majority of the population is still rural, the jump from rural to urban employment makes a big contribution to growth. As cities grow larger, the second effect—faster gains in urban productivity—begins to dominate, as it operates on a larger base.

For these reasons, making urbanization work well is something that countries that want to grow quickly must learn to do. There are two important parts of making it work. The first challenge is to foster the growth of high-productivity activities that benefit from agglomeration and scale economies in developing country cities. The second involves managing the likely side effects of the economic success of cities—congestion, regional inequality, and high prices of land and housing. Meeting this second challenge is essential for mitigating the divisive impacts of successful economic growth and spreading the benefits of higher economic productivity widely.

Why is productivity higher in cities? Why, in other words, is proximity a source of efficiency? The cost of transport is one obvious reason why economic activity might cluster around a harbor or crossroads. Infrastructure and other public services are also cheaper to provide to densely packed populations. City dwellers may also benefit from knowledge spillovers: some theories predict that the aggregate gains from schooling are greater than the (sum of the) returns to individuals, implying that people learn a lot from each other without paying for it.

In addition to understanding what happens within cities, it is important to grasp what unfolds between them, and between cities and the rural hinterland. Urbanization can pose challenges that extend far beyond a mayor's jurisdiction. The migration from the countryside to the cities may, for example, be uncomfortably quick for people already living in cities, who face sharper competition for common, limited resources. Accommodating these pressures requires investments in infrastructure, often in public goods, which, in turn, tests government's capacity to mobilize new public resources and to shift the balance of spending towards cities. The economic success of cities may result in glaring income gaps between them and the rural hinterland, while making a new economic elite more visible to low-income groups flocking to urban areas. The agglomeration economies that make cities productive usually involve externalities or spillovers. Newcomers to cities impose costs that others must bear, and create benefits that others may capture. These externalities create a bias for an established city that makes it hard for secondary cities to grow, even if it would be more efficient to do so. Such "growing pains" may be part and parcel of the modernization process. But to sustain rapid growth, policy makers need to contain the social and political tensions they create.

"Primacy"—the dominance of one city over all others—is one example. In developing countries, one city (such as Dhaka, Jakarta, Bangkok, or São Paulo) often outstrips the others. Governments often feel obliged to even things out. Should they do so? On the one hand, robust empirical evidence shows that productivity increases with the size of cities. On the other, some empirical evidence suggests that excessive "primacy" may reduce overall growth. Precisely how it does so is not clear, however. Nor is it clear that governments can or should act on this result. This issue sparked considerable discussion in the workshops and remains unsettled among scholars. It may, in any case, be easier to cope with the congestion (and other costs) of large cities than to divert the geography of growth away from one city and toward its rivals. Ideally, we would know much more about when cities become too large to accommodate further growth and how to counteract excessive city size effectively.

Financing Urbanization

Economies rarely grow without their cities growing. But urbanization has its "dark side." According to a UN survey, the vast majority of policy makers resist urbanization rather than welcome it. They would prefer to stem the urban tide and see people return to rural areas. This disaffection with urbanization reflects more than just nostalgia for simpler times. Rapid urbanization brings about real social and political headaches, such as overcrowding, concentrated squalor, crime, street violence, and the quick transmission of disease. Urbanization is probably inevitable and ultimately desirable. The question is not how to stop it, but how to reap its benefits without paying too high a cost.

Infrastructure and public services are part of the answer, and possibly the whole answer. According to some estimates, $40 trillion of infrastructure spending is required to meet the needs of cities in developing countries. Where is that money going to come from? Devising means of financing such vast expenditures is probably the biggest challenge for urbanization policy in developing countries.

The economic benefits of cities are often reflected in property prices. It should therefore be possible for the government to capture a share of these benefits by taxing land or property. It could then spend the proceeds on the infrastructure required to offset some of the costs of cities, such as congestion. Economists find the idea appealing. But local government officials think property taxes are a big headache in practice, and they have not proven to be a rich source of investment finance.

Property taxes are cumbersome, costly to administer, and highly unpopular everywhere. In developing countries, the challenges multiply. The administrative and political demands of property taxes are particularly ill-suited to local governments still building their technical capacity and credibility with the public. In many developing countries, the property market is underdeveloped and overregulated. Large tracts of land languish in public hands. Private transactions are underreported because they are heavily taxed. Rents may be controlled, depressing the value of the real estate. In the absence of reliable market prices, officials must arrive at their own estimation of property values, a job that demands some skill and leaves ample discretion. This discretion in turn opens the door to corruption. Besides, it takes time to raise a significant sum from property and land taxes. In countries with a history of exploitative landlords, heavy property taxes will be strongly resisted. Many properties in rapidly growing cities are informal and unserviced, leaving them out of the tax net. Lastly, property taxes are typically designed to generate a steady stream of income reflecting the flow of benefits to property owners. Financing "lumpy" infrastructure investments with a property tax thus requires the additional hurdle of tapping financial markets, which are usually in an embryonic state when rapid urbanization takes hold. Over the long run, property taxes will likely become a mainstay of local taxation in developing countries as they are in the developed world. But in a transitional phase, these taxes must be supplemented by creative and perhaps unorthodox approaches to urban finance, including some methods used historically in developed countries.

Some countries have raised money by capturing land asset values in transactions with the private sector, be they leases, sales, developer's exactions, or betterment levies. In a fast-growing economy, these transactions can be lucrative, raising large multiples of the sums available from other budgetary sources. In places like Hong Kong, China, the terms of a lease have been tweaked and adjusted to help shape a city, without the heavy-handedness of zoning. Economies and regions around the world—ranging from China; Hong Kong, China; and Singapore to Egypt; South Africa; India; Chile; and the rapidly growing jurisdictions in the western United States—have raised substantial sums to finance infrastructure using these techniques.

There are disadvantages. Asset transactions are inherently limited and should be used for investments rather than recurring costs. Leasing transactions may help shape the city, but long-term leases may also make it difficult to change land-use patterns. There is the potential for abuse and corruption in large one-time transactions involving valuable tracts of urban land. But whatever the relative merits of selling land, leasing it, or taxing property, the alternatives may be worse. In many developing country cities, for example, governments administer large tracts of underused land. This acreage is not put to the best use the market can find for it. Nor does it typically yield the government much revenue. It is a good way to squander a precious asset.

Capturing land asset values is lucrative and fraught with risks. It can reduce the need for central budgetary support that has usually been required for financing major urban infrastructure improvements. But land asset–based finance also needs a supporting framework and supervision from higher levels of government. Whatever specific techniques are deployed, it is unrealistic to expect cities to "go it alone" for financing the infrastructure transformation that is needed to make urbanization work.

Urbanization and Regional Inequalities

The economist Simon Kuznets hypothesized that as countries grow richer, inequality would first rise, then fall, tracing out the so-called "Kuznets curve." The curve has a spatial equivalent: the income gap between urban and rural areas first widens, then narrows. In the United States, for example, regional inequality rose from 1820 to 1940, but declined thereafter. Whether developing economies will repeat this pattern remains to be seen. China took a conscious decision to tolerate inequality in its quest for growth. "We will let some regions and some people get rich first," Deng Xiaoping famously said.

Some urban labor markets cope better than others with the influx of new labor. In the United States, mass immigration was accompanied by rising real wages from 1820. Immigrants from Europe and elsewhere found work in an expanding manufacturing sector that offered plentiful unskilled jobs. With the advent of mechanization in the 1920s, the demand for skills rose. But by that time, American high schools were turning out educated workers and policy makers had partially closed the door to immigration. The important conclusion is that if labor-intensive manufacturing is growing, economies can absorb migrants from the fields or foreign countries relatively easily.

In many developing country cities, most jobs, including those for new migrants, are in the informal sector of the economy. Although informal employment is on the rise in many countries, rich and poor, we know relatively little about the productivity of this sector or the mobility of workers from informal employment to formal jobs. However, research in Africa indicates that informal work in the cities is more productive than agricultural labor, even if it is considerably less productive than formal employment. In Ghana, for example, the differential between informal work in the cities and agricultural work was estimated at 2:1. Few of the workers in the informal sector seemed to escape into formal jobs. But perhaps their children will make the leap. We need further research to find out.

Urbanization also has implications for the position of women. In the United States, it was mostly men who migrated in waves to factory jobs in the cities. But this pattern is not universal. In China, for example, early migrants to the cities were often women. This remains true today in those industries that require refined motor skills. In the long run, cities promote growth, and growth enfranchises women. As incomes rise and female education improves, women have fewer children and enjoy higher rates of employment.

There was considerable discussion of whether government intervention could reduce spatial inequalities, and which policies actually succeed. Policy makers often feel obliged to reduce spatial disparities. But many of these efforts to promote some regions over others did not achieve much. Heavy investments in U.S. highways and targeted regional interventions in the EU may have facilitated convergence. But poorer countries face tighter budget constraints and fewer options. Central governments should probably devote their efforts to helping people move from lagging areas to prospering ones, rather than spending large sums on remote infrastructure that may be underused. Yet very difficult choices arise when regional income inequalities coincide with other social divisions such as ethnicity or religion. In such circumstances, fostering a sense of regional balance may become critical to national cohesion, and policy research thus far offers little firm guidance on how to do this.

Housing and Land Markets

As people move to cities in large numbers, the demand for housing and serviced land in urban areas expands rapidly. Unfortunately, the market rarely meets this demand affordably. Ill-conceived planning laws and building standards coupled with insufficient public finance for infrastructure mean that supply responds sluggishly. As a result, the price of land and housing rises beyond the reach of poor people. Even in desperately poor countries such as Bangladesh, big-city land prices can be comparable to prices in industrialized nations.

The Republic of Korea provides one example of a dramatic effort to raise supply. By the late 1980s, the cost of housing had far outpaced GDP. The ratio of house prices to income reached 13:1, as compared with 3:1 in the United States. The government stepped in. Overnight, 25 percent of the country's land was declared "urban," clearing the way for real estate development, compared with 5 percent before. In addition, 2 million homes were added to the housing stock over seven to eight years. Today, Korea's house-price-to-income ratio is about 3.5:1.

The case of Singapore is also revealing. Singapore's government controlled the land and maintained a near monopoly over house-building. Quite exceptionally, the government could also control migration since the borders of the city and the nation coincided. In contrast to Eastern Europe, where unresponsive state monopolies produced low-quality, high-cost housing, Singapore's public housing was standardized and cheap. Its heavy housing subsidies served both social and economic ends. They brought an end to squalid slums and defused ethnic strife. They also ensured the wage competitiveness of workers in Singapore's small, open economy, which had pinned its hopes on foreign investment and exporting success.

The success of Singapore's housing subsidies is more the exception than the rule, however, and they carried significant risks. Its provident fund, a mandatory saving scheme, was heavily invested in real estate. If Singapore had ever suffered a housing downturn, the consequences might have been disastrous. Fortunately, the economy thrived and home prices did not tumble. Subsidies for housing can become a political necessity, but they are also costly and hard to confine to the poor. Certainly, they should not be seen as a substitute for serious efforts to expand supply, including the supply of public services that often constrain efficient land use. Only a greater supply of serviced land and housing can lower costs, because it helps to solve the problem at its root as well as contain the fiscal burden of subsidies. In Mexico, for example, an upfront subsidy was combined with efforts to provide better infrastructure and security of tenure, allowing households to make investments in their home on their own.

Mortgages can improve households' ability to buy decent housing. But finance relaxes demand constraints only. Unless it is accompanied by measures to increase supply, better finance may result in overshooting prices. This volatility can jeopardize macroeconomic stability. In a typical pattern, strong income growth leads to a rapid increase in housing demand. An injection of liquidity from some source, often overseas, may help overstimulate the market, leading to overoptimism and a dangerous concentration of wealth in real estate. This leaves buyers and bankers dangerously exposed when the bubble bursts, as illustrated by Thailand and Hong Kong, China, in 1997, Shanghai in 2003, and recently in the United States. In Sweden, the relaxation of mortgage-lending regulation left banks overexposed to a housing bubble and very vulnerable in the face of an economic contraction.

Concluding Remarks

Rapid and sustained growth entails rapid and sustained urbanization. But, if mishandled, the growth of cities poses problems that can derail growth. Developing countries must accomplish in a few decades what today's industrialized countries achieved over a century or more. Policy makers are, as the *Growth Report* puts it, navigating uncharted waters with a set of incomplete, sometimes inaccurate, maps.

Their task is made no easier by the data at their disposal. Several speakers at the workshop noted that data on housing and real estate markets in developing countries are woeful, much worse than figures on agriculture, for example. This impedes intelligent consideration of policies. Better data could support stronger research on urban economics, finance, and the real estate market, which has been relatively neglected in developing countries. It is our hope that this volume will help people understand the role of urbanization in growth and tackle the formidable challenges it poses.

A. Michael Spence

Workshop Participants

Abdel-Rahman, Hesham, University of New Orleans
Alm, James, Georgia State University
Angel, Solly, New York University
Annez, Patricia Clarke, World Bank
Arnott, Richard, Boston College
Asabere, Paul, Fox School of Business and Management, Temple University
Bertaud, Alain, Independent Consultant
Bosworth, Barry, The Brookings Institution
Brueckner, Jan, University of California at Irvine
Buckley, Robert, Rockefeller Foundation
Chiquier, Loic, World Bank
Cho, Man, The Korea Development Institute (KDI) School
Deichmann, Uwe, World Bank
De Mello, Luiz, Organisation for Economic Co-operation and Development (OECD)
Duranton, Gilles, University of Toronto
Durlauf, Steven, University of Wisconsin-Madison
Eldhagen, Erik, Swedish International Development Cooperation Agency (SIDA)
Freire, Maria Emilia, World Bank
Green, Richard, George Washington University
Hannah, Lawrence, World Bank
Hegedüs, József, Metropolitan Research Institute, Budapest, Hungary
Henderson, Vernon, Brown University
Hesse, Heiko, World Bank
Hwang, Min, George Washington University

Jaffee, Dwight M., University of California, Berkeley

Kalarickal, Jerry, World Bank

Kharas, Homi, Wolfensohn Center for Development, The Brookings Institution

Kim, Sukkoo, Washington University in St. Louis

Laszek, Jacek, Central Bank of Poland

Leamer, Edward, University of California-Los Angeles

Leipziger, Danny, Growth Commission Vice Chair, World Bank

Logan, John, Brown University

Malpezzi, Steve, University of Wisconsin-Madison

Mulas, Alberto, Sociedad Hipotecaria Federal (SHF), Mexico City

Nowak, Dorota, World Bank

Olsen, Edgar, University of Virginia

Peterson, George, The Urban Institute

Quigley, John, University of California, Berkeley

Rivlin, Alice M., The Brookings Institution

Singh, Smita, William and Flora Hewlett Foundation

Sheppard, Stephen, Williams College

Spence, Michael, Growth Commission Chair, Stanford University

Sridhar, Shri S., National Housing Bank, Government of India

Stephens, Mark, The University of York, United Kingdom

Thalwitz, Margret, Global Partnership Program, World Bank

Sir Dwight Venner, Commissioner, Governor, Eastern Caribbean Central Bank

Van den Noord, Paul, European Commission

Van Order, Robert, University of Michigan

Villani, Kevin E., San Diego State University

Whitehead, Christine, London School of Economics

Wong, Grace, University of Pennsylvania

Wu, Weiping, Virginia Commonwealth University

Yezer, Anthony, George Washington University

Yusuf, Shahid, World Bank

Zagha, Roberto, World Bank

Chapter Summaries

In Chapter 1, Annez and Buckley set the context for the rest of the book. They discuss the broad macro relationships between growth and urbanization as well as some of the well-documented microeconomic findings that underpin these linkages. Despite the clear link between cities and growth, policy makers and the development community are often ambivalent about urbanization (although attitudes differ considerably by region and country). The chapter concludes that the policy debate needs to change the question. Instead of asking whether to promote urbanization or curtail it, the debate should consider how to support the structural shifts that urbanization makes necessary.

In Chapter 2, Anthony Venables examines globalization through the lens of economic geography. The chapter argues that cumulative causation processes are fundamental to understanding growth and development. Such processes derive from spatially concentrated increasing returns to scale, including thick-market effects, knowledge spillovers, sectoral and urban clustering, and self-reinforcing improvements in physical and social infrastructure. These sources of agglomeration have been extensively analyzed in the economic geography literature. They imply that spatial unevenness in economic activity and incomes is an equilibrium outcome. Growth tends to be "lumpy," with some sectors in some countries growing fast while other countries lag. The policy challenge is to lift potential new centers of economic activity to the point where they can reap the advantages of increasing returns and cumulative causation.

Chapter 3, authored by Gilles Duranton, develops a consistent framework for considering the effects of urbanization and cities on productivity and economic growth in developing countries. There is strong evidence that cities bolster productive efficiency in developing countries, just as they do in developed economies. Regarding whether cities promote self-sustained growth, the evidence is suggestive but ultimately inconclusive. These findings imply that the traditional agenda of aiming to raise within-city efficiency should be continued. Furthermore, reducing the obstacles to the reallocation of factors across cities is also desirable.

In Chapter 4, John Quigley discusses the insights from the burgeoning theoretical and empirical literature on urban agglomeration. He reviews the linkages between urbanization and economic development and articulates the relationship between urban density and potential increases in productivity—through specialization, complementarities in production, through the diffusion of knowledge and mimicry, and simply through size and scale. The factors limiting the efficient sizes of cities are analyzed. The chapter reviews empirical knowledge—from underdeveloped countries as well as high-income industrial societies—about the importance and magnitudes of these productivity gains. The analysis documents the close link between gains in economic efficiency and the urbanization of populations in most parts of the world.

Chapter 5, by Sukkoo Kim, examines the question of spatial inequality in the growth process. Spatial inequality is an important feature of many developing countries that seems to increase with economic growth and development. At the same time, there seems to be little consensus on the causes of spatial inequality or on a list of effective policy instruments that may foster or reduce spatial inequality. This chapter examines the theoretical and empirical literature on spatial inequality to learn what we know and do not know about the causes of spatial inequality, to investigate what policies may or may not ameliorate spatial inequality, and to determine whether policy makers can identify and implement policies that promote or reduce spatial inequality.

The next two chapters turn to housing issues. Urbanization and growth bring a new set of forces into play in real estate markets. Oftentimes the result is rapid increases in housing costs, which have both social and political implications. The economic case for intervention in housing markets may be weak, but most governments face considerable pressure to do something about housing to make it more affordable for the middle class and to rid cities of unsightly and unhealthy slums. Choosing the policy response wisely is an important element in managing urbanization.

In Chapter 6, Richard Arnott considers the options for governments to improve housing affordability. He underscores the important role of informality, which limits the fiscal capacity of local governments to invest in infrastructure. Informality also makes it difficult to reach poor households with efficient subsidies. Arnott examines the feasibility of offering the kinds of housing subsidies used in developed countries, especially rental subsidies provided to households. He finds that informality would significantly hamper efficient delivery. Given these constraints, Arnott recommends a focus on providing infrastructure rather than housing for the poor. He also suggests policies that might improve the functioning of urban land markets.

In Chapter 7, Dwight Jaffee discusses the mortgage market, often seen as a solution for improving housing access in developing countries. He examines lessons for developing countries drawn from the recent subprime mortgage crisis in the United States. His chapter identifies failures and scope for better policies at three different levels: (i) mortgage lending to subprime borrowers, (ii) securitization of mortgages, and (iii) financial markets and institutions. He notes that this crisis is similar to others in that it follows financial innovations. He recommends various regulatory actions to limit risks of future crises. These lessons are of relevance to developing countries, which are under growing pressure to reap the benefit of increasingly sophisticated but risky financial instruments.

About the Editors and Contributors

Patricia Clarke Annez is Urban Advisor at the World Bank. With over 20 years of experience there, she has worked in Operations and Finance as well as the central Urban Unit, where she works on strategy and project development and analysis of performance of Bank urban projects. She was a member of the core team of the *World Development Report 1992* on Development and the Environment. She has also worked as an economic and financial advisor for large U.S. and Canadian corporations. She recently published *Financing Cities: Fiscal Responsibility and Urban Infrastructure in Brazil, China, India, South Africa and Poland* (Sage 2007) with George E. Peterson and *Lessons for the Urban Century: Decentralized Infrastructure Finance in the World Bank* (World Bank 2008; with Gwenaélle Huet and George E. Peterson).

Richard Arnott is Distinguished Professor of Economics at the University of California, Riverside. He was at Queen's University from 1975 to 1988 and at Boston College from 1988 to 2007. His areas of research interest include public economics and the economics of information, but the bulk of his research has been in urban economic theory, especially urban land use, housing, and transportation. He has extensive editorial experience, including serving as an editor for *Regional Science and Urban Economics* and *Journal of Economic Geography*.

Robert M. Buckley is a Managing Director at the Rockefeller Foundation, where he helps develop the Foundation's approach to addressing urbanization issues in developing countries. Prior to Rockefeller, he served as an Advisor at the World Bank, where he led the development of new approaches to understanding the ramifications of rapidly increasing urbanization in the developing world. During his years at the Bank, he had the opportunity to work all over the world helping to prepare projects and undertaking studies. The studies have been published in more than 30 academic articles and in a number of Bank studies on development effectiveness, housing policy, and urbanization in transition economies. Buckley also served as the Chief Economist for the U.S. Department of Housing and Urban Development, and has taught at a number of universities including Johns Hopkins University, the Maxwell School at Syracuse University, and the Wharton School at the University of Pennsylvania.

Gilles Duranton holds the Noranda Chair in International Trade and Development in the Department of Economics at the University of Toronto, and is also a Philip-Leverhulme Prize winner (2003). His research interests are both theoretical and empirical. On the theory side, he is interested in the modeling of urban systems and the micro-foundations of agglomeration economies. His empirical work is concerned with the measurement of location and concentration in continuous space, the estimation of urban increasing returns, and the identification of spatial externalities. He served as consultant on regional and urban policy for various European governments and international organizations.

Dwight M. Jaffee is the Willis Booth Professor of Banking, Finance, and Real Estate at the Haas School of Business, University of California, Berkeley, where he has taught since 1991. He previously taught for many years in the economics department of Princeton University. Professor Jaffee is a member of the Haas School's Finance and Real Estate Groups, and co-chair of the Fisher Center for Real Estate and Urban Economics. His primary areas of research include real estate finance (in particular, mortgage-backed securitization and the government-sponsored enterprises) and insurance (in particular, earthquakes, terrorism, and auto). He has served in advisory roles for the World Bank, the Federal Reserve System, the Office of Federal Housing Enterprise Oversight, and the U.S. Department of Housing and Urban Development.

Sukkoo Kim is Associate Professor at the Department of Economics, Washington University in St. Louis. He is also a Research Associate in the Development of the Economy Program at the National Bureau of Economic Research. His areas of interest are economic history, urban and regional economics, and international trade. His current research focuses on understanding the long-run patterns of U.S. economic geography, the rise and growth of the modern business enterprises, the development of institutions in the United States and India, and more recently, the rise of urban primacy in the Americas.

John M. Quigley is the I. Donald Terner Distinguished Professor, and Professor of Economics, at the University of California, Berkeley. He also holds appointments in the Goldman School of Public Policy and the Haas School of Business. He directs the Berkeley Program on Housing and Urban Policy. His current research is focused on the integration of real estate, mortgage, and financial markets; urban labor markets; housing; spatial economics; and local public finance.

Michael Spence is Senior Fellow, the Hoover Institution, and Philip H. Knight Professor Emeritus of Management, Graduate School of Business, Stanford University. He was awarded the Nobel Memorial Prize in Economic Sciences in 2001. Mr. Spence was Philip H. Knight Professor and Dean of the Stanford Business School from 1990 to 1999. Since 1999, he has been a partner at Oak Hill Capital Partners. From 1975 to 1990, he served as Professor of Economics and Business Administration at Harvard University. Mr. Spence was awarded the John Kenneth Galbraith Prize for excellence in teaching in 1978 and the John Bates Clark Medal in 1981 for a "significant contribution to economic thought and knowledge." He was appointed Chairman of the Economics Department at Harvard in 1983 and served as the Dean of the Faculty of Arts and Sciences from 1984 to 1990. At various times, he has served as a member of the editorial boards of *American Economics Review, Bell Journal of Economics, Journal of Economic Theory,* and *Public Policy.* Professor Spence is the Chair of the Commission on Growth and Development.

Anthony J. Venables is the BP Professor of Economics at the University of Oxford and Director of the Centre for the Analysis of Resource Rich Economies. He is a Fellow of the British Academy and of the Econometric Society. He has formerly worked as chief economist in the U.K. Department for International Development, as Professor at the London School of Economics, and as research manager of the trade research group in the World Bank. He has published extensively in the areas of international trade and spatial economics, including work on trade and imperfect competition, economic integration, multinational firms, and economic geography.

Acknowledgments

The editors are most grateful for the strong support provided by the sponsors of the Commission on Growth and Development: the Governments of Australia, Sweden, the Netherlands, and the United Kingdom, and The William and Flora Hewlett Foundation and The World Bank Group. Danny Leipziger, Vice President of the Poverty Reduction and Economic Management Network, and Kathy Sierra, Vice President of the Sustainable Development Network in the World Bank, were generous in providing resources for this effort. We are much obliged to the participants in the workshops on Urbanization and Housing Markets sponsored by the Commission, especially the chapter authors and Uwe Deichmann of the World Bank for their numerous and diverse insights and the time they dedicated to engaging in discussions of the issues. Roberto Zagha, secretary of the Commission, was a constant source of good ideas, encouragement, and stimulation. He has a gentle way of bringing out the best in others while keeping a razor sharp focus on the central driving issues at hand. The level of discussion and the quality of the papers that follow reflect his enthusiasm and wisdom.

A team of colleagues in the Growth Commission secretariat, Muriel Darlington, Diana Manevskaya and Dorota Nowak, were dedicated to making every aspect of the Commission's work successful. They gave us what felt like undivided attention in organizing the workshops and producing this book—just one of many Growth Commission activities with pressing deadlines and low tolerance for error. The whole process was only possible due to their marvelous organization and steady hard work. Diana Manevskaya, in particular, did a beautiful job in assisting with the editorial process, displaying good sense, good taste, and boundless dedication to finishing well and on time. Jerry Kalarickal and Oriane Raulet provided expert research assistance in preparing the book for publication. Aziz Gökdemir was pragmatic, accommodating, and rigorous in preparing the manuscript for publication. He never missed his deadlines and was very kind when we occasionally needed to shift ours. Stephen McGroarty oversaw the publication process with great skill. We thank Simon Cox of the *Economist* for his excellent work on the preface.

We would like to pay a special tribute to the late Edward M. Gramlich. He was Senior Fellow at the Urban Institute at the time of his death, and had been Provost and Professor of Economics at the University of Michigan, and Governor of the Federal Reserve System of the United States, to name just a few of the important responsibilities confided to him. He brought us many valuable insights in the early stages of preparing this volume although the sudden onset of his final illness prevented further participation. His words at his confirmation hearing in 1997 for the Federal Reserve appointment offer inspiration for anyone responsible for policy: "Sometimes, one's advice must be weighted toward economic practicality, sometimes toward humanity. A good economist should know how to balance both objectives." We would like to dedicate this volume to his memory.

Michael Spence
Patricia Clarke Annez
Robert M. Buckley

Abbreviations

AGOA	African Growth and Opportunity Act
APR	annual percentage rate
CDI	City Development Index
CDPO	constant proportion debt obligation
CERAP	China Economic Research and Advisory Programme
CDO	collateralized debt obligation
CP	commercial paper
CRA	credit rating agency
EU	European Union
FHA	Federal Housing Administration
FICO	Fair Isaac Company
FMA	foreign market access
GDP	gross domestic product
GNMA	Government National Mortgage Association, Ginnie Mae
GSE	government-sponsored enterprise
HMDA	Home Mortgage Disclosure Act
HOEPA	Homeowners Equity Protection Act
HUD	U.S. Department of Housing and Urban Development
LP	Loan Performance
LTCM	Long-Term Capital Management
MBS	mortgage-backed securities
MOC	Mortgage Origination Commission
OECD	Organisation for Economic Co-operation and Development
OFHEO	Office of Federal Housing Enterprise Oversight
OTC	over-the-counter
PPI	private participation in infrastructure

RESPA	Real Estate Settlement and Procedures Act
SIV	structured investment vehicle
TILA	Truth in Lending Act
UNFPA	United Nations Population Fund
UN-HABITAT	United Nations Human Settlements Programme
VA	Veterans Administration
WDI	World Development Indicators

CHAPTER 1
Urbanization and Growth: Setting the Context

Patricia Clarke Annez and Robert M. Buckley

Urbanization and growth go together: no country has ever reached middle-income status without a significant population shift into cities. Urbanization is necessary to sustain (though not necessarily drive) growth in developing countries, and it yields other benefits as well. But it is not painless or always welcomed by policymakers or the general public. Managing urbanization is an important part of nurturing growth; neglecting cities—even in countries in which the level of urbanization is low—can impose heavy costs.

In terms of development and growth theory, urbanization occupies a puzzling position. On the one hand, it is recognized as fundamental to the multidimensional structural transformation that low-income rural societies undergo to modernize and to join the ranks of middle- and high-income countries. Some models, such as Lucas's (2004, 2007), explicitly consider how urbanization affects the growth process (primarily through the enhanced flow of ideas and knowledge attributable to agglomeration in cities. In a more historical treatment, Landes (1969,

The authors would like to thank the participants in the two workshops organized by the Growth Commission on urbanization and housing—especially the contributors to this volume, and Uwe Deichmann, Danny Leipziger, Mike Spence, and Roberto Zagha for useful discussions, comments, and insights. We are indebted to Jerry Kalarickal and Oriane Raulet for excellent research assistance.

cited in Williamson 1987, p. 6) situates urbanization as an essential ingredient in modernization:

> Industrialization . . . is at the heart of a larger, more complex process often designated as *modernization*. Modernization comprises such developments as urbanization . . . ; the so-called demographic transition; the establishment of an effective, fairly centralized bureaucratic government; the creation of an educational system capable of training and socializing the children of a society . . . ; and of course, the acquisition of the ability and means to use an up-to-date technology.

On the other hand, urbanization is a relatively little-studied area of development economics and policy, as Burgess and Venables (2004, p. 4) note:

> Spatial concentration is most dramatically demonstrated by the role of urbanization, and of mega-cities, in development. . . . despite the massive diseconomies associated with developing country mega-cities, there are even more powerful economies of scale making it worthwhile for firms to locate in these cities. Urbanization is one of the clearest features of the development of manufacturing and service activity in developing countries, yet discussion of urbanization is strangely absent from economic analyses of growth and development.

This volume includes six chapters based on state of the art papers written on topics related to urbanization and growth for the Commission on Growth and Development. To provide context to this rich collection, this chapter begins by examining some basic facts about urbanization and growth, some of them based on the historical experience of today's high-income countries. It then reviews some of the debates that have influenced thinking about the role of urbanization in development. It concludes with a discussion of the institutional, political, and policy challenges that developing countries face as they work through the structural change that urbanization precipitates.

Urbanization and Growth: The Historical Record

Widespread urbanization is a recent phenomenon. In 1900 just 15 percent of the world's population lived in cities. The 20th century transformed this picture, as the pace of urban population growth accelerated very rapidly in about 1950. Sixty years later, it is estimated that half of the world's people lives in cities.

Despite this rapid change, urbanization is not out of control: in terms of population growth rates, the "worst" is over. Urban population growth rates peaked at 3.7 percent a year in 1950–75 and slowed notably thereafter (National Research Council 2003). Nevertheless, given the growing base of people living in cities, annual population increments in absolute numbers are very large—and to many, alarming. UN projections predict that urban populations in developing countries will be growing by more than 65 million people a year between 2000 and 2030 (UN 2006).

Urbanization has long been viewed with ambivalence. In 1800 Thomas Jefferson wrote to Benjamin Rush: "I view great cities as pestilential to the morals, the health and the liberties of man. True, they nourish some of the elegant arts; but the useful ones can thrive elsewhere" (Peterson 1984). Twenty years later Percy Bysshe Shelley wrote, "Hell is a city much like London." More recently, Paul Bairoch (1988), the great chronicler of urbanization throughout history, and Bert Hoselitz (1955), the editor of *Economic Development and Cultural Change,* wrote of "parasitic cities" and their ill effects in developing countries. This perspective has often been shared by the popular press. A 2003 *Newsweek* cover story suggested that urbanization in Asia was exploding and potentially a curse. A 2007 UN publication on population reveals deep skepticism about urbanization among policymakers in developing countries: 88 percent of survey respondents from less developed countries reported that the spatial distribution of their population was unsatisfactory. This number declined from 95 percent in 1976, although over the same period the number of countries with policies actively seeking to reduce migration to cities grew, from about 44 percent to 74 percent. The most intense concerns and most activist policies are in the least developed countries (see annex 1).

Arthur Lewis (1977, p. 32) expressed concerns about the costs of urbanization but saw it as unavoidable. "Urbanization would not be inevitable if we could spread industry around the countryside instead of concentrating it in towns, but this is easier said than done. . . . One can work hard at establishing rural industries, but except in police states, this is bound to be limited."

Lewis's sense of inevitability is borne out by experience: very few countries have reached income levels of $10,000 per capita before reaching about 60 percent urbanization (figure 1.1). This relation has changed little since 1960 (see annex 2). This simple bivariate regression explains at least 55 percent of variability across countries, suggesting that urbanization is a very strong indicator of all aspects of productivity growth over the long run, although clearly this simple statistical relation does not establish causality.

Figure 1.1 Urbanization and Per Capita GDP across Countries, 2000 (1996 dollars)

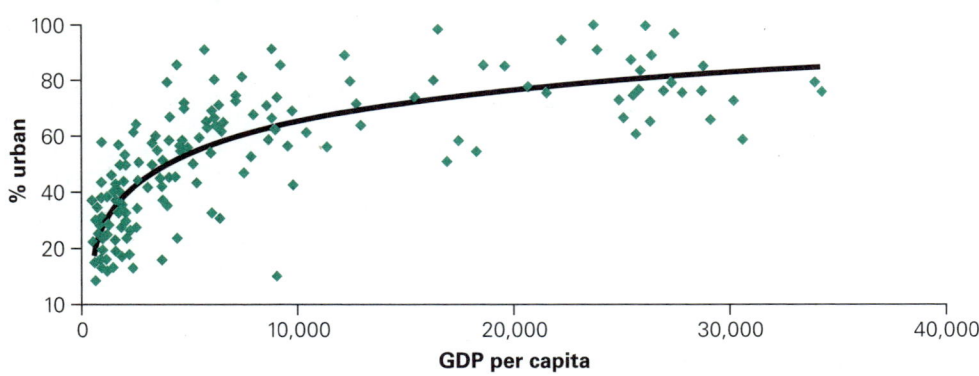

Source: Data on urbanization: World Bank *World Development Indicators* 2005. Data on per capita GDP: Heston, Summers, and Aten n.d.; Penn World Table Version 6.2; Center for International Comparisons of Production, Income and Prices at the University of Pennsylvania, real 1996 GDP per capita (chain), September 2006 (http://pwt.econ.upenn.edu/).

The relation between urbanization and income across countries is striking, but it does not shed much light on what countries should expect as they urbanize. Historical data provide some insights into the evolution of urbanization and per capita income over time. In the United States, urbanization rates and per capita income moved together until about 1940, when urbanization reached close to 60 percent; thereafter per capita income expanded much more rapidly (figure 1.2). Presumably, in the initial phases, when urbanization rates and per capita income increase at roughly the same rates, productivity increases reflect shifting resources from lower-productivity rural activities. In later phases rapid productivity gains reflect mainly improvements within industries and services (Romer 1986; Lucas 1988; Quigley 1998).

Rapidly growing developing countries have followed a similar path, although the rapid take-off in per capita incomes in China (figure 1.3) took place at an urbanization rate about half that of the United States. Both urbanization and economic take-off have been much more rapid in China than in India (figures 1.4 and 1.5).

Urbanization is not necessarily accompanied by the rapid and steady growth that China and India experienced. Brazil started on a path similar to that of the United States and China, with a very rapid increase in productivity starting in the late 1960s, when urbanization stood at about 50 percent (figure 1.6). Income growth was not sustained, however,

Figure 1.2 Urbanization and Per Capita GDP in the United States, 1880–2006

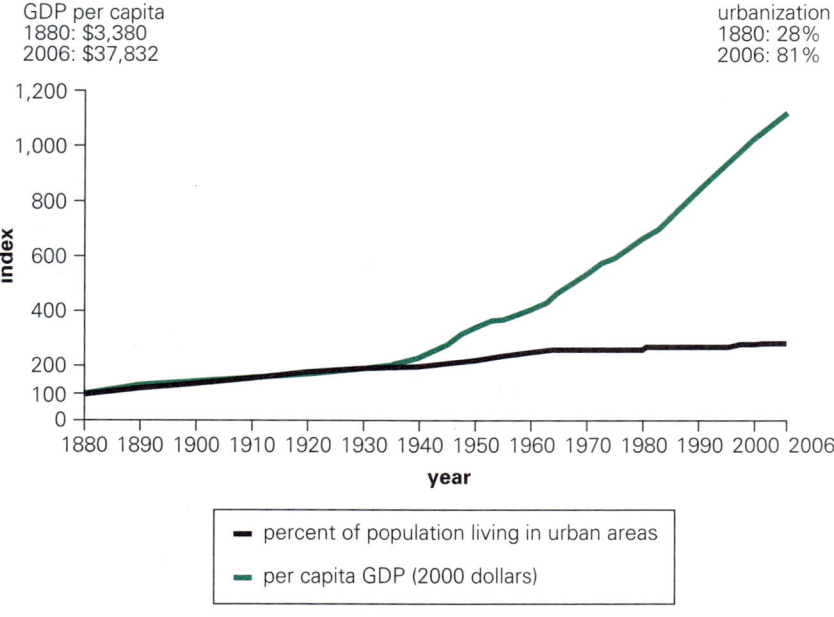

Source: U.S. Census, http://www.census.gov/population/censusdata/table-4.pdf; Johnston and Williamson (2005). Adapted from Malpezzi and Lin (1999).

Note: Both times series are indexed to 100 in the initial year. The *y* value of each series thus shows the percentage change since that time.

Figure 1.3 Urbanization and Per Capita GDP in China, 1960–2004

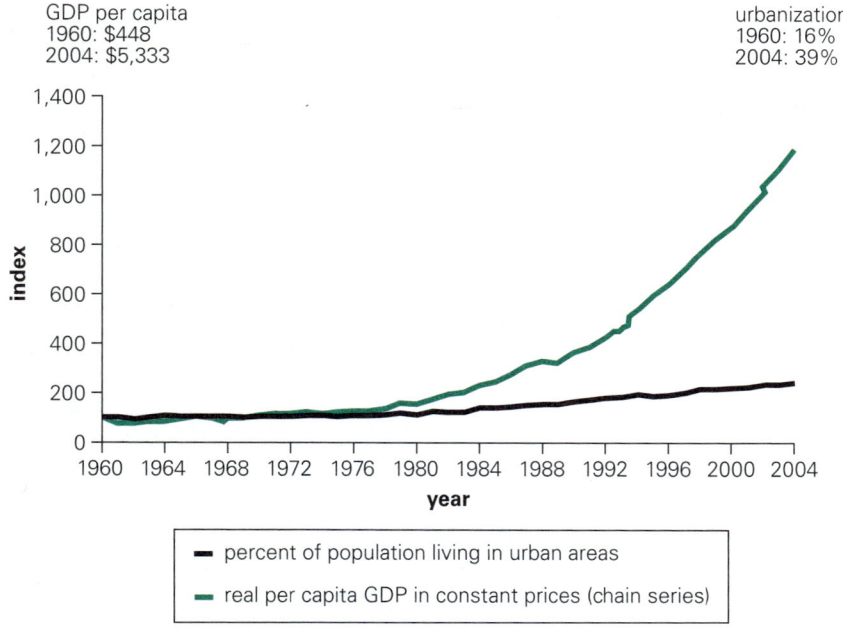

GDP per capita
1960: $448
2004: $5,333

urbanization
1960: 16%
2004: 39%

— percent of population living in urban areas
— real per capita GDP in constant prices (chain series)

Source: See figure 1.1.

Note: Both times series are indexed to 100 in the initial year. The *y* value of each series thus shows the percentage change since that time.

Figure 1.4 Rural Population in China and India, 1980–2006

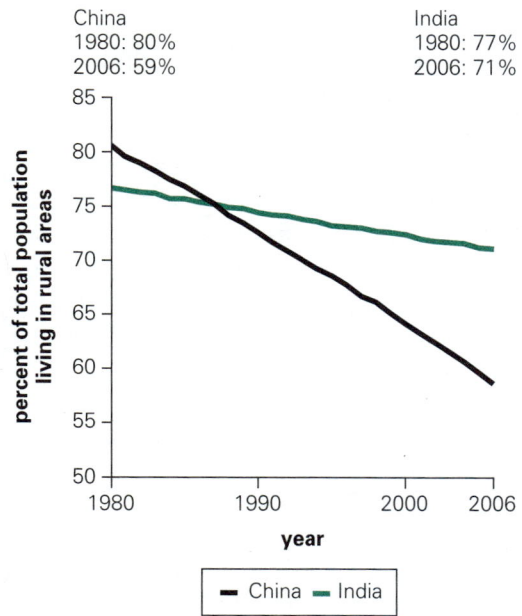

China
1980: 80%
2006: 59%

India
1980: 77%
2006: 71%

— China — India

Source: See figure 1.1.

Figure 1.5 Per Capita Income in China and India, 1980–2006

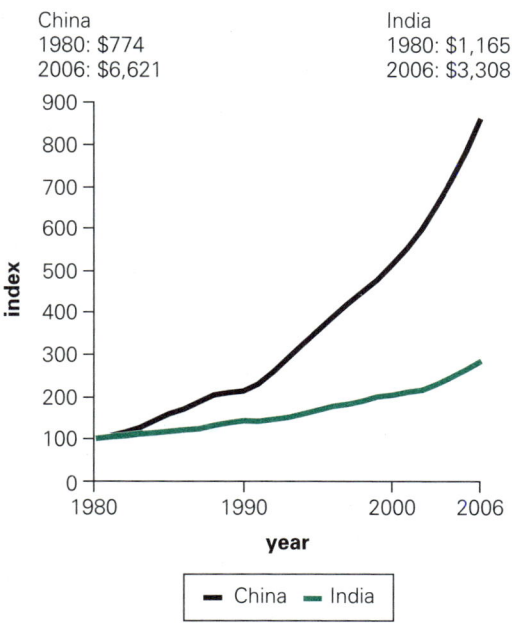

China
1980: $774
2006: $6,621

India
1980: $1,165
2006: $3,308

— China — India

Source: World Bank, World Development Indicators.

Note: Both times series are indexed to 100 in the initial year. The *y* value of each series thus shows the percentage change since that time.

Figure 1.6 Urbanization and Per Capita GDP in Brazil, 1960–2003

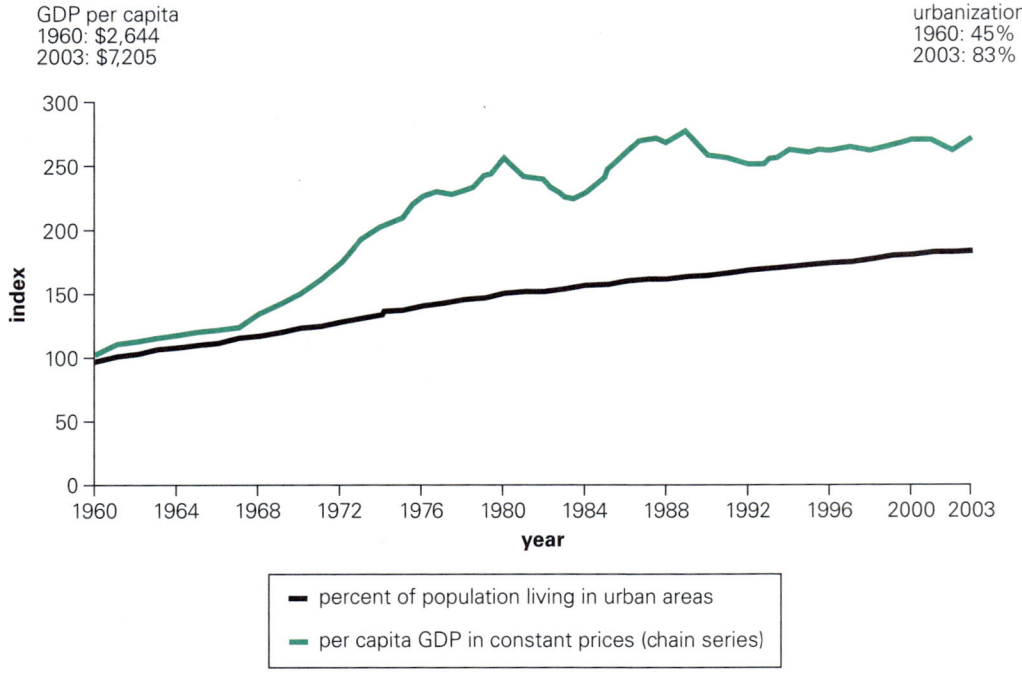

GDP per capita
1960: $2,644
2003: $7,205

urbanization
1960: 45%
2003: 83%

— percent of population living in urban areas

— per capita GDP in constant prices (chain series)

Source: See figure 1.1.

Note: Both times series are indexed to 100 in the initial year. The *y* value of each series thus shows the percentage change since that time.

illustrating the fact that urbanization is far from a sufficient condition for continued rapid growth. The structural shift from rural activities to more-productive urban-based industry and services, clearly well advanced in Brazil, is an essential part of modernization. More is needed to drive the later stages of the growth process.

Kenya (figure 1.7) illustrates a different phenomenon: urbanization without growth.[1] The level of urbanization in Kenya in 1960 was extremely low, at just 7 percent. Urbanization proceeded rapidly from this small base, but it still remains low, at about 20 percent. Per capita income has stagnated. Urbanization has clearly not been pulled by productive industrialization in Kenya; other factors are at work. Several countries in Africa have experienced this phenomenon, which is otherwise rare.[2]

Which of these two patterns predominates? How should stagnation in the face of rapid urbanization be interpreted? In 109 countries with

1 Fay and Opal (2000) document this phenomenon in Africa.
2 Weeks (1994) argues that special factors account in part for Africa's rapid rates of urbanization in the immediate postcolonial period. Colonial prohibitions on migration to cities in East Africa—and control of population movements more broadly—were deeply resented. A one-time stock adjustment that may have had little to do with economic factors took place in the early years to compensate.

Figure 1.7 Urbanization and Per Capita GDP in Kenya, 1960–2003

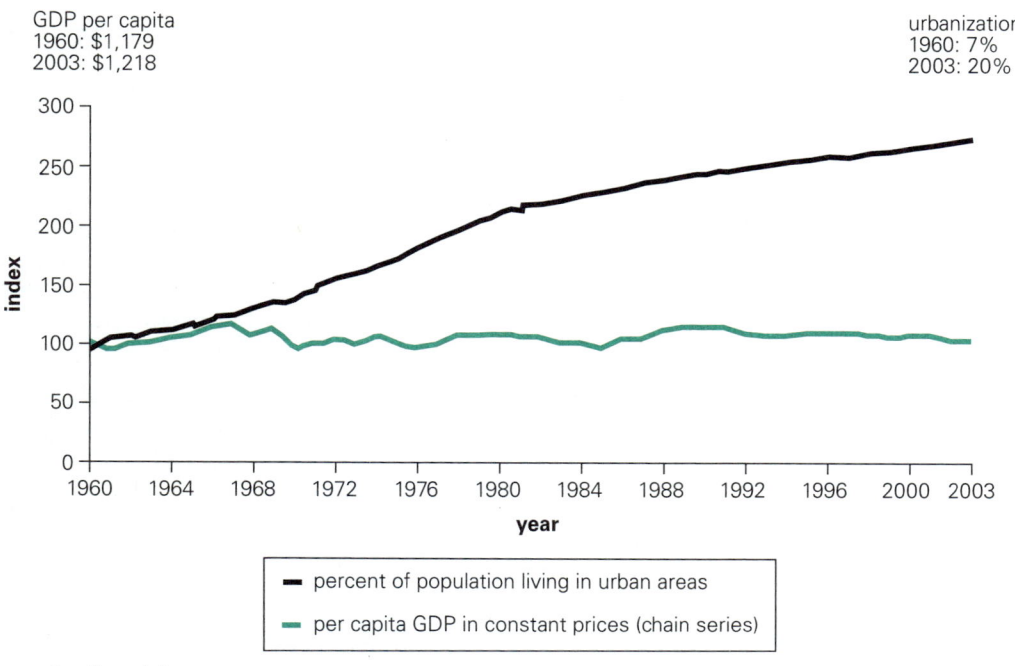

GDP per capita
1960: $1,179
2003: $1,218

urbanization
1960: 7%
2003: 20%

Legend:
— percent of population living in urban areas
— per capita GDP in constant prices (chain series)

Source: See figure 1.1.

Note: Both times series are indexed to 100 in the initial year. The *y* value of each series thus shows the percentage change since that time.

populations of more than 1 million, both urbanization and per capita income growth rose between 1960 and 2003; in the majority of these countries, income per capita grew more rapidly than urbanization (World Bank 2005; UN 2007). In only 25 countries was income growth negative and outpaced by urbanization. What has come to be termed "pathological urbanization"—substantial structural population shifts without growth—is not common. Moreover, urbanization in these cases tends to reflect problems elsewhere in the economy.

Most of the countries experiencing urbanization without growth are small African countries at low levels of urbanization or failed states. This group of countries figures significantly in the work of Collier (2006, 2007) and Barrios, Bertinelli, and Strobl (2006). Collier offers a number of explanations for the poor growth performance of a range of African countries. Geographic factors—including climate, soils, and the failure to achieve a green revolution—and national boundaries play very significant roles. Barrios, Bertinelli, and Strobl analyze cross-country time-series data to test hypotheses on what drives urbanization. Their global cross-country analysis shows that downward trends in rainfall have a positive and significant effect on urbanization, although this effect is present in Africa only. Slow-growing, rapidly urbanizing countries in Africa may thus be experiencing "push" rather than "pull" urbanization, resulting from agricultural stress. This diagnosis leads to a rather different set of policy prescriptions than one pointing to pathological urbanization driven by overprivileged cities, articulated in the *World Development Report 1999/2000* (World Bank 2000, p. 130) as follows:

> National governments have often tried to influence the pace or location of urbanization. Often these efforts consisted of shifting resources from agriculture to finance the expansion of "modern" economic sectors—usually manufacturing—which were concentrated on cities. Urban workers in the formal sector benefited from food and housing subsidies and government-sponsored unemployment and pension schemes, while rural populations received low prices for their crops and had little access to government support. Such misplaced efforts are part of the reason Africa has seen urbanization with very little economic growth.

Starving the cities is a futile and damaging response if cities are refuges from stress in the countryside. So, too, is assuming that benign neglect of urban infrastructure will do little harm, particularly when the basic service level in African cities has been deteriorating for more than 25 years (Banerjee and others 2007). The central government often must play a critical role in making the transition to healthy cities and healthy urban finance (box 1.1).

As disturbing as the rare cases of urbanization without growth are, there is little evidence to suggest that even in these cases urbanization exacerbates poverty. In both East Asia and Sub-Saharan Africa, for example—two regions with dramatically different growth experiences—the poverty headcount has declined with urbanization (figures 1.8–1.11). Evidence from East Asia indicates that urbanization with high growth dramatically reduced overall and urban poverty headcounts. In Africa urbanization, accompanied by very low growth, is concentrating poor people in cities rather than the countryside. Even so the poverty headcount has declined somewhat in the process of urbanization. With the exception of Europe and Central Asia—which was highly urbanized for the entire period and experienced an increase in poverty during the depths of the crisis of the late 1990s—other regions display similar patterns (see annex 3).

The sectoral composition of GDP growth across countries confirms a strong link between rapid growth and a structural shift from agriculture to urban activities (manufacturing and services). Examination of the sectoral composition of growth in countries that, over the long term, are growing rapidly enough to converge with the United States in per capita income (that is, growing by more than about 2 percent a year) shows that this linkage is widespread.[3] In every one of these countries, one or both of the urban sectors led the growth process; no country has sustained high growth driven primarily by agriculture. In the subset of "high-growth" countries that experienced average annual GDP growth of at least 7 percent for at least 25 years, as identified by the report by the Commission on Growth

---

3 Long term is defined here as 20 years or more or for as long as data on the sectoral decomposition of GDP are available in the *World Development Indicators*.

Figure 1.8 Urban and Rural Poverty Headcount in East Asia, 1993–2002

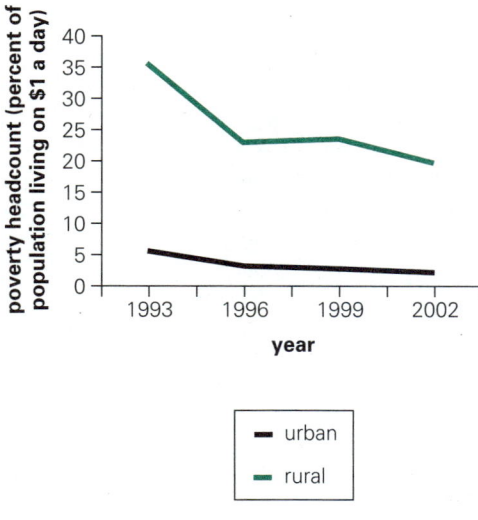

Source: Ravallion, Chen, and Sangraula 2007.

Figure 1.9 Per Capita GDP, Urban Share of Population, and Poverty Headcount in East Asia, 1993–2002

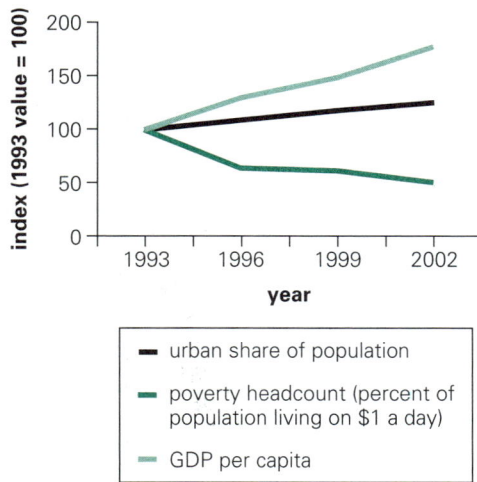

Source: Ravallion, Chen, and Sangraula 2007.

Figure 1.10 Urban and Rural Poverty Headcount in Sub-Saharan Africa, 1993–2002

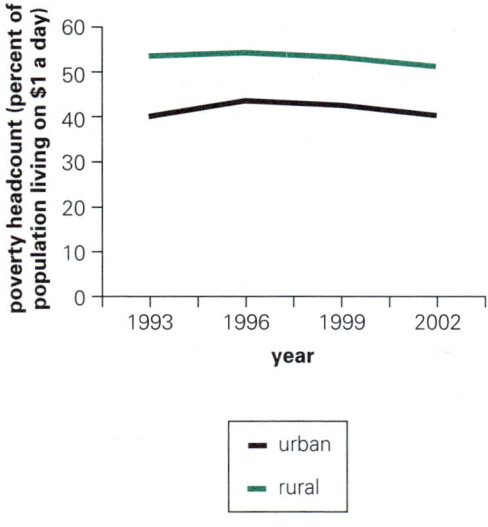

Source: Ravallion, Chen, and Sangraula 2007.

Figure 1.11 Per Capita GDP, Urban Share of Population, and Poverty Headcount in Sub-Saharan Africa, 1993–2002

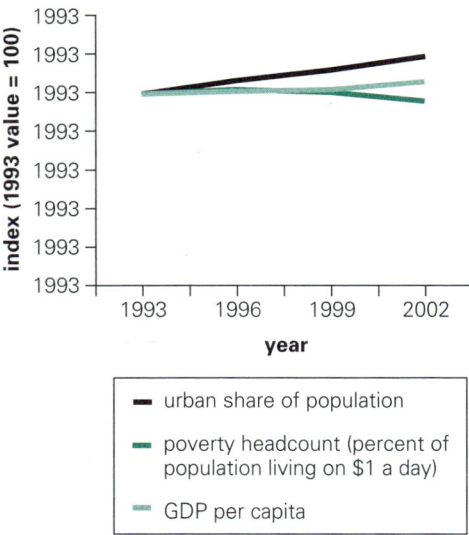

Source: Ravallion, Chen, and Sangraula 2007.

and Development (2008), industry and services dramatically outpaced agriculture in all cases (figure 1.12). Across the developing world, the urban sector drives growth: according to the National Research Council (2003), 86 percent of the growth in value-added in developing countries between 1980 and 1998 came from services and manufacturing.

Box 1.1 The Role of Finance in Cleaning Up Britain's "Killer Cities" in the 19th Century

Britain's cities suffered from high mortality rates for most of the 19th century. The causes of and cures for the problems that made cities so lethal were well known[a] and the economic arguments well crafted and debated in Parliament decades before much was done about them. Britain's cities were cleaned up only when the central government stepped in to alleviate the binding financial constraint in cities. In this story lies an important lesson about building urban infrastructure, especially those lumpy discrete investments in networks that expand the limits at which congestion costs outweigh agglomeration benefits. Neither the municipal finance systems that worked before the urban transition nor those suitable for cities in a demographic steady state will necessarily generate finance for investments in local public goods that more than pay for themselves in economic terms.

During the early 19th century, while the Industrial Revolution was in full swing, cities in Britain grew rapidly. Rural–urban migration in the early 19th century was comparable to rates observed in developing countries in the postwar period (about 1–2 percent a year). One might have expected these population shifts to have attracted capital to cities. In fact, social overhead capital stocks per capita declined during the 70 years up to 1830. As Williamson (1990, p. 273) notes, "Britain had accumulated an enormous deficit in her social overhead stocks by pursuing industrialization on the cheap."

This underinvestment had a high cost in human mortality. In 1841 infant mortality rates were 25–50 percent higher and the crude death rate 5.6 per thousand higher in England's major cities than in the rural hinterland, with most of the difference explained by crowding, city size, and density. The crude death rate differential declined dramatically by 1906 and disappeared by the 1920s.

The high mortality in cities had important costs beyond the obvious human and social toll. It created a spatial mismatch in labor supply, reducing the supply of labor in cities, where labor was needed, and fueling migration from rural areas. High rural–urban wage differentials, driven by strong demand for labor in cities, are evidence of a costly disequilibrium in the labor market.[b]

These costly losses persisted through most of the 19th century. Why were investments in social overhead infrastructure not made sooner? Through 1820 the costs of the Napoleonic Wars might explain part of this crowding out, according to Williamson (1990). The lumpy and long-term investments needed in infrastructure investments were more sensitive to interest rates than were investments in manufacturing. Later the attractive private returns to foreign investments (such as the railroads in the New World) may have won out over investment in social infrastructure, with high social but low private returns. Still, the economic returns to these investments were competitive. Estimates for the United States indicate that annual rates of return to water and sanitation investments there were 6–16 percent—much higher than the 4–5 percent earned on stocks or railroad bonds. Although government intervention makes sense in such situations, local authorities in Britain did not make these investments until much later.

Ignorance of the economic costs of inaction cannot explain local government delays in cleaning up "killer cities." The Great Sanitation Debate, prompted by the Chadwick Report of 1842, had already sensitized the middle and upper classes to the terrible plight of the urban poor. The report offered well-established technical solutions in water and sewerage and even computed cost–benefit ratios for investments using the concept of (if not the term) human capital. It made a compelling case for reform on economic and technical grounds, pulling together information and analysis that had been known for decades. According to the report, investment in urban infrastructure would yield three types of payoff. First, water and sanitation investments would be worthwhile for the rich, because reduced mortality and morbidity would reduce Poor Law expenditures and check the threat of diseases that could spread to the rich. Second, these investments would be worth the expenditure for the poor, because they would improve their health and reduce their doctors' bills. Third, better infrastructure would provide a net benefit for the nation, because the value of saving a human life far exceeded the costs of investing in sanitation.

Despite the strong net benefits, the infrastructure investments the report recommended were not made for decades. The poor could not make these investments—for reasons that are still relevant today in developing country cities. They could not internalize all the benefits of the investments, because upgrading infrastructure for one residence had little impact if neighbors did not follow suit. Moreover,

Box 1.1 Continued

capital markets were unlikely to lend to poor households against future health and productivity improvement. These factors combined with low homeownership rates and high transience to prevent the poor from tackling the problem themselves.

The better-off and the polity also failed to make the investments for 20 years after the debate had been launched. Public finance constraints were critical to this delay. The legal framework did not support long-term borrowing for local authorities until the revisions of the Municipal Acts starting in the 1830s, making it difficult for local governments to tap capital markets. Moreover, the inefficient and unjust tax system—resembling in many respects those in place in thousands of developing country cities today—made it difficult for local governments to take collective action even when it became possible to borrow.

Votes for the city councils that made the investment decisions at the time were based on ratable value; the electorate was thus very narrow. In Birmingham only 3 percent of the population was eligible to vote in 1861; in Leeds just 13 percent of the population could vote. The local taxes voted by these councils were assessed on the basis of the rental value of property. As a result, people with rental income were taxed much more heavily than others. The evidence even suggests that these taxpayers disproportionately made their way into the local councils to protect themselves from excessive taxation (Wohl 1983). Concerns about the costs of sanitation spending were well founded. The city of Leicester, a center for hosiery manufacture, began cleaning up the town in the mid-19th century partly because of the need for clean water for hosiery production.[c] Tax rates went up more than tenfold during this period.

The impasse was finally overcome in the 1860s, thanks to two factors. First, economic growth greatly increased the tax base. Ratable value in Manchester increased by a factor of almost 3.5 between 1840 and 1880 (Wohl 1983). Second, the central government stepped in to provide low-interest long-term loans for investments in water and sanitation.[d] This central government subsidy made investments more attractive and more equitably redistributed the tax burden for infrastructure improvements with high social value. The ramp-up in borrowing and investment was substantial: on average, annual borrowing by local authorities tripled between 1863 and 1873, doubling once again into the early 1890s. In Exeter the sewage treatment system started in 1896 cost about nine times the amount spent for excrement removal over the previous several decades.

Source: Williamson 1990; Wohl 1983.

a. Understanding the epidemiology of the great cholera outbreaks of the 19th century took some time. How it was done is a fascinating story.

b. It is highly unlikely that this wage differential can be attributed to "urban bias." Nineteenth-century policies such as the Corn Laws actually favored agriculture; industry had negative effective protection, and social overhead capital expenditures favored the countryside, not the cities

c. The city of Tiruppur, India, a major hosiery export center in India, offers a fascinating parallel. Tiruppur was a pioneer in a public-private partnership for a major water supply project begun in the mid-1990s. Tiruppur was considered an especially favorable case, because the exporters' business was booming and their willingness to pay for clean water quite exceptional. Even so the project took years to negotiate, and ultimately some of the waste water treatment investments could not be completed because of high costs.

d. The transformation to modern sewerage systems in Britain's cities also has a public-private ownership dimension. It was difficult for municipalities to operate sewer systems without assurance of adequate water flow—of marginal interest to a private water supplier. In the second half of the 19th century, local authorities were helped by legislation that made it easier for them to purchase private water companies. Only five local authorities in England and Wales had public water companies in 1840; by 1871 a third of local authorities had public water supply (Wohl 1983).

Simply because agriculture has consistently grown more slowly than other sectors does not imply that it should be neglected. Good agricultural growth performance may accompany strong performance in other sectors, as the China and Thailand cases in figure 1.12 show. Productivity advances in agriculture offer scope for freeing up labor to work in manufacturing and services. Because the poor are disproportionately represented among those

Figure 1.12 Growth Rates in Agriculture, Manufacturing, and Service Sectors in Selected High-Growth Economies

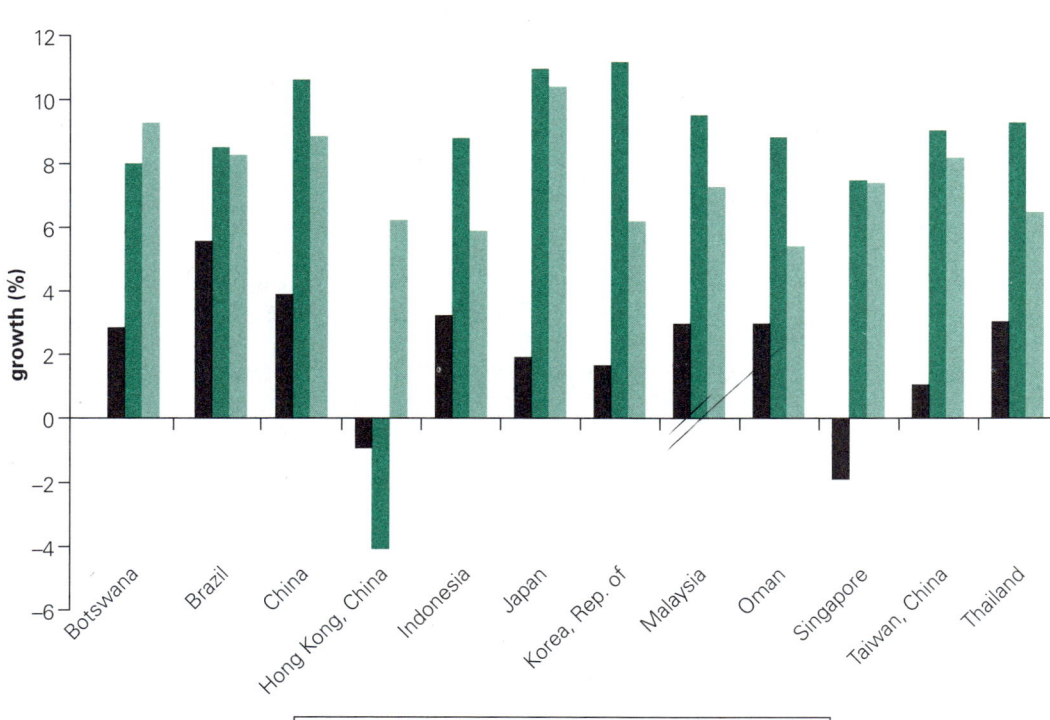

Source: World Bank, *World Development Indicators 2007;* for Brazil: calculation using data from the *World Tables 1976*, World Bank and Institute of Applied Economic Research (IAER), Brazil, http://www.ipeadata.gov.br; for Japan: calculation using data from the *World Tables 1976*, World Bank, and Maddison, Angus, 2001: *The World Economy: A Millennial Perspective.* Paris: OECD.

Note: Growth rates are based on GDP in constant domestic prices. The calculations apply for different periods indicated in parentheses because of differences in availability of consistent data: Botswana (1965–2006); Brazil (1955–73); China (1965–2006); Hong Kong, China (2000–06); Indonesia (1960–2005); Japan (1955–73); Korea, Rep. of (1970–2006); Malaysia (1970–2006); Oman (1988–2004); Singapore (1975–2006); Taiwan, China (1965–2006); Thailand (1960–2006).

whose livelihoods depend on agriculture, making agriculture more productive can have powerful effects on poverty.

That said, the evidence is very strong that development strategies that seek to limit the growth of or neglect cities in order to focus on agricultural development are settling for lower rates of growth. Even among countries that have grown the most rapidly over the past 20 years or so, long-term agricultural growth rates never exceeded 5 percent, a rate of growth that is common in services and manufacturing. Dealing with urbanization and accommodating cities that grow rapidly because the dynamic manufacturing and services sectors locate there is an inevitable part of achieving sustained high growth.

Why Do Rapidly Growing Sectors Locate in Cities?

Industry and services are concentrated in cities. These sectors grow more rapidly than other sectors, so cities must be important to growth. But there is more to this relation. A large body of literature explains why industry and services locate in cities.[4] The chapters by Gilles Duranton, John Quigley, and Anthony Venables discuss the role of agglomeration economies and the functioning of labor markets in cities, highlighting both productivity impacts and linkages with the growth process.

As Quigley points out in chapter 4, the fundamental question in urban economics is why people voluntarily live in close proximity to one another when there are costs to competing for land. The simple answer has two parts: efficiency gains and consumption benefits. Recent theoretical and empirical work provides a sense of the nature and significance of these gains.

The earliest concept of efficiency gain was geographical. Cities have long tended to locate around waterways to exploit transportation cost advantages. In the United States and Western Europe, for example, cities on the coasts, major rivers, or the Great Lakes were vital to industrial development. During the postwar period, coastal megacities have dominated most Asian economies (an exception is India). In Japan urban and industrial growth concentrated in the Tokkaido coastal corridor (Tokyo, Nagoya, and Osaka).[5] The concentration of producers and suppliers in this area enabled innovations such as just-in-time production techniques. Industrial development concentrated in the Seoul/Pusan region of the Republic of Korea and in the Taipei/Kaoshing region of Taiwan (China). In Indonesia, Malaysia, and Thailand, growth concentrated in export-oriented labor-intensive industries in the metropolitan megacities of Jakarta, Kuala Lumpur, and Bangkok. In China development has concentrated in Shanghai and the Pearl River Delta (Mohan 2006; Yusuf, Evenett, and Wu 2001). As the Asian megacity complexes have shown, location effects driven by transportation costs also tend to cumulate into other advantages, a process Burgess and Venables (2004) describe in detail.

Economies of scale offer both efficiency and consumption advantages to urban economies, manifested in several ways. Process industries, such as chemicals, steel, and automobiles, operate more effectively at higher volumes; for this reason they have traditionally been established in urban areas. Economies of scale in input markets affect a wide range of industries. Specialized services—such as accounting, tax advice, and intellectual property management—are easier to obtain in large cities. Specialization among input producers may also allow cost reductions, making local purchasers of their inputs more productive. Public services such as hospitals, theaters, orchestras, and sports stadiums require a critical mass of consumers to make them economically viable. The density of urban areas increases the range of such amenities.

---

4 Quigley (1998) provides a succinct summary of these advantages and the supporting literature. Fujita and Thisse (2002) and Duranton and Puga (2004) provide a detailed treatment of the theory of agglomeration economies.

5 By 1970 almost 60 percent of the urban population lived along this corridor. This concentration reduced the cost of infrastructure investments, which would have been much costlier with a more balanced spatial growth strategy.

Economies of scale in cities also reduce transaction costs. High densities in cities allow both workers with differentiated skills and firms with specific needs to reduce their search costs. This effect can operate even if all producers operate at constant returns to scale and there are no technological externalities (Acemoglu 1996). Operating in a dense urban environment offers efficiencies through the impact of large numbers on risks of fluctuating demands for both labor and products. If these fluctuations are imperfectly correlated across firms, both firms and individuals benefit from locating in cities. Spells of unemployment can be shorter and demand shocks and inventory costs lower in such environments.

Agglomeration effects in cities affect knowledge sharing. By bringing together large numbers of people, cities facilitate the kinds of face to face interactions needed to generate, diffuse, and accumulate knowledge, especially in industries that experience rapid technological change. This aspect of urban agglomeration economies has received less theoretical and empirical attention, but it has promise to be one of the more significant drivers behind dynamic growth in developing country cities.

The theoretical advantages of cities are not limited to high-income countries. Jane Jacobs put this simply and eloquently, noting, "Cities, not countries, are the constituent elements of a developing economy and have been so from the dawn of civilization" (1984, p. 32). In developing countries poor transportation and communication infrastructure tend to magnify the advantages of cities over the countryside. Location advantages can thus be even more valuable there than in developed countries. As developing countries seek to compete in increasingly integrated world markets, even static advantages conferred by cities help firms penetrate export markets, as Venables notes in chapter 2. The report by the Commission on Growth and Development (2008) underscores the significance of penetrating export markets as one of the key elements of sustained, rapid growth. Weak infrastructure could heighten the congestion disadvantages of cities as well, which may affect the optimal size of developing country cities. As Duranton (chapter 3) and Quigley (chapter 4) argue, however, there is no strong prima facie argument that urbanization has weaker advantages in developing countries than in high-income countries.

The empirical evidence on the presence of agglomeration economies in developed countries is strong. Rosenthal and Strange (2004) provide a comprehensive survey of the literature.[6] Most of the work in this area focuses on the United States and to a lesser extent Europe; a relatively few studies cover developing countries. Researchers show that doubling city size increases productivity across industries (urbanization economies) in the United States by 3–8 percent. Work that uses statewide data from the United States finds that a doubling of density is associated with a roughly 5 percent increase in productivity. Similar work for Europe finds the impact of density to be comparable (4.5 percent).

---

6   The discussion below draws heavily on Rosenthal and Strange (2004).

Henderson's (1986) work on Brazil and the United States finds that agglomeration effects tend to affect industries concentrated in a city (localization economies) more than all industries (urbanization economies). The effects in Brazil were broadly comparable with those in the United States. Within-industry agglomeration effects were such that without any other increases in inputs, productivity increased roughly 1 percent for every 10 percent increase in the number of workers employed in an industry in a given city. While this effect may seem small, it implies that by moving from a city with 1,000 workers to one with 10,000 workers, a firm would increase its productivity by a factor of 90. Overman and Venables (2005) summarize the results of studies on urbanization and localization economies in a variety of developing countries. Apart from one anomalous study that indicates localization diseconomies in India, the results, including those of other studies for India, are broadly the same.[7]

As in developed countries, evidence of localization economies in developing countries is somewhat stronger than for urbanization economies. One significant exception is high-tech industries in Korea, where a one standard deviation increase in the index of city diversity increases productivity 60 percent (Henderson, Lee, and Lee 2001). This finding is particularly interesting because Korea has had very strong growth performance even after reaching middle-income status. These findings on localization economies in developing economies are reinforced by case studies on spatial clusters of firms (Overman and Venables 2005).

The importance of the informal sector may distinguish cities in developing countries from those in developed countries. Some critics argue that informality is unproductive and raises the costs to the formal sector, crowding out agglomeration economies. In fact, the little evidence available on agglomeration economies in the informal sector suggests that it also benefits from agglomeration and that informal operators generally have a positive impact on their formal sector counterparts.

Studies on developed countries have tried to pinpoint the distance over which agglomeration economies affect productivity. The evidence points to rapid geographical attenuation of localization economies—beyond 5 miles in some studies, beyond 50 kilometers in others—with the distance varying by industry. Different types of agglomeration economies, such as knowledge spillovers and labor market pooling, have different geographic scopes. These narrow geographic agglomeration effects help explain why dense urban areas emerge in spite of congestion costs and why there is so much spatial concentration of economic activities. In the continental United States, for example, only 2 percent of the land area is covered by the urban built environment, home to 75 percent of the population (Henderson 2005; Rosenthal and Strange 2004).

---

7 The India result is difficult to explain, because of the high geographical concentration of industry in the same data sample.

Several studies have shown that city characteristics can affect productivity over as much as 20 years (see Rosenthal and Strange 2004). The main channel for these intertemporal effects is thought to be knowledge spillovers. Work on the United States has sought to understand the substantial urban wage premium—30 percent in one study—by differentiating the impact of selection (cities attract the best and brightest) from the impact of agglomeration for workers with long experience in cities. Correcting for selection narrows the wage differential to a still substantial 20 percent. Workers with longer experience in the city earn a premium over recent arrivals, a finding that is consistent with the view that knowledge-based agglomeration effects last a long time. Interestingly, these studies also find that when experienced workers leave large cities, their wages in the new location are higher the larger the size of the city of previous residence.

Other findings related to labor productivity (also discussed in Rosenthal and Strange 2004) come from studies that differentiate the "rat-race effect" from the selection effect. This research finds that cities do indeed attract professionals who work harder on average at all ages (the selection effect). When rewards for hard work are high and rivalry exists, young professionals put in even more hours than more experienced professionals (the rat-race effect). These results offer yet another dimension to the urbanization-productivity relation: cities make people work harder.

The notion that cities offer knowledge functions has been extended to consider innovation in products and processes. Using French data, Duranton and Puga (2001) validate their model of "nursery" cities, showing that large diverse cities can be good at providing the incubation function. Once firms find the ideal production process, industries eventually relocate in smaller specialized cities with lower-cost profiles.

The results on knowledge spillovers—which are particularly relevant for the growth process—are consistent with some of the stylized facts in developing countries, even if all the effects have not yet been validated econometrically. There is, for example, strong evidence of higher productivity in cities and persistent geographical advantage, as Venables notes in chapter 2 (see also Venables 2007). China's coastal cities enjoy a large income advantage—a factor of two to one over other urban areas—demonstrating strong geographic and cumulative urban agglomeration advantages (figure 1.13). These intracity differentials are in addition to the significant productivity advantage of urban areas over rural areas in China.

Evidence from Bangladesh provides further confirmation of productivity advantages in large cities in developing countries. Green (2007) examines variations in changes in household expenditures across 64 districts in Bangladesh. He controls for a number of variables that enhance productivity, including the literacy rate, the infant mortality rate, male and female school attendance rates, a measure of semifeudal large landholdings, the level of urbanization, the use of irrigation technology, initial-period expenditure levels, the percentage of households with electricity, and initial-period expenditure inequality. He finds that distance from Dhaka explains

Figure 1.13 Income Advantages of Coastal Metropolitan Regions in China, 2000

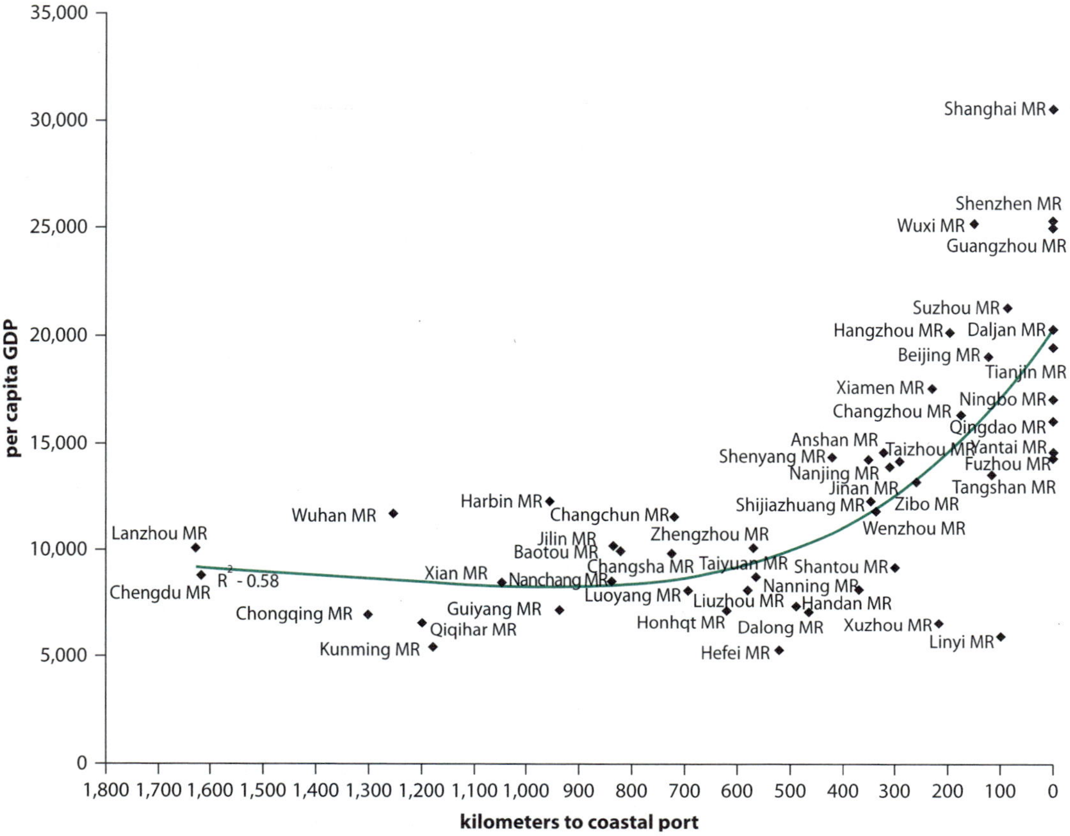

Source: Leman 2005, cited in Gill and Kharas 2007.

Note: The figure shows the situation of 53 metropolitan regions (MRs) in China in 2000.

a significant amount of the residual differences in expenditure growth, with every 100 kilometers from Dhaka reducing expenditure growth by a full percentage point.

Overman and Venables (2005, p. 5) suggest that large cities probably play a "nursery" role in developing country cities, even if the process of research and development and innovation is not identical to that in rich countries. They state:

> Nevertheless, entrepreneurs in low-income countries must also engage in a process of innovation and learning. Their focus is on what Rodrik (2004, p. 9) calls cost discovery: "What is involved is not coming up with new products and processes, but discovering that a certain good, already well established in world markets, can be produced at home at low cost.". . . The urban nature of these cost discovery processes remains largely unexplored. However, Hausmann and Rodrik's (2002) emphasis on tacit knowledge (the kind that cannot be easily codified in to blueprints) in the self discovery process strikes a chord with urban economists who have long seen such knowledge as playing a key role in the information spillovers that occur within cities. This suggests that,

just as for their developed country counterparts, this process of cost discovery is likely to be significantly easier in the information rich environment of large, diverse urban areas.

Hausmann and Rodrik (2002) document an extreme degree of specialization and clustering of exports in Bangladesh; the Dominican Republic; Honduras; Republic of Korea; Pakistan; and Taiwan, China. According to Venables (2007), these patterns suggest that local agglomeration economies are at work in determining international trade patterns. Disaggregated at the six-digit SIC level, the top four product lines account for at least 30 percent of exports to the United States by each of these countries. Moreover, there is very little overlap in export specialization across similar countries.

The evidence from developing countries should be much better than it is. Nonetheless, it shows that the same sorts of agglomeration economies are at work in poor countries as those that are much better documented in richer countries. A few important policy indications emerge from these findings:

- Cities offer productivity advantages that are both static and dynamic. Hence it makes little sense to discourage or try to reverse urbanization. Rural development cannot be a substitute for healthy urbanization. Indeed, it is hard to imagine that much rural-based industry could thrive for export in today's competitive trade environment. The rapid urbanization and growth of large cities in developing countries show that, on balance, the powerful economies of scale and other agglomeration effects at work outweigh the very substantial diseconomies associated with developing country megacities. The urbanization process needs support to help reduce congestion costs. Focusing on making urbanization work would be more productive than trying to stop it.

- The productivity advantages of cities are driven largely by externalities. As a result, market outcomes may be productive, but the size distribution of cities is likely to be inefficient, as the clustering effects described above drive cities to become too large. Chapter 3, by Duranton, sets forth the theory and discusses the empirical analysis of these effects. Unfortunately, in practice, little is known about either the costs of excessive city size or what does and does not work to encourage development of more-efficient new cities. Some interesting research on China (Au and Henderson 2006a, 2006b) suggests that from an economic viewpoint, it is much more costly to be undersized than oversized. This work indicates that real output per worker is quite flat at sizes larger than the optimum city size, so that the costs of a given population reduction below the optimum are nearly three times higher than the cost of adding that same population above the optimum. But much more work is needed on this issue.

- Caution is in order when seeking to decentralize productive activities from large cities. Overman and Venables (2005), Duranton (chapter 3), and Venables (chapter 2) argue instead for a neutral stance that avoids favoring the main city and possibly a policy that signals to private investors the desired location for a new city. This approach may not fully address important practical issues for policymakers. When capacity, both financial and technical, is scarce, governments have to make choices about where to locate infrastructure investments and where to improve services. Many efforts to develop secondary cities have been wasteful. In contrast, China's strategy of favoring coastal cities in the early reform phase reaped rich growth rewards. Because part of the special privileges accorded those cities included the means to finance infrastructure improvements, the worst congestion costs were avoided more successfully than in many other countries (Peterson 2005). Without more research and a more systematic understanding of experience, the danger of cities becoming too large remains difficult to document. Identifying effective policy instruments to address it is thus problematic. If concerns about primacy or cities being too large become an excuse for neglecting necessary urban infrastructure investments, such policies will be very costly.

- The realization of agglomeration economies in fast-growing cities is likely to give rise to very significant spatial inequalities in productivity and income, across regions and cities, between rural and urban areas, and within cities. As a result, policymakers will face important noneconomic concerns, such as political and ethnic tensions, which must be balanced against the economic benefits of productive cities. In chapter 5 Sukkoo Kim discusses the economics of spatial inequalities, how they have evolved over time, and how policies to address them have fared.

Traditional Arguments against Urbanization

Urbanization is inextricably linked to industrialization and modernization, both historically and among rapidly growing developing countries today. There are good economic reasons for this relation, supported by both theoretical and empirical work. Cities have been shown to support high-productivity and high-growth activities in ways that rural areas simply cannot. Despite this evidence, there is discomfort with the urbanization process, and few countries have an explicit policy stance that proactively seeks to incorporate cities in the growth process. Part of the discomfort may be explained by three influential, but largely erroneous, beliefs about urbanization in developing countries:

- Rural–urban migration is unmanageable.
- Rural–urban migration is unproductive.
- Urban growth is driven by pro-urban bias rather than economic fundamentals.

These conjectures emerged in the 1960s, as urban population growth in developing countries was reaching its peak; they have continued to influence policy thinking since. It is worth briefly reviewing the evidence that has emerged since these views became influential.

Is Rural–Urban Migration Unmanageable?

It is commonly argued that developing countries have disastrously overurbanized or are urbanizing at calamitous rates. In fact, their experience has been fairly conventional in important respects (Williamson 1988; National Research Council 2003). The urban share of population in developing countries has been rising since about 1850. Urban population growth in developing countries peaked between 1950 and 1975 and is predicted to continue to decline. During the period of peak growth, the share of urban population increased from 17 to 28 percent (Preston 1979)—nearly identical to the increase that took place in high-income countries in the last quarter of the 19th century (Williamson 1988). Rural–urban migration rates for developing countries as a group in the postwar period were comparable to those in the United Kingdom during the Industrial Revolution (about 17–18 percent).

Developing country experience is distinctive in one important dimension: the total urban population increase over the period is much higher. Urban populations in developing countries increased by 188 percent between 1950 and 1975—a much larger increase than the 100 percent for developed countries between 1875 and 1900. This high population growth in developing countries reflects a demographic success story: the dramatically rapid transition to lower mortality rates that developing countries experienced in both rural and urban areas in the postwar period. In early 19th-century Britain, the rate of natural increase was far lower in cities than in the countryside, because death rates were so high. This made migration a far more important source of population growth, accounting for 60 percent of the increase (Williamson 1990). In contrast, in developing country cities, immigration accounts for only about 40 percent of population growth (National Research Council 2003).[8] Far from being overwhelmed by excessive migration, developing country cities have experienced migration patterns similar to those that occurred elsewhere, although they were also accompanied by rapid natural increase.

Rural–urban migration rates vary considerably across developing countries and over time (figure 1.14). Latin America, the first region to experience rapid migration, achieved the highest rates of urbanization in the 1960s–80s period, peaking in the 1970s. The subsequent decline reflected the already high rate of urbanization (more than 75 percent) and probably the economic slowdown that began in the 1980s.

Africa's rates of migration peaked sooner, in the 1960s; rates have declined by half since then.[9] Already in the 1980s, before the advent of major structural adjustment programs in Africa that reduced "urban bias,"

---

8   This is true of the median country. For data on different developing country regions, see table 1.1.

9   Unfortunately, these decompositions of urban population growth across a range of developing countries have not been brought up to date, and the coverage of the censuses on which they are based is very uneven, especially in Africa. It would be very useful to have more systematic analysis of how these trends have evolved over the past 20 years and more recent census data for many African countries. Satterthwaite (2007) discusses these issues in detail.

Figure 1.14 Estimated Rural-Urban Migration Rates in Africa, Asia, and Latin America, 1960s–1980s

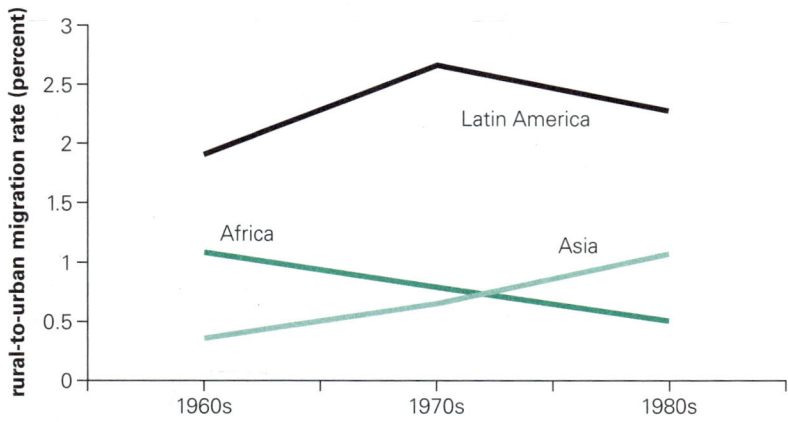

Source: Data from Chen, Valente, and Zlotnik 1998, cited in National Research Council 2003.

Note: Africa includes North Africa and Sub-Saharan Africa.

migration accounted for only a quarter of total urban population growth in Africa (table 1.1). Thus while the share of urban population has steadily increased in Africa, often without economic growth, both migration rates and the share of urban population growth accounted for by migration appear to be in secular decline. The high rates of urbanization in Africa are driven primarily by the high overall rate of population growth—the highest of any region of the world (UNFPA 2007)—and by the relatively small size of the urban population.

Asia experienced a significant secular increase in both migration rates and the share of population growth attributable to migration. These demographic shifts, combined with rapid economic growth, have been accompanied by substantial reductions in poverty in both rural and urban areas. This evidence on regional patterns, based on incomplete data for a number of countries, can be seen only as indicative. It nonetheless suggests that migration rates are neither exploding nor responding perversely to economic signals. Migration rates are rising where economic growth is robust.

Table 1.1 Percentage of Annual Urban Population Growth Attributable to Internal Migration, by Region

Region	1960s	1970s	1980s
Asia	40.4	46.7	63.6[a]
Latin America	40.1	40.5	33.9
North and Sub-Saharan Africa	41.2	40.6	24.9
Developing countries	40.3	44.1	54.3

Source: Data are from Chen, Valente, and Zlotnik (1998), cited in White and Lindstrom (2005).
Note: The regions follow UN definitions. Africa includes both North and Sub-Saharan Africa.
a. The figure for Asia excluding China in the 1980s is 48.9 percent.

Urban populations are growing in Africa primarily as a result of demographic pressure—more so than in any other region. Strategies that seek to manage urban population growth by directing resources away from basic urban services to make cities less attractive to migrants are, in this light, misdirected.

Cities in developing countries have coped far better than was expected when urbanization took off. Urban populations in least developed countries increased by 1.7 billion between 1950 and 2000. Yet the cities of 60 million predicted by Davis, Park, and Bauer (1962) have not yet materialized. The growth of cities in the developing world has placed unprecedented demands on urban services. The common perception of urbanization is colored strongly by images of slums, grinding urban poverty, traffic jams, and air pollution. In fact, however, as Mohan and Das Gupta (2003) argue, developing countries have coped with these demands surprisingly well—even in the face of rapidly growing urban populations, difficult fiscal conditions, and tight constraints on human resource capacity. During the 1990s more than 250 million people in China, India, Indonesia, Korea, and the Philippines were provided with access to clean water, and nearly 300 million gained access to sanitation. Between 1990 and 2000, 32 million people were provided with clean water supply and 23 million people with improved sanitation facilities in Brazil. Coverage rates for these urban services increased in all these countries during the 1990s. Per capita electric power consumption in many countries has increased steadily and substantially, tripling between 1980 and 2000 in China and in the Islamic Republic of Iran and increasing by a factor of more than eight in Indonesia.

The incidence of poverty in cities also declined over this period of rapid urban growth. East Asia lifted unprecedented numbers of people from poverty (see figure 1.8). In Bangladesh the incidence of poverty in Dhaka fell 14 percent during the 1990s, while population grew at 6 percent a year (World Bank 2007b). As chaotic as Dhaka's urban development seems to be, its residents are leaving the ranks of the poor in large numbers.

This evidence should not be interpreted to suggest that urbanization gives no cause for concern. What it does show is that the track record of coping with high rates of urban growth is no disaster. Mohan and Das Gupta (2003, p. 15) put it well:

> Thus there is nothing to fear from the rapid urbanization expected in the next twenty to thirty years, and beyond. We know that we can cope with the unprecedented Asian urban challenge. However, this is not a call for complacency, but is a fact that should give us confidence for the future.

Is Rural–Urban Migration Counterproductive?

The Harris-Todaro model emerged in the late 1960s (Todaro 1969; Harris and Todaro 1970).[10] It proved very influential as an intuitive explanation for the large informal service sector in developing country cities, which

---

10 Williamson (1988) and Lall, Selod, and Shalizi (2006) offer comprehensive critical reviews of the literature in this area, on which this discussion draws.

were viewed as harboring hidden unemployment. The model was pessimistic about urbanization, arguing that rural–urban migration was counterproductive because migrants moved for the wrong reasons—and did so on a continual basis. Rural–urban wage gaps reflected not only productivity differences but also artificially high wages that attracted too many migrants. Rather than offering economic benefits, migration to cities and the eventual closing of the wage gap merely resulted in more workers waiting through unproductive spells of unemployment or underemployment in a bloated service sector. This vision contrasts sharply with work on rural–urban migration during the Industrial Revolution in the United Kingdom. Using a computable general equilibrium model, Williamson (1990) estimates that labor market imperfections prevented migration and led to a deadweight loss of more than 3 percent of GDP.

Worst of all, the Harris-Todaro model predicted that because workers came to the city to participate in a lottery, hoping for formal sector jobs, creating employment only made the problem worse by improving the odds in the lottery and attracting more migrants whose productivity was lower in the cities than in the countryside (the Todaro paradox). This conclusion was particularly important for policy, because it argued against making cities attractive, implicitly endorsed measures to discourage or reverse migration, and reinforced the tendency of poverty and development programs to focus on rural areas.

The Harris-Todaro model has been very influential. It turns out, however, that evidence supporting the predicted link between urban unemployment and migration—and hence their broader pessimism about the economic impacts of urbanization—is weak. Many of the critical assumptions and predictions of the model have not been supported by subsequent empirical studies of labor markets in developing countries. Richer and more plausible alternative models of migration have since emerged. Models of family migration strategies that send workers to the city, for example, show that interactions with the countryside upon migration to the city have been significant. Yet the absence of such interaction is critical to the Todaro paradox (Stark and Lucas 1988; Stark and Levhari 1982). Evidence of wage rigidity in the formal sector has been questioned. Real wage erosion in a number of African countries started in the 1970s (Weeks 1994). Even in Africa institutionalized high wages turn out to have been limited largely to East and Central Africa, where they represent the legacy of high wage policies under the British colonial regime and a short period of trade union power following independence.[11] In West Africa there was a minimal and sometimes even negative urban income premium as colonialization ended. The data do not support rising wage gaps between industry and agriculture, a necessary premise for increases in unemployment in the face of urban job creation. Moreover, contrary to the model's prediction, as soon as they get

---

11 Measures to reduce high labor turnover in the westernized sectors of British East Africa included a high wage policy whose goal was to provide sufficient income to support a family in the urban areas (Weeks 1994).

jobs, migrants tend to earn more than they did in the countryside. Studies provide empirical support for some behaviors embodied in the model—such as migration responding to wage differentials—but the evidence that the Todaro paradox actually holds in developing countries is weak (Lall, Selod, and Shalizi 2006).

Also damaging to the Harris-Todaro argument are the findings of Williamson (1988), who argues that the "problem" that the model was intended to explain was exaggerated. A number of studies show that the growth of the service sector in developing country cities was neither disproportionate nor composed primarily of unskilled "surplus labor" from the countryside. Once early surveys indicating growing unemployment in developing countries in the 1960s were revised, little support remained for the concept of high and rising unemployment in cities. Nor was there ever much evidence that recent migrants were more likely to be unemployed than others in the city labor force.

The poor performance of some African economies experiencing rapid urban growth rates may have contributed to the enduring appeal of the Harris-Todaro model, which despite its flaws "influenced policy for decades" (Lall, Selod, and Shalizi 2006, p. 47). In 25 of the 56 countries Collier (2007) terms "Africa+ countries"—countries that are falling behind—urbanization without growth has occurred. However, both weaknesses in the model and its inability to explain underlying demographic trends argue against using it as the hypothesis of first resort.

Other economic constraints may have more substantial effects on economic performance. Reducing fertility may be a better policy response to high urban population growth than reducing migration (Chen, Valente, and Zlotnik 1998). If a low-income agrarian economy suffers from agricultural distress or civil unrest, migrants are likely to be pushed into cities, resulting in temporarily high unemployment or a proliferation of low-productivity service sector jobs as migrants barely get by. High commodity prices may lead to overvalued exchange rates and resource shifts to the nontraded sector in cities. In such cases remedies such as suitable macroeconomic or agricultural policies should at least be explored before assuming that reducing the attractiveness of cities by withholding investments in basic amenities is the best policy response.

The economic stagnation in a number of African countries is a disturbing trend even if growth rates are indeed driven by climate and conflict rather than high wages and better services in cities. Part of getting growth back on track should be taking a view of how cities will ultimately serve as platforms for growth. Allowing secular deterioration in basic services, as has happened in many of these countries, may well compromise prospects for achieving this goal.

Is Urban Bias Widespread and Enduring?

The concept of urban bias—closely linked to the notion of pathological urbanization and migration—has been very influential in guiding aid and development programs away from cities. Lipton's (1976) work on urban bias, which is both simple and sweeping, is the most influential articulation of the concept. Lipton argues that policy distortions favor city growth, harming the rural poor while encouraging excessive migration to cities. Industrial protection, cheap credit, and subsidized local services financed out of general tax revenues are among a long list of policies that presumably shift economic activity to cities. Empirical work has focused largely on measuring urban bias (see Agarwala 1983; Little, Scitovsky, and Scott 1970).

Rural bias is rarely discussed, but there is no logical reason why distorting policies might not sometimes favor the countryside unduly. The existence of urban bias has virtually ceased to be an empirical policy question; it is often simply assumed to be present if the poor continue to be disproportionately represented in the countryside (see, for example, Majumdar, Mani, and Mukan 2004). By this logic, focusing on how cities can facilitate industrialization and growth should be a lower priority, cities should fend for themselves, and subsidization of urban areas should be avoided (subsidization of rural areas is rarely questioned). This simplification of thinking about urbanization policy is what has made the concept of urban bias most problematic.

In practice, the concept of urban bias groups a host of policies, all of which might have merit in specific circumstances but often do not. The antidote to such bias often involves focusing on the poor in the countryside and avoiding subsidies in cities, even if many of the poor live and work there. This approach does not distinguish between subsidies to public services that make cities livable and productive (common even in high-income countries) and subsidies to specific industries and food products, where the case for government intervention is much weaker. Rather than examine each of those policies that fit under the "urban bias" umbrella on its merits, the response has been to focus development spending on the countryside and avoid support to cities. Rural and urban areas are pitted against each other, with development policy conceived as a zero-sum game for dividing the subsidy pie. Lost is the notion that the rapid growth that only urban areas can produce will reduce poverty and add to the revenue base to finance assistance to the rural poor. Moreover, the focus on avoiding urban bias has diverted attention from understanding some of the institutional and social constraints that may have driven policies that created urban bias in the first place.

The example of Africa is instructive. Many of the stylized features of urban bias were present in the early postcolonial period in many African countries. Weeks (1994) argues that much of this bias, such as high formal sector wages, reflected specific political imperatives and institutional constraints following independence rather than an explicit strategy to favor cities. In some East African countries, unions played an important role in the independence struggle—and expected rewards after independence. As a reaction to colonial policy, countries sought to industrialize and build prestigious public works, which naturally meant investing in cities. Given the structure of the economy, agriculture was the only sector that could generate much tax revenue. Very weak government administrations in the immediate postcolonial period had limited fiscal options. Weeks argues that taxing external trade was attractive because it was simple. In contrast, administering direct taxes on farm income—difficult in the best of circumstances—posed insurmountable difficulties in Africa right after independence. As a result many governments resorted to highly distorting marketing boards to extract fiscal resources indirectly. While all of these measures undoubtedly hurt agriculture, many of them reflected very real constraints on fiscal instruments. Reducing these distortions, which attracted so much attention under the guise of urban bias, did not lead to a resumption of growth. Significant constraints to growth—related to geography, climate, and colonial history—apparently lay elsewhere (Collier 2007).

Structural Transition and Urbanization

These insights from Africa's experience highlight issues at the crux of managing urbanization productively in developing countries. Urbanization involves millions of individual decisions about where to live and work. It usually accompanies positive economic developments, such as industrialization and entry into export markets. Sometimes, as appears to be the case in some parts of Africa, it may respond to adversity in agriculture or to social conflicts. Measures to slow the urbanization process have almost always failed, because they sought to thwart a response to strong economic rewards or pressures.

Whatever the driving forces, people typically move to cities well before the institutions emerge to accommodate an orderly urbanization process. Urbanization therefore nearly always involves a host of messy problems—unsightly, unsafe, or unhealthy development; congestion; skyrocketing land prices; and highly questionable real estate practices—at least for a while. Many of these problems are perceived as failures, although they often emerge in the face of economic success. To make modern cities work, a transformation, not incremental change, in fiscal and administrative institutions, is needed, and it often comes in response to a crisis of some kind. The following sections examine some of the most important structural transitions that urbanization requires.

Mobilizing support for urbanization. Political economy makes it harder to adopt policies that support urbanization—more so in some places than others. According to Lewis (1977), in 19th-century Argentina, the landed aristocracy that emerged with the development of foreign-financed agricultural exports was a major constraint to the development of industry and the creation of a supporting environment in cities. By contrast Australia, dominated from the outset by urban communities, was able to put in place policies to make industry profitable and build the cities to support it. In countries in the early stages of urbanization, governments, especially democratic governments, may find themselves pressed to invest tax dollars in infrastructure for growing cities that are essential to the economic future of the country but currently house only a minority of the population.

Historically, the governments of economically dynamic cities often operated with political models that explicitly or implicitly contested economic and political power with higher levels of government. Pirenne (1922) documents both the economic dynamism in cities and the deep-seated conflicts between governance systems that supported trade in cities and protection in the countryside in medieval and Renaissance Europe. In Bangladesh and India, important independence leaders held prominent positions in local government during the independence struggle.[12] DeLong and Shleifer (1993) provide empirical support for earlier findings that cities governed by absolutist governments (princes) experienced lower economic growth (measured by growth in city size) than cities governed by more market-friendly systems (merchants) in the 800 years preceding the Industrial Revolution. These historical differences between city governments and nation-states have often slowed the transition to policies and governance structures that are well suited to providing the local public goods growing cities require.

Financing public goods. Fiscal constraints can profoundly affect the scope of feasible urbanization policy. Cities require public goods to manage the high densities that engender agglomeration economies. Productive and healthy urbanization requires finance to support lumpy investments in expensive networked infrastructure. The demand for these public goods arises just as industrialization is also making substantial claims on resources (Linn 1982). For these reasons, there is an historical tendency for urbanization to coincide with foreign borrowing (Lewis 1977). In the best of circumstances, local public goods are not easy to finance at the city level. National governments can typically mobilize fiscal resources with less distortion of labor market and investment decisions than local governments, hence the case for fiscal federalism (see, for example, Broadway 2001). In theory, optimal land taxation could be used to finance local public goods, but doing so is difficult in practice in developing countries. A public finance system that works for cities with stable populations does not necessarily generate the resources needed to modernize rapidly growing cities.

Cities in low-income countries have large informal economies that are difficult to tax, as Richard Arnott notes in chapter 6. This informality is often a natural outcome of accommodating rapid population and economic growth in cities. Widespread informality undermines myriad elements of traditional local finance, including land taxation, recorded real estate transactions, and transparent market-based land valuations, to name a few.

---

12 Pandit Nehru, Sardar Patel, Acharya Gidvani, and Subash Chandra Bose, all Congress Party leaders in the fight for independence, held prominent positions in major municipal corporations in the 1930s.

The drivers of informality are many. Institutional capacity to protect property rights, enforce regulations, and manage planned urban expansion is weak. In Bangladesh, for example, Siddiqui (1997) estimates that it would take nearly 50 years to clear the existing backlog in land records. Meanwhile Dhaka's population was growing at 6 percent a year (World Bank 2007b). Many, sometimes most, low-income residents of cities are often too poor to live in housing built to standards the authorities consider decent enough to regularize. Local governments do not have the resources to finance the investments needed to provide services to all, yet no residence can be considered formal without these services. The result is that many inhabitants of cities live in informal areas and fall outside the public finance net. They usually pay for services at far higher prices than formal service providers charge. They pay—often dearly—for protection to remain irregular; as long as they remain informal, their payments do not contribute to the fiscal base. As Arnott suggests, widespread informality in cities can lead to a vicious circle of weak fiscal base and very inadequate infrastructure.

This narrowing of the local tax base dramatically complicates the politics of raising local revenues. The constraints identified in box 1.1 in 19th-century Britain were overcome only when central subsidies were provided to ease the local fiscal burden of making economically sound investments in sanitation. Paris's experience illustrates another source of public finance—land transactions—and shows how fragile such resources can be if property holders rebel (box 1.2). While reforming its fiscal system in the 1990s to reassert central fiscal control, China still left local governments scope to use land appreciation as a form of capital finance in booming economies. The resulting expansion of urban infrastructure has been nothing short of dramatic, even if extensive waste and significant risks have been part of the process (see Gao 2007; Su and Zhou 2007). Brazil financed a substantial expansion of urban water and sanitation facilities in the 1970s and 1980s with a system of centralized planning, regulation, and financing, almost doubling sanitation coverage in a decade. With the slowdown of economic growth in the 1980s and decentralization, however, the system was restructured, and investments have declined (Cortines and Bondarovsky 2007).

A sound system of public finance for local public goods does not emerge naturally in poor urbanizing countries. Making this transition effectively deserves more attention in the development process and requires central government support in some form.

Modernizing real estate and financial markets. Rapid urbanization and economic growth require a third significant transition: the modernization of real estate markets and systems for financing them. Rapid increases in low-skill, low-wage jobs that fuel growth in developing country cities lead to influxes of low-income city residents who need housing convenient to their work. The businesses offering jobs need land for shops and factories. Because of agglomeration economies, they all want to locate in the same places. A functional real estate market is essential for allocating this resource to

Box 1.2 How Baron Haussman Financed the Modernization of Paris

In the early 19th century, the population of Paris, which had hitherto grown very slowly, expanded rapidly, doubling in 50 years. Conditions of life for the vast majority of the population were miserable and unhealthy. Three cholera epidemics had ravaged the city. The first and worst, in 1832, killed 20,000 people, nearly 3 percent of the population. The casualties included the prime minister, Casimir Perier, but the lower classes suffered disproportionately from the disease, giving rise to considerable social unrest. The Revolution of 1848, seen as an urban uprising against crowding, miserable housing, and high rents, lent urgency to the renovation of Paris. Emperor Louis Napoleon made the modernization of Paris his priority, appointing George Eugene Haussman as prefect of the Seine in June 1853 to achieve this goal.

With the strong support of the emperor, Haussman remade the face Paris—at no small cost. Haussman estimated that over 18 years, he spent 44 times the annual budget of the city on capital works (Pinkney 1957). Others estimate that the capital spending for Haussman's series of improvements was equivalent to the annual budget of France for an entire year (Marchand 1993).

Yet in many ways the finances of Paris at the time Haussman started his work resembled the meager budgets of poor developing country cities today. In the preceding 30 years, while the population had soared, revenues and expenditures, although broadly in balance, stagnated. Seventy percent of revenue came from indirect taxes, primarily the *octroi*, a medieval tax charged on entry into the city (Marchand 1993). Ten percent of all revenues were paid to the central government. About two-thirds of the population was exempt from direct taxation, considered too destitute to pay. Spending on capital investment and maintenance was limited to about 15 percent of the total budget. This fiscal environment was hardly ripe for the transformational change Haussman envisaged and the 16-fold increase in capital spending needed to achieve it.

Changes in the expropriation laws offered Haussman the wherewithal both to remake the city and to finance it expeditiously. In 1852 a new law was passed permitting expropriation of entire blocks, not just rights of way. Each expropriation required passage of a law, however, making the process extremely cumbersome. Later that year this law was modified to allow expropriation by imperial decree. Haussman used these powers liberally. As he remade Paris's layout and infrastructure, he resold any surplus expropriated land at a handsome profit, thus financing his operation through the value created from his public works. Haussman's profits were estimated at four times the original subsidy provided by the state (Marchand 1993). Up until 1858 this method was successful. But landowners eventually moved the Council of State to respond. It rendered a decision that all improved lands had to be resold to their original owners at the original price at expropriation, notwithstanding the change in market value the improvements had effected. In 1860 the courts handed down a decision that expropriation payments had to be paid immediately, not at eviction, thus advancing the costs of expropriation by several years (Marchand 1993).

These two decisions created new pressures on cash flow and forced Haussman to go to both the capital markets and his suppliers to fund further operations (Pinkney 1957). Relying on these arrangements alone was a less robust financial model, and rising real estate prices, a byproduct of Haussman's success, made it far more difficult and expensive to complete the later phases of his work. Ultimately, the city became heavily indebted and Haussman ran afoul of the city council, as it asserted its rights of oversight and control. Jules Ferry, a republican deputy, immortalized the dark view of Haussman's financial engineering in *Les Comptes Fantastique de Haussman*. Combining the debts Haussman incurred and debts for reparations of the war of 1870, the debt per inhabitant in Paris was twice that in New York and three times that in London by the end of the 19th century (Marchand 1993). It was only the inflation of the interwar period that eventually reduced the debt burden, ruining many bondholders.

Source: Marchand 1993; Pinkney 1957.

its best use. Yet the capacity of the formal real estate market to respond is limited in most developing countries, for many reasons.

A number of features of the typical developing country city combine to make housing supply much less responsive than it should be. Traditional systems of land ownership, registration, and taxation are rarely able to accommodate a high volume of transactions and rapid turnover in land use. Planning, zoning, and building standards resemble those of high-income European cities. These standards make housing that is affordable for most of the city population illegal and do little to alleviate the chaotic conditions in these neighborhoods. To compound the problem, the military or parastatals often control large parcels of economically valuable land in the cities, effectively taking this land off the market. Infrastructure service providers often have neither the finance nor the capacity to expand and upgrade network infrastructure to provide for occupying land at high densities. Conversion of agricultural land surrounding cities can be both burdensome and socially contentious. In such environments countries successfully tapping the global market to industrialize will find that growth in the demand for housing and land in cities far outstrips the supply response.[13] A very common result is high real estate prices, in some cases comparable to those in large cities in high-income countries—even in very poor countries like Bangladesh (Buckley and Mathema 2007; Buckley and Kalarickal 2006; World Bank 2007b). These market outcomes create great social and political pressures for governments to do something, even when the problem is a byproduct of economic success.

In chapter 6 Arnott discusses some of the options for governments facing these problems. There are no easy fixes for addressing this kind of market imbalance driven by structural change. It is too costly for the government to provide housing directly for low- and middle-income groups on a wide scale. In most cases, government housing projects are built to unrealistic standards, and they rarely reach truly low-income households. Singapore's extraordinary experience of providing public housing for virtually all needy residents benefited from exceptional circumstances, such as full government control of land and the absence of a hinterland. The most effective programs in developed countries (rental subsidies) are difficult to use when informal economic activity is widespread.

Despite these difficulties, developing country governments must do something to improve urban living conditions in the short run. The response should involve providing basic infrastructure and reasonable security of tenure for the poorest; limiting subsidies for public housing programs, which do not reach the neediest in typical market conditions; and improving basic infrastructure networks to allow a healthy expansion in sought-after cities. In the medium term, governments can often do more by doing less. Unrealistic planning standards marginalize lower-income residents by making legal housing unaffordable (Bertaud 2008). Tight planning norms and strong demand in real estate markets combine with weak institutions and corruption to make real estate development expensive and slow, weakening the supply response just when it needs

---

13 Immigration to wealthy countries is another aspect of globalization that has a strong impact on real estate markets. Remittances from nationals living abroad, which are often invested in real estate, may drive prices well above the capacity of local wage earners to pay (Buckley and Mathema 2007).

to be stronger. As incomes increase, fiscal capacity improves, institutions evolve, and the elasticity of land supply and purchasing power for good housing increase. It is at this stage that standards closer to those of rich countries become feasible.

This transition can be long and painful. It can be helped along through financial innovation. When properly documented, real estate assets are excellent candidates for finance. Because these assets are long lived, they offer good investments for institutions with long-term liabilities. They offer some of the best collateral for borrowing. Long-term mortgage finance can dramatically improve households' capacity to purchase decent housing. Mortgage markets have developed and liberalized very rapidly in the past 20 years (Buckley and Kalarickal 2006). This market now extends to developing countries, with mortgage credit growing at more than 20 percent a year in China and India in recent years (Buckley and Kalarickal 2006). For long-run development, these changes are necessary and beneficial. But as with all financial innovations, in the short term there is scope for both instability and abuse. In chapter 7 Dwight Jaffee examines a highly visible and recent example of this cycle—the subprime mortgage crisis in the United States—drawing lessons from it for developing countries. While the subprime crisis seems unique to the U.S. mortgage market, finding the right balance between financial innovation that heightens the risk of a painful crisis and financial repression that rations financial services, typically depriving the neediest, is a universal challenge.

Two factors make managing innovation in mortgage markets in developing country cities particularly tricky. First, inelastic supply is often the primary constraint in urban real estate markets in developing countries. Mortgage finance, while helpful to individual purchasing households, operates on the demand side. If the supply response is price insensitive in key real estate markets, in the short run expanding access to mortgage finance may simply create more pressure on demand and prices. Without measures to enhance a supply response, policymakers may be disappointed in the ultimate impact of expanding mortgage credit on housing prices and affordability. Rapid expansion of mortgage finance in highly regulated or poorly functioning real estate markets may even run the risk of financing an asset price bubble. Moreover, when access to market-rate mortgage credit is introduced in environments characterized by high levels of informality, the reach of mortgage finance beyond the highest income classes can be very limited.

Second, importing financial innovation to developing countries in the area of mortgage finance can be very risky. Argentina, for example, issued mortgage-backed securities as early as 1996. Because the local financial sector was seen to have a number of shortcomings for such issues, the securities were sold in international markets denominated in U.S. dollars (Chiquier, Hassler, and Lea 2004). Because they placed foreign exchange risk with borrowers ill-equipped to manage it, these securities fared poorly during the economic crisis in Argentina, when mortgage liabilities were converted to the rapidly devaluing peso. As was also the case with public-private partnerships for infrastructure, devaluation of the exchange rate created an untenable situation in the local mortgage market, with costly disruptions to long-term market development. These difficulties are significant but should not be seen as reasons to avoid liberalization altogether. They are reasons for proceeding with caution, recognizing that local circumstances in both the financial sector and real estate markets must figure strongly in strategies to navigate a sensitive but necessary transition.

Concluding Remarks

The tensions that urbanization creates and the structural shifts it puts into motion suggest why developing country policy makers do not always welcome rapid urbanization. Viewed from the long perspective of history, urbanization is necessary for achieving high growth and high incomes. In its early stages urbanization is beneficial, but it can also be painful. Managing urbanization will affect politics, social norms, institutional change, and the broader financial system. Policymaking in this environment is rife with problems of the second best. Shaping strategies that make cities work for the national economy will demand pragmatism and sensitivity to what is viable in a given context, but such strategies will reap large rewards.

Annex 1: Results from UN Inquiry among Governments on Population and Development, Various Years

The following tables are from *World Population Policies 2007*, published by the United Nations Department of Economic and Social Affairs/Population Division.

Table A1.1 Government Views on the Spatial Distribution of the Population: 1976, 1986, 1996, and 2007

	A. By level of development							
	(Number of countries)				(Percentage)			
Year	Major change desired	Minor change desired	Satisfactory	Total	Major change desired	Minor change desired	Satisfactory	Total
World								
1976	78	55	17	150	52	37	11	100
1986	75	71	18	164	46	43	11	100
1996	80	57	55	192	42	30	29	100
2007	100	66	29	195	51	34	15	100
More developed regions								
1976	4	19	11	34	12	56	32	100
1986	3	18	13	34	9	53	38	100
1996	11	15	22	48	23	31	46	100
2007	18	19	12	49	37	39	24	100
Less developed regions								
1976	74	36	6	116	64	31	5	100
1986	72	53	5	130	55	41	4	100
1996	69	42	33	144	48	29	23	100
2007	82	47	17	146	56	32	12	100
Least developed countries								
1976	27	15	0	42	64	36	0	100
1986	26	22	0	48	54	46	0	100
1996	30	12	6	48	63	25	13	100
2007	32	16	2	50	64	32	4	100

Table A1.1 (continued)

	B. By major area							
	(Number of countries)				(Percentage)			
Year	Major change desired	Minor change desired	Satisfactory	Total	Major change desired	Minor change desired	Satisfactory	Total
Africa								
1976	36	12	0	48	75	25	0	100
1986	34	17	0	51	67	33	0	100
1996	33	13	6	52	63	25	12	100
2007	39	12	2	53	74	23	4	39
Asia								
1976	14	19	4	37	38	51	11	100
1986	11	24	3	38	29	63	8	100
1996	17	18	11	46	37	39	24	100
2007	24	17	6	47	51	36	13	100
Europe								
1976	2	17	10	29	7	59	34	100
1986	2	15	12	29	7	52	41	100
1996	10	13	20	43	23	30	47	100
2007	17	16	11	44	39	36	25	100
Latin America and the Caribbean								
1976	22	4	1	27	81	15	4	100
1986	24	8	1	33	73	24	3	100
1996	16	7	10	33	48	21	30	100
2007	13	14	6	33	39	42	18	100
North America								
1976	0	1	1	2	0	50	50	100
1986	0	1	1	2	0	50	50	100
1996	0	0	2	2	0	0	100	100
2007	0	1	1	2	0	50	50	100
Oceania								
1976	4	2	1	7	57	29	14	100
1986	4	6	1	11	36	55	9	100
1996	4	6	6	16	25	38	38	100
2007	7	6	3	16	44	38	19	100

Table A1.2 Government Policies on Internal Migration into Urban Agglomerations: 1976, 1986, 1996, and 2007

	A. By level of development									
	(Number of countries)					(Percentage)				
Year	Raise	Maintain	Lower	No intervention	Total	Raise	Maintain	Lower	No intervention	Total
	World									
1976	4	0	39	40	83	5	0	47	48	100
1986	2	1	50	41	94	2	1	53	44	100
1996	3	5	55	60	123	2	4	45	49	100
2007	5	5	112	50	172	3	3	65	29	100
	More developed regions									
1976	2	0	11	7	20	10	0	55	35	100
1986	1	1	8	9	19	5	5	42	47	100
1996	3	3	8	17	31	10	10	26	55	100
2007	2	2	17	23	44	5	5	39	52	100
	Less developed regions									
1976	2	0	28	33	63	3	0	44	52	100
1986	1	0	42	32	75	1	0	56	43	100
1996	0	2	47	43	92	0	2	51	47	100
2007	3	3	95	27	128	2	2	74	21	100
	Least developed countries									
1976	0	0	11	15	26	0	0	42	58	100
1986	0	0	7	19	26	0	0	27	73	100
1996	0	0	17	17	34	0	0	50	50	100
2007	0	0	32	11	43	0	0	74	26	100

	A. By level of development									
	(Number of countries)					(Percentage)				
Year	Raise	Maintain	Lower	No intervention	Total	Raise	Maintain	Lower	No intervention	Total
	Africa									
1976	0	0	18	19	37	0	0	49	51	100
1986	0	0	16	17	33	0	0	48	52	100
1996	0	1	22	18	41	0	2	54	44	100
2007	0	0	36	10	46	0	0	78	22	100
	Asia									
1976	1	0	4	0	5	20	0	80	0	100
1986	1	0	12	6	19	5	0	63	32	100
1996	0	0	18	9	27	0	0	67	33	100
2007	3	3	30	6	42	7	7	71	14	100
	Europe									
1976	2	0	11	6	19	11	0	58	32	100
1986	1	1	8	6	16	6	6	50	38	100
1996	3	3	7	13	26	12	12	27	50	100
2007	2	2	15	20	39	5	5	38	51	100
	Latin America and the Caribbean									
1976	1	0	6	13	20	5	0	30	65	100
1986	0	0	13	6	19	0	0	68	32	100
1996	0	0	8	15	23	0	0	35	65	100
2007	0	0	21	10	31	0	0	68	32	100
	North America									
1976	0	0	0	1	1	0	0	0	100	100
1986	0	0	0	2	2	0	0	0	100	100
1996	0	0	0	2	2	0	0	0	100	100
2007	0	0	0	2	2	0	0	0	100	100
	Oceania									
1976	0	0	0	1	1	0	0	0	100	100
1986	0	0	1	4	5	0	0	20	80	100
1996	0	1	0	3	4	0	25	0	75	100
2007	0	0	10	2	12	0	0	83	17	100

Annex 2: Urbanization Rates and Per Capita GDP, 1960–2000 (1996 Dollars)

Figure A2.1 Urbanization and Per Capita GDP across Countries, 1960–2000 (1996 Dollars)

a. 1960

$y = 18.695 \text{ Ln}(x) - 109.62$

$R^2 = 0.5415$

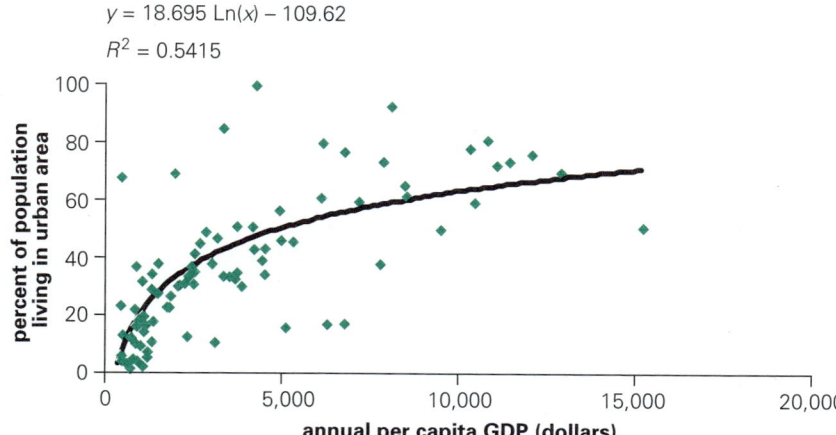

b. 1970

$y = 18.09 \text{ Ln}(x) - 105.88$

$R^2 = 0.5678$

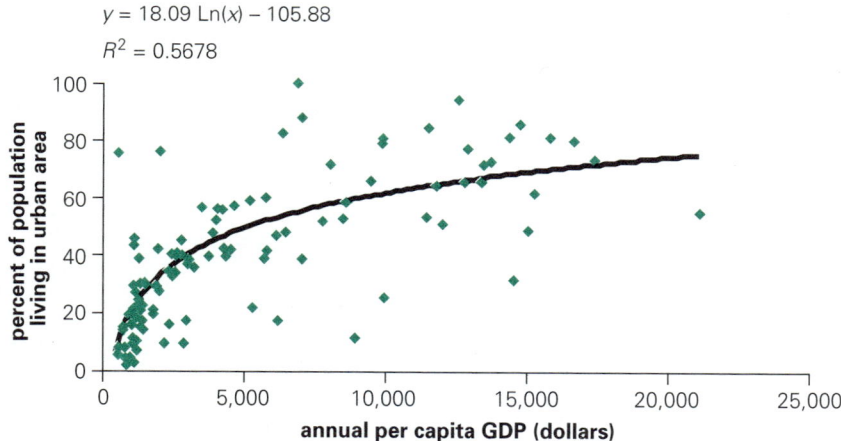

c. 1980

$y = 16.855 \text{ Ln}(x) - 94.377$

$R^2 = 0.6087$

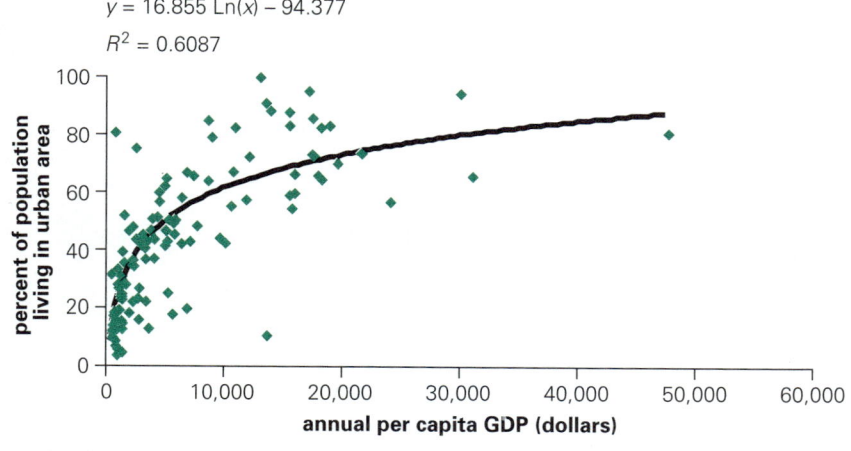

Figure A2.1 (continued)
d. 1990

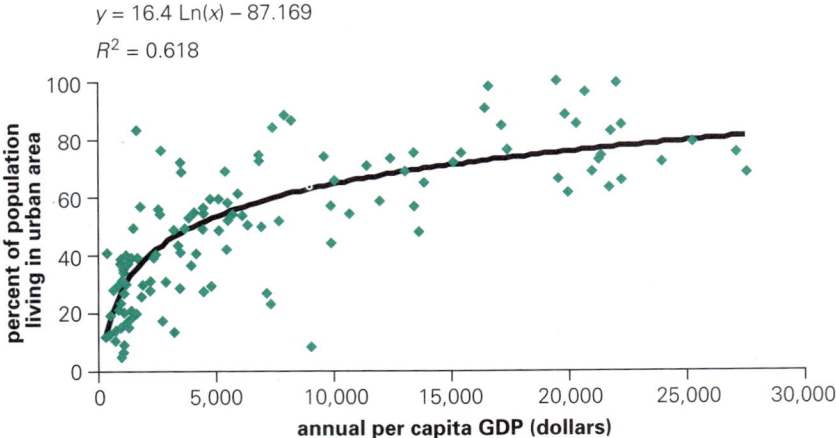

$y = 16.4\ \text{Ln}(x) - 87.169$

$R^2 = 0.618$

e. 2000

$y = 14.92\ \text{Ln}(x) - 72.665$

$R^2 = 0.5705$

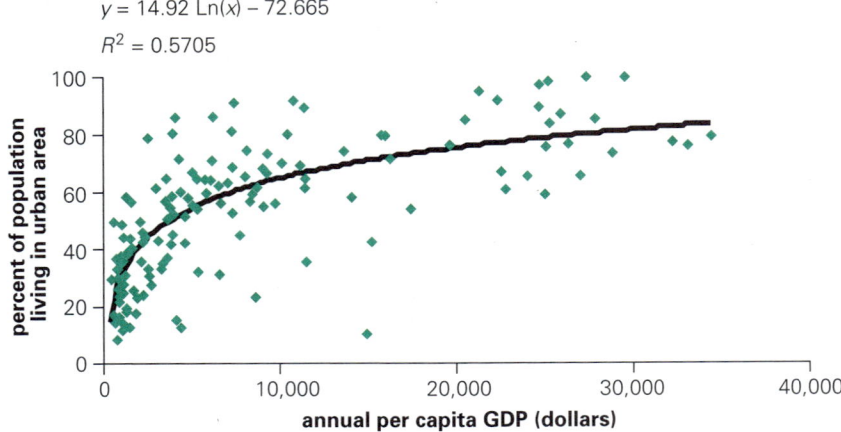

Annex 3: Regional Poverty Incidence in Urban and Rural Areas, by World Region, 1993–2002

Figure A3.1 Poverty Headcount in Latin America and the Caribbean, 1993–2002

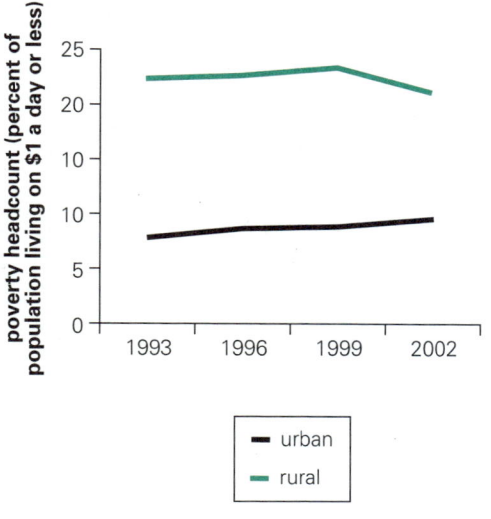

Source: Ravallion, Chen, and Sangraula, 2007.

Figure A3.2 Poverty Headcount, Urban Share of Population, and Per Capita GDP Indexes for Latin America and the Caribbean, 1993–2002

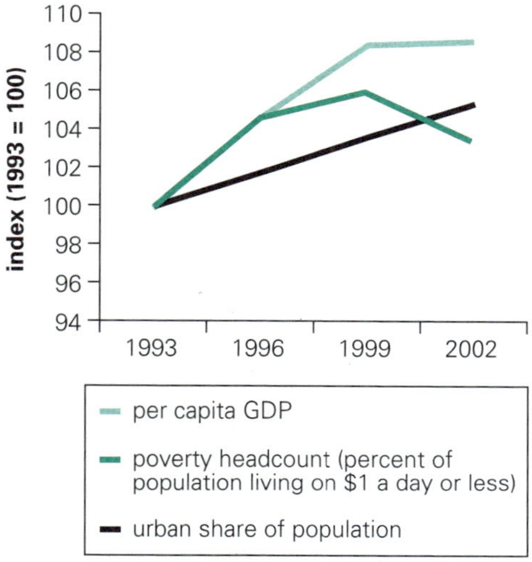

Source: Ravallion, Chen, and Sangraula, 2007.

Figure A3.3 Poverty Headcount in South Asia, 1993–2002

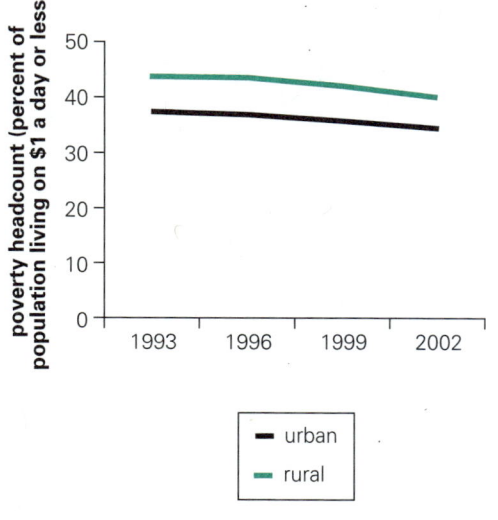

Source: Ravallion, Chen, and Sangraula, 2007.

Figure A3.4 Poverty Headcount, Urban Share of Population, and Per Capita GDP Indexes for South Asia, 1993–2002

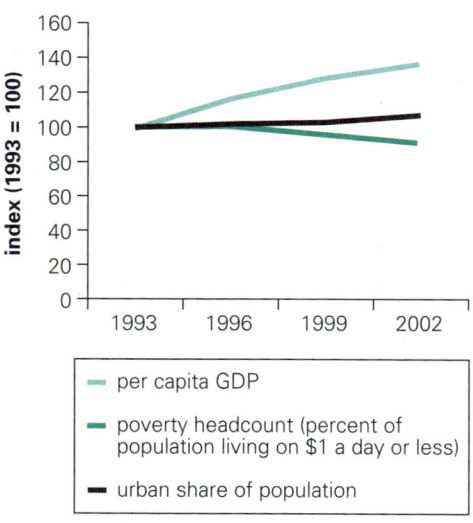

Source: Ravallion, Chen, and Sangraula, 2007.

Figure A3.5 Poverty Headcount in Europe and Central Asia, 1993–2002

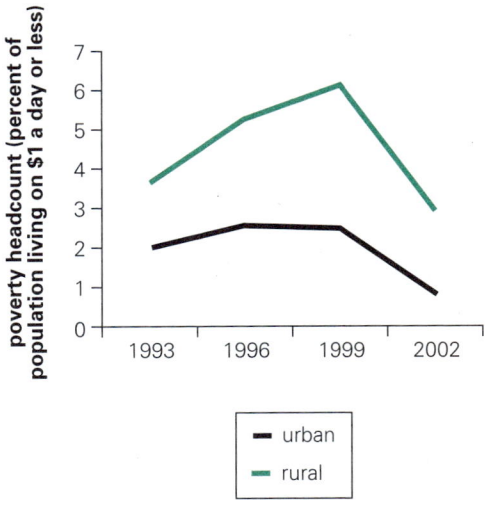

Figure A3.6 Poverty Headcount, Urban Share of Population, and Per Capita GDP Indexes for Europe and Central Asia, 1993–2002

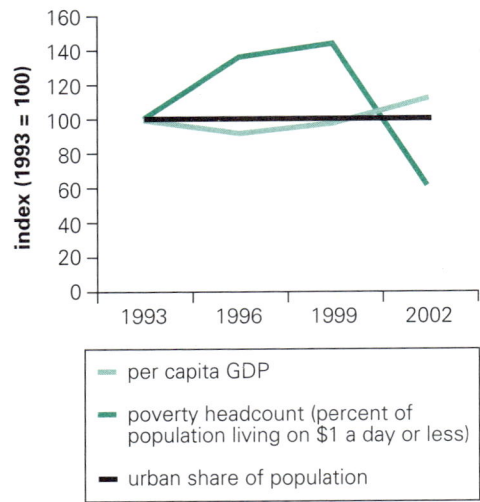

- per capita GDP
- poverty headcount (percent of population living on $1 a day or less)
- urban share of population

Figure A3.7 Poverty Headcount in the Middle East and North Africa, 1993–2002

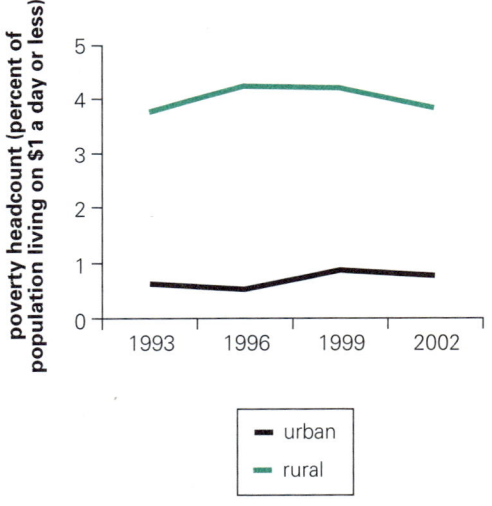

Figure A3.8 Poverty Headcount, Urban Share of Population, and Per Capita GDP Indexes for the Middle East and North Africa, 1993–2002

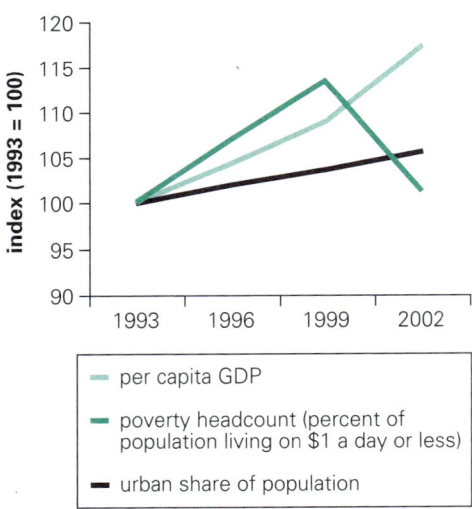

- per capita GDP
- poverty headcount (percent of population living on $1 a day or less)
- urban share of population

References

Acemoglu, Daron. 1996. "A Microfoundation for Social Increasing Returns in Human Capital Accumulation." *Quarterly Journal of Economics* 111 (3): 779–804.

Agarwala, R. 1983. "Price Distortions and Growth in Developing Countries." World Bank Working Paper 575, Washington, DC.

Au Chun-Chung, and J. Vernon Henderson. 2006a. "Are Chinese Cities Too Small?" *Review of Economic Studies* 73 (3) (256) (July): 549–76.

———. 2006b "How Migration Restrictions Limit Agglomeration and Productivity in China." *Journal of Development Economics* 80 (2) (August): 350–88.

Bairoch, Paul. 1988. *Cities and Economic Development: From the Dawn of History to the Present*. Chicago: University of Chicago Press.

Banerjee, S., Q. Wodon, A. Diallo, T. Pushak, H. Uddin, C. Tsimpo, and V. Foster. 2007. "Affordability and Alternatives: Modern Infrastructure Services in Africa." Infrastructure Diagnostic Study, World Bank, Washington, DC.

Barrios, Salvador, Luisito Bertinelli, and Eric Strobl. 2006. "Climate Change and Rural–Urban Migration: The Case of Sub-Saharan Africa." *Journal of Urban Economics* 60 (3): 357–71.

Becker, Charles, Andrew Hamer, and Andrew Morrison. 1994. *Beyond Urban Bias in Africa*. London: James Curry.

Bertaud, Alain. 2008. http://alain-bertaud.com.

Broadway, Robin. 2001. "Intergovernmental Fiscal Relations: The Facilitator of Fiscal Decentralization." *Constitutional Political Economy* 12 (2): 93–121.

Buckley, Robert, and Jerry Kalarickal. 2006. *Thirty Years of World Bank Shelter Lending: What Have We Learned?* Directions in Development Series, World Bank, Washington, DC.

Buckley, Robert, and Ashna Mathema. 2007. "Is Accra a Superstar City?" World Bank Policy Research Working Paper 4453, Washington, DC.

Burgess, Robin, and Anthony J. Venables. 2004. "Towards a Microeconomics of Growth." World Bank Working Paper 3257, April, Washington, DC.

Chen, N., P. Valente, and H. Zlotnik. 1998. "What Do We Know about Recent Trends in Urbanization?" In *Migration, Urbanization, and Development: New Directions and Issues*, ed. R. E. Bilsborrow, 59–88. New York: United Nations Population Fund.

Chiquier, Loic, Olivier Hassler, and Michael Lea. 2004. "Mortgage Securities in Emerging Markets." World Bank Policy Research Working Paper 3370, Washington, DC.

Collier, Paul. 2006. "Africa: Geography and Growth." Department of Economics, Centre for the Study of African Economies, Oxford University, Oxford.

———. 2007. *The Bottom Billion: Why the Poorest Countries Are Failing and What Can Be Done About It*. Oxford: Oxford University Press.

Commission on Growth and Development. 2008. *The Growth Report: Strategies for Sustained Growth and Inclusive Development*. Washington, DC: World Bank.

Cortines, Aser, and Sandra Bondarovsky. 2007. "Mobilizing Finance for Urban Sanitation Infrastructure in Brazil." In *Financing Cities: Fiscal Responsibility and Urban Infrastructure Finance in Brazil, China, India, Poland and South Africa*, ed. George Peterson and Patricia Clarke Annez. New Delhi: Sage Publications.

Davis, Kingsley, Richard Park, and Catherine Bauer. 1962. *India's Urban Future: Selected Studies*. Berkeley: University of California Press.

DeLong, Bradford, and Andrei Shleifer. 1993. "Princes and Merchants: City Growth before the Industrial Revolution." *Journal of Law and Economics* 36 (October): 671–702.

Duranton, Gilles, and Diego Puga. 2001. "Nursery Cities: Urban Diversity, Process Innovation, and the Life-Cycle of Products." *American Economic Review* 91 (5): 1454–77.

———. 2004. "Micro-foundations of Urban Agglomeration Economies." In *Handbook of Regional and Urban Economics*, vol. 4, ed. J. Vernon Henderson and Jean-François Thisse. Amsterdam: Elsevier B.V.

Fay, Marianne, and Charlotte Opal. 2000. "Urbanization without Growth: A Not So Uncommon Phenomenon." *Policy Research Working Paper* 2412, World Bank, Washington, DC.

Fujita, Masahisa, and Jean-François Thisse. 2002. *Economics of Agglomeration*. Cambridge: Cambridge University Press.

Gao, Guo Fu. 2007. "Urban Infrastructure Investment and Financing in Shanghai." In *Financing Cities: Fiscal Responsibility and Urban Infrastructure Finance in Brazil, China, India, Poland and South Africa,* ed. George Peterson and Patricia Clarke Annez. New Delhi: Sage Publications.

Gill, Indermit, and Homi Kharas. 2007. *An East Asian Renaissance: Ideas for Economic Growth*. Washington, DC: World Bank.

Green, Richard. 2007. "Urbanization, Primacy, and Productivity in Bangladesh." World Bank, South Asia Sustainable Development, Urban, Water and Sanitation Unit, Washington, DC.

Harris, J. R., and M. Todaro. 1970. "Migration, Unemployment, and Development: A Two-Sector Analysis." *American Economic Review* 60 (1): 126–42.

Hausmann, R., and Dani Rodrik. 2002. "Economic Development as Self-Discovery." NBER Working Paper 8952, National Bureau of Economic Research, Cambridge, MA.

Henderson, J. Vernon. 1986. "Efficiency of Resource Usage and City Size." *Journal of Urban Economics* 19 (1): 4770.

———. 2005. "Urbanization and Growth." In *Handbook of Economic Growth*, vol. 1b, ed. Philippe Aghion and Steven N. Durlauf. Amsterdam: Elsevier.

Henderson, J. Vernon, Todd Lee, and Yung Joon Lee. 2001. "Scale Externalities in Korea." *Journal of Urban Economics* 49 (3): 479–504.

Heston, Alan, Robert Summers, and Bettina Aten. 2006. Real 1996 GDP per Capita (Chain), Penn World Table Version 6.2. Center for International Comparisons of Production, Income and Prices, University of Pennsylvania, Philadelphia. http://pwt.econ.upenn.edu/.

Hoselitz, Bert. 1955. "Generative and Parasitic Cities." *Economic Development and Cultural Change* 3 (3): 278–94.

Jacobs, Jane. 1984. *Cities and the Wealth of Nation: Principles of Economic Lives*. New York: Random House.

Johnston, Louis D., and Samuel H. Williamson. 2005. "The Annual Real and Nominal GDP for the United States, 1790–Present." Economic History Services, October. http://www.eh.net/hmit/gdp/, consulted March 2007.

Lall, Somik, Harris Selod, and Zmarak Shalizi. 2006. "Rural–Urban Migration in Developing Countries: A Survey of Theoretical Predictions and Empirical Findings." World Bank Policy Research Working Paper 3915, Washington, DC.

Landes, D. S. 1969. *The Unbound Prometheus*. Cambridge: Cambridge University Press.

Leman, Edward. 2005. "Metropolitan Regions: New Challenges for an Urbanizing China." Paper prepared for the World Bank and Institute of Applied Economic Research Urban Research Symposium, Brasilia, April 4.

Lewis, W. Arthur. 1977. "The Evolution of the International Economic Order." Discussion Paper 74, Research Program in Development Studies, Woodrow Wilson School, Princeton University, Princeton, NJ.

Linn, Johannes. 1982. "The Costs of Urbanization in Developing Countries." *Economic Development and Cultural Change* 30 (3): 625–48.

Lipton, Michael. 1976. *Why Poor People Stay Poor: Urban Bias in World Development*. Cambridge, MA: Harvard University Press

Little, I. M. D., T. Scitovsky, and M. Scott. 1970. *Industry and Trade in Some Developing Countries*. Oxford: Oxford University Press

Lucas, Robert E., Jr. 1988. "On the Mechanics of Economic Development." *Journal of Monetary Economics* 22 (1): 3–42.

———. 2004. "Life Earnings and Rural–Urban Migration." *Journal of Political Economy 112* (1, pt. 2): S29–S59.

———. 2007. "Trade and the Diffusion of the Industrial Revolution." Frank D. Graham Memorial Lecture, Princeton University, Princeton, NJ, March.

Maddison, Angus. 2001. *The World Economy: A Millennial Perspective*. Paris: Organisation for Economic Co-operation and Development.

Malpezzi, Stephen, and Zhengou Lin. 1999. "Urban Transitions and Endogenous Growth." Center for Urban Land Economics Research, University of Wisconsin, Madison.

Majumdar, M., A. Mani, and S. W. Mukan. 2004. "Politics, Information, and the Urban Bias." *Journal of Development Economics* 75 (1): 137–65.

Marchand, Bernard. 1993. *Paris: Histoire d'une ville*. Paris: Editions du Seuil.

Mohan, Rakesh. 2006. "Asia's Urban Century: Emerging Trends." Keynote Address, Conference on Land Policies and Urban Development. Lincoln Land Institute, Cambridge, MA, June 5.

Mohan, Rakesh, and Shubhagato Das Gupta. 2003. "The Twenty-First Century: Asia Becomes Urban." Keynote Address, World Bank Urban Research Symposium, Washington, DC, December 15.

National Research Council. 2003. *Cities Transformed: Demographic Change and Its Implications for the Developing World. Panel on Urban Population*

Dynamics, ed. Mark R. Montgomery, Richard Stren, Barney Cohen, and Holly E. Reed. Committee on Population, Division of Behavioral and Social Sciences and Education. Washington, DC: National Academies Press.

Newsweek. 2003. "Boom Times: Is Asia's Urban Explosion a Blessing or a Curse?" Special Edition: October–December.

Overman, H. G., and Anthony J. Venables. 2005. *Cities in the Developing World*. Department for International Development, London.

Peterson, George E. 2005. *Intergovernmental Fiscal Systems and Sub-National Growth: China*. Report prepared for the World Bank, Washington, DC, and the Department for International Development, London.

Peterson, Merill D. 1984. *Thomas Jefferson: Writings*. New York: Library of America.

Pinkney, David H. 1957. "Money and Politics in the Rebuilding of Paris, 1860–1870." *Journal of Economic History* 17 (7): 45-61.

Pirenne, Henri. 1922. *Early Democracies in the Low Countries: Urban Society and Political Conflict in the Middle Ages and the Renaissance*. New York: W. W. Norton.

Preston, S. H. 1979. "Urban Growth in Developing Countries: A Demographic Reappraisal." *Population and Development Review* 5 (2): 195–215.

Quigley, John. 1998. "Urban Diversity and Economic Growth." *Journal of Economic Perspectives* 12 (2):127–38.

Ravallion, Martin, Shaohua Chen, and Prem Sangraula. 2007. "New Evidence on the Urbanization of Absolute Poverty." World Bank Policy Working Paper 4199, Washington, DC.

Rodrik, Dani. 2004. "Industrial Policy for the 21st Century." CEPR Discussion Paper 4767, Centre for Economic Policy Research, London.

Romer, Paul. 1986. "Increasing Returns and Long-Run Growth." *Journal of Political Economy* 94 (5): 1002–37.

Rosenthal, Stuart, and William C. Strange. 2004. "Evidence on the Nature and Sources of Agglomeration Economies." In *Handbook of Regional and Urban Economics*, vol. 4, ed. J. Vernon Henderson and Jean-François Thisse. Amsterdam: Elsevier.

Satterthwaite, David. 2007. "The Transition to a Predominantly Urban World and Its Underpinnings." Paper presented at the UNU WIDER project workshop, "Beyond the Tipping Point: Development in an Urban World," October 18–20, London.

Siddiqui, Kamal. 1997. *Land Management in South Asia: A Comparative Study*. Karachi: Oxford University Press.

Stark, Oded, and David Levhari. 1982. "On Migration and Risks in LDCs." *Economic Development and Cultural Change* 31 (1): 465–81

Stark, Oded, and Robert E. Lucas Jr. 1988. "Migration and Remittances and the Family." *Economic Development and Cultural Change* 36 (3): 191–96

Su, Ming, and Quanhou Zhou. 2007. "China: Fiscal Framework and Urban Infrastructure Finance." In *Financing Cities: Fiscal Responsibility and Urban Infrastructure Finance in Brazil, China, India, Poland and South Africa*, ed. George Peterson and Patricia Clarke Annez. New Delhi: Sage Publications.

Todaro, M. 1969. "A Model of Labor, Migration, and Urban Employment in Less Developed Countries." *American Economic Review* 59 (1): 138–48.

UN (United Nations). 2006. *World Urbanization Prospects: The 2006 Revision.* http://esa.un.org/unup.

———. 2007. *World Population Policies.* Department of Economic and Social Affairs, Population Division. New York: United Nations Publishing.

UNFPA (United Nations Population Fund). 2007. *State of World Population 2007: Unleashing the Potential of Urban Growth.* New York: UNFPA.

Venables, Anthony. 2007. "Shifts in Economic Geography and Their Causes." Department of Economics, Oxford University, Oxford. Paper prepared for the 2006 Federal Reserve Symposium, Jackson Hole, WY.

Weeks, John. 1994. "Economic Aspects of Rural–Urban Migration." *Urbanization in Africa: A Handbook*, ed. John Tarver. London: Greenwood Press.

White, Michael J., and David P. Lindstrom. 2005. "Internal Migration." In *Handbook of Population*, ed. Dudley L. Poston and Michael Micklin. New York: Kluwer Academic Press.

Williamson, Jeffrey A. 1987. "Did England's Cities Grow Too Fast during the Industrial Revolution?" Discussion Paper 1311, Harvard Institute of Economic Research, Cambridge, MA.

Williamson, Jeffrey G. 1988. "Migration and Urbanization." In *Handbook of Development Economics*, vol. 1, ed. H. Chenery and T. N. Srinivasan. Amsterdam: Elsevier.

——— . 1990. *Coping with City Growth during the British Industrial Revolution* Cambridge: Cambridge University Press

Wohl, Anthony S. 1983. *Endangered Lives: Public Health in Victorian Britain.* Cambridge, MA: Harvard University Press.

World Bank. 1976. *World Tables 1976.* Washington, DC: World Bank.

———. 2000. *World Development Report 1999/2000: Entering the 21st Century.* Washington, DC: World Bank.

———. 2005 and 2007a. *World Development Indicators.* Washington, DC: World Bank.

———. 2007b. *Dhaka: Improving the Living Conditions of the Urban Poor.* Washington, DC: World Bank.

Yusuf, Shahid, Simon J. Evenett, and Weiping Wu. 2001. *Facets of Globalization: International and Local Dimensions of Development.* Washington, DC: World Bank.

CHAPTER 2
Rethinking Economic Growth in a Globalizing World: An Economic Geography Lens

Anthony J. Venables

The role of trade in economic growth—especially exports from the modern sector—has become increasingly clear. The Asian experience is well documented, and a number of recent studies point to the role of exports in growth accelerations. For example, Jones and Olken (2008) identify growth accelerations and show that they are associated with an average increase of 13 percentage points in the share of trade in income (over a five-year period), as well as an acceleration of the rate of transfer of labor into manufacturing. Pattillo, Gupta, and Carey (2005) point to the association between growth accelerations and trade in Sub-Saharan Africa (see also Hausmann, Pritchett, and Rodrik 2005).

This chapter draws on recent work in trade and economic geography to provide a lens through which to assess trade, globalization, and economic growth. It investigates how globalization shapes countries' growth prospects and draws some policy implications. The analysis in this chapter is based on three facts about the technology of trade and modern sector production. The first is that modern sector activity is surrounded by increasing returns to scale deriving from many sources, including social and political as well as narrowly economic. The second is that space still matters, both in

The author thanks the participants at the Growth Commission meeting for helpful comments.

defining the geographic scope of these increasing returns and in shaping economic relationships more broadly. The third is that globalization is changing the nature of international trade, in particular by facilitating the fragmentation of production. These facts are discussed in the next section of the chapter.

The chapter then draws out implications from these facts and argues that they support a view of the world different from that offered by standard trade or growth theory, although consistent with the evidence. In particular, there are equilibrium disparities between regions of the world and also between subregions within a country. Rapid economic growth can occur, and is likely to be associated with modern sector export growth. It will typically be "lumpy" in three senses. In geographic space, it will be uneven being concentrated in some countries, regions, or cities. In product space, these regions are likely to be narrowly specialized, perhaps even specializing in a few tasks rather than production of integrated products. Temporally, growth will be rapid, but only once some threshold level of capabilities has been reached. Growth will tend to be sequential rather than parallel, that is, with selected regions growing very fast while others lag behind. Furthermore, there will be a tendency for both middle-income regions and very low-income regions to be left behind in this process.

The final section of the chapter discusses policy implications, focusing on two questions. The first is, how can countries or regions get to the threshold at which they become attractive as export bases for manufacturing, and at which they start to benefit from increasing returns to scale? Discussion of this question is based on urbanization and on African export diversification. The second question is, how should we understand the economic relationship between regions or countries? Are developments in one region complementary or competing with developments in another?

Modern Trade and Production

We start by outlining three facts about the technology of modern trade that underlie the thinking in the chapter.

Increasing Returns to Scale

Standard economic modeling draws heavily on the assumption of diminishing returns to scale, although increasing returns are inherent to much modern sector activity.[1] Increasing returns arise through a variety of mechanisms, some narrowly technical and others related to wider socioeconomic feedbacks. Increasing returns may be internal to the firm (average costs falling with the length of the production run), but their implications for the performance of the economy are greatest if they are external (that is, occur-

---

1   There is an enormous body of work on increasing returns, dating from (at least) the work of Young (1928).

ring between rather than within economic units). What are the sources of such external economies of scale?

One category is technological externalities, such as knowledge spillovers. Knowledge spillovers occur when one firm is able to benefit from the knowledge capital of another. The mechanism through which knowledge transfer occurs may be labor mobility, face-to-face social contact between workers, or observation of the practices of other firms. Such effects are particularly important in innovation-intensive activities. A large body of literature points to the spatial concentration of innovative activities (Audretsch and Feldman 2004). Location-specific knowledge spillovers also arise if firms learn about the characteristics (for example, the productivity) of the location, and are unable to keep their knowledge private, as in the "self-discovery" story of Hausmann and Rodrik (2003). This may be learning about real characteristics of locations, or may simply be a "herding" story as firms choose to copy the location decisions of other (successful) firms.

Possibly more important than technological externalities are pecuniary externalities. In an imperfectly competitive market there are allocative inefficiencies, and these inefficiencies may depend on the size of the market. Increasing returns arise if increasing the size of the market reduces these inefficiencies. This can occur in the goods markets. For example, there is a tradeoff between having firms large enough to achieve internal economies of scale without becoming monopolists. Increasing market size shifts this tradeoff, allowing benefits of both large-scale and more intense competition, and as a consequence firms will be larger, will operate at lower average costs, and will set lower prices. If firms have different productivity levels, an increase in the size of the market and the associated increase in competition will cause higher-productivity firms to grow and lower-productivity firms to exit. This argument supports the empirical finding that much of the gain from trade liberalization comes from a change in the mix of firms within each sector, favoring high-productivity firms at the expense of low-productivity firms (see Bernard and others 2007).

A larger market will also support a greater variety of products. These price and variety effects benefit consumers and also, if the goods are intermediates, benefit firms in downstream sectors. For example, a larger market will support a greater variety of specialized input producers, tailoring their products to the needs of other firms. Downstream firms benefit from this variety, while upstream firms benefit from the large number of downstream firms. This is simply a modern restatement of old ideas of forward and backward linkages: firms benefit from proximity to both suppliers and customers (see Fujita, Krugman, and Venables 1999).

In addition to efficiency gains deriving from the size of the goods market, there are also gains from operating in a large labor market. The larger the pool of workers a firm can access the more likely it is to be able to find the exact skills that suit its needs (see Amiti and Pissarides 2005). If firms are subject to idiosyncratic shocks, then a larger labor market will expose workers to less risk, increasing the probability of reemployment if they are made redundant. More importantly, a large labor market will increase the incentives for workers to undertake training. This argument, like some of those in the product market, turns on increased intensity of competition. In a small market workers who acquire specialist skills may be "held up" by monopsonistic employers, in which case there is no incentive for them to invest in skills. The presence of a large number of potential employers removes this threat of opportunistic behavior, thereby increasing training incentives (Matouschek and Robert-Nicoud 2005).

A further set of arguments, relating to density of activity as much as to scale of activity, has to do with communication between workers. In many activities face-to-face communication is extremely important (Matouschek and Robert-Nicoud 2005). Such contact enables higher frequency interchange of ideas than is possible by e-mail, phone, or videoconference. Brainstorming is hard to do without the ability to interrupt and use parallel means of communication—oral, visual, and body language. Face-to-face contact is also important for building trust, by observing the body language and a range of other characteristics of one's interlocutor. By breaking down anonymity, face-to-face contact enables networks of the most productive workers to develop and promotes partnerships and joint projects between these workers. All these considerations enhance productivity.

Increasing returns are common in the provision of public sector goods and services. The simplest mechanism is technological: many publicly provided services are also public goods, which by definition have declining average costs. An important twist on this is that many inputs—including public services and utilities—have a complementary relation when used in production (see Kremer 1993). Efficiency in production of goods requires the continuous supply of electricity, water, roads, and security. If any of these inputs is subject to increasing returns, returns to scale for the package as a whole are amplified.

Increasing returns in the provision of public sector goods, services, and institutions are also based on a broader argument. Provision of fundamental governance services—protection of property rights, maintenance of economic and personal security, and the rule of law—is often suboptimal. One factor determining the quality of the institutional environment for doing business is the level of demand by firms for a high-quality environment, which creates positive feedback. The larger the business sector, the greater the demand for a good business environment, the greater the political payoff from providing these governance services and the better the ensuing business environment. If the initial position was suboptimal, this feedback is a source of increasing returns: the larger the sector, the closer provision will be to the optimal level.

Spatial Frictions and Economic Geography

The second fact about modern trade and globalization is that distance still matters. This can be seen most clearly by thinking about the externalities cited in the previous subsection, almost all of which are spatially limited.

Many knowledge spillovers occur within very concentrated economic regions—clusters and districts within cities. "Self-discovery" is, by definition, the discovery of the characteristics of a particular location. Labor market effects operate within a travel-to-work area. Public goods and utilities are typically not easily traded across space. Institutional effects operate partly at the national level but also at the level of provinces, cities, or special economic zones. The key element of "distance" is slightly different in each of these contexts. Distance matters because it raises the monetary and time cost of trading goods, moving workers, or spreading ideas. It also underlies jurisdictions and hence man-made barriers to mobility.

The product market mechanisms are the ones for which globalization has most obviously reduced the importance of distance, although even here it is far from eliminated. Small trade frictions can be used by firms as a way of softening competition, as witnessed by the long-running struggle to turn the European Union into a truly integrated market. Distance has an important effect in choking off trade flows; gravity models of trade suggest that the full costs of trade are far higher than those suggested by simply looking at tariffs or transport costs (see Anderson and van Wincoop 2004). Part of the cost is associated with time-in-transit. Just-in-time management techniques have increased the cost of slow or uncertain delivery times: Hummels (2001) estimates the cost of time-in-transit for manufactures to be nearly 1 percent of the value of goods shipped for each day in transit.

The spatial dimension provides a way of estimating the quantitative importance of increasing returns. A well-established body of literature measures the productivity advantages of large urban centers. A recent survey of that literature (Rosenthal and Strange 2004) reports a consensus view that over a wide range of city sizes, doubling city size is associated with a productivity increase of some 3–8 percent. This is a large effect—moving from a city of 50,000 inhabitants to one of 5 million is predicted to increase productivity by more than 50 percent. Analysis of the spatial scale of these effects indicates that they are quite concentrated: work on the United Kingdom suggests that they attenuate rapidly beyond 45 minutes driving time (Rice, Venables, and Pattachini 2006). Effects also vary across sectors, generally being larger in higher-technology sectors.

Fragmentation

A third characteristic of globalized trade is fragmentation, also known as unbundling or splitting the value chain. Fragmentation refers to the fact that the different stages of producing a final good are now often performed in many different countries. Particular tasks may be outsourced (or offshored) and undertaken in different places. Fragmentation is a response to differences in productivity or factor prices; it may take place within a single multinational firm or through production networks of supplier firms (see Arndt and Kierzkowski 2001; Grossman and Rossi-Hansberg 2006; Markusen and Venables 2007).

Although widely reported, solid evidence on the extent of fragmentation is hard to obtain. For the United States it is estimated that just 37 percent of the production value of a typical American car is generated in the United States. Grossman and Rossi-Hansberg (2006) report that the share of imports in inputs to U.S. goods manufacturing doubled to 18 percent over a 20-year period. In China it is estimated that domestic value added amounts to about 60 percent of the value of exported goods (the figure falls to less than 30 percent in the electrical, communications, and transport sectors) (Cuihong and Jianuo 2007). It is estimated that up to 78 percent of East Asian trade is in intermediate goods.

Fragmentation means that comparative advantage now resides in quite narrowly defined tasks. This is highly beneficial for developing countries, particularly when accompanied by learning effects and increasing returns to scale. It means that countries do not have to acquire capability in all stages of an integrated production process but can instead specialize in a narrow range of tasks, mastery of which requires a much easier learning process.

Implications for Growth and Development

What are the implications of these facts for the world economy and for growth? There are several important points.

Equilibrium Disparities

Diminishing returns to scale are a force for convergence. A city or country that offers high returns to firms or workers will attract inflows of these factors, this reducing their returns and giving convergence to equilibrium. A consequence of this is that an economic model dominated by diminishing returns offers no theory of international or spatial inequality. Some exogenous reason may be postulated as to why regions differ, but economic processes then tend to reduce these differences.

Spatially concentrated increasing returns offer a very different view. If a city or country offers high returns to firms or workers then they are attracted to the area, this increasing their returns further and amplifying any initial differences. The process may be unbounded: some regions could empty out altogether, with all world production of some commodity taking place in a single location. Alternatively, if beyond some point diminishing returns dominate scale effects, the process would be bounded. Thus, cities eventually run into diminishing returns because of congestion costs. Production of a good is not (generally) concentrated in a single location but dispersed across several locations because of transport costs (or time differences) in supplying world demand from one place. The most important source of diminishing returns to concentration of activity is that the prices of immobile factors are bid up, reducing the return to mobile factors. In the urban context, land prices increase, making the city less attractive to mobile workers. In the international context, wages rise, making a country less attractive to mobile firms.

But whether bounded or unbounded, the point is that increasing returns create a force for divergence. Locations may be identical in their underlying characteristics, but economic forces make them different as the economy "self-organizes" into clusters. Differences in prices of immobile factors and income levels are then an equilibrium outcome, not a transient consequence of some initial difference.

Wage Gradients

The fact that the benefits of increasing returns to scale and access to large markets depends on proximity to centers of activity means that one should expect to observe wage or income gradients as one moves from central to peripheral locations. Redding and Venables (2004) use international trade data and a gravity model to measure each country's access to foreign markets. They then compare this measure with per capita income. Several points stand out from this relation (figure 2.1). The first is the empty bottom right part of the figure: good geography (in the sense of good market access) prevents countries from having low incomes. Among countries with good market access there is a wage gradient within the European Union and a similar one (at lower income) for transition economies. In the top left, it is clear that a substantial number of countries have escaped the problem of poor foreign market access. Some have done so as a result of good endowments of natural resources; others have done so as a result of the large own-market effect, which reduces the impact of distance from other sources of demand. Adding other controls (factor endowments, physical geography, and social, political, and institutional variables) and undertaking a number

Figure 2.1 GDP Per Capita and Foreign Market Access

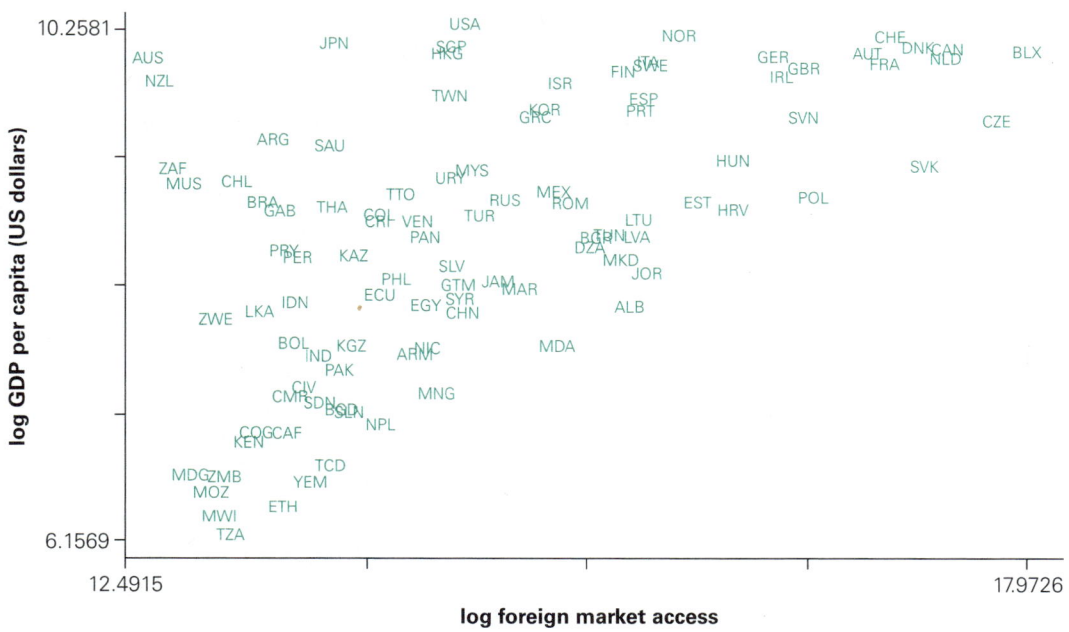

of robustness checks, Redding and Venables conclude that proximity to foreign markets is a statistically significant and quantitatively important determinant of income levels. This finding is consistent with the work of Frankel and Romer (1999), who use geography as an instrument for the effect of trade on income.

Lumpy Growth

What does economic growth look like in this world? It has three characteristics, each of which is a sort of lumpiness.

The first is that growth is lumpy or uneven across space. Rather than growing in parallel, regions will have a tendency to grow in sequence. Some countries or regions may grow rapidly, as increasing returns set in and they transit from one "convergence club" to another. Other countries will be left out of the process. To see the logic behind this, suppose that the world is divided between high-income countries, which have manufacturing activity, and low-income countries, which do not. This is an equilibrium, because wages in the high-income countries are matched by the high productivity associated with scale, so there is no incentive for any firm to relocate. Now suppose that some growth process—for example, technical progress—is going on in the world economy as a whole that is raising income and hence demand for manufactures. This increases employment and raises wages in the manufacturing regions until a point is reached at which the productivity advantage of being in an existing cluster is outweighed by the higher wages in the cluster. It then becomes profitable for some firms to relocate, but where do they go? Spatially concentrated increasing returns mean that they will tend to cluster in a single newly emergent manufacturing location. A situation in which all countries gain a little manufacturing is unstable; a country that gets even slightly ahead will have the advantage, attracting further firms. Running this process through time, countries join the group of high-income nations in sequence. Each country grows fast as it joins the club, and is then followed by another country, and so on.

The strict sequence of countries should not be taken literally; the key insight is that the growth mechanism does not imply more or less uniform convergence of countries, as has been argued by some economic growth theorists (see, for example, Lucas 2000). Instead, growth is sequential, not parallel, as manufacturing spreads across countries and regions. Which countries go first, and the order in which countries join the high-income club, is determined by a range of factors related to endowments, institutions, and geography. Proximity to existing centers may be an important positive factor accounting for development in Eastern Europe and regions of China, East Asia, and Mexico.[2] Institutional failure, a bad macroeconomic environment, and civil war are powerful negative factors.

---

2 Puga and Venables (1999) investigate the implications of market size and trade barriers. They assess the export-oriented versus import-substituting manufacturing development. Kremer and Chamon (2006) build a model of a development queue.

The second aspect of lumpiness is that growth is uneven over time. Small initial differences between countries may mean that some countries get ahead while others are left behind for a long period of time. Countries that fall below some threshold—in terms of investment climate and institutional quality—will not participate in the process.

The third feature of lumpiness is that growth may be lumpy across products, because it is likely to be concentrated in particular sectors. This type of lumpiness occurs as many of the sources of increasing returns are sector specific, requiring the acquisition of skills and capacity in narrowly defined sets of products or tasks. A corollary of narrow specialization is that growth will be highly export dependent. This is consistent with the Asian experience, and with the empirical work on growth accelerations (for example, Hausmann, Pritchett, and Rodrik 2005) that we noted above. Hausmann and Rodrik (2003) provide direct measures of the sectoral concentration of exports. They look at exports to the United States by Bangladesh, the Dominican Republic, Honduras, Pakistan, the Republic of Korea, and Taiwan (China), using data at the highly disaggregated six-digit level (for example, "hats and other headgear knitted or from textile material not in strips"). Even at this very fine level of disaggregation there is a high level of specialization. For each of these countries, the top four product lines account for more than 30 percent of exports to the United States, and there is little overlap in the top product lines of similar countries (only six product lines are in the top 25 for both Bangladesh and Pakistan; Bangladesh is successful in exporting shirts, trousers, and hats, while Pakistan does well in bed linen and footballs). Hausmann and Rodrik conclude that "for all economies except possibly the most sophisticated, industrial success entails concentration in a relatively narrow range of high productivity activities."[3]

Initial Difference: Who Gains and Who Is Left Behind?

The preceding argument emphasizes that inequalities could emerge even between similar (or ex ante identical) countries. Given that there are underlying differences between countries, what sort of countries might expect to do well and which countries poorly as a result of globalization? We make just two points.

The first is that some countries have failed to meet the necessary conditions for full integration in the global economy and inclusion in production networks. The obvious comparison is between the performance of much of Asia and of Africa. Asian manufacturing has crossed the threshold, and diversification into exports of manufactures has raised wages and been contagious across the region. In Africa this process has yet to start. Africa has lagged behind partly because its economic reforms lagged those of Asia: in the 1980s, when Asia first broke into global markets, no mainland African country provided a comparable investment climate. Lumpiness in

---

3 Imbs and Wacziarg (2003) note that the degree of diversification increases in the earlier stages of diversification before declining.

the development process means that these initial differences translate into very large differences in outcomes and may create long lags before Africa can attract modern sector activity. A number of African cities, such as Accra, Dakar, Dar es Salaam, Maputo, and Mombassa, now offer investment climates as good as those offered earlier in Asia. However, these cities now face the obstacle that Asia has a head start, benefiting from clusters of shared knowledge, availability of specialist inputs, and pools of experienced labor. Africa's potential export locations do not have these advantages; they therefore face an entry threshold (or chicken-and-egg) problem. Until clusters are established, costs will be higher than those of Asian competitors; because costs are higher, individual firms have no incentive to relocate.

A second point is that globalization tends to benefit the extremes and squeeze the middle. It permits a finer division of labor, enabling the highest-skilled countries to concentrate on skill-intensive tasks, and the lowest-skilled to concentrate on low-skill tasks, subject to crossing a capability threshold. What happens to middle-income countries during this process? They do not have an extreme comparative advantage to exploit and at the same time are faced with changing terms of trade, largely as a result of increased supply from Asia. Price changes of this magnitude have benefited consumers worldwide, but they have also put pressure on producers. The pressure has fallen primarily on producers in middle-income countries, which produce goods that are technologically relatively unsophisticated. This is one of the reasons why globalization appears not to have benefited many middle-income countries (Summers 2006).

The relative income gains of people in countries at different points in the world income distribution are illustrated vividly in figure 2.2, based on

Figure 2.2 Changes in World Income Distribution

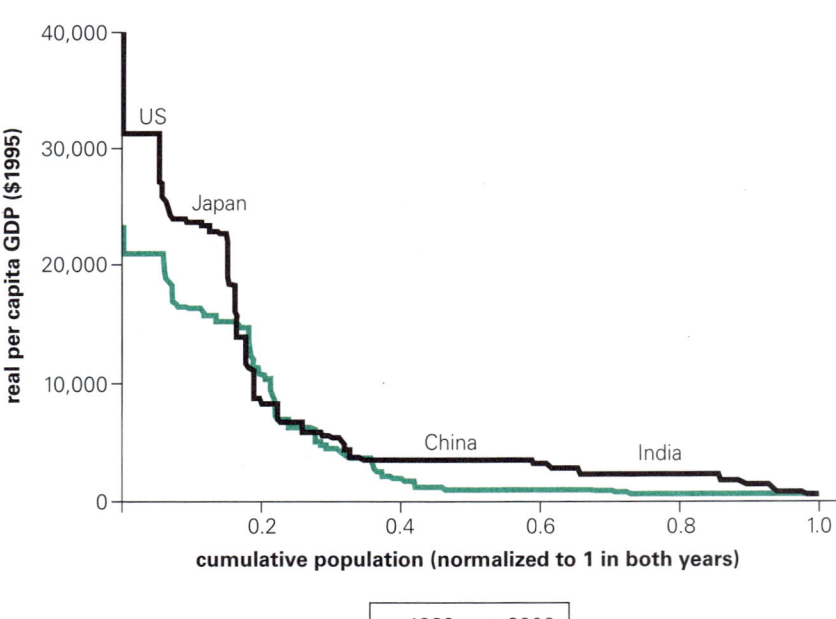

Leamer (2007). The horizontal axis shows cumulative population shares, with the poorest country at the extreme right and the richest at the extreme left; the vertical axis shows per capita income. Comparison of income distributions in 1980 and 2000 indicates that the populations of high- and low-income countries did relatively well while those in middle- and very-low-income countries saw no progress.

Of course, this figure masks much detail; it would be incorrect to attribute all changes to globalization. But it illustrates the two points posited above. First, the lowest-income countries have remained below the threshold and failed to experience income growth. Second, the finer division of labor that is facilitated by globalization encourages specialization at extremes while tending to squeeze the middle.

Policy Issues: Threshold Effects and Coordination Failures

What are the policy implications of the economic environment that we have described? There are multiple market failures and plenty of arguments for policy intervention. But spatial policy—regional policy in particular—has generally been a failure. Researchers in new economic geography have been hesitant to make policy recommendations. This chapter will not venture far outside that tradition.

At least two difficult sets of issues need to be understood in thinking about policy. One has to do with the threshold effects and coordination failures that arise in the presence of external economies of scale, and we discuss them in this section. The other has to do with linkages and spillover effects: how do changes in one country or region affect other countries and neighboring regions? We discuss this issue in the following section.

The world described here is one of lumpiness and extreme specialization. This means that it is difficult to get started in a new industry or location even if an activity would be viable once scale economies were attained. There are several policy responses to this problem. The first is to increase both the confidence with which investors view future benefits and the ability to borrow against future returns. The second is to internalize any external benefits that new entrants create. The third is to offer temporary support through some form of industrial policy. These options are analyzed through two examples: the growth of new cities and prospects for African export diversification.

Threshold Effects: Growing an Urban Structure

Cities have high productivity and, in many developing countries, enjoy rapid economic growth. But economies of scale are balanced against diseconomies of urban congestion and pollution, suggesting that there is an optimal urban size. Little is known about what this size is; it varies according to geography, industrial structure, and governance (Au and Henderson 2004). Threshold effects suggest, however, that there may be a tendency for cities to become larger than is optimal, because external economies of scale make it hard to start new cities. Small cities do not benefit from urban-scale economies; they are therefore unattractive to firms and as a consequence fail to grow into large cities. Instead, migration flows into existing cities, leading to the growth of megacities. Because new urban centers are hard to establish, existing cities grow well beyond their optimum scale, possibly to the point at which, at the margin, diseconomies such as congestion outweigh positive economies of scale. Such an outcome is clearly inefficient. The policy question is, how should the growth of new cities—or the deconcentration of existing ones—be promoted?

Two market failures are likely to be present in this situation. One is that increasing returns to scale give rise to externalities, so that the benefits *created* by a single economic agent (a migrant to the city or a relocating firm) are not internalized. The other is that the benefits *received* by a single economic agent (these are reciprocal externalities, so firms and migrants receive as well as transmit benefits) accrue over time and their future development will be highly uncertain. These two issues require different policy responses, and let us take the second one first.

When does it become worthwhile for a single small firm or individual to make a decision to invest in a new city?[4] Investment will take place sooner the more confident investors are in the future development of the city and the greater is their ability to capture the future economic benefits, most obviously by having secure property rights to the land on which the investment takes place. Investment will also occur earlier the easier it is for an individual to borrow against these future benefits. These are all areas in which policy can have a direct and important impact. The first may require government investment, which plays the dual role of constructing the new urban infrastructure and signaling to investors that a particular city (as compared with numerous other potential city sites) is one in which there is a commitment to growth. Given this, long-term property rights in urban land and access to credit are standard prescriptions for making markets work.

Adopting these measures increases the incentives to be an early mover from an existing megacity to a new secondary city, but it does not move the economy to a first-best optimum. Investors invest in the expectation of receiving the external benefits of a dynamic growing city, but they are not capturing the benefits of the externalities they create. There are two textbook solutions to this problem. One is to internalize these benefits through large developers, who buy up the land in the city, attract firms and immigrants, and then take all the land rents. The other is for the public sector to offer subsidies for the creation of external benefits. In practice, neither of these solutions is likely to be satisfactory. Developers play this role in shopping malls and office developments but are unlikely to be large enough to capture more than a fraction of the benefits of a city. Public subsidies to the

---

4   This section draws on Henderson and Venables (2008).

myriad externalities created by urban activity are expensive, difficult to target, subject to abuse, and consequently difficult to recommend.

The important point to take away from this discussion is that even without compensating for externalities, policy can move a large part of the way toward efficiency just by adopting the first set of policy measures. Creating confidence that a particular urban site will develop and establishing property rights so that forward-looking individuals will be induced to invest in the site solves the coordination failure, even if it does not internalize the externality.

Threshold Effects: Can Africa Export Manufactures?

Threshold effects matter for countries, as well as for cities. As we argued above, Africa has, at least until recently, been below the threshold required to be an attractive location from which to source imports.

What is the role for policy? A number of observations follow by analogy with the discussion of cities. Provision of a good business environment and appropriate infrastructure has direct benefits; it may also signal commitment to development. Government may reinforce commitment by high-level engagement—the idea of a "developmental state." Concentrating attributes in a particular location—perhaps a special economic zone—has two advantages. The first is that provision of a full set of high-quality complementary inputs and utilities is relatively cost-effective; complementarity means that it is better to provide inputs well in one place than half as well in two places. The second advantage of a special economic zone relates to the discussion of urbanization. In the long run there are efficiency gains from clustering activity; in the short run it is important to signal this by committing to a particular location.

Active industrial policy that goes beyond these measures is controversial. There are multiple market failures in the environment we have described, and hence there is a case for intervention to reduce coordination failure and internalize externalities. But direct interventions are hard to target, difficult to withdraw, and subject to political economy manipulation. An alternative policy instrument that merits consideration is trade preferences (Collier and Venables 2007). Unlike other forms of industrial policy, trade preferences in Organisation of Economic Co-operation and Development (OECD) markets are under the control of OECD governments. This gives them several major advantages over policies available to African governments to provide the (temporary) advantage needed to get cluster formation. First, such policies are relatively immune to recipient country political economy problems, because they are set by foreign, not domestic, governments. There is thus no way in which their level can be escalated in support of failing firms. Second, because trade preferences support exports, they offer a performance-based incentive: firms benefit only if they export. Firms therefore face the discipline—on quality as well as price—imposed by international competition. Rodrik (2004) argues that this discipline was an important positive factor underlying the success of export-oriented strategies relative to import substitution. Third, such policies are fiscally costless to African governments and virtually costless to OECD governments; they do not compete with government spending on social needs or aid.

Current trade preferences are not particularly successful in promoting the growth of manufacturing export clusters. They typically set conditions that are at variance with some of the characteristics of modern international trade identified above. As we saw, much world trade now takes the form of trade in tasks, with production fragmented across many countries and high levels of intermediate trade. This fragmentation is potentially beneficial for Sub-Saharan Africa, because it is much easier to develop capabilities and grow economies of scale in a narrow range of tasks than in integrated production of an entire product. However, most preferential trading schemes have rules of origin that prohibit this sort of trade, insisting that a high proportion of value added (or transformation) be performed within the country or region and ruling out sourcing intermediate inputs from the lowest cost source (often China). The implication for preferential trading schemes is that rules of origin must be liberal enough not to exclude countries from participation in such production networks.

The second point is that preferences should be open to countries that are close to the threshold of developing globally competitive clusters of activity. Preference schemes that just favor the least developed countries have the effect of excluding countries such as Ghana and Kenya, which have just arrived at the threshold and are manifestly more likely to develop manufacturing exports than are Liberia or Somalia. The effect of concentrating on the least developed countries is therefore to exclude precisely those African countries best placed to take advantage of preferences for export diversification.

In practice, if preferences are offered with rules of origin allowing specialization in tasks, and open to members beyond least developed countries, will export diversification occur in response? These conditions are offered by one policy regime, the special rule for apparel of the African Growth and Opportunity Act (AGOA). The evidence suggests a strong export response, with apparel exports from Kenya, Lesotho, Madagascar, and countries in southern Africa soaring from about $300 million to $1,500 million a year (Collier and Venables 2007).

Policy Issues: Spatial Linkages and Spillover Effects

Some countries stand little chance of breaking directly into world manufacturing export markets, perhaps because of very low starting positions, and perhaps because of natural geography, such as being landlocked. These economies are relatively dependent on the performance of their neighbors. This is an aspect of a larger question: given some established pattern of economy activity between cities or regions, what are the spatial linkages between regions? At one level this is a straightforward question of comparative statics. How do the effects of some exogenous or policy change spread out across regions? Yet it is one about which all the answers are not known. This is partly because the policy shock needs to be clearly specified: is it contained within one region, does it affect many regions, or is it an "integrative shock" that affects regions only through its effect on the links between them? Even given the specification of the policy shock, the presence of increasing returns means that comparative statics analysis is difficult; effects can be qualitatively ambiguous, depending in a delicate way on characteristics of the regions and the linkages between them.

Spatial Linkages: Complementary or Competing Regions?

How does change in one region affect neighboring regions? An analytical structure to address this question was developed in work for the British government, and deals with the effects of shocks (such as infrastructure or house supply) on the region directly affected, and on other regions (Overman, Rice, and Venables 2007). The work provides a simple diagrammatic framework within which inter-region linkages could be analyzed. The framework is based on three key relationships that shape inter-region linkages. The first is the employment-earnings relationship, a within-region relationship relating earnings in a region to the size of its labor force; the relationship may be increasing or decreasing, depending on returns to scale. The second is the employment–cost of living relationship; within a region, how does additional population change the cost of living? Some factors make the effect negative (more intense competition and more varieties of nontraded goods mean that an economically large region has a lower cost of living); others, mainly commuting costs and the prices of land and houses, make it positive. The third relationship is migration; an inter-regional relationship, measuring the responsiveness of population to regional differences in real earnings.

Depending on the shape of these relationships equilibrium could be stable or unstable. Concentrating, for obvious reasons, on stable equilibria, regions may have either a complementary or a competing relation with one another. When regions are complementary, the effects of a positive shock that originates in one region spread across other regions. Thus an increase in productivity in one region will trigger in-migration, which tends to dampen the productivity increase in the region while increasing productivity in other regions. When regions are competing, economic adjustment has the opposite effect, amplifying the impact of a productivity shock in one region while causing productivity in other regions to fall. This might arise because increasing returns mean that an increase in the labor force is associated with *higher* productivity and equilibrium is restored only by large changes in population and regional living costs.

Understanding whether parameters are such that regions are complementary or competing is fundamental for evaluating policy. The British government launched debate on whether to relax planning regulations to allow more house building in the booming southeast of England. If regions are in a competing relation, allowing more housing construction will increase house prices in the region and amplify regional differentials. The mechanism is population inflow combining with increasing returns to scale to generate higher earnings, this inducing further population inflow until choked off by higher house prices.

Although this example may not be directly relevant to developing countries, it contains several lessons. First, it is possible to synthesize key relationships from the many theoretical models in this area in a simple "reduced form" manner. The way in which these relationships interact to determine inter-regional linkages can then be studied in a straightforward way. Second, these relationships are amenable to empirical investigation. By looking at both the separate relationships and the behavior of the system as a whole, researchers can determine whether regions are competing or complementary. Third, doing this research is a necessary input for undertaking regional policy; without it, even the signs of a response to policy change are unknown. These approaches need to be applied to developing countries, to analyze the problem of lagging regions in a rapidly growing economy, for example. Doing so requires both analytical work on the main channels through which regions are linked and empirical work establishing whether regions are complementary or competing.

Integrative Shocks: A Force for Convergence or Divergence?

Much spatial policy deals not with shocks within a region, but shocks aimed at changing the relationship between regions—for example trade policy or road and communications improvements. What is known about the effects of such integrative shocks?

Here, too, there are ambiguities. Under some circumstances a reduction in trade costs between two regions reduces disparities; under other circumstances it may increase them. The mechanisms derive from the interplay between product markets and factor markets. The product market mechanism is that firms want to locate where there is good market access. If one region is slightly larger than the other, then reducing trade costs will cause firms to move to the larger location, and to export to the smaller one. Differences between regions are therefore amplified. The factor market mechanism is that firms relocate in response to wage differences, and will be more likely to relocate to a low-wage region the lower are trade costs. Putting these effects together in a general equilibrium framework (in which both the location of demand and wage rates may be endogenous) typically yields an inverse U-shaped relation between trade costs and regional disparities. Reducing trade costs from a high to an intermediate level tends to increase dispersion. But reducing them from an intermediate level to a low level will reverse this, leading to convergence.

What does the evidence show? There has been a continuing worry in Europe that centripetal forces would dominate, drawing activity into the center of the European Union at the expense of peripheral regions. In fact, most recent research suggests that trade costs are low enough for further reductions to have the effect of reducing rather than increasing disparities. This EU-based work leaves issues open for developing countries.

Conclusions

There are many reasons for variation in the prosperity of countries and regions. Some factors are truly exogenous—first-nature geography—and others are a function of political and institutional history. On top of these exogenous factors, we need to place a theory of the location of economic activity. International trade theory gets us part of the way, and the new economic geography approach broadens this out to capture (in a micro-founded and evidence-based way) endogenous variations in productivity. This approach offers an explanation of the emergence of disparities between countries and regions, and offers an explanation of their persistence. It suggests that even as globalization causes dispersion of activity, so economic development will be in sequence, not in parallel; some countries will experience rapid growth while others will be left behind. At the micro level, it points to the importance of overcoming coordination failures and threshold effects in growing new cities and in establishing new industries in developing economies.

This literature provides a basis for new and innovative thinking about policy, but a note of caution is essential. Policy is difficult because there are multiple market failures. Even in the simple world of theory, policy does not map continuously (and perhaps not even uniquely) into outcomes, since there is rapid change and there may also be multiple equilibria. Comparative statics may depend in a delicate way on characteristics of the economy. But the fact that policy is not straightforward is not surprising to researchers of growth and development, and the lens of economic geography provides some further insights for grappling with these problems.

References

Amiti, M., and C. A. Pissarides. 2005. "Trade and Industrial Location with Heterogeneous Labor." *Journal of International Economics* 67(2): 392–412.

Anderson, J., and E. van Wincoop. 2004. "Trade Costs." *Journal of Economic Literature* 42(3): 691–751.

Arndt, S. W., and H. Kierzkowski, eds. 2001. *Fragmentation: New Production Patterns in the World Economy*. Oxford: Oxford University Press.

Au, C-C., and J. V. Henderson 2004. "Are Chinese Cities Too Small?" Department of Economics, Brown University, Providence, RI.

Audretsch, D., and M. Feldman. 2004. "The Geography of Innovation." In *Handbook of Urban and Regional Economics*, vol. 4., ed. J. F. Thisse and J. V. Henderson. Amsterdam: North Holland.

Bernard, A., J. Jensen, S. Redding, and P. Schott. 2007. "Firms in International Trade." *Journal of Economic Perspectives* 21(3): 105–30.

Collier, P., and A. J. Venables. 2007. "Rethinking Trade Preferences: How Africa Can Diversify Its Exports." *World Economy* 30(8): 1326–45.

Cuihong, Y., and P. Jianuo. 2007. *Input Dependence of Foreign Trade*. Beijing: Chinese Academy of Sciences.

Frankel, J. A., and D. Romer. 1999. "Does Trade Cause Growth?" *American Economic Review* 89(3): 379–99.

Fujita, M., P. R. Krugman, and A. J. Venables. 1999. *The Spatial Economy: Cities, Regions and International Trade*. Cambridge, MA: MIT Press.

Grossman, G. M., and E. Rossi-Hansberg. 2006. "The Rise of Offshoring: It's Not Cloth for Wine Any More." Department of Economics, Princeton University, Princeton, NJ.

Hausmann, R., and D. Rodrik. 2003. "Economic Development as Self-Discovery." *Journal of Economic Growth* 72: 603–33.

Hausmann, R., L. Pritchett, and D. Rodrik. 2005. "Growth Accelerations." *Journal of Economic Growth* 10(4): 303–29.

Henderson, J. V., and A. J. Venables. 2008. "The Dynamics of City Formation." NBER Working Paper 13769, National Bureau of Economic Research, Cambridge, MA.

Hummels, D. 2001. "Time as a Trade Barrier." Department of Economics, Purdue University, Lafayette, IN.

Imbs, J., and R. Wacziarg. 2003. "Stages of Diversification." *American Economic Review* 93(1): 63–86.

Jones, B., and B. Olken. 2008. "The Anatomy of Start-Stop Growth." *Review of Economics and Statistics* 90(3): 582–87. Available online at http://www. mitpressjournals.org/doi/abs/10.1162/rest.90.3.582.

Kremer, M. 1993. "The O-Ring Theory of Economic Development." *Quarterly Journal of Economics* 108(3): 551–75.

Kremer, M., and M. de Carvalho Chamon. 2006. "Asian Growth and African Development." *American Economic Review Papers and Proceedings* 96(2): 400–04.

Leamer, E. E. 2007. "A Flat World, a Level Playing Field, a Small World after All, or None of the Above? Review of Friedman." *Journal of Economic Literature* 45(1): 83–126.

Lucas, R. E. 2000. "Some Macroeconomics for the Twenty-First Century." *Journal of Economic Perspectives* 14: 159–68.

Markusen, J., and A. J. Venables. 2007. "Interacting Factor Endowments and Trade Costs: A Multi-Country, Multi-Good Approach to Trade Theory." *Journal of International Economics* 73: 333–54.

Matouschek, N., and F. Robert-Nicoud. 2005. "The Role of Human Capital Investments in the Location Decisions of Firms." *Regional Science and Urban Economics* 35(5): 570–83.

Overman, H. G., P. G. Rice, and A. J. Venables. 2007. "Economic Linkages across Space." Centre for Economic Performance Discussion Paper 0805, London School of Economics and Political Science.

Pattillo, C., S. Gupta, and K. Carey. 2005. "Sustaining Growth Accelerations and Pro-Poor Growth in Africa." IMF Working Paper 195, International Monetary Fund, Washington, DC.

Puga, D., and A. J. Venables. 1999. "Agglomeration and Economic Development: Import Substitution versus Trade Liberalisation." *Economic Journal* 109: 92–311.

Redding, S. J., and A. J. Venables. 2004. "Economic Geography and International Inequality." *Journal of International Economics* 62(1): 53–82.

Rice, P. G., A. J. Venables, and E. Pattachini. 2006. "Spatial Determinants of Productivity: Analysis for the Regions of Great Britain." *Regional Science and Urban Economics* 36(6): 727–52.

Rodrik, D. 2004. "Industrial Policy for the Twenty-First Century." John F. Kennedy School of Government, Harvard University, Cambridge, MA.

Rosenthal, S. S., and W. C. Strange. 2004. "Evidence on the Nature and Sources of Agglomeration Economies." In *Handbook of Urban and Regional Economics*, vol. 4, ed. V. Henderson and J. Thisse. Amsterdam: North Holland.

Summers, L. 2006. "The Global Middle Cries Out for Reassurance." *Financial Times*, October 29.

Young, A. A. 1928. "Increasing Returns and Economic Progress." *Economic Journal* 38(150): 527–42.

CHAPTER 3
Are Cities Engines of Growth and Prosperity for Developing Countries?

Gilles Duranton

Urban policy interventions in developing countries often have two objectives. The first is to make cities "work better" by improving the provision of local public goods, from sewerage to public transport. The second is to limit urbanization, the movement of people from rural areas to already crowded cities. This dual agenda is driven by the idea that the priority for policy should be to alleviate the grim life of urban dwellers in developing countries and slow the growth of cities to prevent more misery.

Although there is no doubt about the abysmal conditions in the slums of Nairobi or Calcutta, is the gloomy outlook of many governments in developing countries about their cities justified? More precisely, do cities favor economic efficiency? Do cities and urbanization bolster self-sustained growth?

An integrated theoretical framework is developed to answer these questions. The framework starts from the idea that the entire urban system is an equilibrium outcome (though one in which politics and other institutional features arguably play fundamental roles). A simple graphical device is pre-

Comments and feedback from Richard Arnott, Gustavo Bobonis, Bob Buckley, Vernon Henderson, Frédéric Robert-Nicoud, Cam Vidler, and especially Patricia Annez and Keith Head, are very much appreciated.

sented to describe the main feedbacks. The framework is then expanded to focus on a number of specific features of cities in developing countries. This highly tractable and flexible framework is also used to interpret the existing evidence about cities and urbanization in developing countries.

To the first question—do cities foster (static) economic efficiency?—the answer from the literature is a resounding yes. Cities provide large efficiency benefits, and there is no evidence that they systematically hurt particular groups. This result provides support for the first pillar of traditional urban policies (improving the functioning of cities). The importance of efficiency benefits from cities also suggests that restricting urbanization entails losses. The theoretical framework presented here also underscores key complementarities in urban policy and cautions about a number of pitfalls.

The second question—what are the dynamic benefits generated by cities?—is more difficult to answer. The evidence suggests that cities can spur economic growth as long as the largest city in a country does not become too large relative to the others. Although this evidence is not strong enough to provide the basis for radical policy initiatives, it raises further doubts about policies that take a negative stance toward cities and discourage labor mobility.

The priority for policy should be to prevent or curb the worst imbalances in urbanization rather than attempt to slow or reverse it. Broadening the focus from within-city to between-city efficiency suggests that reducing the obstacles to the reallocation of factors and activities across cities is a highly desirable policy objective.

In conclusion, there is nothing wrong with the first traditional pillar of urban policy in developing countries, although possibly not for the reasons commonly put forth in its defense. Instead of restricting the influx of people into cities, the second pillar of urban policies in developing countries should be to favor the mobility of resources across cities and regions while avoiding their concentration in a very large dominant city (known as a "primate" city).

The rest of this chapter is organized as follows. The next section presents the graphical framework and discusses the main policy issues. The second section reviews the empirical evidence about greater economic efficiency in cities. It also expands the framework to discuss urban features that are salient in developing countries, such as primate city favoritism and dual labor markets. The third section examines the evidence about the effects of cities on the dynamics of growth and development. The last section discusses a number of policy issues and offers some conclusions.

A Simple Graphical Framework of Urban Development

This section presents the main framework of analysis. It then analyzes the framework's main welfare properties before turning to a number of practical policy considerations.

Modeling Cities

Economic theories concerned with cities have a common underlying structure, with three elements: a spatial structure, a production structure, and some assumptions about the mobility of goods and factors.[1] These elements are necessary for any model of cities to be well specified.

Spatial structure. It is often convenient to distinguish between the internal and external geography of cities. Internal geography is concerned with land, housing, infrastructure, and internal transport. External geography is concerned with the development of new cities and the way in which cities are located relative to one another and to the location of natural resources.[2]

Production structure. It may be tempting to specify an aggregate production function that directly relates primary factors to final output, as is customary in much economic analysis. This standard simplification is often inadequate, however, because cities are characterized by increasing returns to scale and the way in which such increasing returns are generated has potentially important policy implications. In particular, detailed assumptions are needed about labor, the nature of products, the production function of individual firms, the input-output structure that links firms, and how firms compete.

Three main mechanisms can be used to justify the existence of increasing returns in cities (Duranton and Puga 2004). First, a larger city allows for a more efficient sharing of indivisible facilities (such as local infrastructure), risks, and the gains from variety and specialization. For instance, a larger city makes it easier to recoup the cost of infrastructure or, for specialized input providers, to pay a fixed cost of entry. Second, a larger city allows for better matching between employers and employees, buyers and suppliers, partners in joint projects, or entrepreneurs and financiers. This can occur through both a higher probability of finding a match and a better quality of matches when they occur. Third, a larger city can facilitate learning about new technologies, market evolutions, or new forms of organization. More frequent direct interactions between economic agents in a city can thus favor the creation, diffusion, and accumulation of knowledge.

This typology of sources of urban increasing returns concerns the mechanism at stake (sharing, matching, learning). It differs from the traditional Marshallian "trinity" (Marshall 1890) of spillovers, input-output linkages, and labor pooling, which is concerned with where agglomeration effects take place (the market for labor, the market for intermediates, and a largely

---

1   The material in this subsection is adapted from Combes, Duranton, and Overman (2005).

2   Depending on the focus of the analysis, some aspects need to be explained in great detail while others can be modeled very simply. Models that emphasize market access often propose a detailed modeling of the external geography of cities. In contrast, models that focus on housing supply usually assume a very simple external geography and pay more attention to the internal geography of cities and the micro issues related to the operation of land markets. Both the internal and external geography of cities is often taken as exogenous. This may be true in the short run but need not be the case in the long run, as distances within and between cities can be modified following changes in policy or technology.

absent market for ideas). The two typologies complement one another, because the three mechanisms highlighted above (and their associated market failures) can take place in different markets. Good policies require knowing about both the type of market failures at play and the markets in which they take place.

Hence the first general feature that emerges from the literature is that many different mechanisms can generate urban increasing returns. The second main feature highlighted by the literature is that sources of urban increasing returns are also sources of urban inefficiencies. For instance, specialist input producers in a model of input-output linkages may not be remunerated for increasing the choice of inputs in a city. In a matching framework, firms are not compensated for increasing the liquidity of their local labor market. With learning spillovers, workers are not rewarded for the knowledge they diffuse around them. More generally, private and social marginal returns do not usually coincide in a city. This means that urban production is inefficient, in the sense that it does not make the best possible use of local resources.

These two features have important implications. The pervasiveness of market failures hints at a strong role for policy. However, the appropriate corrective policies depend on the exact mechanism at play. The corrective policies associated with urban knowledge spillovers are not the same as those correcting for imperfect matching on the labor market. Given that many mechanisms generate similar outcomes, identifying the precise sources of urban agglomeration and their associated market failures is extremely difficult (Rosenthal and Strange 2004). In terms of policies, this suggests extreme caution when trying to "foster" agglomeration effects. From a modeling perspective, the fact that a variety of mechanisms can generate urban increasing returns is very good news, because one expects agglomeration economies to be a robust feature of cities. This also suggests that one can assume the existence of urban increasing returns without having to rely on a specific mechanism.

Mobility of goods and factors. Assumptions about mobility, both within and between cities, are critical. They need to cover the geographical mobility of goods, services, primary factors, ideas, and technologies. The extent to which material inputs and outputs are tradable clearly varies across sectors. Among primary factors land is immobile, although its availability for different uses (for example, housing versus production) is endogenous. Capital is often taken as highly mobile, with (roughly) the same supply price everywhere. As emphasized below, the (imperfect) mobility of labor, both geographically and sectorally, is a fundamental issue that warrants careful treatment. The mobility of ideas and technologies determines how production varies across space.

The "3.5-Curve" Framework of Urban Development

A simple model of a city in an urban system is presented here. This model, which is in the spirit of Henderson (1974), can be represented graphically.

The wage curve. The first key relation is the city aggregate production function relating total output in a city to its inputs. If the three factors of production are land, labor, and capital, and land is perfectly immobile while capital is perfectly mobile, the focus of attention needs to be on labor. Rather than considering output per worker as a function of the size of the urban labor force, it is technically equivalent, but more fruitful in terms of interpretation, to focus on an inverse demand for labor that relates the wage of workers to the size of the urban labor force.

The wage in a city is increasing in the size of the urban labor force, reflecting the existence of urban agglomeration externalities (figure 3.1). The intensity of urban increasing returns is measured by the slope of the

Figure 3.1 Baseline Case for Typical City

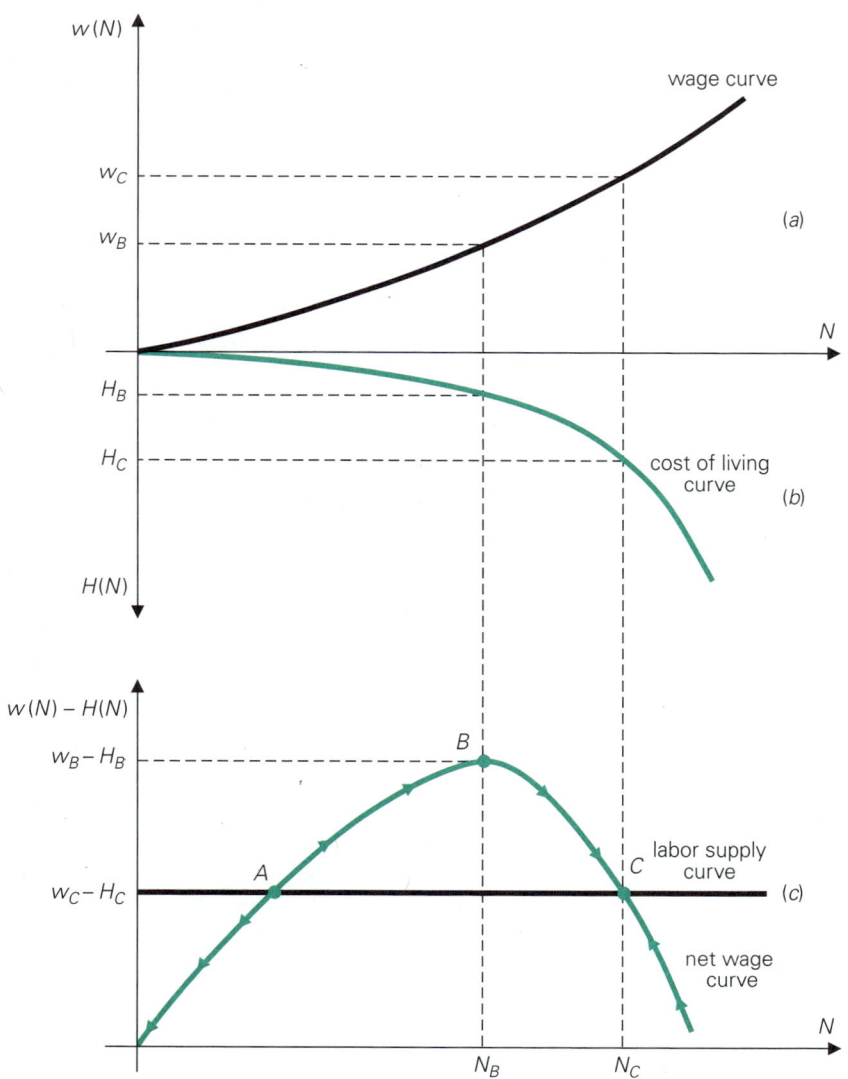

wage curve. Because the nature and intensity of increasing returns differs across industries, the shape of the wage curve varies across industries.

This upward-sloping wage curve stands in sharp contrast to "neoclassical" wage curves, which slope downward. Urban increasing returns have received considerable theoretical attention. Modeling cities in this way is consistent with the fundamental stylized fact that most, if not all, measures of productivity per capita increase with city size (see below for a discussion of the evidence in developing countries). Higher productivity in larger cities can explain why a disproportionate share of economic activity takes place in a small number of places rather than spreading uniformly over space, as would be predicted by a neoclassical model.

The concentration of employment fosters urban productive efficiency. However, human concentration is not the only determinant of urban efficiency, which also relies on a broad range of infrastructure from roads and international airports to well-functioning rental markets for commercial property. Hence the wage curve can differ across cities because of differences in infrastructure and local institutions. Level differences for the wage curve can also occur because of natural endowments and a set of other factors discussed below. As also made clear below, differences in the wage curve lead to cities of different sizes in equilibrium.

The cost of living curve. The second relation relates the costs of living in a city to its employment size. The main components of the cost of living are the cost of commuting, housing, and other consumption goods. It seems reasonable to assume that commuting costs increase with population, because a larger population implies longer commutes and more congested roads. A larger population is also expected to drive up the cost of land and thus of housing. Under some conditions (clarified below), a larger city with a higher cost of land also implies higher retail costs and thus a higher price for consumption goods and other nontradables.

In figure 3.1 the cost of living is increasing in the size of the urban labor force, reflecting increasing urban crowding.[3] For reasons that will become obvious, this curve is drawn with a reversed Y-axis. The precise shape of the cost of living curve is driven by the details of the specific mechanisms that underpin it and is ultimately an empirical matter. However, that the cost of living should increase with population is intuitively obvious. As discussed below, the empirical literature strongly supports this notion.

Beyond its shape, the level of the cost of living curve is also of fundamental importance. First, like the wage curve, the cost of living curve is riddled

---

3 An increase in productivity, which raises local wages, may be expected to have a positive effect on the demand for land and thus on its price. If commuting is paid in units of time, higher wages also lead to a higher shadow cost of commuting. Hence an upward shift in the wage curve implies a downward shift in the cost of living curve. One can ignore these issues by assuming that the cost of living is paid in monetary terms only and that housing consumption per household is fixed. More formal modeling either ignores these effects or suggests that they are second order and thus do not completely offset the direct effect of a shift to the wage curve. In what follows, these effects are ignored in order to keep the exposition simple.

with market failures. For instance, unpriced urban congestion implies an inefficiently high cost of living for any level of population. Poorly defined property rights can also prevent the efficient densification of cities, because investors may be reluctant to invest in property upgrading when, for example, they face a risk of expropriation. Second, a low cost of living in a city relies on a vast number of local public goods. In this respect the provision of roads and public transport to ease commuting is important. The provision of many other public goods of a less capital-intensive nature, such as security or air quality, also matters. Like the wage curve, the cost of living curve is also expected to differ across cities, because cities differ in their natural geography, availability of land, and so forth.

The net wage curve. One can think of the wage curve as representing labor market earnings and of the cost of living curve as representing the expenditure associated mainly with housing and commuting. The difference between the two curves is represented in figure 1 by the net wage curve.[4] This difference is bell-shaped in the figure, corresponding to the case in which agglomeration economies dominate crowding costs for a small population while the reverse occurs for a large population. For this to be the case, the wage curve must be steeper than the cost of living curve before a certain threshold and flatter beyond that point. At this threshold net wages reach their peak (point B in figure 1). This peak can be interpreted as identifying a "pseudo-optimal" city size that maximizes net wages per capita in the city.[5] This is only a "pseudo-optimum" (also called a constrained optimum) rather than a true optimum because of the existence of market failures in production and the cost of living. These market failures imply that the wage and cost of living curves in figure 1 are not as high as they could be.

The labor supply curve. The last curve of figure 3.1 is an inverse labor supply curve. For any level of net wage, it indicates the amount of labor supplied in the city. For simplicity labor supply is assumed to be a function of city population; labor force participation decisions are ignored. The curve essentially captures the migration response to the wage in the city under consideration. A flat labor supply curve implies perfect mobility. In a fully urbanized country, labor mobility takes place primarily across cities, and the labor supply curve of one city mainly reflects conditions in other cities. In a country not yet fully urbanized, labor mobility mostly implies

---

4   This curve is the difference between two other curves and thus not an independent relation, hence the "3.5 curve" name for this framework. Rather than measuring the cost of living curve in units of the numéraire, one could view it as a price index. In that case using the difference between the two curves would be warranted only when using a log scale for both the wage and the cost of living curves. Alternatively, the net wage curve could be modified to represent the ratio of the wage to the cost of living.

5   With no natural obstacle to city creation, it is reasonable to aim at maximizing per capita surplus rather than total city surplus. Note also the implicit assumption that labor is the sole factor of production, because the surplus accruing to labor is equated to the total surplus. It is easy, albeit cumbersome within this graphical framework, to consider other factors of production.

rural–urban migration, and the labor supply curve of a city mainly reflects the conditions of rural hinterlands. (This important issue is returned to below.) City-specific effects, such as amenities, shift this curve: more attractive cities face a labor supply curve that is below that of less attractive ones, because workers accept a lower net wage and are compensated by higher amenities.

Equilibrium. The equilibrium of the model in the absence of any policy intervention can now be derived. The intersection between the labor supply and net wage curves determines the equilibrium. It corresponds to a situation in which workers obtain the net wage they require to come to and stay in the city. This intersection between these two curves may not be unique: in figure 3.1 the labor supply curve first cuts the net wage curve from above (at point A) and then from below (at point C). Point A is not a stable equilibrium. It is easy to see that a small increase in the population raises the net wage, which attracts more workers, raising net wages. This process continues until the city reaches point C. By the same token, a small decrease in the population leads population and wages to fall to zero. A similar argument verifies that the equilibrium at point C is stable. Once the equilibrium population in the city (N_C) is established, one can trace upward to the wage and cost of living curves to read off the equilibrium wage (w_C) and the cost of living (H_C).

Three important points must be addressed before turning to welfare and policy issues. First, to the extent that agglomeration effects take place within sectors, cities have a tendency to specialize. To see this, it is useful to consider two hypothetical activities in a city. These two activities are entirely unrelated, and each has its own productivity curve and a given initial level of employment. Workers in both activities face the same cost of living, because everyone is competing for the same land. The two activities generally offer different wages, however. If this is the case, workers are expected to leave the activity with the lower net wages and move to the other activity. This movement happens only when the city is specialized in a single activity.[6] More generally, it is inefficient to have "disjoint" activities in the same city, because they bring no benefit to one another and crowd one another's land market. The economic composition of cities is expected to reflect this. Hence should agglomeration effects take place mostly within sectors, cities should be specialized. If instead agglomeration effects take place at a broad level of aggregation with strong linkages across sectors, more diversity should be observed.

Second, different wage (and cost of living) curves lead naturally to cities of different sizes. A higher wage curve for a city implies a higher net wage curve and, in turn, a larger equilibrium population. Similarly, cities special-

---

6 Should, for some unspecified reason, the two activities have the same returns, a small employment shock, positive or negative, in either of the two activities creates a small asymmetry between the two activities and leads to full specialization.

ized in sectors with stronger agglomeration economies will also reach a higher equilibrium population.[7]

Third, the analysis of cities is inherently a general equilibrium problem, in which the researcher has to look beyond the direct effect of a change and assess the induced changes that follow. Doing so is possible only if there is a clear analytical framework within which the various effects interact.

Welfare in the 3.5-Curve Framework

This subsection discusses the main welfare issues. It should be viewed more as a way to reach a deeper understanding of the framework than a practical policy guide. General policy issues are addressed in the next subsection before turning to specific policy problems in a development context.

Uncompensated externalities in production. The first source of inefficiencies stems from the production structure itself. The microeconomic foundations of the increasing returns operating inside cities are associated with market failures. First, the indivisibilities at the heart of sharing mechanisms generate a number of inefficiencies. Like all indivisibilities, they imply that only a limited number of players enter the market. This results in imperfect competition and the (socially inefficient) exploitation of market power. If new entrants increase the diversity of, say, local inputs, they are unlikely to reap the full benefits of this increase in diversity. Firms are also expected to make their entry decision on the basis of the profits they can make rather than the social surplus they create. Under imperfect competition, this is inefficient.

Second, with matching mechanisms, a different set of market failures is at play. For instance, firms neglect the positive effects of their vacancies on the job search of workers.

Third, many possible market failures are associated with learning mechanisms. Under imperfect intellectual property rights protection, firms are likely to invest too little in knowledge generation. In the absence of rewards for knowledge diffusion, too little of it takes place. Firms in cities may also be reluctant to train their workers if, for example, they expect them to be poached by competition in the future.

These are only a few of the inefficiencies that can occur when production takes place under increasing returns. If these inefficiencies were suppressed, wages would increase in the city for any level of employment. Starting from the thin wage curve, solving for the inefficiencies in production leads to the thick line in panel (i) of figure 3.2.

Uncompensated externalities in the cost of living. The second source of market failures is related to the cost of living curve. If the private marginal costs paid by residents were equal to the social marginal costs (that is, the costs

---

7   See Duranton (2007) and Rossi-Hansberg and Wright (2007) for models in which technological shocks on the wage curve generate realistic distributions of city populations.

Figure 3.2 Welfare Analysis

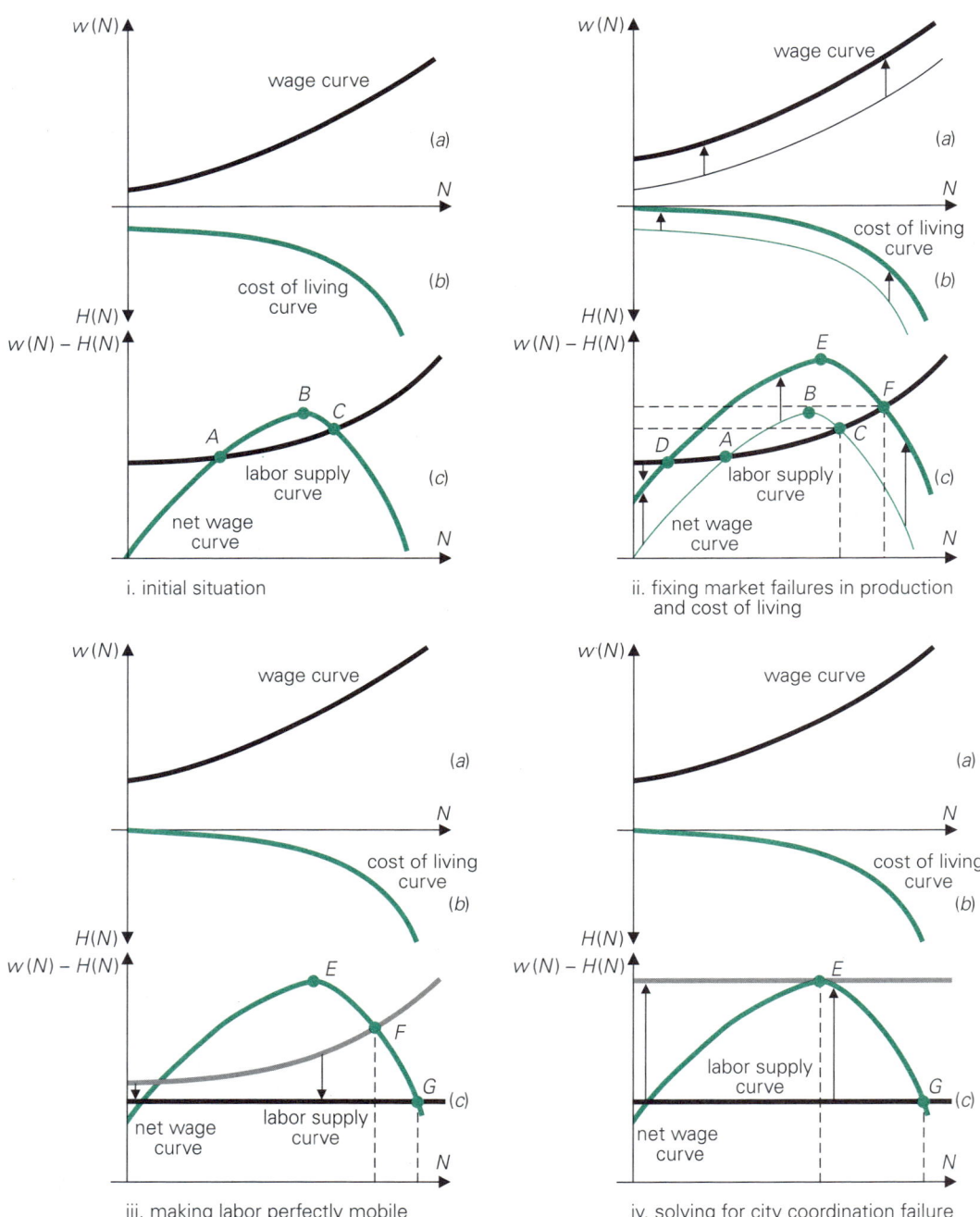

i. initial situation

ii. fixing market failures in production and cost of living

iii. making labor perfectly mobile

iv. solving for city coordination failure

to the economy), there would be no inefficiency in the cost of living. Given no congestion, a perfectly functioning land market, and redistribution of the land surplus, this equality between private and social marginal costs holds naturally. Empirically, one expects none of these three assumptions to be satisfied: as cities become more crowded, congestion becomes more important; land markets are subject to significant frictions and are strongly regulated through planning and zoning regulations; and increases in land values are not taxed away.[8]

The main implication of congestion and frictions in the land market is that in the absence of corrective policy, the cost curve is distorted. With proper corrective policies, it should be possible to reduce the cost of living for any population level in the city. For instance, a congestion tax would reduce the level of traffic congestion in the city and increase the total surplus. Starting from the thin cost of living curve in panel (ii) of figure 3.2, fixing the inefficiencies in the cost of living leads to the thick line.

A higher wage and a lower cost of living imply a higher net wage curve, as shown in panel (iii) of figure 3.2. Following elimination of the market failures in production and cost of living, the net wage curve and the labor supply curve intersect at points D and F (rather than A and C). The net wage curve has its maximum at point E instead of B. Like A, point D indicates an unstable equilibrium. The only stable equilibrium is at point F. At this new equilibrium the net wage is higher than at point C. Population is also higher, because solving for the inefficiencies in production and cost of living makes the city more attractive. The labor supply response implies that workers migrate to the city.

The extent to which a higher net wage curve leads to a larger population versus a higher net wage depends on the slope of the labor supply curve. Perfect mobility (a flat supply curve) implies that all of the gains from curbing the inefficiencies in production and cost of living are translated into a larger population and more crowding. In the absence of mobility, a vertical labor supply curve implies that the upward shift of the net wage curve leads only to higher net wages. After elimination of the inefficiencies associated with production and the cost of living, the equilibrium at F does not coincide with the first-best equilibrium at point E.

Barriers to migration. The third source of inefficiency is related to the labor supply curve and thus to the migration process. The labor supply curve is driven by two sets of forces. First, it echoes the net wage in the rest of the economy. For many developing countries one expects the labor supply curve to largely reflect rural earnings. In this case a higher net wage in rural areas implies a higher labor supply curve. Second, barriers to migration are reflected in the labor supply curve. More costly mobility implies a higher and steeper labor supply curve.

Eliminating obstacles to mobility in panel (iii) of figure 3.2 thus leads to a lower and flatter labor supply curve. As a result, the equilibrium shifts to point G. This new equilibrium implies a larger population and a lower net

---

8 Traffic congestion is a major form of congestion in cities but by no means the only one. Most local public goods, from parks to cultural events, and many amenities, are also subject to negative congestion externalities. Poorly defined property rights over urban land also constitute a critical issue in many developing countries.

wage than the previous equilibrium at point F. The net wage decreases because reducing barriers to mobility makes it easier for newcomers to settle in the city. Because point F is already in the region in which the marginal agglomeration gains are dominated by the marginal losses in urban crowding, an influx of newcomers reduces the welfare of existing residents.

This negative result underscores a fundamental policy issue. Urban economies are second-best economies. Nothing guarantees that eliminating a market failure always brings a city closer to optimality. Solving for the market failures in the wage and cost of living curves and removing barriers to migration is not enough to lead a city to its first-best efficiency, because another market failure prevents cities from reaching their optimal size. Unless this market failure is also eliminated, reducing the barriers to mobility may not improve welfare in a city.[9]

The city coordination failure. The equilibrium with no policy intervention (point C in panel (i) of figure 3.2) is not efficient; it is located to the right of the pseudo-optimum (point B). Without any corrective policy, existing cities are too large with respect to the pseudo-optimum size; employment concentrates in too few cities that are too large.

The reason behind this inefficiency is coordination failure. Fixing the inefficiencies embedded in the wage, cost of living, and labor supply curves does nothing to address the city coordination failure. In panel (iii) of figure 3.2, the equilibrium size (point G) is still inefficiently large compared with the first-best (point E). It is easy to understand why this inefficient situation can be sustained. No one wants to move alone and develop a new city, because doing so would mean forming a very small and thus very unproductive city. It is worthwhile to move to a new city only if it is already large enough or if a large enough group of workers and firms decides to coordinate their move. The creation of such a new city would be desirable for everyone, because existing cities would become smaller and thus able to offer higher net returns. The problem is that in the absence of corrective policy (or market for cities), there is no mechanism to coordinate the movement of workers to new cities.

To solve this governance problem and reach the first-best equilibrium at E, two solutions can be envisioned. The first alternative is to directly restrict the population size of the city. Doing so implies rejecting residents and sending them to places where they will be worse off. Depending on where these rejected residents go, this can increase the cost of living in other cities or increase rural population, arguably reducing agricultural earnings. This solution is thus a partial equilibrium response to the city coordination failure that generates negative general equilibrium effects.

The second alternative is to create new cities and coordinate the move of residents to these new cities. This creation of new cities implies a reduction in the population of previously oversized cities and an improvement in

---

9   Even though welfare in the city under consideration decreases, aggregate welfare increases. This point is made clear below.

the welfare of the remaining residents. Should new cities be populated by rural migrants, this would also imply a decrease in the rural population, arguably increasing agricultural earnings. Higher welfare outside the city implies a higher labor supply curve. In this case the general equilibrium effects are positive.[10] New cities can be created until the labor supply curve hits the net wage curve at point E. At this stage the entire urban system is fully efficient.

Practical Policy Considerations

It is now time to take a more practical look at urban policies. A fundamental policy question should first be answered: Should policymakers bother about cities at all? Cities are riddled with market failures: production is inefficient, congestion is rife, and overcrowding is expected to be the rule. The welfare analysis presented above also makes clear that full urban efficiency is extremely hard to achieve. Hence there is a strong temptation to view the "urban problem" in developing countries as an unmanageable pathology and neglect cities.

Doing so would be wrong. The presence of numerous inefficiencies implies only that cities are much less efficient than they could be and that there are important gains from well-designed urban policies. Furthermore, existing urban inefficiencies do not imply that cities are less efficient than their rural alternatives: the very success of cities in developing countries points to the opposite. However suboptimal they may be, cities typically offer higher returns and better long-term opportunities than other areas. Neglecting cities and restricting their access can have only negative consequences: a worsening of urban inefficiencies and "overcrowded" rural areas, which implies low returns to agriculture and an exacerbation of rural poverty.

Two important points need to be made about the wage curve. First, it reflects a number of evolutions that are determined well beyond the city itself. To take a simple example, many developing countries have policies that distort agricultural prices relative to manufacturing prices. Because cities in developing countries specialize in manufacturing and services, any increase in relative manufacturing prices is likely to translate into higher urban wages and thus a higher wage curve. This should lead to larger cities. More generally, national technology and government policies are reflected in the wage curve of any particular city, affecting its level and, sometimes, its slope.[11]

---

10 General equilibrium effects (that is, what happens outside the city) matter and play a fundamental role. Changes outside the city under consideration affect the labor supply curve and thus its equilibrium. These interdependencies can mean that a worsening of the situation outside the city (that is, a lower labor supply curve) leads to an influx of new residents and a worsening of the welfare in the city as well. The importance of general equilibrium effects also implies that improving the functioning of only one city makes it grow but has ambiguous implications for welfare in this city. As a better-functioning city becomes attractive, new residents can crowd out all the gains.

11 An example is modern telecommunication technologies, which may affect the intensity of agglomeration effects.

Second, the existence and growth of cities is driven by a variety of mechanisms whose relative importance is extremely difficult to identify empirically. The market failures associated with these mechanisms require different corrective policies. For instance, corrective policies aimed at dealing with labor market matching problems have nothing to do with those aimed at fostering knowledge diffusion. Put differently, some corrective policies for inefficiencies are needed about which almost nothing is known. This suggests some caution.[12]

Given the limited possibilities for policy to raise the wage curve, the cost of living curve is a more promising area of action for city governments, for several reasons. Many of the key determinants of the cost of living curve, such as traffic congestion, are reasonably well identified. From sewerage to public transport, there are many components of the cost of living curve for which local governments can make a big difference. The cost of living curve also has to do with poorly defined property rights and the inefficient operations of the land market (this issue is dealt with at greater length below). Finally, many other policies of local governments, such as the provision of public goods and amenities, are reflected into the cost of living curve. For these reasons, the cost of living curve is the traditional area of expertise of city governments and should remain so.

Turning to labor mobility, it is clear that a flatter labor supply curve can potentially lead to important welfare gains by allowing workers to move from low net wage areas to high net wage cities.[13] This increase in mobility is best carried out by central governments, because any city that unilaterally increases labor mobility may decrease its welfare. This prescription of greater labor mobility runs contrary to many policies in developing countries that restrict internal migration. This issue is developed in the next two sections.

The last prescription of the framework regards the fact that cities tend to be too large in equilibrium. This calls for the creation of new cities and

---

12 These market failures are likely to occur in all cities. Creating a more efficient labor market or favoring the diffusion of knowledge is more appropriate for central rather than local governments. The main tool for local governments with respect to the wage curve should be the provision of productive local public goods. (A complete discussion of this issue, including the qualifications that apply to the preceding statement, is well beyond the scope of this chapter. See Epple and Nechyba 2004 and Helsley 2004 for reviews.)

13 An important technical caveat applies here. In the absence of pure externality in the wage and cost of living curves, it is always good from an efficiency (and welfare) perspective to have workers move from low-wage (rural) areas to high-wage (urban) areas. This result holds even for cities that have decreasing returns, because the difference between the net wage curve and the labor supply curve exactly measures the social marginal gain associated with one additional migrant in the city. This is no longer true in the presence of pure externalities. In this case a new worker into the city can raise the wages of all other workers (through agglomeration effects) but also increase their cost of living. If the increase in the cost of living associated with the externality is very large, the private gains from the move for the migrant and the higher wages for all workers can be more than offset by the cost of living loss to all the other inhabitants. Given how large spatial disparities can be in developing countries (Aten and Heston 2005), the congestion externalities would need to be extremely large for migration from poor to rich areas not to raise overall output. This case remains to be made empirically.

the coordination of their settlement. This recommendation should be taken with extreme caution. Experiences with city creation in developing countries, particularly capital city creation, have often led to mixed (or worse) results. While new cities in the United States are often created by private developers (Henderson and Mitra 1996), few developing countries appear to be able (or willing) to follow suit. Moreover, developing countries already appear to host many very small cities. The challenge is thus to increase growth in small cities.[14]

What's Special about Cities in Developing Countries?

The framework can be applied to cities in developed as well as developing countries. This section presents some empirical evidence on developing countries in support of this framework. It then explores some specific features of cities in developing countries.

Empirical Support for the Framework

The literature offers support for all the main building blocks of the framework proposed here: an upward-sloping wage curve, a cost of living that rises with city size, a bell-shaped net wage curve, and some labor mobility driven by net wage differentials. A large body of literature documents the existence of agglomeration economies in developed economies (see Rosenthal and Strange 2004 for a review). The main conclusion of this literature is the finding of scale economies of 3–8 percent (that is, a 10 percent increase in the size of an activity in a city raises productivity in this activity by 0.3–0.8 percent). These agglomeration effects take place both within sectors (localization economies) and between sectors (urbanization economies). The results for developing countries are usually similar, although far less research about agglomeration economies has been conducted in such settings.

Agglomeration effects. Studies of agglomeration economies in developing countries regress some productivity outcome in cities (and sectors) on city measures of economic activity within or across sectors. (See Rosenthal and Strange 2004 and Combes and others 2008 for details about this type of methodology.) Following Henderson's 1988 study of localization economies in Brazil, several studies have found quantitative evidence of localization effects. Henderson, Lee, and Lee (2001) find localization economies for industries, particularly traditional industries, in the Republic of Korea.

---

14 One could argue that all cities, small and large, are already oversized. There is no contradiction if one acknowledges that cities should reach their pseudo-optimal size. The growth and industrialization of small cities is all the more important because developing countries often have an international comparative advantage in mature manufacturing sectors. Small and mid-size cities are natural locations for such activities (Henderson 1997).

Similar evidence is provided by Lall, Shalizi, and Deichmann (2004) for India and by Deichmann and others (2005) for Indonesia. Additional evidence about localization effects can be found in a number of case studies looking at a wide variety of countries and sectors (see Overman and Venables 2005 for references).

There is also evidence of urbanization economies in developing countries. Henderson, Lee, and Lee (2001) show that they matter for advanced sectors in the Republic of Korea. There is also evidence of urbanization economies for India. They appear rather weak in Lall, Funderburg, and Yepes (2004) but much stronger in Lall, Koo, and Chakravorty (2003). Deichmann and others (2005) find mild evidence of urbanization effects in Indonesia for a number of sectors. The results of Au and Henderson (2006a, b) on Chinese cities are also consistent with a mix of localization and urbanization economies. This literature is discussed in Henderson (2005), Overman and Venables (2005), and Quigley (chapter 4 in this volume), who provide detailed reviews of agglomeration findings for developing countries (see References for additional comments).

Strong localization economies are expected to foster the growth of specialized cities, while strong urbanization economies foster the growth of diversified cities. Evidence of both localization and urbanization economies is consistent with the existence of diversified cities and specialized cities in developing countries.[15]

These studies can be criticized on two grounds. First, they usually do not control for the individual (observed and unobserved) characteristics of workers. It could be that measured agglomeration effects reflect only the sorting of more productive workers in larger and more specialized cities rather than true agglomeration economies. Using French data, Combes, Duranton, and Gobillon (2008) show that such sorting is empirically important and goes a long way toward accounting for observed spatial disparities. Controlling for sorting does not make agglomeration effects vanish, however.

Second, most of the findings concern the formal sector. Including the informal sector more widely in future household surveys would be helpful. At this stage one can note only that the linkages between formal and informal sector firms are often intense, which suggests that agglomeration effects are generated within both sectors, with benefits that accrue to both. The case study evidence that supports the existence of agglomeration effects also strongly supports the idea that the informal sector is a strong contributor.

Evidence on the cost of living curve is scarce. Early work by Thomas (1980), Henderson (1988), and Richardson (1987) shows a rapid increase in the cost of living with city size. These findings are confirmed by more recent work by Henderson (2002a), who looks at a broader cross-section of

---

15 Despite strong evidence about localization economies, it seems that there are few specialized cities in developing countries relative to the United States. Other factors, such as high transport costs, must be invoked to explain these weak patterns of urban specialization.

cities. He finds the elasticities of various cost of living measures to cities size to be between 0.2 and 0.3.[16] Timmins (2006) develops a novel methodology to infer the "true" cost of living from widely available data using a model of location choice. Applying his approach to Brazilian data, he finds that the cost of living increases with city size above a certain threshold.[17]

The evidence about the net wage curve is thin. The main difficulty is that with sufficient labor mobility, one would expect all cities to be on the decreasing portion of the net wage curve, following the stability argument presented above. Having most cities on the decreasing portion of the net wage curve is consistent with the findings of Da Mata and others (2007) on Brazil. Au and Henderson (2006a, b) provide direct evidence from Chinese cities of net returns to size being bell-shaped. They exploit the fact that the Chinese government has imposed strong barriers to labor mobility, which have constrained urban growth.[18] As a result a steep labor supply curve is expected in China. Provided it is steep enough, some cities can be too small in equilibrium, and a bell-shaped net wage curve can be estimated.

Interestingly, Au and Henderson find that Chinese cities tend to be significantly undersized. This results in large income losses. They also find that the net wage curve is quasi-flat after its maximum. This suggests that cities may become grossly oversized under free mobility but that the costs of being oversized are small (unlike the costs of being underpopulated).

Migration. The mechanism that underlies the labor supply curve has been widely studied. Greenwood (1997) provides a general survey of internal migrations in developed and developing countries. Lall, Selod, and Shalizi's (2006) review focuses on developing countries. A key finding of the literature is that internal migration flows in developing countries are consistent with an upward-sloping labor supply curve. Representative of this literature, Brueckner (1990) and Ravallion and Wodon (1999) find that the direction of migration flows is consistent with differences in net wages. In their work on Bangladesh, Ravallion and Wodon (1999) also address the slope of the net wage curve by documenting persistent differences in living standards across areas, despite the absence of formal barriers to mobility.

Closer to the spirit of the labor supply curve in the framework presented here, Da Mata and others (2007) estimate a population supply function for Brazilian cities. They find the elasticity of population to income per capita

---

16 These elasticities, like those for the wage curve, are estimated for observed (that is, equilibrium) sizes. It is therefore unsurprising that the cost-of-living elasticities with respect to population are higher than the wage elasticities: this is exactly what the framework predicts should happen in equilibrium.

17 He also finds that the cost of living decreases with population below the threshold. This suggests that the cost of living is high in large cities and small in isolated places.

18 Although the absolute numbers for Chinese cities look impressive, urbanization has proceeded at a slow pace compared with many other countries during their industrial takeoff. During the past several years, China's urban population has grown at about 3–4 percent a year—much more slowly than the 5–6 percent growth experienced in Brazil, Indonesia, and the Republic of Korea at a comparable stage. In cross-country analysis China's urbanization rate is very low relative to its level of GDP (Henderson, Quigley, and Lim 2007).

to be between 2 and 3. This is quite elastic but still far from perfect mobility. Barrios, Bertinelli, and Strobl (2006) show that in Sub-Saharan Africa there is a direct link between climate, which directly affects living standards in rural areas, and urban growth. Their finding is consistent with an important role for shocks that shift the labor supply curve up or down (Poelhekke 2007). It also suggests that in less advanced countries, the labor supply curve is driven largely by living conditions in the countryside rather than in other cities.[19] This is consistent with the traditional notion of surplus labor (Lall, Selod, and Shalizi 2006).

Another conclusion that can be drawn from Barrios, Bertinelli, and Strobl is more subtle. They show a negative correlation between urban growth and the welfare of urban dwellers. This negative correlation may explain why many developing country governments attempt to restrain urbanization. However, this correlation is not causal. Negative agricultural shocks lower the labor supply curve, causing workers to flock to cities, thereby lowering urban welfare. Hence cities can still offer efficiency benefits despite a negative correlation between urban growth and urban net wages. Preventing rural dwellers from moving to cities will make them worse off.

Development of new cities and size of existing ones. The theoretical literature has recently made progress on efficient city development (Henderson and Venables 2006). Little empirical work has been done, however. Using data on world cities spanning several decades, Henderson and Wang (2007) use a 100,000 population threshold to track the entry of new cities. Several interesting findings emerge. First, in a typical country the rate of growth in the number of cities is not statistically different from that of population growth. This suggests that new cities do indeed rise; the rough proportionality between the entry of new cities and population growth is reassuring. Of course, this does not say much about the efficiency of the process of city creation, beyond ruling out the notion that it is entirely dysfunctional. Henderson and Wang also show that the emergence of new cities is favored by democratization and government decentralization; it is slowed by a large fraction of educated workers. With world urban population growing by about 100 million per year, there is no doubt that those issues deserve further attention.

There is scant evidence about cities being too large. Very strong barriers to labor mobility have made Chinese cities too small, according to Au and Henderson (2006a, b). No other study looks at this question without making heroic assumptions about what the optimal city size is. In light of the framework presented above and its predictions about cities being oversized, casual observation of cities in developing countries reveals some apparently puzzling facts with respect to city size. Many megacities in developing coun-

---

19 The corollary of this is that worsening rural conditions, which lower the labor supply curve, lead to "urbanization without growth," as documented for instance in Fay and Opal (1999).

tries, such as Karachi, are arguably "too large." But most cities in developing countries are much smaller. In Thailand, for instance, only one city has a population of more than 300,000. How is it that both Bangkok, with a population nearing 6 million, and the fifth-largest city in Thailand, Chiang Mai, with a population of about 150,000, could both be too large? The answer lies in primate city favoritism and market access.

Primate City Favoritism

Urban primacy is a well-known feature of urbanization in developing countries (see, for example, Henderson 2005). To explain why the largest city in so many developing countries is often disproportionately larger than the second-largest city, the literature has focused on two arguments, protectionist trade policies and political and institutional factors.

Urban primacy is sometimes attributed to protectionist trade policies. In the model of Krugman and Livas Elizondo (1996), trade liberalization reduces urban primacy because it allows all cities to import differentiated goods from abroad. This equalization of market potential reduces the tendencies for the agglomeration of manufacturing in a single core city.

This model relies on very specific assumptions. Rather than equalizing market potential, it seems more reasonable to assume that trade liberalization gives privileged market access to coastal cities or cities close to trading partners. In this case inland primate cities can obviously see their dominance reduced by trade liberalization. Mexico City, which served as a motivating example to Krugman and Livas Elizondo (1996), may be an illustration of this. In contrast, coastal primate cities can see their dominance reinforced by trade liberalization (Fujita and Mori 1996). The primacy of Buenos Aires, for example, was not diminished by trade liberalization. The effects of trade policy are thus ambiguous.

Consistent with this theoretical ambiguity, empirical support for trade-based explanations of urban primacy is weak. Studies that find a negative effect of trade on primacy often do so because they fail to control properly for other channels that can influence primacy and are correlated with trade (see, for example, Moomaw and Shatter 1996). The better and more recent studies (Ades and Glaeser 1995; Nitsch 2006) suggest that trade plays no systematic role with respect to urban primacy.

Instead, political and institutional factors appear to be at the root of the primacy phenomenon. There is strong evidence of a positive association between unstable and undemocratic regimes and urban primacy (Ades and Glaeser 1995; Davis and Henderson 2003). The exact underlying mechanism(s) is nevertheless not fully elucidated. The story is often told in terms of dictatorial regimes bribing the residents of the primate city because they are afraid of being overthrown by social unrest. Direct evidence about this mechanism is lacking. Furthermore, this type of explanation implicitly assumes fairly strong state institutions able to tax their countryside and redistribute the proceeds to the primate city. It may be argued that undemocratic and unstable regimes are weak and favor primate cities by default.

Primate city favoritism can work through a myriad of small decisions, from underpriced gasoline and better provision of local public goods to better business opportunities for government cronies in the primate city (Henderson and Becker 2000; Henderson 2002a, b). In this respect, the many regulations and permits that govern economic activity in most developing countries could play an important role. Being close to a center of power makes it easier to obtain permits or to circumvent the need for them. A complementary explanation points to better road infrastructure linking the primate city to the rest of the country (Saiz 2006).

Primate city favoritism can readily be incorporated into the framework presented here. For simplicity favoritism (or the lack thereof) is assumed to primarily affect wages (a similar argument could be developed for the cost of living curve). Earnings are higher than they would otherwise be in the favored cities. They are also lower than they would otherwise be in other cities, because favoritism comes at a cost to them (figure 3.3). With the cost of living curve the same in both cities, the net wage curve of the favored city is above that of the nonfavored city. It is then easy to see that the equilibrium size of the favored city is larger than that of the nonfavored city.[20] Because of general equilibrium effects, the labor supply curve is also lower than it would be in the absence of favoritism.

The potentially large misallocation of resources associated with primate cities suggests that policies to reduce urban primacy are needed.[21] Dealing effectively with this problem will be difficult, however, for several reasons. First, primate city favoritism manifests itself in many different ways, and there is no definite evidence about which channels matter most. The Korean experience hints that administrative deregulation may be a powerful tool with which to reduce urban primacy (Henderson, Lee, and Lee 2001). Red tape may be costly for all businesses but more so for those located far away from the main center, so that deregulation is more beneficial to them.

Second, the political economy associated with urban primacy may be very difficult to break. Cronies who benefit from their proximity to political power are unlikely to easily accept a leveling of the playing field.

Third, the theoretical findings of Henderson and Venables (2006) suggest that governments may play a role in anchoring expectations about which secondary cities are developed. Their development may then alleviate primacy. However, anchoring expectations about future urban development may be subject to time inconsistencies and an inefficient political economy.

---

20 In figure 3 the favored city is larger but not disproportionately larger than the nonfavored city. A flatter downward sloping portion of the net wage curve can make this difference much larger. According to Au and Henderson (2006a), the net wage curve is empirically rather flat beyond its maximum in China.

21 Such policies have been attempted for a long time. However, many policies, such as the relocation government activities, did not provide the right incentives for residents to relocate and took place in a framework of highly controlled labor mobility.

Figure 3.3 Primate Cities Favoritism

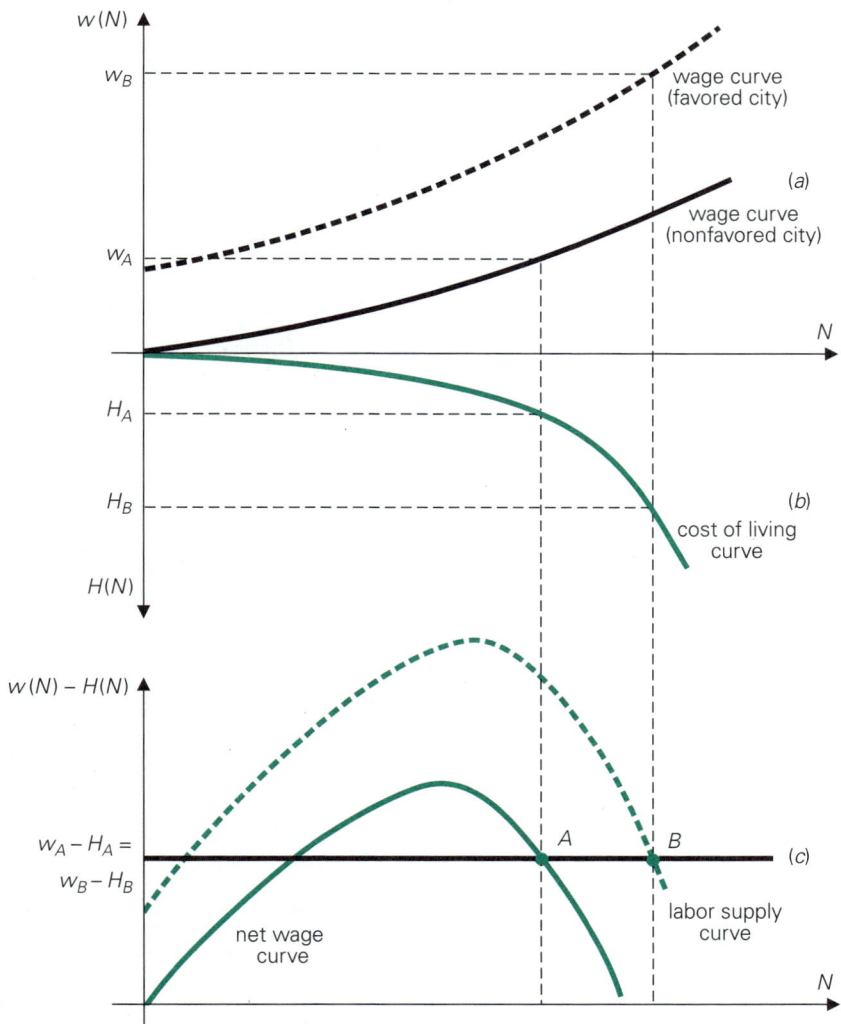

Internal Market Access

The proposition that good access to markets matters can be traced back at least to Harris (1954). It was recently revived by Krugman (1991). This body of work, referred to as the New Economic Geography, is summarized in Fujita, Krugman, and Venables (1999), Baldwin and others (2004), and Combes, Mayer, and Thisse (forthcoming).

The minor adaptation of Krugman's (1991) model presented here considers two regions and two sectors. Agriculture produces a homogenous good under constant returns in the hinterland of each region. For simplicity this good is assumed to be perfectly tradable and is produced by immobile workers. In each region there is a city in which manufacturing firms operate under increasing returns. Each monopolistically competitive firm employs mobile manufacturing workers to produce a different variety of differentiated product, which is demanded by consumers in both regions. Manufacturing varieties are costly to transport between regions, so that firms' sales have a home-market bias.

The wage of manufacturing workers is determined as follows. Consider a "high" level of transport costs, a reasonable assumption for most developing countries.[22] Because of high transport costs, producers in each city are partly insulated from imports from the other regions. Producers in a city can thus charge high prices, which in turn imply high manufacturing wages locally. If manufacturing expands, the regional market becomes more crowded. This happens because, although the expansion of manufacturing implies a larger urban market, the size of the local market (that is, the whole region) does not increase proportionately (remember the fixed agricultural sector in the hinterland). Furthermore, with high transport costs, very little of the increase in manufacturing output is exported. When transport costs are high, manufacturing wages decrease with the size of the urban manufacturing workforce.

This alone would lead to a downward sloping wage curve and a complete dispersion of manufacturing. However, it seems difficult to completely write off the efficiency effects of urban agglomeration described above. This suggests that the wage curve is determined by opposing forces (market access versus agglomeration economies). Put differently, as a city grows, its regional market becomes more crowded, so that the prices of locally produced goods decline (which reduces urban wages), but it also becomes more efficient (which raises urban wages).

Assume that market access effects dominate agglomeration effects in small markets and that the reverse holds in large markets. This implies a wage curve that first slopes downward and then upward (figure 3.4). (This case is examined because it has more interesting implications than its opposite.) To defend it, one could argue that negative market crowding effects can be very strong at the margin in a very small market and much milder if many firms are already operating in a market. It could also be argued that a minimum city size is needed for agglomeration economies to take place.

Transport costs affect not only the wage curve (through the production of goods) but also the cost of living curve (through their consumption). A small isolated city may face very low housing and commuting costs. However, consumption goods can be very expensive, because most of them need to be shipped in, at a very high cost. As the city grows and produces more, the price of manufactured goods declines, because a smaller proportion of them need to be imported.

Other components of the cost of living, such as housing and commuting, increase with city size. Forces are thus pushing in opposite directions. It seems reasonable to assume that higher housing and commuting costs even-

---

22 Details about this case and a complete explanation of the low transport cost case can be found in Combes and others (2005). The tradeoff between the two main forces described below is resolved differently when transport costs are low.

Figure 3.4 Internal Market Access

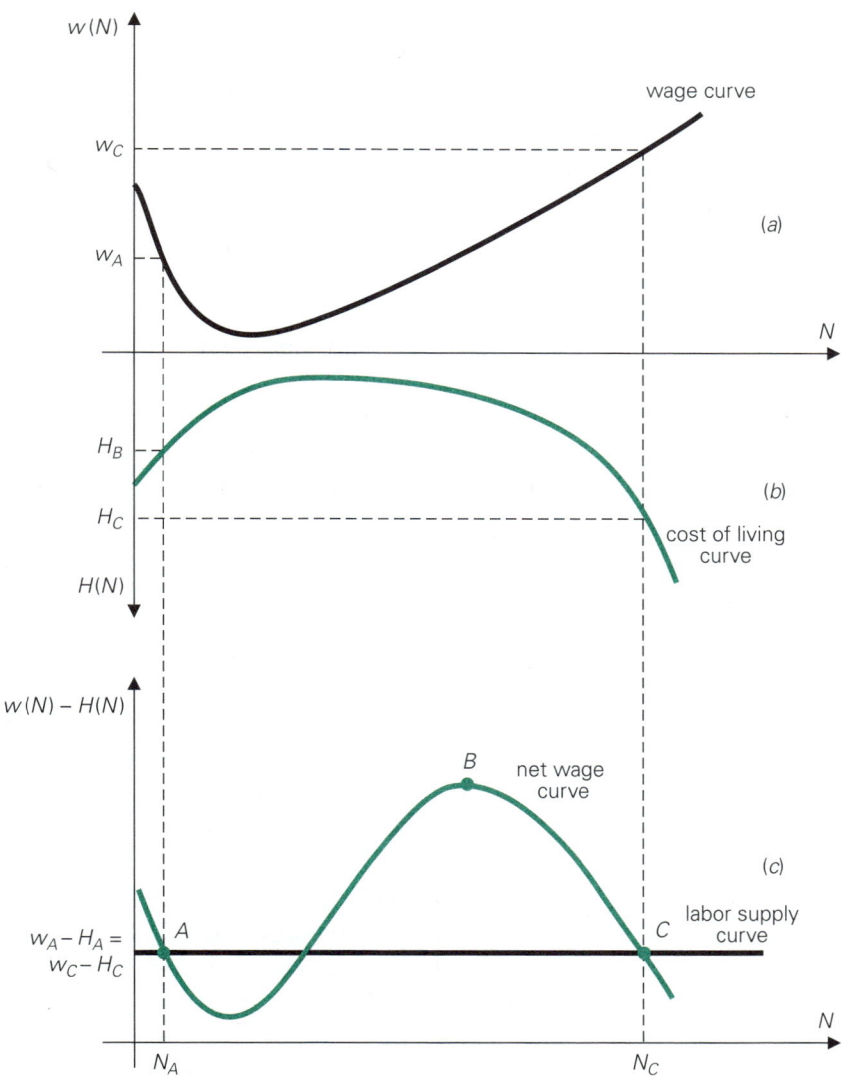

tually dominate when cities grow very large. This suggests that the cost of living first decreases and then increases as cities grow (see figure 4).

Subtracting the cost of living from the wage implies that the net wage first decreases then increases before decreasing again with city size.[23] In figure 3.4 the net wage curve and the labor supply curve intersect three times. Ignoring the unstable equilibrium in the middle, two stable equilibria remain. Cities are either very small (point A) or much larger (point C), with

---

23 This requires the wage curve to decrease faster initially than the cost of living as the city grows. We expect this to happen because manufacturing wages are expected to decline proportionately to the price of local manufacturing goods whereas the cost of living in the city is expected to decrease less than proportionately because the prices of the agricultural good and imported manufacturing are unchanged while the other components of costs of living increase.

the optimal city size (point B) somewhere in between. The novelty in figure 3.4 is the existence of small cities whose growth is limited by strong crowding on the product market and insufficient agglomeration effects. This crowding is in turn caused by high transport costs and the difficulty the cities face exporting their output.

The representation in figure 3.4 is important because it provides a strong rationale for the coexistence in many developing countries of small stagnant cities and large primate cities. High costs of trade between cities may also explain why cities in developing countries may not be as fully specialized as cities in developed countries. Urban specialization makes little sense when the costs of intercity trade are very high.

The literature offers strong empirical support regarding the importance of market access for cities in developing countries. Using two different approaches, Lall, Koo, and Chakravorty (2003) and Lall, Funderburg, and Yepes (2004) underscore the importance of market access in India. Strong effects of market access are also found in Brazil (Lall, Funderburg, and Yepes 2004; Da Mata and others 2007) and Indonesia (Deichmann and others 2005; Amiti and Cameron 2007). This within-country evidence is complemented by a large body of literature that looks at the importance of market access at the country level (Head and Mayer 2004; Redding and Venables 2004). The evidence on the shape of the cost of living curve is much thinner, although the article that currently defines the frontier on the topic (Timmins 2006) finds strong evidence for Brazilian cities of nonlinear cost of living curves taking the shape hypothesized above.

What are the policy implications of these findings? Improving market access implies better access to other markets, but it is also synonymous with a loss of protection for local firms. Depending on which effect dominates, the wage curve can shift upward or downward. Better market access for small isolated cities also implies a less steeply decreasing wage curve, so that a flatter wage curve (at least in its early part) is expected. With better access, one would also expect a lower cost of living. On balance, for small cities better market access implies a flatter and possibly higher net wage curve. This in turn implies that the small city equilibrium at point A should shift to the right (city growth) or even disappear entirely, making point C the only stable equilibrium. With broad-based gains from better market access, one should also expect a higher labor supply curve through general equilibrium effects. As a result of a higher labor supply curve, the equilibrium size of large cities would decrease. The final outcome could be smaller large cities but a larger number of them.

In practice market access is improved by two sets of policies. The first involves building and developing roads and other transport infrastructure, such as airports and high-speed train lines. The second involves removing impediments to trade across regions, from administrative hurdles to cartelized distribution networks.

A number of caveats must be kept in mind about these policies. First, most specifications in the empirical literature are not derived directly from theory (Head and Mayer 2004, 2006). Put differently, the importance of market access has been established, but it is still unclear how it works. Second, the development of road networks may have perverse effects. Linking small cities to large economic centers increases the market potential of small cities, but it may increase that of large cities even more, thereby reinforcing rather than reducing primacy. The U.S. experience nonetheless suggests large productivity gains can be associated with the development of an integrated transport network (Fernald 1999). Third, improving market access may also have some effects at a geographical scale greater than cities. A key prediction of modern regional economics is that lower transport costs can lead first to increased regional agglomeration and then to decreased regional agglomeration for even lower levels of transport costs (Fujita, Krugman, and Venables 1999; Combes, Mayer, and Thisse forthcoming). However, better transport infrastructure may create a group of winning cities in core regions and a group of cities left behind in the periphery.[24] One could think of coastal Chinese cities versus hinterland cities or high-plateau cities in Colombia versus cities on the Colombian Caribbean coast.

In summary, urban primacy is often attributed to a dysfunctional political economy leading to primate city favoritism. There is much empirical support for this explanation. A complementary explanation points to high internal trade costs leading to either large or small cities. Much of the evidence is consistent with this explanation as well. In both cases a reduction in urban primacy is desirable. Achieving it by reducing primate city favoritism may be effective, but doing so is hard to implement politically. Improving market access for isolated cities may be politically easier to achieve, but the precise effects of better access are more difficult to predict, because improved access may reinforce primacy.

Migration and Dual Labor Markets

The framework developed above assigns a positive (and equalizing) role to internal migrations and labor mobility. This is in contrast with some of the academic literature and much of the policy reality in developing countries. From internal passports in China and the "nativist" policies of Indian states to resettlement policies in Africa and Latin America, there is a strong bias against free labor mobility in many developing countries. Restricting the movement of labor is not the right answer if cities become too large, as shown above.

Another justification for antimobility policies rests on the existence of dual labor markets. This argument, first developed by Harris and Todaro (1970), has been extremely influential in policy circles. Theoretically, it works as follows. There is a formal sector with a fixed number of urban

---

24 Baldwin and others (2004) analyze the theoretical ambiguities concerning the effects of transport costs on regional agglomeration. See Fujita and Mori (2005) for a systematic study of how transport costs can affect cities in a regional setting.

jobs that pay a high wage (w_A in figure 3.5). In rural areas workers receive lower earnings, represented by the labor supply curve (figure 3.5). This initial earnings gap between the rural and the formal urban sector causes workers to move to the city.

Should there be only as many migrants to the city as there are jobs in the formal sector, the city would end up at the social optimum, point A in figure 3.5. However, when the city is at point A it cannot be in equilibrium, because the net wage is above that in rural areas. If there are more workers than available jobs in the formal sector, the model assumes that jobs are randomly allocated among city residents. The lucky ones obtain jobs in the formal sector, while the unlucky ones obtain jobs in the informal sector of the same city. This informal sector offers a lower wage, w. In this case workers keep moving to the city until the expected wage they receive minus

Figure 3.5 Harris-Todaro Migrations

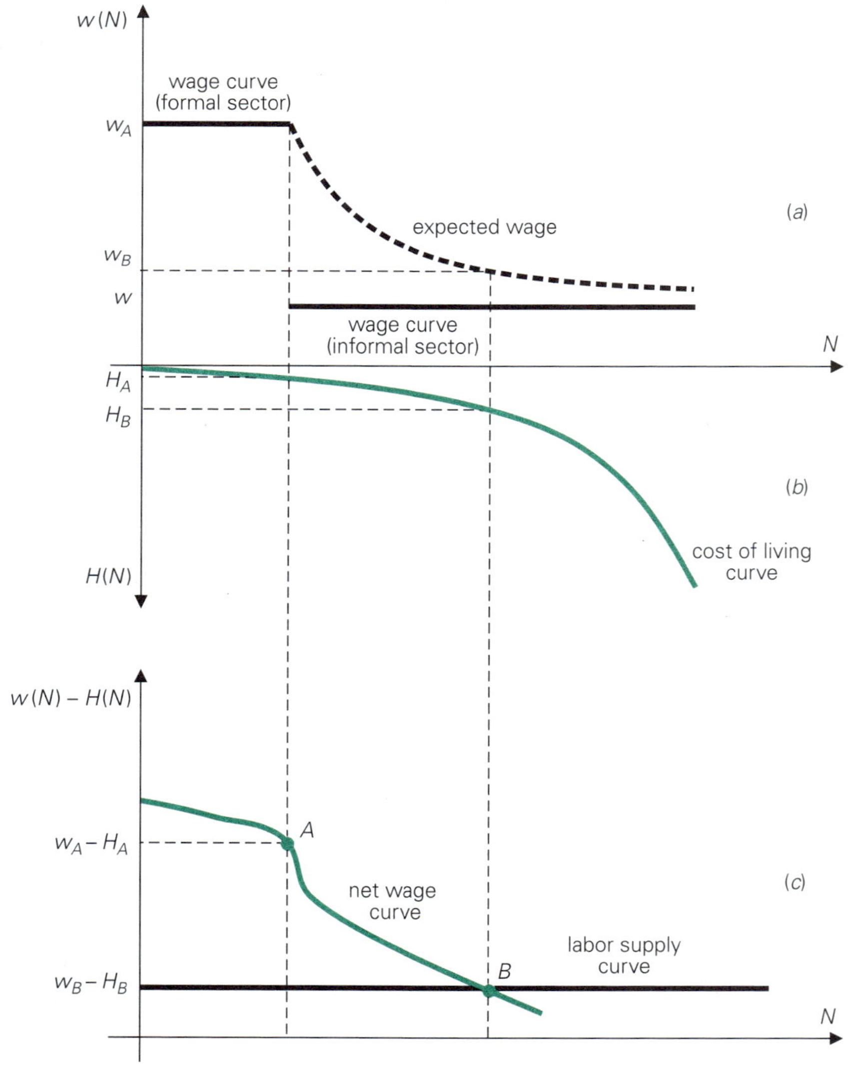

the cost of living (that is, their expected net wage) intersects with the labor supply curve (point B).[25] It is easy to see that this equilibrium entails cities that are too large. The main difference with the baseline case explored above is not that cities are too large—that was the case in the baseline as well—but that it makes sense to curtail entry into the city.

Although appealing, the Harris-Todaro argument can be criticized on a variety of grounds (see Lall, Selod and Shalizi 2006 for an in-depth analysis and empirical references). Workers end up in the informal sector because of wage rigidities in the formal sector. Trying to solve a problem that occurs in the labor market by restricting the mobility of workers is not the most direct solution and is likely to have a number of unwanted side effects.[26] The stark assumptions of the Harris-Todaro model also bias it toward generating overmigration to cities. In the model, workers are risk neutral and formal sector job are randomly allocated. In the real world, workers are arguably risk averse and know that formal sector jobs are not randomly allocated, so that only those with high chances of obtaining such jobs are expected to move. The fact that the formal and informal sectors appear quite segmented in most developing countries reinforces this point. Furthermore, there is no empirical support for the downward-sloping wage and net wage curves predicted by figure 3.5, as made clear above. All this suggests that the main argument used to restrict labor mobility is relatively weak.

To go beyond a mere rejection of Harris and Todaro, one needs to ask why restrictions on labor mobility are so widespread in developing countries. One possibility is that policy makers have overzealously applied their ideas. In such a case policies can change after showing the weakness of their underpinnings. Another possibility is that restrictions on labor mobility may be part of a political economy equilibrium. In this case better policies would be much more difficult to implement. More needs to be known about this issue to understand the nature of the challenge for labor mobility and how it may be overcome.

Dual Housing Markets

The last key feature of cities in developing countries is the existence of a dual housing sector, consisting of formal sector housing and squatter settlements (also referred to as slums, invasions, and shanty towns).[27] In some large cities in developing countries, more than half the population live in squatter settlements, where they face very poor (or no) public services provision, insalubrious living conditions, and a number of constraints associated with the precariousness of their housing.

---

25 The figure follows the approach of Brueckner and Zenou (1999), who explicitly consider a land market. The presence of a land market already reduces the tendency of cities to become too large compared with the most basic versions of the Harris-Todaro model.

26 This rigidity is also partly attributable to a very large and spatially concentrated public sector. Restricting urbanization is not the way to deal with a dysfunctional public sector.

27 A distinction can be drawn between illegal settlements, in which residents have property rights, and true squatter settlements, in which they do not. Although this distinction is important to design policies, it remains in the background below for simplicity.

Squatter settlements are often associated with the idea of low-cost and low-quality housing. If these were its only characteristics, such housing would simply reflect the poverty of some urban dwellers, who opt out of the formal housing sector because they cannot afford it. Policy decisions regarding what to do with squatter settlements would largely be choices about how much redistribution to do (or not to do) and whether it is best to effect the redistribution through subsidized housing and public services or by other means.

These issues are important, but there is more to squatter settlements than this. First, it has been widely argued that poorly defined or poorly enforced property rights over urban land, which make squatter settlements possible, could also affect a wide range of other economic outcomes. De Soto (2000) argues that a lack of effective formal property titles prevents residents of squatter settlements from using their housing as collateral and is thus a major barrier to enterprise development. Although the evidence of the existence of these financial constraints is disputed, Di Tella, Galliani, and Schargrodsky (2007) find that the lack of titles has important effects on the beliefs of people and thus their economic behavior. Field (2007) finds that it also affects the female labor supply. Durand-Lasserve and Selod (2007) provide a detailed review of a broad range of effects associated with the lack of effective titles.

Second, squatter settlements may be the outcome of policy distortions. Henderson (2007) argues that binding minimum lot size is responsible for the growth of squatter settlements in Brazilian cities. Malpezzi (1999) also cites the prevalence of rent controls, which limit the expansion of the rental market.

Third, once the absence of public services or their very poor quality is taken into account, squatter settlement may not be so cheap. For instance, water in slums often needs to be bought at a very high price from local water distributors. Without titles, squatters must also often pay a steep price for some form of protection.

It is possible to expand the theoretical framework to gain some insights into dual housing markets based on the last two points. Figure 3.6 assumes a standard upward-sloping wage curve that applies to all city residents.[28] It shows three cost of living curves. The dotted curve represents the cost of living in the formal sector in the absence of exclusionary zoning. Exclusionary zoning (for example, minimum lot size in Brazil) raises the cost of living in the formal sector, yielding the solid cost of living curve. The alternative to the formal sector is a squatter settlement. The cost of living in a squatter settlement is represented by the dashed line. Because of the high cost of the

---

28 In many cities with squatter settlements, a significant proportion of slum dwellers work in the formal (production) sector. As a first-order approximation, the assumption is made here that all workers benefit from agglomeration effects. A more refined version of figure 3.6 would take into account the possibility that slums may often be located far from the main places of work and poorly served by public transportation. In such a case slum dwellers would be less likely to benefit from agglomeration effects.

Figure 3.6 Dual Housing Sector

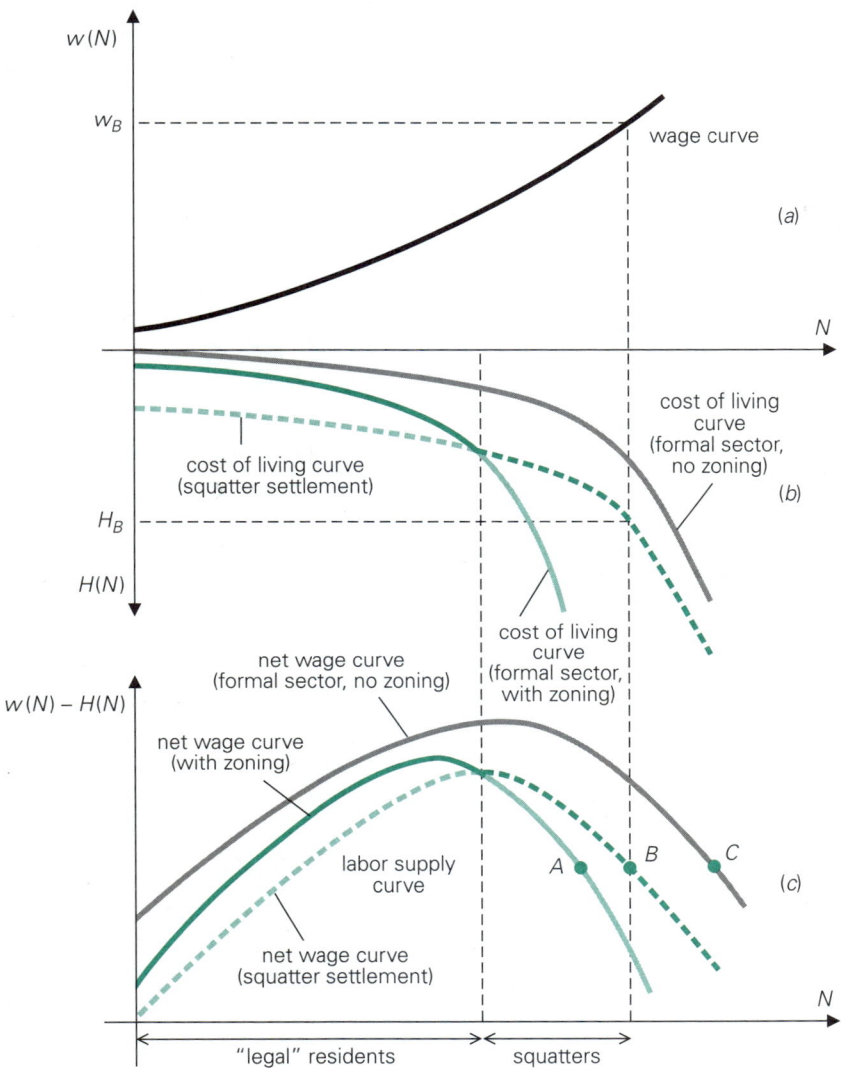

substitutes for missing public services and other expenses, the cost of living in squatter settlements is higher than in the formal sector in the absence of exclusionary zoning. The cost of living in squatter settlements is also higher than the cost of living in the formal housing sector with exclusionary zoning for small cities but lower than in large cities. The main reason for this result is that the higher cost of "public" services in squatter settlements is rather insensitive to city size whereas the economy in land rent made by squatting is more likely to increase with city size.

In the absence of exclusionary zoning, the cost of living is always lower in the formal sector, and no one would choose to live in a squatter settlement. The net wage curve corresponding to this situation is the dotted thin curve in figure 3.6. The city equilibrium is reached at point C.

With exclusionary zoning it is cheaper to live in the formal sector than in squatter settlements when the city is small, but it becomes more expensive to do so when the city grows. The thick line in figure 3.6 represents the minimum cost of living under exclusionary zoning. This line is solid (that is, represents the formal sector) for small cities and dashed for larger cities, because they expand through squatter settlements.

Under exclusionary zoning the net wage curve is the maximum of the net wage offered by the formal housing sector or squatter settlements. It is represented by the thick continuous and dashed curve in figure 3.6. The equilibrium for the city is at point B. Below the *X*-axis, one can read the city population that resides in the formal sector and in squatter settlements.

This analysis suggests a number of policy implications. Imposing regulatory constraints in the formal housing sector may reduce the equilibrium size of the city, but a good fraction of this reduction is crowded out by the growth of squatter settlements. The equilibrium for the city is at point B, not point A, as originally intended. Removing unnecessary constraints in the formal housing sector is socially desirable, because it lowers the cost of living and hence raises the net wage curve and eliminates squatter settlements. Furthermore, improving the situation in a single city only is not enough to raise net wages, because a higher net wage curve may keep hitting the same labor supply curve at a larger population. General equilibrium effects matter.

Titling policies are also desirable, because poorly defined property rights have a range of other negative side effects. After solving disputes over land ownership and the financing of the titles handed out, the main issues with titling policies are how to avoid further preemptive invasions driven by the expectation of a future title and how to ensure that there is a local tax counterpart to legalized titles. In some respect the problems in dealing with illegal settlements are the same as those of urban favoritism. There are many dimensions associated with this phenomenon, and it is not clear yet which matter most empirically. As with urban favoritism, there is also a political economy of illegal settlements with vested interests that benefit from slums, either directly, by charging their residents, or indirectly, by providing expensive substitutes for missing public services. These vested interests often pose formidable challenges.

Do Cities Matter for Growth?

The framework presented above is expanded in this section to try to determine if cities and urbanization affect the long-run rate of economic growth. The implications of this extension are then used to review the empirical literature on cities and growth.

Extending the Framework

To keep the analysis simple, a multiperiod setting in which workers are initially endowed with some human capital is considered. Each period workers spend part of their time working. They consume their labor market earnings at the end of each period. They also spend part of each period learning, so that the following period they start with a higher level of human capital and are more productive. Workers work and learn in the city in which they are located.

These ideas are captured in the upper part of figure 3.7, which shows two curves. The first is the wage curve used earlier. It represents the labor market earnings of a worker depending on the size of the city. The second curve is the wage expansion curve. It represents the (discounted) value of the increase in human capital, as a function of city size. This curve is referred to as the expansion curve. (For reasons that will become clear below, it is more convenient to represent this wage expansion as an absolute amount rather than a relative amount.)[29] In each new period, the wage curve for a

Figure 3.7 Learning in Cities

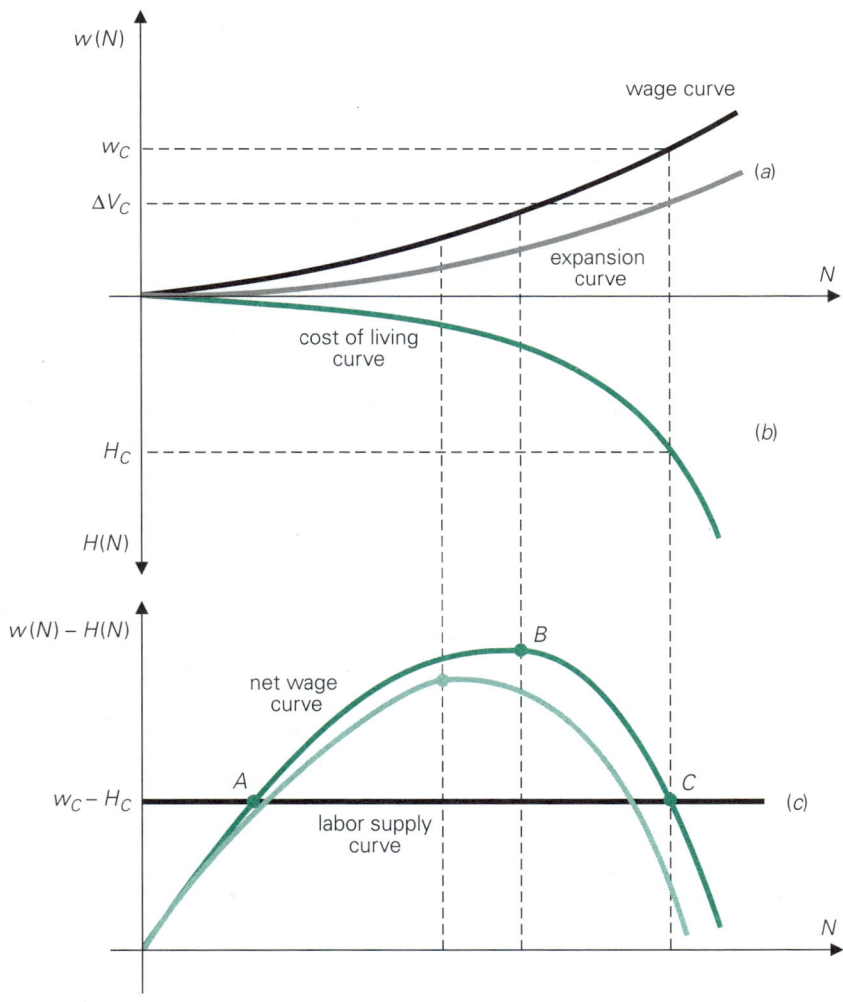

---

29 The two key equations of all growth models are the production function and the accumulation equation. The wage curve captures the production function, while the expansion curve is a version of the accumulation equation.

given worker in a city shifts upward as a function of the increase in human capital during the previous period.

Before proceeding, a number of remarks are in order. First, how much time is spent working and learning is set exogenously. Allowing workers to make decisions about their time allocation would only reinforce the results derived below, because workers are expected to spend more time learning where the returns to learning are the highest.

Second, because workers entirely consume their labor market earnings in each period, there are no savings. Human capital is the only factor that is accumulated.

Third, the expansion curve, which captures the discounted value of learning during the period, is known to workers. The value of what is learned during the current period may depend on how much is learned in subsequent periods (as there may be some intertemporal substitutability or complementarity in learning). This value of current learning also depends on future location choices. The extent to which human capital is transferable across cities is discussed below.

Figure 7 shows an upward-sloping curve that is flatter than the wage curve. This particular shape can be thought of as a theoretical possibility for now. Three different sets of factors may influence the shape of the expansion curve.

The first are national factors that affect economic growth in the entire country. Institutions or aggregate research and development are often argued to be the main engines of aggregate growth. When growth is entirely orthogonal to cities, the discounted value of the increase in human capital is the same everywhere. Hence when location does not matter (as in most of the growth literature), the expansion curve is flat.

With a flat expansion curve, the issues of growth and urbanization can be treated separately. Urban issues can be dealt with the tools developed above; the dynamic framework just described boils down to a standard (spaceless) model of economic growth. To understand this result, note that a flat expansion curve at the current period implies that the wage curve shifts upward the next period. Following this, the net wage curve also shifts upward by the same amount. Because the same wage increase takes place everywhere, the labor supply curve shifts upward in the same way. As a result the equilibrium city size is unchanged.[30]

---

30 The cost of living is paid in terms of the good used as the numéraire and is thus not affected by human capital accumulation. Should the cost of living be paid in units of time (assuming that commuting requires time and not energy), this benchmark, for which cities play no role in growth, would look different. Cities with higher-productivity labor would raise the opportunity cost of commuting and thus scale the cost of living up. As a result a complete separation between economic growth and the urban structure is obtained only when the expansion curve is a scaled version of the wage curve. In this case the equilibrium the following period would involve scaling the wage and cost of living curves by the same factor. The net wage and labor supply curves would be scaled in the same way, leading equilibrium city size to remain unchanged.

With a flat expansion curve, the long-run behavior of the economy depends on how human capital is accumulated. With decreasing returns to the accumulation of human capital, this model is equivalent to a standard Solow (1956) model using human capital instead of physical capital as a factor of accumulation. In this case the economy converges to a constant level of output. With constant returns in the accumulation of human capital, this model then becomes similar to the endogenous growth framework of Lucas (1988). The main result is that a constant positive growth rate of output can be sustained. In this steady state, cities can affect the level of output but not its growth rate. In short, growth takes place in cities, but cities do not constitute the engine of growth.

The second set of factors are city-specific factors that may affect the expansion curve in each city individually. As discussed above, the static urban increasing returns associated with an upward-sloping wage curve can be justified theoretically by a number of mechanisms: sharing, matching, and learning. These mechanisms may play a similar role with respect to the expansion curve, suggesting that this curve may be upward sloping rather than flat. Learning mechanisms seem particularly relevant here. The higher frequency of interactions taking place in cities may spur learning and the accumulation of human capital, which make cities more efficient in the future.

Since Jacobs (1969) and more recently Lucas (1988), this assumption of dynamic increasing returns in cities sustained by some form of human capital externalities or knowledge spillovers has been at the heart of the theoretical literature that views cities as engines of growth (see, for example, Eaton and Eckstein 1997; Black and Henderson 1999; Glaeser 1999; Bertinelli and Black 2004; Rossi-Hansberg and Wright 2007). Duranton and Puga (2004) provide a detailed review of how cities can favor the creation, accumulation, and diffusion of knowledge.

What are the implications of the upward-sloping expansion curve of figure 3.7? The cost of living curve is the same as in the previous figures. The net wage curve now has three components. The net wage that workers consider in their location choice for the period is the sum of the wage and the wage expansion minus the cost of living. As wage expansion is defined as the net present value of the increase in human capital in the current period, these three items are measured consistently. The resulting bell-shaped net wage curve intersects with the labor supply curve at points A and C. As in previous figures, only C is a stable equilibrium.

The net wage curve in figure 3.7 looks similar to that in figure 3.1. There is, however, a fundamental difference: the net wage curve now captures urban efficiency from both a static and a dynamic perspective. The (static) net wage curve associated with the wage curve and the cost of living curve (but excluding the expansion curve) is represented by the thin dotted curve in figure 3.3. The maximum of the net wage curve for the dynamic model at point B is larger than for the static model, because a larger city now brings about greater efficiency in the current period as well as the promise of greater efficiency in the future. The benefits from agglomeration are thus stronger than they would be in the absence of dynamic effects and the optimal city size is larger.[31]

This result suggests that taking a purely static perspective to assess whether cities are oversized is misleading. Lucas (2004) proposes a model of urban–rural migration and learning in which rural workers optimally migrate to cities. Early on their urban wage is very low. In a Harris-Todaro (1970) framework, this would be interpreted negatively as urban unemployment. However, these migrants spend their early time in the city accumulating human capital, which allows them to become more productive later. Hence with learning, restricting migration to cities has negative dynamic consequences.

Turning to the long-run dynamics of the model, the wage curve in the next period sums the current wage curve and the wage increase associated with rising human capital. In turn a higher wage curve implies a higher net wage curve. If the labor supply curve does not move, because surplus rural labor receives a constant wage, the equilibrium size of the city increases. Eventually, the exhaustion of surplus rural labor should imply an upward shift of the labor supply curve following the increase in human capital of all workers in all cities. Because of more learning in larger cities, the wage curve is expected to become steeper over time. A steeper wage curve implies that the maximum of the net wage curve shifts to the right as workers in the city accumulate human capital.

In this case, following Black and Henderson (1999), it is possible to envision the following long-run dynamics under full urbanization. In each period the net wage grows by the same amount in all cities. This implies that both the labor supply and the net wage curves keep shifting up at the same rate. The increase in the slope of the wage curve also implies a relative rightward shift of the peak of the net wage curve (figure 3.8). This type of dynamics also suggests that the labor supply curve will eventually intersect with the net wage curve at its peak. In this case the learning that takes place in cities leads to both economic growth and the (optimal) population growth of cities, which in turn fuels economic growth through the expansion curve.

Both national and city-specific factors have been mentioned. Arguably, interactions between cities (aside from those taking place through the shifts of the labor supply curve) also matter. They are examined following a look at the empirical relevance of what has been discussed so far.

The Empirics of Growth and Cities

The dynamic framework presented here relies on the existence of some human capital externalities in cities, which underpin the upward-sloping expansion curve. These externalities affect the learning of workers and

---

31 An extension could consider congestion effects specific to learning. For instance, the physical crowding of a city is time consuming and implies that there is less time available to learn and accumulate human capital. In this case (net) dynamic efficiency no longer monotonically increases with city size.

Figure 3.8 Growth in Cities

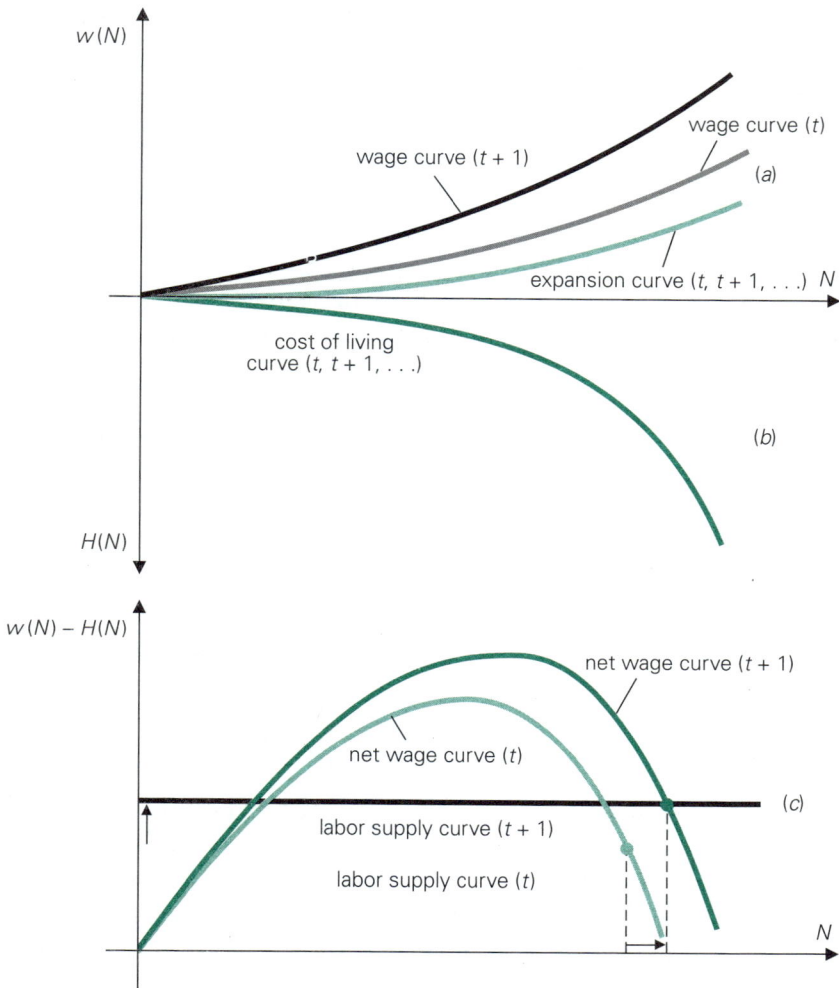

imply that the urban structure affects aggregate economic growth. What is the empirical evidence on these three elements?

Human capital externalities in cities. A large body of literature investigates human capital externalities in cities. Most of the studies look at cities in the United States or other developed countries (an exception is Conley, Flyer, and Tsiang 2003, who look at Malaysia; see Moretti 2004 and Duranton 2006 for surveys). The key findings can be summarized as follows. There is a strong association between the average level of human capital in cities and individual wages, after controlling for individual characteristics. The effects are relatively large. Estimates of social returns to education of the same magnitude as private returns are not uncommon. This relation between urban human capital and individual wages is particularly strong when urban human capital is measured by the share of university graduates in the city. While these facts are firmly established, the direction of causality is less clear. Nonetheless, there is reasonable evidence that causality runs from city-level human capital to individual wages. Whether the literature has really identified human capital externalities (as opposed to other complementarities) is far less clear, because these externalities are notoriously hard to identify empirically. Direct evidence about the channels of transmission of those effects is still missing.

Learning in cities. Another body of literature looks more specifically at learning in cities. Its empirical findings are very suggestive, albeit limited largely to the United States. Glaeser and Maré (2001) show that there is an urban wage premium, which workers retain when they move back to smaller cities or rural areas. Peri (2002) and Wheeler (2006) document that wage growth is stronger in cities, particularly for young educated workers. This finding is consistent with the learning in cities hypothesis. It could also reflect the self-selection of workers with rapid career progressions in cities for reasons unrelated to learning. This does not seem to be the case. Freedman (2007) shows that this type of result holds even when controlling for the fact that some workers may experience higher wage growth independently of their location. Thus both the literature on human capital externalities and that on learning in cities provide suggestive micro-based evidence of an upward-sloping expansion curve in cities. This evidence is not decisive, however, and comes nearly exclusively from developed countries.

Urban structure and economic growth. The empirical growth literature has not been particularly successful at disentangling the causes of long-run growth (see Durlauf, Johnson, and Temple 2005, for a critical review). Sadly, this literature has paid almost no attention to cities and urbanization as possible determinants of growth.

One study, Henderson (2003), uses a reasonable cross-section of countries and sound econometric methods to look at the aggregate dynamic effects of cities and urbanization.[32] It draws two main conclusions. First, urbanization per se does not affect economic growth. Second, urban primacy has large effects on economic growth. The first conclusion is unsurprising and confirms a broad consensus that urbanization is a benign transition that to a large extent follows but does not profoundly affect the process of development. The second conclusion is more provocative. Henderson finds that an increase in urban primacy by one standard deviation (15 percent) from the mean (31 percent of the urban population living in the largest city) reduces the rate of GDP growth by about 1.5 percent a year. These are large effects. They are also interesting from a policy perspective, because urban primacy can evolve relatively quickly.

The main issue in any such investigation regards the direction of causality. A strong negative statistical association between urban primacy and growth may not be surprising. A strong causal effect is. To deal with causal

---

32 Using the same data, Bertinelli and Strobl (2003) replicate and confirm some of the findings of Henderson (2003) using nonparametric techniques.

issues, one needs to find good instruments for urban primacy (variables that determine urban primacy but are not otherwise correlated with economic growth). The variation in urban primacy caused by these exogenous variables can then be used to assess the causal effect of primacy on growth. Unfortunately, it is hard to think of any variable that would determine primacy and be otherwise uncorrelated with economic growth. The key determinants of urban primacy—political variables—are expected to have a strong independent effect on economic growth.

Henderson (2003) proceeds as follows. He takes the first difference of all his variables to get rid of any permanent country effects that would be correlated with both economic growth and urban primacy. Then, using a generalized method of moments estimation technique, he instruments changes in urban primacy by lagged primacy levels from 10 or 15 years before. This estimation technique yields large effects of urban primacy on economic growth. Economic growth first increases and then decreases with urban primacy.

The idea that, for low levels of primacy, a larger primate city should foster economic growth is easy to interpret in the framework presented here. Through the workings of the expansion curve, a larger city implies greater learning for more workers. Provided that there is also a diffusion of this learning to other cities (an issue discussed below), a positive relation between aggregate growth and the relative size of the main city occurs naturally. The second part of the relation, when the effect of primacy becomes detrimental to growth, is more puzzling in light of the above framework.

Henderson's (2003) results are compatible with two possible interpretations. The first is that the urban structure has a direct effect on economic growth. In this case, one needs to consider a situation like that depicted in figure 4, where differences in market access lead to two possible equilibria for cities. In this situation of cities that are either small or very large, consider an expansion curve that first slopes upward and then downward. The downward-sloping section of the expansion curve could be explained by some congestion in learning as the city grows very large. In this case small cities could be too small for efficient learning to take place and the primate city too large. With this interpretation of the relation between primacy and growth, promoting growth simply entails reducing the size of the primate city and increasing the size of smaller cities. All cities would then end up on a higher point on the expansion curve.

A second possible interpretation of Henderson's results is that the factors that drive urban favoritism also affect the expansion curve.[33] Imagine, for

---

33 To understand why these two explanations are compatible with Henderson (2003), a technical aside is necessary. First, it can be argued that Henderson's first-differencing conditions out all static explanations in which institutions (a possible missing variable) would explain both long-run growth and primacy. Henderson instruments change in urban primacy by lagged primacy. Past levels of primacy are good predictors of current changes. The key issue is whether these instruments are otherwise uncorrelated with changes in the rate of growth. This is an open question. Although Henderson shows that overidentification tests are easily passed, time-varying factors closely related to primacy could be at the root of both primacy and growth.

instance, that red tape is at the root of urban primacy. Dealing with government regulations is much easier for firms when they are located in the capital city because of greater proximity to bureaucrats. Under such circumstances red tape leads to a higher wage curve for the favored city, which becomes primate as a result. Red tape may have a detrimental effect on growth everywhere (albeit less so in the primate city). It may also imply a very low expansion curve, leading to very slow growth.

With this second interpretation of the findings on primacy and growth, the policy implications differ. A forced reduction of the size of the primate city is unlikely to have much of a dynamic effect, because it does not deal with the root cause behind the low expansion curve. Here the growth problem is not caused by primacy itself but by urban favoritism, which causes both primacy and low growth. There is scant evidence with which to distinguish between the two interpretations; the second one is consistent with the conclusions drawn above regarding urban favoritism.

Diffusion, Mobility, and Growth

A key limitation of the approach taken so far is that it views each city as an island of growth, typically assuming that each city can generate economic growth by and for itself. It is critical to understand how knowledge flows across places.[34]

A first line of argument is to recognize that the expansion curve may not be driven by overall city size, as in figure 7, but by the concentration of "innovation inputs." Duranton and Puga (2001) argue that modern cities can be divided into two groups, cities in which innovation takes place ("nursery cities," with very diverse production structures) and cities that specialize in the production of a particular set of goods. In developed economies the past 50 years have also seen a growing separation between business centers, which host headquarters and business services, and production cities, which host production plants (Duranton and Puga 2005).

In this type of framework, preventing urban dispersion by favoring a primate city or slowing the development of secondary cities prevents the efficient concentration of innovation inputs (scientific personnel, research facilities, and so forth) in nursery cities without too much crowding out from other activities. This leads to a lower expansion curve in those cities and slower growth there. It also affects secondary cities, because the lack of innovation in nursery cities implies a lack of new ideas, new products, and new production processes to be transmitted to secondary centers.

This type of claim is hard to evaluate empirically. There is good evidence from the Republic of Korea that mature manufacturing quickly moved out of Seoul and relocated to secondary cities after urban favoritism was reduced (Henderson 2002b, 2005). Brazil appears to be following a similar path, albeit more slowly (Da Mata and others 2005). In many other countries this

---

34 Flows of knowledge between developed and developing countries are also fundamental but beyond the scope of this chapter (see Keller 2004).

process of urban change appears to be even slower, if it takes place at all. There may also be a temptation to forcibly concentrate innovation inputs in some cities to create some centers of excellence (or innovation clusters). These policies are unlikely to be successful because of the difficulty of replicating the subtle alchemy of nursery cities.

The second line of argument focuses on knowledge flows within countries. The framework developed above relies on human capital being both embedded in workers (as in the traditional definitions) and "in the air" (following Marshall 1890) in the form of human capital externalities. More precisely, knowledge is assumed to be both embedded in people and acquired by direct contact with "those who know." The corollary of this idea is that flows of people are also flows of knowledge. Hence more learning, and thus a higher expansion curve, can be achieved through the mobility of skilled labor across cities.[35] This argument has been modeled in the context of the mobility of employees across firms (Combes and Duranton 2006; Franco and Filson 2006) but not yet across cities. Empirically, Møen (2005) and Freedman (2007) show that technological progress is indeed associated with the movement of skilled workers between firms. Job-hopping appears to benefit job-hoppers and their industry, if not their employers. Almeida and Kogut (1999) show that long-distance flows of knowledge, as tracked by patent citations in the U.S. semiconductor industry, coincide with the movement of star scientists across firms in different cities. Agrawal, Cockburn, and McHale (2006) show that scientists who leave a city continue to be cited by those working there. They are gone but not forgotten.

To the extent that these findings on highly skilled workers in the United States also apply to highly skilled workers in developing countries, a number of tentative policy conclusions can be drawn. First, the general working of the labor market, and more specifically the covenants that restrict labor mobility, can play an important role in hindering the diffusion of knowledge within and across cities. Lack of labor mobility between the main city and secondary cities, especially in the most skilled segments of the labor market, may be an important contributor to both urban primacy and the backwardness of secondary cities. With limited labor mobility across cities, nearly all skilled labor may go to the main city and stay there. The main city then becomes an island of more advanced knowledge with a much higher wage curve. As highly skilled workers remain in the primate city, their knowledge does not percolate to other cities. These other cities then stay behind technologically, remaining small and unattractive because of their low wage curve. This situation can persist even in the absence of formal impediments to labor mobility, because the technological backwardness of small cities may provide little incentive for skilled workers to relocate there.

---

35 Models of urban growth generally ignore this issue. Eaton and Eckstein (1997) is an exception. They assume that human capital accumulation in cities is driven by the "knowledge base" of the city, taken to be total human capital in the city plus the discounted sum of human capital of other cities. They do not provide a well-specified mechanism regarding these knowledge interactions across cities, which they model only as a pure externality.

The two-way mobility of skilled labor across cities seems important to foster the geographical diffusion of technologies, but it may not be the only channel. Although most of the evidence concerns countries and not regions within countries, there is a good case to be made that more trade in goods is associated with higher growth and convergence across places. In a cross-country setting, Wacziarg and Welch (2003) show that increased openness has large positive effects on growth and investment. Alcalá and Ciccone (2004) show that the positive growth effects of trade work through total factor productivity. The effects found by Alcalá and Ciccone (2004) and much of the earlier literature in cross-country settings are large. Moving from the 20th percentile of openness to the median raises productivity by 160 percent, according to Alcalá and Ciccone (2004). With no evidence of weaker effects when openness is already high, this suggests that there are potentially large dynamic gains from removing impediments to trade within developing countries.

Finally, there is very strong evidence that productivity growth is linked to the process of creation and destruction at the firm level (Davis, Haltiwanger, and Schuh 1996; Foster, Haltiwanger, and Krizan 2001; Bartelsman, Haltiwanger, and Scarpetta 2004). In particular, resources need to flow from less-productive to more-productive firms and allow new entrants to rise and challenge incumbents. Analysis of this process of reallocation lies well beyond the scope of this chapter. Nonetheless, it is important to note that in developed countries there is a strong spatial dimension to this process of reallocation, as industries tend to change location when their technology evolves (Duranton 2007). An important conclusion is that hindering the movement of factors across firms, including across firms in different cities, may have large dynamic costs.

Policy Conclusions

Several recommendations emerge from the static analysis presented in the first part of this chapter. It suggests that policymakers should eliminate primate city favoritism; improve urban efficiency, in order to lower the cost of living curve by dealing with urban crowding and providing public goods; eliminate the biases that lead to squatter settlements with a reasonable titling policy and urban deregulation; improve market access between cities by developing transport infrastructure and lowering impediments to trade; and not discourage internal migration, which fosters an efficient allocation of the population and has an equalizing effect across places.

By underscoring the need for better public service delivery and the importance of housing and commuting issues, this set of recommendations is consistent with some of the objectives of many existing urban policies. The main difference is that the baseline framework also emphasizes labor mobility. This emphasis is strongly at odds with existing urban policies, which often seek to reduce labor mobility and more generally to promote some form of stability.

Another novelty of the static framework is that it underscores the possible effects that technological, institutional, or policy-driven changes can have on cities. The urban equilibrium is determined by the interplay of the wage, cost of living, and labor supply curves. These curves are determined by a wide array of forces, all of which can affect cities indirectly.

As shown in the second part of this chapter, taking a more dynamic perspective does not fundamentally alter the recommendations of more static approaches.[36] It leads one to put even more emphasis on the mobility of people and goods across places. This emphasis on mobility and flexibility in factor allocation and reallocation should also arguably be part of any modern growth agenda. Hence although at some fine level of detail, static and dynamic approaches to urban policy may conflict, these divergences are minor from a practical perspective. It is also important to note that an urban perspective on economic growth does not appear to conflict with any broader growth agenda.

That said, implementing a broad-ranging urban agenda aimed at bolstering economic growth raises a number of problems. The first is that such an agenda is rather demanding, because it includes raising the efficiency of public good provision, lowering barriers to mobility, improving market access to allow secondary cities to develop, and so forth. The second difficulty is that the political economy of many of these issues often represents a formidable obstacle to change. Hence politics and other more mundane feasibility constraints, such as the limited capabilities of many governments, require establishing priorities. The framework presented here shows that cities operate in a second-best world, where fixing one problem may not result in any tangible improvement locally. Policy makers are thus faced with the dilemma that doing everything at once may not be possible whereas a step-by-step approach may not be effective.

Growth agendas often identify a number of "growth drivers" that need to be fostered. It may be more fruitful to think about constraints and bottlenecks that need to be removed. The theoretical framework developed here can be useful in identifying constraints to harmonious urban development.[37] Because constraints and bottlenecks are likely to differ across countries, so will the diagnostic approach and the urban strategy. The main caveat is that static constraints to urban development, such as a gridlocked city, are for all to see, while dynamic constraints are much more difficult to identify.

Who should be in charge of implementing any "cities and growth" agenda? The emphasis here on the mobility of goods and factors across cities suggests that central governments should have a prominent role in promoting labor mobility, developing infrastructure, and removing impediments to internal trade. But cities also have important parts to play to improve the

---

36 The distinction between "static" and "dynamic" is blurred. For instance, the construction of the U.S. interstate system should be viewed conceptually as a one-time improvement. But Fernald (1999) estimates that it generated about 1 percentage point of annual GDP growth over a period of nearly 20 years, arguably a long-run effect.

37 The framework presented here and its extensions could be developed as a diagnostic tool in the spirit of Hausmann, Rodrik, and Velasco (2005).

life of their residents and minimize their cost of living. This division of labor between central and local governments is unlikely to remain free of tensions. There is a fundamental asymmetry between primate and secondary cities. Unlike primate cities, no secondary city can alone have an effect on the entire urban system. Moreover, there is considerable heterogeneity in the capabilities of secondary cities to design and implement local policies that would be consistent with a national growth agenda.

References

Ades, Alberto F., and Edward L. Glaeser. 1995. "Trade and Circuses: Explaining Urban Giants." *Quarterly Journal of Economics* 110 (1): 195–227.

Agrawal, Ajay, Iain Cockburn, and John McHale. 2006. "Gone but Not Forgotten: Knowledge Flows, Labor Mobility, and Enduring Social Relationships." *Journal of Economic Geography* 6 (5): 571–91.

Alcalá, Francisco, and Antonio Ciccone. 2004. "Trade and Productivity." *Quarterly Journal of Economics* 119 (2): 613–46.

Almeida, Paul, and Bruce Kogut. 1999. "Localization of Knowledge and the Mobility of Engineers in Regional Networks." *Management Science* 45 (7): 195–227.

Amiti, Mary, and Lisa Cameron. 2007. "Economic Geography and Wages." *Review of Economics and Statistics* 89 (1): 15–29.

Aten, Bettina, and Alan Heston. 2005. "Regional Output Differences in International Perspective." In *Spatial Inequality and Development,* ed. Ravi Kanbur and Anthony J. Venables. New York: Oxford University Press.

Au, Chun-Chung, and J. Vernon Henderson. 2006a. "Are Chinese Cities Too Small?" *Review of Economic Studies* 73 (3): 549–76.

———. 2006b. "How Migration Restrictions Limit Agglomeration and Productivity in China." *Journal of Development Economics* 80 (2): 350–88.

Baldwin, Richard E., Rikard Forslid, Philippe Martin, Gianmarco I. P. Ottaviano, and Frédéric Robert-Nicoud. 2004. *Economic Geography and Public Policy.* Princeton, NJ: Princeton University Press.

Barrios, Salvador, Luisito Bertinelli, and Eric Strobl. 2006. "Climatic Change and Rural-Urban Migration: The Case of Sub-Saharan Africa." *Journal of Urban Economics* 60 (3): 357–71.

Bartelsman, Eric, John Haltiwanger, and Stefano Scarpetta. 2004. "Microeconomic Evidence of Creative Destruction in Industrial and Developing Countries." Department of Economics, University of Maryland, College Park.

Bertinelli, Luisito, and Duncan Black. 2004. "Urbanization and Growth." *Journal of Urban Economics* 56 (1): 80–96.

Bertinelli, Luisito, and Eric Strobl. 2003. "Urbanization, Urban Concentration and Economic Growth in Developing Countries." Research Paper 03/14, Centre for Research in Economic Development and International Trade (CREDIT), University of Nottingham, United Kingdom.

Black, Duncan, and J. Vernon Henderson. 1999. "A Theory of Urban Growth." *Journal of Political Economy* 107 (2): 252–84.

Brueckner, Jan K. 1990. "Analyzing Third World Urbanization: A Model with Empirical Evidence." *Economic Development and Cultural Change* 38 (3): 587–610.

Brueckner, Jan K., and Yves Zenou. 1999. "Harris-Todaro Models with a Land Market." *Regional Science and Urban Economics* 29 (3): 317–39.

Combes, Pierre-Philippe, and Gilles Duranton. 2006. "Labor Pooling, Labor Poaching, and Spatial Clustering." *Regional Science and Urban Economics* 36 (1): 1–28.

Combes, Pierre-Philippe, Gilles Duranton, and Laurent Gobillon. 2008. "Spatial Wage Disparities: Sorting Matters." *Journal of Urban Economics* 63 (2): 723–42.

Combes, Pierre-Philippe, Gilles Duranton, Laurent Gobillon, and Sébastien Roux. 2008. "Estimating Agglomeration Economies with History, Geology, and Worker Effects." Department of Economics, University of Toronto.

Combes, Pierre-Philippe, Gilles Duranton, and Henry G. Overman. 2005. "Agglomeration and the Adjustment of the Spatial Economy." *Papers in Regional Science* 84 (3): 311–49.

Combes, Pierre-Philippe, Thierry Mayer, and Jacques Thisse. Forthcoming. *Economic Geography.* Princeton, NJ: Princeton University Press.

Conley, Timothy G., Frederick Flyer, and Grace R. Tsiang. 2003. "Spillover from Local Market Human Capital and Spatial Distribution of Productivity in Malaysia." *Advances in Economic Analysis and Policy* 3 (1).

Da Mata, Daniel, Uwe Deichmann, J. Vernon Henderson, Somik V. Lall, and Hyoung Gun Wang. 2005. "Examining the Growth Patterns of Brazilian Cities." Policy Research Working Paper 3724, World Bank, Washington, DC.

———. 2007. "Determinants of City Growth in Brazil." *Journal of Urban Economics* 62 (2): 252–72.

Davis, James C., and J. Vernon Henderson. 2003. "Evidence on the Political Economy of the Urbanization Process." *Journal of Urban Economics* 53 (1): 98–125.

Davis, Steven J., John C. Haltiwanger, and Scott Schuh. 1996. *Job Creation and Destruction.* Cambridge, MA: MIT Press.

De Soto, Hernand. 2000. *The Mystery of Capital: Why Capitalism Triumphs in the West and Fails Everywhere Else.* New York: Basic Books.

Deichmann, Uwe, Kai Kaiser, Somik V. Lall, and Zmarak Shalizi. 2005. "Agglomeration, Transport, and Regional Development in Indonesia." Policy Research Working Paper 3477, World Bank, Washington, DC.

Di Tella, Rafael, Sebastian Galliani, and Ernesto Schargrodsky. 2007. "The Formation of Beliefs: Evidence from the Allocation of Land Titles to Squatters." *Quarterly Journal of Economics* 122 (1): 209–41.

Durand-Lasserve, Alain, and Harris Selod. 2007. "The Formalisation of Urban Land Tenure in Developing Countries." Paris School of Economics.

Duranton, Gilles. 2006. "Human Capital Externalities in Cities: Identification and Policy Issues." In *A Companion to Urban Economics,* ed. Richard J. Arnott and Daniel P. Mcmillen, 24–39. Oxford: Blackwell.

———. 2007. "Urban Evolutions: The Fast, the Slow, and the Still." *American Economic Review* 97 (1): 197–221.

Duranton, Gilles, and Diego Puga. 2001. "Nursery Cities: Urban Diversity, Process Innovation, and the Life Cycle of Products." *American Economic Review* 91 (5): 1454–77.

———. 2004. "Micro-Foundations of Urban Agglomeration Economies. In *Handbook of Regional and Urban Economics*, vol. 4, ed. Vernon Henderson and Jacques-François Thisse, 2063–17. Amsterdam: North-Holland.

———. 2005. "From Sectoral to Functional Urban Specialization." *Journal of Urban Economics* 57 (2): 343–70.

Durlauf, Steven N., Paul A. Johnson, and Jonathan W. Temple. 2005. "Growth Econometrics." In *Handbook of Economic Growth*, vol. 1A, ed. Philippe Aghion and Steven N. Durlauf, 555–677. Amsterdam: North-Holland.

Eaton, Jonathan, and Zvi Eckstein. 1997. "Cities and Growth: Theory and Evidence from France and Japan. *Regional Science and Urban Economics* 27 (4–5): 443–74.

Epple, Dennis, and Thomas Nechyba. 2004. "Fiscal Decentralization." In *Handbook of Regional and Urban Economics*, vol. 4, ed. Vernon Henderson and Jacques-François Thisse, 2423–80. Amsterdam: North-Holland.

Fay, Marianne, and Charlotte Opal. 1999. "Urbanization without Growth: A Not-So-Uncommon Phenomenon." Policy Research Working Paper 2412, World Bank, Washington, DC.

Fernald, John G. 1999. "Roads to Prosperity? Assessing the Link between Public Capital and Productivity." *American Economic Review* 89 (3): 619–38.

Field, Erica. 2007. "Entitled to Work: Urban Property Rights and Labor Supply in Peru." *Quarterly Journal of Economics* 122 (4): 1561–602.

Foster, Lucia, John C. Haltiwanger, and C. J. Krizan. 2001. "Aggregate Productivity Growth: Lessons from Microeconomic Evidence." In *New Developments in Productivity Analysis*, ed. Charles R. Hulten, Edwin R. Dean, and Michael J. Harper, 303–72. Chicago: National Bureau of Economic Research and University of Chicago Press.

Franco, April M., and Darren Filson. 2006. "Spin-Outs: Knowledge Diffusion through Employee Mobility." *Rand Journal of Economics* 37 (4): 841–60.

Freedman, Matthew. 2007. "Location Decisions in a Changing Labor Market Environment." Department of Economics, University of Maryland, College Park.

Fujita, Masahisa, Paul R. Krugman, and Anthony J. Venables. 1999. *The Spatial Economy: Cities, Regions, and International Trade*. Cambridge, MA: MIT Press.

Fujita, Masahisa, and Tomoya Mori. 1996. "The Role of Ports in the Making of Major Cities: Self-Agglomeration and Hub-Effect." *Journal of Development Economics* 49 (1): 93–120.

———. 2005. "Transport Development and the Evolution of Economic Geography." *Portuguese Economic Journal* 4 (2): 129–56.

Glaeser, Edward L. 1999. "Learning in Cities." *Journal of Urban Economics* 46 (2): 254–77.

Glaeser, Edward L., and David C. Maré. 2001. "Cities and Skills." *Journal of Labor Economics* 19 (2): 316–42.

Greenwood, Michael J. 1997. "Internal Migrations in Developed Countries." In *Handbook of Population and Family Economics*, vol. 1B, ed. Mark R. Rosenzweig and Oded Stark, 647–720. Amsterdam: North-Holland.

Harris, Chauncy D. 1954. "The Market as a Factor in the Localization of Industry in the United States." *Annals of the Association of American Geographers* 44 (4): 315–48.

Harris, John R., and Michael P. Todaro. 1970. "Migration, Unemployment and Development: A Two-Sector Analysis." *American Economic Review* 60 (1): 126–42.

Hausmann, Ricardo, Dani Rodrik, and Andrés Velasco. 2005. "Growth Diagnostics." John F. Kennedy School of Government, Harvard University, Cambridge, MA.

Head, Keith, and Thierry Mayer. 2004. "The Empirics of Agglomeration and Trade." In *Handbook of Regional and Urban Economics,* vol. 4, ed. Vernon Henderson and Jacques-François Thisse, 2609–69. Amsterdam: North-Holland.

———. 2006. "Regional Wage and Employment Responses to Market Potential in the EU." *Regional Science and Urban Economics* 36 (5): 573–94.

Helsley, Robert W. 2004. "Urban Political Economics." In *Handbook of Regional and Urban Economics*, vol. 4, ed. Vernon Henderson and Jacques-François Thisse, 2381–421. Amsterdam: North-Holland.

Henderson, J. Vernon. 1974. "The Sizes and Types of Cities." *American Economic Review* 64 (4): 640–56.

———. 1988. *Urban Development: Theory, Fact and Illusion.* Oxford: Oxford University Press.

———. 1997. "Medium-Size Cities." *Regional Science and Urban Economics* 27 (6): 583–612.

———. 2002a. "Urban Primacy, External Costs, and the Quality of Life." *Resource and Energy Economics* 24 (1): 95–106.

———. 2002b. "Urbanization in Developing Countries." *World Bank Research Observer* 17 (1): 89–112.

———. 2003. "The Urbanization Process and Economic Growth: The So-What Question." *Journal of Economic Growth* 8 (1): 47–71.

———. 2005. "Urbanization and Growth." In *Handbook of Economic Growth*, vol. 1B, ed. Philippe Aghion and Steven N. Durlauf, 1543–91. Amsterdam: North-Holland.

———. 2007. "Exclusion through Informal Sector Housing Development." Department of Economics, Brown University, Providence, RI.

Henderson, J. Vernon, and Randy Becker. 2000. "Political Economy of City Sizes and Formation." *Journal of Urban Economics* 48 (3): 453–84.

Henderson, Vernon, Todd Lee, and Yung Joo Lee. 2001. "Scale Externalities in Korea." *Journal of Urban Economics* 49 (3): 479–504.

Henderson, J. Vernon, and Arindam Mitra. 1996. "The New Urban Landscape: Developers and Edge Cities." *Regional Science and Urban Economics* 26 (6): 613–43.

Henderson, J. Vernon, John Quigley, and Edwin Lim. 2007. "Urbanization in China: Policy Issues and Options." Department of Economics, Brown University, Providence, RI.

Henderson, J. Vernon, and Anthony J. Venables. 2006. "The Dynamics of City Formation." Department of Economics, Brown University, Providence, RI.

Henderson, J. Vernon, and Hyoung Gun Wang. 2007. "Urbanization and City Growth: The Role of Institutions." *Regional Science and Urban Economics* 37 (3): 283–313.

Jacobs, Jane. 1969. *The Economy of Cities*. New York: Random House.

Keller, Wolfgang. 2004. "International Technology Diffusion." *Journal of Economic Literature* 42 (3): 752–82.

Krugman, Paul R. 1991. "Increasing Returns and Economic Geography." *Journal of Political Economy* 99 (3): 484–99.

Krugman, Paul R., and Raúl Livas Elizondo. 1996. "Trade Policy and the Third World Metropolis." *Journal of Development Economics* 49 (1): 137–50.

Lall, Somik V., Richard Funderburg, and Tito Yepes. 2004. "Location, Concentration, and Performance of Economic Activity in Brazil." Policy Research Working Paper 3268, World Bank, Washington, DC.

Lall, Somik V., Jun Koo, and Sanjoy Chakravorty. 2003. "Diversity Matters: The Economic Geography of Industry Location in India." Policy Research Working Paper 3072, World Bank, Washington, DC.

Lall, Somik V., Harris Selod, and Zmarak Shalizi. 2006. "Rural–Urban Migration in Developing Countries: A Survey of Theoretical Predictions and Empirical Findings." Policy Research Working Paper 3915, World Bank, Washington, DC.

Lall, Somik V., Zmarak Shalizi, and Uwe Deichmann. 2004. "Agglomeration Economies and Productivity in Indian Industry." *Journal of Development Economics* 73 (3): 643–73.

Lucas, Robert E., Jr. 1988. "On the Mechanics of Economic Development." *Journal of Monetary Economics* 22 (1): 3–42.

———. 2004. "Life Earnings and Rural–Urban Migration." *Journal of Political Economy* 112 (1, Part 2): S29–S59.

Malpezzi, Stephen. 1999. "Economic Analysis of Housing Markets in Developing and Transition Countries." In *Handbook of Regional and Urban Economics*, vol. 3, ed. Edwin S. Mills and Paul Cheshire, 1791–864. Amsterdam: North-Holland.

Marshall, Alfred. 1890. *Principles of Economics*. London: Macmillan.

Møen, Jarle. 2005. "Is Mobility of Technical Personnel a Source of R&D Spillovers?" *Journal of Labor Economics* 23 (1): 81–114.

Moomaw, Ronald L., and Ali M. Shatter. 1996. "Urbanization and Development: A Bias toward Large Cities?" *Journal of Urban Economics* 40 (1): 13–37.

Moretti, Enrico. 2004. "Human Capital Externalities in Cities." In *Handbook of Regional and Urban Economics*, vol. 4, ed. Vernon Henderson and Jacques-François Thisse, 2243–91. Amsterdam: North-Holland.

Nitsch, Volker. 2006. "Trade Openness and Urban Concentration: New Evidence." *Journal of Economic Integration* 21 (2): 340–62.

Overman, Henry G., and Anthony J. Venables. 2005. *Cities in the Developing World*. Department for International Development, London.

Peri, Giovanni. 2002. "Young Workers, Learning, and Agglomerations." *Journal of Urban Economics* 52 (3): 582–607.

Poelhekke, Steven. 2007. "Urban Growth, Uninsured Risk, and the Rural Origins of Aggregate Volatility." European University Institute, Fiesole, Italy.

Ravallion, Martin, and Quentin Wodon. 1999. "Poor Areas, or Only Poor People?" *Journal of Regional Science* 39 (4): 689–711.

Redding, Stephen, and Anthony J. Venables. 2004. "Economic Geography and International Inequality." *Journal of International Economics* 62 (1): 63–82.

Richardson, Harry W. 1987. "The Costs of Urbanization: A Four-Country Comparison." *Economic Development and Cultural Change* 35 (3): 561–80.

Rosenthal, Stuart S., and William C. Strange. 2004. "Evidence on the Nature and Sources of Agglomeration Economies." In *Handbook of Regional and Urban Economics*, vol. 4, ed. Vernon Henderson and Jacques-François Thisse, 2119–71. Amsterdam: North-Holland.

Rossi-Hansberg, Esteban, and Mark L. J. Wright. 2007. "Urban Structure and Growth." *Review of Economic Studies* 74 (2): 597–624.

Saiz, Albert. 2006. "Dictatorships and Highways." *Regional Science and Urban Economics* 36 (2): 187–206.

Solow, Robert M. 1956. "A Contribution to the Theory of Economic Growth." *Quarterly Journal of Economics* 70 (1): 65–94.

Thomas, Vinod. 1980. "Spatial Differences in the Cost of Living." *Journal of Urban Economics* 8 (2): 108–22.

Timmins, Christopher. 2006. "Estimating Spatial Differences in the Brazilian Cost of Living with Households' Location Choices." *Journal of Development Economics* 80 (1): 59–83.

Wacziarg, Romain, and Karen Horn Welch. 2003. "Trade Liberalization and Growth: New Evidence." NBER Working Paper 10152, National Bureau of Economic Research, Cambridge, MA.

Wheeler, Christopher H. 2006. "Cities and the Growth of Wages among Young Workers: Evidence from the NLSY." *Journal of Urban Economics* 60 (2): 162–84.

CHAPTER 4
Urbanization, Agglomeration, and Economic Development

John M. Quigley

In 2007 the United Nations Population Fund released a report forecasting rapidly rising levels of urbanization over the next two decades, especially in the developing world. It noted that for the first time in history, more than half the world's population resides in urban areas. The same year UN-HABITAT issued a report highlighting the slums and deplorable living conditions in cities in developing countries. That report (UN-HABITAT 2007) estimated that by the end of 2007 there would be more than 1 billion slum dwellers, most of them living in developing countries. It claims that in many cases the economic circumstances of urban migrants are worse than those of rural peasants. In 2003 the United Nations surveyed member governments eliciting their attitudes toward urbanization. It found that the "vast majority" of these governments would have liked to shift populations back to rural areas and to stem the tide of urbanization.

Is urbanization actually bad for development? If life in urban areas were worse for urban dwellers than the life they left behind, presumably they would leave the city. So why all the fuss about urbanization and development?

The author is grateful to Patricia Annez and Robert Buckley for their comments, as well as to Vernon Henderson and Stephen Malpezzi.

This chapter considers the evidence on the mechanisms increasing economic efficiency in cities and examines the record of cities in facilitating economic output and in improving the consumption opportunities available to urban residents. Much of this evidence is based on observations from highly developed countries, but a growing body of evidence is based on analyses of developing countries. The evidence clearly supports the conclusion that cities are important facilitators of economic growth, increased productivity, and rising incomes in poor and rich nations alike. Policies to facilitate, not inhibit, urbanization are likely to improve economic conditions in developing countries. The analysis suggests a variety of broad polices that would improve resource allocation and increase incomes in such countries.

Why Cities?

Why do people and firms choose to locate in cities? A uniform distribution of populations over space would reduce competition for locations and thus the rents paid by households and firms, making both better off (Starrett 1974). There must therefore be compensating benefits of urban location—cost reduction, output enhancement, utility gains—to make dense location and the payment of location rent rational choices for households and firms.

The putative utility gains from urbanization have been the subject of much speculation and analysis by noneconomists. In vivid prose Jane Jacobs (1969) argues that the potential for variety in consumption is valuable to consumers. As long as the higher density of cities is associated with greater variety—in people, goods, and services—there are some utility gains to those who value diversity. These gains compensate consumers for some or all of the increased location rents in cities. It is not hard to incorporate a taste for variety into economists' models of consumer preferences (Quigley 1998 and 2001 explore some of these models).

The productivity gains, cost reductions, and output enhancements associated with collocation have been the subject of extensive analysis by economists. The historical reasons for city formation and the rationalization for the payment of location rents emphasize transport costs and internal economies of scale to the exclusion of other factors (see, for example, Hoover 1975). Transport costs refer to those incurred in delivering inputs (raw materials and labor) to industrial sites as well as the costs of delivering outputs (finished products) to local, national, and world markets. It is no accident that many of the large cities of the world developed along waterways, where ocean vessels facilitated lower-cost shipment of products to far-flung markets, or along trade routes, at entrepôts where the transshipment of products had already been established (Rappaport and Sachs 2003).

After the Industrial Revolution the internal scale economies arising from factories and production facilities provided a new rationale for urbanization. The factory system replaced cottage industry. The new division of labor required larger facilities and more workers at these facilities for the production of commodities. The economies of scale in the wool industry dictated large mills near cheap water power and nearby workers. The development of denser settlements—industrial plants and tenements—allowed firms to operate at scales at which average costs could be reduced. Aggregate rents and the higher wages paid by firms to workers were more than offset by the value of increased output. The growth of many large cities in the developed world in the 19th and early 20th centuries (Detroit, Manchester, Pittsburgh) reflects the importance of internal economies of scale.

Cities and Growth

If transport costs and internal scale economies were the only economic rationale for cities, the effects of urbanization on economic growth more generally would be limited. The economic importance of cities would be determined strictly by the technologies available for transport and production. Reductions in travel cost and in the scale of the "best practice" manufacturing plant surely would have made cities less important to the health of national economies during the past century.

In fact, the importance of cities to the modern economy hardly emphasizes internal scale economies at all. Instead, the emphasis is on external effects, spillovers, and external economies of scale, factors that have all become more important with increased industrialization, technical progress, and economic development.

These external effects can be characterized along a variety of dimensions. One useful taxonomy distinguishes among productivity gains arising from specialization; from transaction costs and complementarities in production; from education, knowledge, and mimicking; and from proximity to large numbers of other economic actors.

Specialization

The gains from specialization arise because denser aggregations of urban communities (conurbations) with a larger number of firms producing in proximity can support firms that are more specialized in producing intermediate products. Specialization can lead to enhanced opportunities for cost reduction in goods production when the production of components of intermediate goods can be routinized or the components of final products mechanized or automated, for example. The gains from specialization extend to the production of services as well. Specialized legal services, for example, may be provided more efficiently by firms that concentrate in specific areas (taxation, copyright law, secured transactions, and so forth). In both intermediate goods and services, specialization increases the opportunities for cost reduction.

The potential gains from specialization are further enhanced by the opportunities for sharing inputs among firms, opportunities that are facilitated by larger and denser urban areas. Specialized services—repair, printing, advertising, communications—can be provided to a wide spectrum of producers if the density of establishments is high enough.

These external gains from specialization may arise because firms producing for final demand are themselves more spatially concentrated by industry or product, giving rise to localization economies. But they may also arise because firms producing diverse goods for final demand are more densely packed in space, giving rise to urbanization economies. In either case the environment permits more specialization among firms producing intermediate goods and services, which leads to cost reductions.

Transaction Costs and Complementarities

Externalities arising from lower transaction costs and better complementarities in production can emerge because larger urban scale can facilitate better matches between worker skills and job requirements or between intermediate goods and the production requirements for final output. In the labor market, for example, better opportunities for skill matches reduce the search costs of workers with differentiated skills and of employers with differentiated demands for labor. Complementarities in production between physical and human capital suggest that when the pool of urban workers has a larger stock of human capital, firms that expect to employ these workers will invest more in physical capital. With costly search and imperfect matching in urban labor markets, some low-skill workers will end up working with more physical capital, making them more productive and raising their incomes. The return on workers' human capital and employers' physical capital thus rises with the stock of human capital in the city, even when production at each worksite is characterized by constant returns to scale.

The same principle—externalities arising from better matches in larger urban environments—applies to specialized machines in production and to entrepreneurs in firms. Better matches can also reduce the potential losses from bankruptcy by making it easier to resell equipment.

Education, Knowledge, and Mimicking

The notion of complementarities in labor market matching can be distinguished from externalities arising from the collocation of workers with similar education and skills in dense urban areas. The effects of aggregate levels of schooling in urban areas on aggregate output may be distinguished from the effects of individuals' schooling on their individual earnings. Productivity spillovers—educated or skilled workers increasing the productivity of other workers—may arise in denser spatial environments regardless of whether the urban industrial structure is diversified or specialized. The diffusion of techniques among firms, the copying and innovation in style, and the genealogy of patents among firms are all examples of local externalities in production fostered by urban density and the concentration of skilled workers. These economies may arise with spatial concentration by industry (localization economies) or higher densities of diverse industries (urbanization economies).

The Law of Large Numbers

Considerable cost savings may arise simply from the presence of large numbers of economic actors in close proximity. To the extent that fluctuations in demand are imperfectly correlated across firms in an urban labor market, employment can be stabilized, because some firms will be hiring workers while other firms will be laying workers off. To the extent that fluctuations in demand for products are uncorrelated across buyers, firms need to carry less inventory, because some consumers will be buying while others will not. The decisions of large numbers of imperfectly correlated economic actors in close proximity can provide a form of natural insurance.

The basic insight from the law of large numbers is straightforward; it is possible to get a better estimate of the moments of a distribution with a larger sample size. This allows all economic actors to make decisions based on better information. This is true on the buying and selling sides of markets for purchasing inputs, storing intermediate products, and selling outputs.

Limitations on City Sizes

The external effects of the urban environment on productivity described above all point to larger and denser accommodations and indicate that there is a strong positive relation between urbanization and economic development. What are the limits, if any, to the extent of urbanization? What are the efficient sizes of cities? At least three sources limit the size of cities and affect the efficiency of city sizes: land and transport costs, unpriced externalities of urban life and higher densities, and explicit public policies affecting the gains from urbanization.

Land and Transport Costs

Important factors limiting city sizes arise from the same technological considerations that spawn cities in the first place. Increased housing and land prices mean that the attractiveness of larger cities for residents declines, holding the wages offered constant. (Any decline in the attractiveness of cities will, of course, be less pronounced if the consumption externalities of cities are large.) The wages offered as cities expand must increase enough to offset the higher costs workers must bear if they choose to live and work in these locations. The efficiency gains in production from higher densities must be at least as large as the increased wage payments required. Together with wages and output prices, housing and land prices limit the efficient sizes of cities.

Unpriced Externalities of Urban Density

The increased transport costs and higher densities of cities may bring their own externalities. If these are large enough, they will limit the extent of urbanization. Of course, if these externalities are unpriced, they will fail to limit urbanization sufficiently. In developed countries air pollution from vehicles is typically underpriced; until recently congestion in cities was rarely priced. Externalities from vehicle accidents are seldom priced. In developing countries there may be additional external costs of higher-density living in the form of higher risks of disease, epidemics, or fires, all of which are not priced. To the extent that these factors are underpriced in cities, potential rural migrants do not face the marginal costs of urban life. Hence migration will be excessive and cities larger than their efficient sizes.

Explicit Policies

Explicit governmental policies, especially in developing countries, may provide strong indirect incentives affecting the extent and distribution of urbanization. Governments in many developing countries favored producers and consumers in urban areas at the expense of rural and agricultural workers (by imposing below-market prices for agricultural output and above-market prices for urban products, for example). The structural adjustment policies widely adopted since the 1980s have greatly reduced the scope for this urban bias and the distorted migration signals inherent in these subsidies, but some policies still favor certain cities, particularly national capitals. Policies favoring the locations that benefit elites and bureaucrats may be adopted as a result of rent-seeking behavior or corruption. Questionable policies may include direct public investments in plant, equipment, or infrastructure simply because certain cities are favored by elites; capital controls on investment across cities; and differences in rules imposed on cities for access to capital markets or for obtaining licenses and permissions. In some countries—for example, China—restrictions include explicit limitations on labor mobility as well.

Summary

All of the factors suggest why productivity is higher in larger cities than in smaller cities. Larger cities permit greater specialization and admit more complementarities in production. They facilitate spillovers and learning within and across industries. And they facilitate sharing and risk pooling by their very size.

Even given the potential negative externalities of larger cities, these factors suggest that real wages in larger cities in developed and developing countries will exceed those in smaller cities. Urban productivity will be higher than rural productivity, and the differential will facilitate migration from the labor-surplus hinterland to more productive urban areas.

Early models of rural–urban migration, beginning with Kuznets, recognized that the free flow of labor from unproductive agriculture to urban employment tended to equalize wages and was a vital part of the development process. In the 1970s analysts emphasized the importance of minimum wage rules in cities and the tendency toward equalization of expected wages across sectors. These models, beginning with that of Harris and Todaro (1970), reconciled high levels of wages and worker productivity with unemployment in cities in developing countries. Inexplicably, the reasoning behind these models has been used by some to "justify" actions by governments in developing countries that limit mobility to productive cities rather than remove barriers to competition in the labor market. Indeed, agrarian romantics with an antiurban bias often compare high levels of official unemployment in cities with "official" statistics from rural areas that ignore disguised rural unemployment (see Lall, Selod, and Shalizi 2006, especially pp. 47–48, for a more balanced discussion of the issue of bias that also suggests that the concern is greatly overblown).

Empirical Evidence on Productivity Gains

Despite the attention paid to agglomeration economies—going back to observations by Marshall in the 1890s—verification of efficiency gains by direct observation initially proved difficult, even using data from advanced economies. A number of early studies estimating aggregate production functions are suggestive, but most of these efforts lacked critical data (such as measures of capital stock), which made inferences about the importance of external effects problematic (see Eberts and McMillen 1999; Rosenthal and Strange 2004).

More recent work using micro data sets on firms and establishments in the United States has overcome most of these measurement problems. Henderson's (2003a, 2003b) analyses of machinery and high-tech industries, for example, tests for the presence of localization economies (agglomeration within an industry) and urbanization economies (agglomeration across industries) by estimating plant-level production functions. Using a panel of plants across counties and metropolitan areas makes it much easier to test for the effect of local conditions on the productivity of plants and their levels of output. Henderson's results show that productivity in single-establishment firms is higher as a result of localization economies.

Even with appropriate micro data, however, simple statistical models may lead to misleading inferences. If agglomeration economies do enhance firm productivity, more talented entrepreneurs will seek out these more productive locations. More sophisticated statistical methods are needed to account for this simultaneity. Henderson handles the problem by applying more appropriate statistical methods of estimation in his study of high-tech and machinery industries, but the instruments he relies on (measures of the local environment) are weak, rendering the statistical results problematic.

Greenstone, Hornbeck, and Moretti (2007) solve this identification problem. They study the effects of the opening of "million-dollar plants" on the productivity of nearby plants, using a panel of establishments from the same data source used by Henderson. For each of the million-dollar plants, they collect information on the county chosen for investment and on the county that had been under final consideration by the parent firm but not ultimately selected. The authors find clear evidence of a discontinuity in total factor productivity in plants after the opening of a large plant nearby. Total factor productivity rose in preexisting plants located in the "winning" counties but not the "losing counties," confirming the existence of urbanization economies. This finding is important.

A variety of less direct approaches have been employed to make inferences about agglomeration. Rosenthal and Strange (2004), among others, study the location of firm births. To avoid the problems associated with the data on factor inputs (including the legacy of sunk capital), they investigate new establishments. This plausibly allows them to take the existing economic geography of regions as exogenous. Their results suggest that births are substantially more likely to occur where there is a concentration of firms in the same industry (see also Carlton 1983). To the extent that profit-seeking entrepreneurs are drawn to more productive locations, this result emphasizes the importance of localization economies.

The study of the spatial distribution of wages and rents may provide indirect evidence on economies of agglomeration. The marginal product of labor and wages will be higher in more productive regions. Analogously, locations where industrial rents are higher are those with offsetting differentials in productivity. Wheaton and Lewis (2002) use U.S. data on wages, Gabriel and Rosenthal (2004) use U.S. data on rents, and Dekle and Eaton (1999) use data from Japanese prefectures to document agglomerative economies.

Patterns of employment growth may provide indirect evidence of the importance of agglomeration. If agglomeration economies enhance productivity, more productive regions will grow more rapidly than less productive regions. Glaeser and others (1992) use aggregate employment data from U.S. metropolitan areas to confirm these effects. Henderson, Kuncoro, and Turner (1995) conduct a more precise test using employment in manufacturing.

Economists have studied the mechanisms transmitting these urbanization and localization efficiencies. Perhaps the clearest evidence of external effects in local labor markets comes from education and training. Early studies by Rauch (1993), testing the Lucas (1988) hypothesis, identified the external effects of schooling on wages in cross-sectional models of wage determination, using U.S. cities as units of observation. Moretti (2004) extends this analysis to explain longitudinal as well as cross-sectional variations in wages across labor markets.

Perhaps the most persuasive evidence of the importance of educational externalities comes from Moretti's (2004) analysis of educational spillovers and productivity in the United States. This research is based on the estimation of total factor productivity and the effects of education at the level of the individual plant or establishment.

These productivity findings are confirmed, at least roughly, in a study of the service sector by Arzaghi and Henderson (2006). They analyze advertising firms in Manhattan, documenting the substantial increases in productivity attributable to the networking opportunities arising from the proximity of similar firms.

It has been widely reported that incomes have grown more rapidly in U.S. cities with high initial levels of human capital (see, for example, Glaeser and others 1992). This finding is consistent with skill acquisition and diffusion through the interaction of workers in denser urban areas (Duranton and Puga 2001; Glaeser and Maré 2001).

Lacking direct observations on workers' interactions, economists have examined one important paper trail of these interactions: data on patent applications and awards. Patent applications list the addresses of the holders of antecedent patents as well as the addresses of patent applicants. This makes possible the study of the localization of patents and the analysis of the decay of patent citations as a function of the distances between firms and between inventors (Jaffe, Trajtenberg, and Henderson 1993). This work provides explicit confirmation of the importance of geographic spillovers in the development of new knowledge.

Anthropological studies by sociologists and others have observed worker interactions in dense locations. The results of Saxenian's (1994) study of highly educated workers in Santa Clara County, California (Silicon Valley), and along Route 128 (the technical corridor outside Boston) are broadly consistent with those of quantitative investigation by economists.

Corroboration from Developing Countries

Many of the models reported in the previous section have been adapted, extended, and applied using data from developing countries. Much of this work has been pioneered by Vernon Henderson and his collaborators. Using detailed industrial census data, Henderson (1988) estimates the extent and importance of agglomeration economies in Brazil. He finds clear evidence of external economies of scale at the two-digit industry level. (The fact that in some cities a single industry is dominant, meaning that factor prices and populations are endogenously determined, is a major limitation.) This work is similar to (but much more primitive than) the work of Greenstone, Hornbeck, and Moretti (2007) using U.S. data. In a more recent analysis of city growth in Brazil, Henderson and his collaborators analyze aggregate data for 123 cities over three decades beginning in 1970 (Da Mata and others 2007). Using an ambitious model of the structure of supply and demand for output at the municipal level, the authors estimate relations describing the evolution of city sizes in Brazil and their decennial growth. The empirical results indicate that increases in the sizes of local markets and their access to domestic markets have very strong effects on the growth rates of cities. Improvements in labor force quality and in the initial levels of educational attainment significantly affect economic growth, extending the conclusions of Glaeser and others (1992).

Other direct investigations of agglomeration and productivity have been undertaken in China, Indonesia, India, and the Republic of Korea. Henderson, Lee, and Lee (2001) report evidence of localization economies for Korean industry, including transport and traditional industry. They analyze metropolitan-level data for 23 Korean industries in 5 major groups between 1983 and 1993, a time of rapid deconcentration of economic activity from Seoul to smaller metropolitan areas. They estimate aggregate production functions by using census estimates of capital stock and labor and testing for the importance of the potential urbanization and localization economies provided in Korean cities. Their results confirm the importance of localization economies in Korean industry, especially in heavy industry and transportation. They also find significant localization economies in machinery and high-tech industries and, to a lesser extent, in traditional manufacturing. Lee and Zang (1998) find similar results by applying somewhat different statistical models to the same basic source of data.

In related empirical work on Indonesia, Henderson and Kuncoro (1996) report substantial localization economies for many industries and less pronounced urbanization economies. They estimate models of the choice of location for plants and the establishment of small and medium-size firms in Java. Their results indicate that manufacturing plants are much more likely to choose locations that include mature establishments and plants in the same or related industries. These results are consistent with the work on firm births in the United States by Rosenthal and Strange (2001), who report that entrepreneurs actively seek out localization and agglomeration to improve productivity and profits.

Deichmann and others (2005) extend Henderson and Kuncoro's work by analyzing a large sample of plant locations for the entire country. Their statistical analysis documents the importance of localization economies and the influence of existing firms in the same industry in affecting location choice. The econometric results suggest the importance of existing backward linkages to suppliers in determining location choice. Urbanization economies per se are much less important.

Simulations based on these statistical results illustrate the difficulties faced by lagging regions in attracting new economic activity. Au and Henderson (2006) use aggregate data on some 285 Chinese cities to estimate the effects of urban agglomeration on productivity, using detailed data on GDP by metropolitan area in three categories. The aggregate productivity relation exhibits an inverted U shape in metropolitan size and scale, as expected. The estimated urban agglomeration benefits are high, and it appears that a large fraction of cities in China are undersized, as a result of migration controls imposed at the national level. These results are consistent with earlier and less complete work by Chen (1996). Some of the policy implications of this line of research are discussed in CERAP (2007).

The evidence from India includes an analysis of the relation between urban populations and total factor productivity by state and industry over a 16-year period (Mitra 2000). Of more significance, perhaps, is the analysis of plant-level data by Lall, Koo, and Chakrovorty (2003), who use micro data on establishments from the 1998 Indian Survey of Industries to estimate the parameters of a translog cost function. They provide direct separate estimates of the elasticity of costs with respect to four different measures of agglomeration for eight industrial groupings and three size classes of plants. The results provide strong support for the importance of urbanization economies in reducing costs per unit of output. The fact that this result holds across all industries and plant size classes suggests that urbanization economies may apply to other developing economies as well.

Summary

The quality of the evidence from developing countries cited above is probably lower than that obtained from developed countries, if only because more reliable data on economic activity are available for a longer period for developed countries. Nevertheless, the quantitative results obtained in developing countries in Asia and Latin America are remarkably consistent with those obtained in developed economies. Comparable evidence from developing countries in Africa is conspicuously absent (Collier 2007).

Urbanization and localization do support increases in productivity. Of course, it may be that the economic returns to mimicking successful ideas or investments are especially high in developing countries, where mimicking could result in too little entrepreneurial activity, a point made by Hausmann and Rodrik (2002, 2006). But there is no systematic evidence that the potential returns to mimicking are greater in poorer countries than in richer ones. As the evidence on patent citations suggests, denser and more specialized local economies may simply generate a larger stock of entrepreneurial capital to be copied.

Of course, none of this evidence establishes a tight causal link between urbanization and economic development (see Henderson 2003a, 2003b for a balanced discussion). Moreover, evidence from elsewhere suggests that urbanization is not a sufficient condition for economic development (Fay and Opal 2000). Nevertheless, it sems quite clear that productivity is enhanced by the localization and urbanization features of cities, in developing economies as well as industrialized countries. The cumulative evidence is overwhelming.

Efficient City Sizes

Given the productivity advantages of larger cities documented in the previous section, one would expect urbanization to be a natural concomitant of increased output and well-being in developing countries. City sizes are determined by the trade-off between the increased productivity and incomes in larger cities on the one hand and the increased rent and transport costs consumers confront on the other. To the extent that rural workers contemplating moving to cities do not adequately account for congestion, pollution, and the risk of epidemics in making their decision, cities will be "too large"—but not by much. Some of these externalities can be eliminated by improved technology or investments in public health.

It is surprising that a cohesive body of literature—or much economic literature at all—relating these externalities to levels of urbanization in developing countries does not exist. Case studies on the linkage between traffic fatalities and economic growth have been conducted (Kopits and Cropper 2005), but no cases studies have examined the link between traffic fatalities and urbanization or investigated the linkage between externalities from traffic fatalities and levels of urbanization. It is relatively straightforward to estimate the correlation between the incidence of health problems and communicable diseases (such as diarrhea and tuberculosis) and urbanization at the country level or to estimate the correlation between access to water and sanitation on the one hand and urbanization on the other. Indeed, Evans (2007) reports that the rate of infant mortality in developing countries is higher in urban slums; many correlations can be investigated on line (using, for example, the World Bank's WDI Online). Although these correlations barely hint at the causal mechanisms at work, the results are widely interpreted as if there were a causal mechanism. Absent definitive analysis, at this point one can conclude only that unpriced externalities are probably a bit more important in distorting migration flow to cities in developing countries than in developed countries. These distortions can be reduced in all countries by direct pricing or the imposition of indirect levies, such as urban property taxes.

What about the explicit policies of governments? Explicit policies of developing countries have inappropriately favored cities at the expense of agriculture, interfering with economic development. The most direct accusation of urban bias was made three decades ago, by Lipton (1976; see also Lipton 1993). Distorting price signals through macroeconomic and national trade policies that raise value added in the urban sector when value added is computed using local prices provide incentives for inefficiently high levels of urbanization; valuing urban products at inflated prices and rural products at deflated prices can make the productivity advantages attributed to cities illusory.

It is not clear how these price distortions can be measured (see Becker and Morrison 1999) or how the implications of this bias could be tested directly. But after two decades of structural adjustment policies advocated by international organizations, it is clear that in most developing countries price liberalization has caused local relative prices to converge closer to world prices, reflecting economic scarcity. Indeed, the World Bank's 1991 treatise on urban policy documents the contemporaneous effects of structural adjustment policies in removing artificial price advantages of cities and reducing the economic circumstances of the poor in cities in developing countries.

The controversy over policies to undo distortions in relative prices seems dated. But certain limited aspects of "bias" in development policies—such as government policies that favor particular cities or regions for political or ideological reasons—may be of continuing concern.

A remarkable regularity observed across systems of cities is the rank-size rule, according to which the product of the city rank in the size distribution and the city population is roughly constant. This means that the second-largest city in a country is half the size of the first and so forth. This relation (more generally, a power relation) has proved robust over time in the United States (Dobkins and Ioannides 1998) and other countries as well as across countries (Rosen and Resnick 1980; Soo 2005). Many explanations for the general findings are purely mechanical. Fujita, Krugman, and Venables (1999) describe "nihilistic and simplistic" models that generate this pattern. Gabaix (1999) shows that if, over some range of city sizes, the expected growth rate of population and its variance are independent of size, the distribution of city sizes follows a simple power relation. Puga (1998) hypothesizes that the higher costs of spatial interaction and the less elastic labor supply in the 19th century help explain why a smaller share of the national population lives in large old European cities than in large cities in developing countries. As Puga stresses, the nature of increasing and decreasing returns to city size govern the size distribution of cities in the long run. Where, for example, there are stronger external economies of scale in cities, the distribution of city sizes will be more uneven. The exact relation between economies of scale in production and the distribution of city sizes remains elusive, however.

Considerable evidence suggests that political variables affect the distribution of city sizes. Soo's (2005) analysis of the size distribution of cities in 73 countries suggests that political measures—dictatorial government, measures of political rights and liberties, and the length of time a nation has been independent—are more important than economic variables in explaining deviations from a common exponential relation relating city rank and size.

These results generalize the more primitive analysis by Ades and Glaeser (1995) of the primacy of a single city in national economic life. Ades and Glaeser examine variations in the national population residing in the largest city in a sample of 85 cities over 15 years. Their empirical analysis suggests that countries currently governed by dictatorships have principal cities that are about 45 percent larger than the principal cities found in democracies; democratically governed countries that were governed by dictators in the past have principal cities that are about 40 percent larger than those in countries with no history of dictatorship. These and similar results survive a variety of tests for causality.

Most of the discussion of "excessive" concentration in cities by economists is framed in terms of the extreme primacy of one or a few cities in many developing countries (see Henderson 1999 and the references he cites). Surprisingly, little or none of the criticism is based on the empirical evaluation of externalities in developing countries.

Excessive concentration may be abetted by government policy. The mechanisms by which authoritative governments are able to favor particular cities or regions may be difficult to document, however. These mechanisms include the imposition of weaker benefit–cost tests on infrastructure investment or the relaxation of licensing rules in favored cities, explicit allocation of credit to favored regions, and the adoption of decisions that favor investments by public officials and cronies in national capitals. In this sense there may be an urban bias in government policy, which may adversely affect not only rural areas but also most small and medium-sized cities in developing countries.

Some Conclusions

This review and analysis of the literature reveals the strong relation between urbanization on the one hand and economic productivity and development on the other. Based on extensive analyses of data from the United States and other high-income countries and less extensive analyses of data from developing countries, it suggests that specific mechanisms fostered by urbanization and localization of industry can affect productivity. The evidence does not conclusively show that urbanization is necessary for development or sufficient to increase output and well-being in developing countries, but the case is strong and the causal relation clear.

Urbanization and economic development are intimately related, and the concentration of resources—labor and capital—in cities is a part of this process. To the extent that movements of these factors represent a rational response to market signals about scarcity, there is no reason for concern about the size of any city or the size distribution of cities in general. To the extent that external effects, such as pollution and congestion, are unpriced in cities, conurbations will be too large, but not by much. Public concerns about pricing congested roadways and about water supplies and public health investments to decrease the chances of epidemic are well placed.

From this perspective, the concern with urban slums and low-quality housing, which impose no externalities per se, is less important. Urban poverty in developing countries is not an excuse for adopting policies that limit the extent of urbanization.

It is hard to know how important corruption and antidemocratic policies are in inhibiting or directing flows of factors to and across cities. Their existence in developed as well as developing countries provides a strong argument for allowing natural market forces to determine the spatial distribution of labor and capital. Doing so would cause both the level of urbanization and the level of economic development to increase. Increased urbanization unquestionably facilitates the development process. Explicit policies to discourage urbanization are therefore surely misguided.

References

Ades, A., and E. Glaeser. 1995. "Trade and Circuses: Explaining Urban Giants." *Quarterly Journal of Economics* 110 (1): 195–228.

Arzaghi, Mohammad, and J. Vernon Henderson. 2006. "Networking off Madison Avenue." Working Paper, Department of Economics, Brown University Providence, RI.

Au, Chun-Chung, and J. Vernon Henderson. 2006. "Are Chinese Cities Too Small?" *Review of Economic Studies* 73 (3): 549–76.

Becker, Charles M., Andrew M. Hamer, and Andrew R. Morrison. 1994. *Beyond Urban Bias in Africa: Urbanization in an Era of Structural Adjustment.* Portsmouth, NH: Heinemann.

Becker, Charles M., and Andrew R. Morrison. 1999. "Urbanization in Transforming Economies." In *Handbook of Regional and Urban Economics*, vol. 3, ed. Edwin S. Mills and Paul Cheshire. Amsterdam: North-Holland.

Carlton, Dennis W. 1983. "The Location and Employment Choices of New Firms: An Econometric Model with Discrete and Continuous Endogenous Variables." *Review of Economics and Statistics* 65 (3): 440–49.

CERAP (China Economic Research and Advisory Programme). 2007. "Urbanization in China." Professional Report P07-001, Institute of Business and Economic Research, University of California, Berkeley.

Chen, Y. 1996. "Impact of Regional Factors on Productivity in China." *Journal of Regional Science* 36 (3): 417–36.

Collier, Paul. 2007. *The Bottom Billion: Why the Poorest Countries Are Failing and What Can Be Done about It.* Oxford: Oxford University Press.

Da Mata, Daniel, Uwe Deichmann, J. Vernon Henderson, Somik Vinay Lall, and Hyuong Guanghua Wang. 2007. "Determinants of City Growth in Brazil." *Journal of Urban Economics* 62 (2): 252–72.

Deichmann, Uwe, Kai Kaiser, Somik V. Lall, and Zmarak Shalizi. 2005. "Agglomeration, Transport, and Regional Development in Indonesia." Policy Research Working Paper 3477, World Bank, Washington, DC.

Dekle, Robert, and Jonathan Eaton. 1999. "Agglomeration and Land Rents: Evidence from the Prefectures." *Journal of Urban Economics* 46 (2): 200–14.

Dobkins, Linda, and Yannis Ioannides. 1998. "Dynamic Evolution of the U.S. City Size Distribution." In *The Economics of Cities*, ed. Jean-Marie Huriot and Jacques-François Thisse. New York: Cambridge University Press.

Duranton, Gilles, and Diego Puga. 2001. "Nursery Cities: Urban Diversity, Process Innovation, and the Life Cycle of Products." *American Economic Review* 91 (5): 1454–77.

Eberts, Randall W., and Daniel P. McMillen. 1999. "Agglomeration Economics and Urban Public Infrastructure." In *Handbook of Regional and Urban Economics*, vol. 3, ed. Paul C. Cheshire and Edwin S. Mills. Amsterdam: North-Holland.

Evans, Timothy. 2007. "Research for Urban Health: Towards a Global Agenda." Paper presented at the "Innovation for an Urban World: A Global Urban Summit," Bellagio, Italy, July 3.

Fay, Marianne, and Charlotte Opal. 2000. "Urbanization without Growth: A Not-So-Uncommon Phenomenon." Policy Research Working Paper 2412, World Bank, Washington, DC.

Fujita, Masahisa, Paul Krugman, and Anthony J. Venables. 1999. *The Spatial Economy: Cities, Regions, and International Trade.* Cambridge, MA: MIT Press.

Gabaix, Xavier. 1999. "Zipf's Law for Cities: An Explanation." *Quarterly Journal of Economics* 114 (3): 739–67.

Gabriel, Stuart A., and Stuart S. Rosenthal. 2004. "Quality of the Business Environment versus Quality of Life: Do Firms and Households Like the Same Cities?" *Review of Economics and Statistics* 86 (1): 438–44.

Glaeser, Edward L., Heidi Kallal, José Scheinkman, and Andrei Schleifer. 1992. "Growth in Cities." *Journal of Political Economy* 100 (6): 1126–52.

Glaeser, Edward L., and David C. Maré. 2001. "Cities and Skills." *Journal of Labor Economics* 19 (2): 316–42.

Greenstone, Michael, Richard Hornbeck, and Enrico Moretti. 2007. "Identifying Agglomeration Spillovers: Evidence from Million Dollar Plants." NBER Working Paper w13833, National Bureau of Economic Research, Cambridge, MA.

Harris, John R., and Michael P. Todaro. 1970. "Migration, Unemployment, and Development. A Two Sector Analysis." *American Economic Review* 60 (1): 126–42.

Hausmann, Ricardo, and Dani Rodrik. 2002. "Economic Development as Self-Discovery." NBER Working Paper 8952, National Bureau of Economic Research, Cambridge, MA.

———. 2006. "Doomed to Choose: Industrial Policy as Predicament." John F. Kennedy School of Government, Harvard University, Cambridge, MA.

Henderson, J. Vernon. 1988. *Urban Development: Theory, Fact, and Illusion.* Oxford: Oxford University Press.

———. 1999. "How Urban Concentration Affects Economic Growth." Policy Research Working Paper 2326, World Bank, Washington, D.C.

———. 2003a. "Marshall's Scale Economies." *Journal of Urban Economics* 53 (1): 1–28.

———. 2003b. "The Urbanization Process and Economic Growth: The So-What Question." *Journal of Economic Growth* 8 (1): 47–71.

———. 2005. "Urbanization and Growth." In *Handbook of Economic Growth*, ed. Philippe Aghion and Steven Durlauf. Amsterdam: North-Holland.

Henderson, J. Vernon, and Ari Kuncoro. 1996. "Industrial Centralization in Indonesia." *World Bank Economic Review* 10 (3): 513–40.

Henderson, J. Vernon, Ari Kuncoro, and Matthew Turner. 1995. "Industrial Development in Cities." *Journal of Political Economy* 103 (5): 1067–85.

Henderson, J. Vernon, Todd Lee, and Yung Joon Lee. 2001. "Scale Externalities in Korea." *Journal of Urban Economics* 49 (3): 479–504.

Hoover, Edgar M. 1975. *An Introduction to Regional Economics*, 2nd ed. New York: Alfred A. Knopf

Jacobs, Jane. 1969. *The Economy of Cities.* New York: Random House.

Jaffe, Adam B., Manuel Trajtenberg, and Rebecca Henderson. 1993. "Geographic Localization of Knowledge Spillovers as Evidenced by Patent Citations." *Quarterly Journal of Economics* 108 (3): 577–98.

Kopits, Elizabeth, and Maureen Cropper. 2005. "Traffic Fatalities and Economic Growth." *Accident Analysis and Prevention* 37 (1): 169–78.

Lall, Somik V., Jun Koo, and Sanjoy Chakravorty. 2003. "Diversity Matters: The Economic Geography of Industry Location in India." Policy Research Working Paper 3072, World Bank, Washington, D.C.

Lall, Somik V., Harris Selod, and Zmarak Shalizi. 2006. "Rural Urban Migration in Developing Countries: A Survey of Theoretical Predictions and Empirical Findings." Policy Research Working Paper 3915, World Bank, Washington, DC.

Lee, Y. Jung Joon, and Hyoungsoo Zang. 1998. "Urbanization and Regional Productivity in Korean Manufacturing." *Urban Studies* 35 (11): 2085–99.

Lipton, Michael. 1976. *Why Poor People Stay Poor: Urban Bias in World Development.* Cambridge, MA: Harvard University Press.

———. 1993. "Urban Bias: Of Consequences, Classes and Causality." *Journal of Development Studies* 29 (4): 229–58.

Lucas, Robert E., Jr. 1988. "On the Mechanics of Economic Development." *Journal of Monetary Economics* 22 (1): 3–42.

Mitra, Arup. 2000. "Total Factor Productivity Growth and Urbanization Economies: A Case of Indian Industries." *Review of Urban and Regional Development Studies* 12 (2): 97–108.

Moretti, Enrico. 2004. "Workers' Education, Spillovers and Productivity." *American Economic Review* 94 (3): 656–90.

Quigley, John M. 1998. "Urban Diversity and Economic Growth." *Journal of Economic Perspectives* 12 (2): 127–38.

———. 2001. "The Renaissance in Regional Research." *Annals of Regional Science* 35 (2): 167–78.

Puga, Diego. 1998. "Urbanization Patterns: European vs. Less Developed Countries." *Journal of Regional Science* 38 (2): 231–52.

Rappaport, Jordan, and Jeffrey Sachs. 2003. "The United States as a Coastal Nation." *Journal of Economic Growth* 8 (1): 5–46.

Rauch, James. 1993. "Productivity Gains from Geographic Concentration of Human Capital: Evidence from the Cities." *Journal of Urban Economics* 34 (3): 380–400.

Rosen, Kenneth, and Mitchel Resnick. 1980. "The Size Distribution of Cities: An Examination of the Pareto Law and Primacy." *Journal of Urban Economics* 8 (2): 165–86.

Rosenthal, Stuart S., and William C. Strange. 2001. "The Determinants of Agglomeration." *Journal of Urban Economics* 50 (2): 191–229.

———. 2004. "Evidence on the Nature and Sources of Agglomeration Economies." In *Handbook of Regional and Urban Economics,* vol. 4, ed. J. Vernon Henderson and Jacques-François Thisse. Amsterdam: North-Holland.

Saxenian, AnnaLee. 1994. *Regional Advantage: Culture and Competition in Silicon Valley and Route 128*. Cambridge, MA: Harvard University Press.

Soo, Kwok Tong. 2005. "Zipf's Law for Cities: A Cross-Country Investigation." *Regional Science and Urban Economics* 35 (3): 239–63.

Starrett, David A. 1974. "Principles of Optimal Location in a Large Homogeneous Area." *Journal of Economic Theory* 9 (4): 418–48.

UN (United Nations). 2003. *World Population Policies*. New York: United Nations.

UNFPA (United Nations Population Fund). 2007. *State of World Population 2007: Unleashing the Potential of Urban Growth*. New York: United Nations.

UN-HABITAT. 2007. *The State of the World's Cities Report 2006/2007*. London: Earthscan Publications, Ltd.

Wheaton, William C., and Mark J. Lewis. 2002. "Urban Wages and Labor Market Agglomeration." *Journal of Urban Economics* 51 (3): 542–62.

World Bank. 1991. *Urban Policy and Economic Development: An Agenda for the 1990s*. Washington, DC: World Bank.

CHAPTER 5
Spatial Inequality and Economic Development: Theories, Facts, and Policies
Sukkoo Kim

Although systematic evidence on the extent of spatial inequality in developing countries is still relatively scarce, a growing body of work documents the existence of such inequalities in countries in Africa, Asia, Europe, and Latin America (Kanbur and Venables 2005a, 2005b; Kanbur, Venables, and Wan 2006). Little consensus has emerged, however, on the causes of spatial inequality or the ways in which policy makers should respond to it.

From the standpoint of economic efficiency, spatial inequality may be beneficial or harmful. If it results from regional specialization based on comparative advantage or returns to scale in production, it may be beneficial, because productivity increases. If, however, it is caused by external economies that are not internalized, the level of inequality may not be optimal. Spatial inequality in the form of the excessive concentration of urban population in large primate cities may impose a variety of social ills in society. From the standpoint of equity, it may be socially undesirable if it contributes to social inequality across regions. It may also be socially destabilizing if the regional divergence in economic welfare and political interests contributes to social instability.

What are the causes of spatial inequality? What is the nature of the evidence on its causes? What is the optimal level of spatial inequality? Does

The author is grateful to Patricia Annez for her helpful and thoughtful suggestions.

rapid growth accelerate spatial inequality? Is the rise of spatial inequality necessary for development? To what extent is its rise a short-run or a long-run phenomenon? Do globalization and international trade increase spatial inequality within countries? What can governments do to promote or reduce spatial inequality?

This chapter sheds light on these important questions by reviewing the current state of knowledge on the theories on, empirical evidence about, and policies concerning spatial inequality and development. Although research on spatial inequality in developing countries remains in a nascent stage, there has been an explosion of both theoretical and empirical research on the general causes of spatial agglomeration (Henderson and Thisse 2004). Significant advances have been made in establishing the theoretical micro-foundations of spatial agglomerations; the growth in computing power and advances in empirical methods have greatly expanded the quality of empirical evidence on agglomeration economies.

Innovations in theory continue to dictate scholarly discourse in economics; empirical studies rarely have a decisive impact on policy or theory. Although the amount of empirical evidence has increased substantially in recent years, policy directives are likely to be influenced by a scholar's theoretical perspective and a subjective weighing of the evidence rather than solely by the accumulation of systematic empirical evidence. Because theories that have little proven empirical track record can quickly enter the realm of policy discourse, policy makers must recognize the inherent theory bias in economics. To be able to evaluate the merits of policies proposed by scholars, they must acquire a basic knowledge of developments in the theory of economic geography

Policy makers also need to recognize the interdependent nature of regional and urban spatial inequality. Because the fields of regional and urban economics developed separately, the literature on spatial inequality treats regional inequality and urban inequality as two separate phenomena. The most important reason for this dichotomy is that it is extremely difficult to develop a unified theory of regions and cities in a satisfactory manner (see Fujita, Krugman, and Venables 1999). Only in the extreme case, in which cities are uniform in size and uniformly distributed across regions, is urban inequality expected to have limited impact on regional inequality. In reality both city sizes and their geographic distribution are very uneven.

To the extent that industrial revolution and urbanization go hand in hand, the rise of North–South regional cores and peripheries is likely to be intimately related to urban development. North–South divergence in incomes and industrial structures in the United States in the late 19th and early 20th centuries coincided with more rapid urban development in the North than in the South. At a more regional level, it is impossible to imagine that the city of Chicago would have become the mercantile center of the Midwest in the late 19th century had it not had access to a rich rural hinterland (Cronon 1991). Conversely, for a given population the extent of urban scale economies is likely to influence the number of cities and their geographic distribution across regions. In the United States it probably is not a coincidence that urban densities rose significantly when regional inequality rose and fell considerably when regional inequality fell (Kim 1995, 1998, 2007a).

Policy makers face a bewildering array of empirical evidence on spatial inequality that is difficult, if not impossible, to evaluate. Studies vary greatly in terms of both focus and in their methods of measurement of spatial inequality, which often are not comparable. The problem is most severe for studies of developing countries, where scholars must resort to survey rather than government census data. Although it is extremely challenging to summarize this literature, some important themes emerge. Policy makers need to take into account the dynamic nature of spatial inequality; they must be able to evaluate the impact of foreign trade on spatial inequality; and, perhaps most important, they must understand the role of political institutions on spatial inequality.

This chapter is organized as follows. The next section reviews recent advances in theories of regional and urban spatial inequality. In addition to examining the standard theories of spatial agglomeration, it looks at the impact of trade and political institutions on spatial inequality. The second section reviews the evidence on spatial inequality for developing and developed countries from both regional and urban perspectives. The third section outlines the policy implications and lessons that emerge from the literature on spatial inequality. The last section summarizes the findings and provides suggestions for future research.

Theories of Spatial Inequality

From the perspective of theory, spatial inequality is determined by the location decisions of firms and households. Firms choose locations to maximize profits; households choose locations to maximize job market outcomes and utility. While firms and households generally care about the quality of both their regional and urban environments, there is no widely accepted general theory of spatial location that seems to incorporate regional and urban location decisions in a unified manner (see Fujita, Krugman, and Venables 1999; Fujita and Thisse 2002; Berliant 2007). Rather, the field of economic geography is divided into two fields, regional economics and urban economics (Kim and Margo 2004).

The traditional regional science models based on the central-place theory take a regional-urban perspective, but these models have been discredited for lacking a rigorous theoretical foundation.[1] To the extent that they exist, regional models are based largely on models of international or

---

1 The central-place theory of Christaller (1933) and Losch (1954) seeks to explain the hierarchy of cities and towns (central places) that serve rural markets. It is not an economic model based on optimization and the equilibrium behavior of firms and households but rather a useful descriptive classification scheme, as Fujita, Krugman, and Venables (1999) note.

interregional trade. Although it is impossible to imagine interregional (international) trade in the absence of cities, perusal of standard texts in international trade reveals a complete absence of discussion of cities.[2] Conversely, urban models are devoid of regional location decisions. In the classic Henderson (1974) model, cities are islands that differ only in scale. Study of the size distribution of cities without reference to their locations forms an important research agenda for urban economists.

The various theories of economic geography provide different causal explanations for spatial inequality and elicit different policy responses to combat inequality. Recent theoretical innovations in modeling increasing returns have led to the formalization of many traditional concepts, such as Marshallian externalities (technological spillovers, labor-market pooling, access to nontraded intermediate inputs) and nonpecuniary externalities (forward and backward linkages and market size). This in turn has clarified the forces of spatial agglomeration and dispersion.

In general, spatial inequality is the net result of the balance of forces of concentration and dispersion. From a regional perspective, the centripetal forces of geographic concentration are natural advantages, Marshallian externalities, and nonpecuniary externalities; the centrifugal forces of dispersion are immobility in factors and goods caused by high transportation and communications costs. An urban perspective also considers new costs of concentration in the form of congestion costs that result from the fixed supply of land. Concentration leads to increased housing and commuting costs as well as the costs caused by greater crime, pollution, and exposure to disease.

In addition to presenting the theories of regional inequality, this section explores the impact of globalization and trade on spatial inequality, the influence of institutions on spatial inequality, and the relation between household inequality and spatial inequality. It addresses three important issues. First, while the forces that determine the location of firms and households caused by foreign and domestic trade are identical, citizens rarely view the economic impact of foreign and domestic trade in similar ways. Second, regional differences in institutions may affect regional inequality. The distribution of political and fiscal power among the federal, state, and local governments is also likely to have an impact on urban inequality. Third, household income inequality is an important concern for policy makers. It is therefore important to understand whether spatial inequality contributes to household income inequality.

Theories of Regional Inequality

Two classes of regional economics models yield very different policy implications for dealing with regional inequality. In the first class of models, based on the standard neoclassical assumptions of constant returns to scale

---

2 International and interregional trade models usually do not address cities, because neoclassical models based on comparative advantage cannot be easily adapted to incorporate city formation. Starrett's (1974) theorem demonstrates that regional specialization, cities, and trade cannot be equilibrium outcomes under the standard neoclassical assumptions (see Fujita and Thisse 2002).

and perfect competition, the role of government is limited to infrastructural investments that affect the mobility of goods, labor, and other factors.[3] Governments may have little ability to influence centripetal forces that are based on comparative advantage stemming from technology or resources, but they may be able to increase regional specialization or inequality by reducing the mobility of goods or decrease inequality by lowering the mobility of factors.

In the second class of models—the "new models of economic geography," based on imperfect competition and increasing returns—the potential role for government intervention is significantly higher, for three main reasons.[4] First, as a result of the potential for "cumulative causation" forces, small subsidies can potentially have significant first-order effects.[5] Second, infrastructural investments that increase the mobility of goods, labor, and capital may have significant impact on spatial inequality because of the self-enforcing nature of increasing returns. Third, because the equilibrium market allocations are inefficient in these models, markets will not reach the optimal level of spatial inequality without government intervention.

---

3   The two important neoclassical models of trade, the Ricardian and the Heckscher-Ohlin models, present two different theories of regional inequality based on comparative advantage. In the Ricardian model the source of regional comparative advantage is differences in technologies; in the Heckscher-Ohlin model the source is differences in resource endowments. If goods are mobile but factors immobile, both theories predict a rise in regional spatial inequality based on comparative advantage. In the Ricardian model, if a region possesses absolute advantage in technology, its workers will earn higher wages before or after economic integration; in the Heckscher-Ohlin model, the factor price equalization theorem implies that regional differences in incomes can result only from differences in regional industrial structures. If factors are mobile, all workers will migrate to the region with absolute advantages, leading to interregional convergence.

4   These models, commonly associated with Paul Krugman, contain five essential ingredients: increasing returns to scale that are internal to the firm; imperfect competition (usually Spence-Dixit-Stiglitz monopolistic competition); trade costs (Samuelson's "iceberg form," in which goods melt away by distance); endogenous firm location; and, most important, the endogenous location of demand (Spence 1976; Dixit and Stiglitz 1977; Samuelson 1952). As Head and Mayer (2004) note, the first four ingredients give rise to the agglomeration economies of home market effects; the last ingredient, the endogenous location of demand, creates the well-known process of circular causation that causes core-periphery regions to arise from initially symmetric regions. Krugman's (1991a, 1991b) model includes two regions (North and South) and two goods (agricultural and manufacturing). Agricultural goods are homogenous goods produced under constant returns and perfect competition; manufacturing goods are differentiated goods produced under scale economies and monopolistic competition. The only input to production is labor; agricultural workers are immobile, whereas manufacturing workers are mobile. The transportation costs of agricultural goods are costless and those of manufacturing goods costly. When transportation costs of manufacturing goods are high, regions are symmetric and manufacturing is dispersed in both regions. As transportation costs fall, manufacturing becomes concentrated in one region (the North) and the other region (the South) becomes an agricultural periphery. The intuition is simple: the concentration of manufacturing workers in the North creates larger markets, which in turn reduces the costs of production as a result of economies of scale.

5   Because the models typically contain multiple equilibria, a slight perturbation caused by an industrial subsidy to an industry in a given region may increase spatial inequality dramatically. Even if two regions are initially identical, a slight advantage given to one region through tax subsidies may trigger a sharp rise in spatial inequality between the regions. Because increasing returns create a momentum of their own, in theory cumulative causation should lead to the rise of core-periphery regions (Krugman (1991a, 1991b). There is little empirical support for such a hypothesis.

When the sources of increasing returns are forward and backward linkages rather than market size and internal scale economies in production, it is possible to derive an inverted-U pattern of geographic concentration in which regional inequality first rises and then falls.[6] Forward linkages exist when increased production by upstream firms provides positive pecuniary externalities to downstream firms. Backward linkages exist when increased production by downstream firms provides positive pecuniary externalities to upstream firms. When labor is immobile, an initial decline in the transportation costs of final goods leads to geographic concentration and regional inequality; when transportation costs fall further, regional inequality declines and the location of manufacturing firms becomes more dispersed.[7] Thus at least in principle, a policy that significantly lowers the transportation costs of final goods may, under certain conditions, lead to a long-run reduction in regional inequality.

For policy makers in developing countries these standard models of geography may prove inadequate guides for understanding regional inequality in developing countries. Most of these models are static and do not contain elements of a structural shift in economic activities from agriculture to manufacturing and services, one of the hallmarks of development. Puga (1999) shows that the extent of regional inequality may be limited by manufacturing firms' ability to recruit workers from the agricultural sector. Thus the potential for agglomeration depends critically on the labor mobility of workers between the two sectors. Murata (2002, forthcoming) shows that the level of regional inequality may be constrained by consumer expenditure patterns.[8] Regional inequality generally rises as an economy shifts from agriculture to manufacturing; the degree of the shift may depend on

---

6 See Krugman and Venables (1995), Venables (1996), and Puga (1999). Puga (1999) presents the most general version of the model; Krugman and Venables (1995) and Venables (1996) are derived as special cases. Puga's model is similar to that of Krugman (1991b) in that it has two regions and two goods (agricultural and manufacturing). The agricultural good is homogenous and is produced using labor and land under constant returns to scale in a perfectly competitive market; land is immobile; agricultural goods are freely mobile; consumers have Spence-Dixit-Stiglitz preferences for varieties; and goods are produced with scale economies and can be used both as final consumption goods or intermediate goods for use in the same industry, as in Ethier (1982). This specification captures the idea of forward and backward linkages in the sense of Hirschman (1958).

7 As Puga (1999, p. 324) notes, "At high trade costs firms want to be where final demand is, so they split between regions. At intermediate levels of trade costs firms cluster to exploit cost and demand linkages. However, without interregional labour mobility, agglomeration opens wage differences. At low levels of trade costs, firms want to be where immobile factors are cheaper, so they spread across regions again."

8 Murata models the structural shift from agriculture to manufacturing by introducing nonhomothetic preferences, which, by invoking Engel's law, shift consumer demand from agricultural to manufacturing goods. In this model the preindustrial economy is defined by prohibitive interregional transportation costs. As transportation costs fall with development, the extent of the market increases for manufactured goods and consumers' purchasing power rises as prices fall. Initially, at low demand for manufactures (as a result of low agglomeration economies) manufacturing remains dispersed. As transportation costs continue to fall further, however, the increase in expenditure shares in manufacturing leads to agglomeration forces sufficient enough to create a pattern of core and periphery.

the rapidity with which consumers increase their expenditure shares in manufacturing.

Theories of Urban Inequality

Urban inequality and regional inequality are highly interdependent. Although few models of urban inequality do not address regional inequality, urban inequality affects regional inequality in a variety of ways. First, the well-known urban–rural wage gap leads to regional inequality if there are regional differences in the rates of urbanization; this increase may contribute to growing regional inequality. Second, urban specialization in different industries may contribute to regional inequality if regions possess different types of cities. Third, the size distribution of cities influences regional inequality. If cities are uniformly small, urbanization is likely to have limited impact on regional inequality. However, if cities differ in size, as they usually do, urban inequality may have a major impact on regional inequality. For example, urban primacy or the concentration of a significant share of the urban population in a few central cities will cause regional inequality. Thus policies that reduce the importance of urban primacy are likely to contribute to greater regional equality.

Theories of urban inequality differ from those of regional inequality in one important respect: the treatment of land. Whereas the regional immobility of factors constrains regional inequality by limiting agglomeration economies, the most important limiting factor for urban scale or inequality is the cost of congestion associated with land. As firms and workers concentrate in one urban location to take advantage of agglomeration economies, they bid up land rents.[9] The optimal city size is determined by the balance between agglomeration economies and congestion costs.

In Henderson's (1974) classic model of the systems of cities, the balance of centripetal forces of Marshallian externalities and centrifugal forces of land rents and commuting costs determine the size distribution of cities. Because externalities are assumed to be industry specific (localization economies), a city specializes in a single industry and its size is determined by the strength of its Marshallian externalities. From this theoretical perspective, urban inequality is likely to rise if localization economies are particularly strong in a few industries and likely to fall if congestion costs are more significant relative to agglomeration forces.

In more recent model of cities, Abdel-Rahman and Fujita (1990) show that if the centripetal force is changed from Marshallian externalities to the Spence-Dixit-Stigliz-Ethier type of pecuniary externalities, similar results in terms of the size distribution of cities arise. In their model city sizes and

---

9   Duranton and Puga (2004) provide a useful list of categories of urban agglomeration economies based on economies of sharing, matching, and learning. The sharing category includes sharing of indivisibilities in the provision of public goods and facilities, the gains from variety, and the gains from individual specialization and risk. The matching category includes improving quality and the chances of matches. The learning category includes knowledge generation, diffusion, and accumulation.

wages are positively related to a variety of intermediate inputs. Unlike in Henderson's (1988) model, however, cities are not of optimal sizes. Urban inequality may rise if the strength of spillovers from forward and backward linkages is significant and concentrated in a few industries.

These two models provide different motivations for why cities specialize or diversify in different industries. In the Henderson (1974) type of model, the nature of Marshallian externalities determines the types of cities. If externalities are of the localization type (specific to industries), cities are likely to be specialized; if externalities are of the urbanization type (specific to cities), cities are likely to be diverse.

In the urban models based on the Spence-Dixit-Stigliz-Ethier type of pecuniary externalities, Abdel-Rahman (1996) shows that the extent of urban specialization or diversification may be a function of intercity transportation costs. When intercity transportation costs are low, cities specialize, in order to take advantage of the agglomeration economies from a greater variety of nontraded inputs; when intercity transportation costs are high, cities become diversified, in order to economize on transportation costs. Thus like regional specialization, urban specialization may be limited by intercity transportation and local congestion costs.

Like the standard models of regional inequality, these models of urban inequality are likely to prove inadequate guides to policy makers for understanding urban inequality in developing countries. Except in the model of Puga (1998), there is no rural–urban interaction or consideration of a structural shift in economic activities from agriculture in rural areas to manufacturing and services in cities. These urban models thus seem disconnected from the classic urban models of development, such as Lewis (1954) and Harris and Todaro (1970). In Lewis (1954) the assumption of an elastic supply of unskilled labor from rural areas fuels industrial development in cities. In Harris and Todaro (1970) rural–urban migration is caused by a politically determined minimum wage in cities. It may result in ex post poor outcomes for migrants if they do not obtain jobs in the formal sector but become unemployed in the informal sector.

In the standard models discussed above, the urban–rural wage gap is determined by the forces of agglomeration economies and diseconomies and transportation costs. Building on the basics of the Harris-Todaro (1970) model, Rauch (1993) provides a different rationale for why urban–rural wage gaps arise. In his model there are two urban sectors (formal and informal) and one rural sector. Wages are highest in the formal urban sector and lowest in the informal urban sector. Ex ante a rural worker will migrate to the city if the expected income is higher in the city; ex post the rural worker will be better off only if he or she lands a job in the former sector. Uncertainties in labor search may thus contribute to the urban–rural wage gap.

Rauch shows that urban inequality may follow an inverted-U pattern, in the spirit of Kuznets (1955). In the early phase of development, when the population is mostly rural, rural incomes are relatively low. Consequently, rural agents are willing to risk underemployment in the informal sector in the hope of landing a higher wage in the formal urban sector job. Because income inequality between the formal and informal urban jobs is higher than inequality between the formal urban and rural sectors, the initial rise in urbanization increases income inequality. However, as the rural population decreases with urbanization, urban–rural wage differentials decline and urbanization rates fall. Rural agents are less willing to incur the risks of underemployment in the informal sector, and income inequality declines.

Trade and Spatial Inequality

Globalization may increase or decrease spatial inequality. In principle, its impact on spatial inequality is the same as that of domestic trade, as discussed above. To the extent that some regions may benefit more from external trade than others, international trade may increase regional spatial inequality. From a neoclassical perspective, unless regions and their cities have identical exposure to trade and similar comparative advantage, foreign trade is likely to increase spatial inequality. Regions and cities that have natural resources for exports or natural advantages, such as proximity to rivers, coasts, and transportation networks, are likely to benefit from external trade, whereas those in remote areas are not.

From an increasing returns perspective, spatial inequality is likely to rise because some regions may capture the benefits of increasing returns from foreign trade while others remain more reliant on domestic trade. Puga and Venables (1999) suggest that under certain circumstances, however, trade liberalization may reduce regional and urban spatial inequality over time in sequential regional waves.[10] Initially, industries concentrate in one region. When the wage gap widens between this region and poorer regions, industry migrates toward one of the poor regions. As a result of agglomeration economies, the migration will be concentrated in only one of these regions. Over time, as the process continues, more poor regions will join the group. Puga and Venables find that both import-substitution policies (increases in tariffs) and trade liberalization (decreases in tariffs) can be used to attract industries for underdeveloped regions but that welfare levels are higher under the trade liberalization scenario.

Using a simple three-location model (two domestic cities and the rest of the world), Krugman and Livas Elizondo (1996) show that foreign trade may also reduce urban inequality. In their model the forces of urban inequality—the centripetal forces of backward and forward linkages—are counterbalanced by the centrifugal forces of commuting costs and land rents. When tariff rates are prohibitively high, the stable equilibrium is the concentration of manufacturing in one primate city. Under this setting the concentration of domestic firms and workers in one city produces sufficiently strong forward and backward linkages to offset the costs of urban congestion. When trade is liberalized, centripetal forces decline, causing

---

10 Puga and Venables's (1999) model is based on the increasing returns model of Krugman and Venables (1995) and Puga (1999).

manufacturing to disperse to the other city. Trade liberalization thus causes the primate city to decline, increasing urban equality.

Institutions and Spatial Inequality

Institutions matter not just for growth and development but also for spatial inequality. Most recent studies focus on understanding the impact of institutions on national development and growth (Engerman and Sokoloff 1997; Acemoglu, Johnson, and Robinson (2001, 2002, 2004), but regional differences in the quality of institutions may also affect economic development within countries, as Banerjee and Iyer (2005), Kapur and Kim (2006), Bruhn and Gallego (2007), and Kim (2007b) show. Political institutions that determine the distribution of power and fiscal resources across federal, state, and local governments can also play major roles in determining spatial inequality (Henderson 2002; Kim 2008).

Scholars have proposed a variety of explanations for why countries or regions possess different institutions. They include accidents of history (North 1990); factor endowments (Engerman and Sokoloff 1997); and climate and native population density (Acemoglu, Johnson, and Robinson 2001, 2002). While differences in the institutions of regions within a country may be more difficult to sustain than those at the international level, regional differences persist even after these differences have been removed.

Especially in developing countries, political institutions are likely to contribute to urban inequality if property rights are easier to establish and defend in cities, where one has access to the legal system. Political corruption and instability may also contribute to urban inequality in the form of urban primacy if proximity to a primate city makes it easier to shield oneself from the threat of violence, to make illegal bribes easier to conceal, or to gain access to information and communication. In a simplified model, Ades and Glaeser (1995) show that the benefits of political primacy are likely to be higher under dictatorships than democracies.

Federalism (the balance of political power among the federal, state, and local jurisdictions) is also likely to matter greatly for spatial inequality. Until the second half of the 20th century, the United States had a weak federal government that gave significant political power to the states and local governments. This American-style federalism is likely to have contributed to spatial equality over time (Kim 2008).[11] In contrast, many countries in Latin America emerged from colonialism with strong federal but weak local governments (Sokoloff and Zolt 2006). Latin American–style federalism is likely to have contributed significantly to spatial inequality over time.

---

11 With the signing of the Constitution, the United States emerged with a relatively weak federal government but strong state governments and an emphasis on states' rights. Between 1850 and 1900, local municipal governments came to dominate government expenditures. In the 20th century the state and federal government became increasingly important over time. American-style federalism still gives significant political and economic power to local and state governments (Kim 2008).

Effect of Household Income Inequality on Spatial Inequality

One of the most important topics of interest in development economics is income inequality, but there is little discussion of the potential relation between spatial inequality and household income inequality. In theory, household income inequality can increase without an increase in spatial inequality if the rise in inequality is solely intraregional. In practice, an increase in spatial inequality is likely to contribute to an increase in household income inequality. Indeed, Kuznets's (1955) argument for the existence of the inverted-U pattern of household income inequality contained a strong geographic component and inspired Williamson's (1965) inverted-U pattern of regional inequality.

For Kuznets the rise in household income inequality with development is caused by a structural shift in the economy from agriculture to manufacturing industries. Kuznets identifies two forces increasing household inequality. First, savings inequality rises, raising increasing income inequality. Second, because household income inequality is higher in urban manufacturing than in rural agriculture, by the logic of industry decomposition identity, the industrial shift leads to higher income inequality. Kuznets argues that as economies mature, the dynamics of the growing economy worked against these forces of household inequality. These dynamics include efforts by governments to reduce the accumulation of the savings of the very wealthy; demographic factors, such as immigration, which reduce the size of the top income bracket; the democratic nature of capitalism, which favors the widening of the entrepreneurial class; and the gradual shift into services, which compresses incomes.

Lindert and Williamson (1985) discuss a number of forces that may be correlated with long-run income equality. Among the most interesting is the following demographic theory. In the early phase of the industrial revolution, there is an elastic supply of agrarian workers (Lewis 1954), who suppress the wages of unskilled industrial workers. Higher fertility, lower infant mortality, and immigration may also lower the wages of unskilled workers during the early industrial period. As the incomes of skilled workers rise, income inequality increases. Later, as the industrial revolution matures and the level of skills per member of the labor force rises, the wages of skilled and unskilled workers converge, causing a decline in income inequality.

Evidence on Spatial Inequality

What does the evidence on regional and urban spatial inequality show? This section begins by briefly describing the measurement of regional and urban spatial inequality. It then presents evidence on regional spatial inequality in developing and developed countries, urban spatial inequality, the relation between regional and urban spatial inequality, and long-run trends. The last three subsections examine empirical evidence on the impact of trade and institutions on spatial inequality and on the relation between household income inequality and spatial inequality.

Measuring Spatial Inequality

The location Gini coefficient is the simplest and most widely used measure for measuring regional inequality (Krugman 1991a). As in the Gini coefficient used to measure household income inequality, its locational counterpart measures the extent to which geographic activity is concentrated.[12]

In recent years several important alternative measures have been proposed. Because an industry may be geographically concentrated for random reasons if it contains a small number of very large firms, Ellison and Glaeser (1997) propose an alternative measure that corrects for an industry's scale economy (also see Maurel and Sédillot 1999). Because regional units are geographically coarse units of observation, Duranton and Overman (2005) develop a distance-based measure that uses the Euclidian distance between every pair of establishments. Brülhart and Traeger (2005) suggest using entropy indices, which are decomposable into within- and between-region components.

To measure urban inequality, scholars have focused on urban productivity and the size distribution of cities. Because wages and productivity are generally positively correlated with city sizes, differences in wages and productivity measure urban inequality. Urban inequality is also often measured using the rank-size distribution of cities. In particular, urban primacy or the concentration of the urban population in the largest cities is often used as a measure of urban inequality. Unfortunately, no measure relates urban inequality with regional inequality.

Evidence on Regional Spatial Inequality

Studies on regional inequality are challenging to summarize, because they differ across many dimensions, such as indices of geographic concentration and geographic units of observation, as well as in their theoretical motivation and empirical specification. In addition, given the difficulty of constructing regional inequality measures that are comparable across many countries, there is no international cross-sectional or panel analysis similar to that used in the urban inequality literature (see below) or the household income literature. As a result, the literature on regional inequality is dominated by country-specific studies.

Because of the scarcity of reliable census data, the evidence for developing countries is often based on survey data. Perhaps because of poor data quality or greater variance in the economic circumstances of developing countries, the evidence on spatial inequality varies widely across countries. In contrast, although there are important variations in the level of spatial inequality, the industrial patterns of spatial localization are fairly similar across many developed countries.

---

12 For a detailed discussion on the properties of the Gini coefficient in the context of household income inequality, see Ray (1998).

Regional inequality in developing countries.

The most striking pattern that emerges from the data on the spatial inequality of developing countries is its varied nature. Country-specific geographic and political factors may play a disproportionately large role in shaping the patterns of spatial inequality in developing countries.[13]

In countries as diverse as China and Mexico, trends in spatial inequality seem to have fluctuated over time until the late 20th century, when inequality rose sharply in both countries. In China inequality rose markedly during the period of the Great Leap Forward and the Great Famine (1952–60), fell during the recovery period, rose during the Cultural Revolution period (1967–76), and fell again during the period of rural reform. Inequality rose substantially with decentralization and the sharp rise in international trade in the 1984–2000 period (Kanbur and Zhang 2005), during which time intraprovince inequality in household incomes and wages rose (Knight, Shi, and Renwei 2006).

In Mexico north-south regional disparities were fairly high in 1970, fell between 1970 and 1985, and rose substantially between 1985 and 1990 (Rodriguez-Pose and Sanchez-Reaza 2005). When Mexico's government imposed high trade barriers as part of its import-substitution industrialization strategy, industrial employment was concentrated in Mexico City. As trade liberalized, industrial activity shifted to the U.S.-Mexico border (Hanson 1997). Hanson (2007) finds that globalization in the 1990s increased geographic labor income inequalities as incomes in states with high exposure to trade benefited relative to those in states with low exposure to trade.

Inequality within regions appears to be as significant as inequality across regions in many countries. Regional inequality rose in the Czech Republic, Hungary, Poland, and the Russian Federation in the 1990s; it was highest in Russia and lowest in Poland (Forster, Jesuit, and Smeeding 2005). The data suggest that the main source of inequality was intraregional rather than interregional variation. In Ecuador, Madagascar, and Mozambique, within-community or intraregional inequality was just as important as between-community or interregional inequality. Elbers and others (2005) find that in all these countries there are considerable variations in inequality across communities and that geographic location is a good predictor of local-level inequality even after controlling for some basic demographic and economic characteristics.

In some countries, such as Brazil, regional spatial inequality was significant but declined between 1981 and 1997 (Azzoni, Menezes-Filho, and Menezes 2005); in other countries regional inequality was stable at relatively low levels. In Peru regional inequality measured using expenditure

---

13 The World Institute for Development Economics Research Project of the United Countries University entitled "Spatial Disparities in Human Development," directed by Ravi Kanbur and Anthony Venables, presents evidence on the extent of spatial inequality in more than 50 developing countries (Kanbur and Venables, 2005a, 2005b). That evidence suggests that spatial inequality increased in many developing countries in recent years.

and literacy was low and remained relatively low between 1972 and 1993 (Escobal and Torero 2005). Regional spatial inequality appears to have declined in the Philippines between 1985 and 2000 (Balisacan and Fuwa 2006), in Indonesia between 1984 and 1999 (Friedman 2005), and in South Africa between 1990 and 2000 (Naude and Krugell 2003).

Regional inequality in developed countries.

The cross-country evidence on regional spatial inequality is much more robust and consistent in developed countries, where the main source of spatial inequality seems to be geographic differences in industrial concentration. Because some industries, such as textiles, are much more geographically concentrated than industries such as food or electrical machinery, spatial inequality is caused by the spatial variations in concentrated industries. Other industries, such as agriculture and mining, tend to contribute to spatial inequality (because natural resources are distributed unequally). In contrast, most services, especially those that serve local markets, tend to reduce spatial inequality.

There is considerable evidence for a long-run inverted-U pattern of regional inequality in the United States, especially in the manufacturing sector. Kim (1995) finds that U.S. regions became more specialized or unequal between the mid-19th and the turn of the 20th century before becoming significantly despecialized in the second half of the 20th century. Similar results are obtained from industrial localization patterns over time. Based on the locational Gini coefficient at the two- and three-digit industry level, Kim (1995) finds that manufacturing industries became more localized between 1890 and the turn of the 20th century but then became significantly more dispersed during the second half of the 20th century.[14] At every point in time, traditional low-tech industries, such as textiles, apparel, and tobacco, were much more localized than medium- to high-tech industries, such as electricity and transportation. Consequently, the gradual shift in manufacturing from low-tech to high-tech industries contributed to the general dispersal of manufacturing over time.

For the aggregate economy, there is some evidence for an inverted-U pattern that peaked a little earlier. Kim (1998) investigates the patterns of regional specialization in all sectors (agriculture, manufacturing, and services). Regional specialization by crops in agriculture rose over time, but the shift in economic activity from agriculture to manufacturing and then to services contributed to a significant convergence in regional industrial structures. The divergence in industrial structures between the north, which specialized in manufacturing, and the south, which specialized in agriculture, accounts for about half of the regional divergence in wages. Regional convergence in wages was significantly correlated with regional convergence in industrial structures.

---

14 Kim (1995) points out that as one moves from two- to four-digit industries, the finer classification of industries is likely to contribute to an apparent rise in localization of industries as a result of simply defining industries more narrowly.

For a more recent period, Ellison and Glaeser (1997) show that even after controlling for the size distribution of plants and the size distribution of geographic areas, industry localization is prevalent for a large majority of industries. At the four-digit industry level, they find that industries such as tobacco, textiles, and leather are most localized and that industries such as furniture and fixtures; paper, printing, and publishing; petroleum and coal; rubber and plastics; stone, clay, and glass; industrial machinery; and instruments are dispersed. Although Ellison and Glaeser use a different index, the patterns of industry localization they find are similar to those found by Kim (1995). At a more aggregate level, Holmes and Stevens (2004) show that mining industries are most localized, followed by construction and manufacturing; services, such as wholesale trade, retail trade, finance, insurance, and real estate, are least localized. The growth of services is thus likely to lead to greater convergence in incomes across regions.

The apparent stable empirical relation in the localization patterns across industries and over time masks the dynamic nature of the spatial economy. New firms are born, old firms die, and existing firms expand/open new plants or contract/close old plants. Dumais, Ellison, and Glaeser (2002) show that geographic concentration (measured by the Ellison-Glaeser index) fell from 0.039 in 1972 to 0.034 in 1992. The variations in the plant life cycle contributed significantly to the variations in the geographic concentration of U.S. manufacturing industries over this period. New firm births accounted for three-fourths of the geographic deconcentration over the 20-year period, as more firms established themselves away from centers of industry. In contrast, firm deaths increased geographic concentration, because the rate of firm closure was higher in the periphery.

Duranton and Overman (2005) show that the level of localization in the United Kingdom depends on the way localization is measured. Using the Ellison-Glaeser index, they find that 94 percent of U.K. industries are localized; using a distance measure, they find that 51 percent of industries are localized, 26 percent are dispersed, and 23 percent do not deviate significantly from randomness. Industry localization patterns at the four-digit industry level in the United Kingdom differ slightly from those in the United States. Textiles, publishing, instruments, and appliances are most localized, whereas food and beverages, wood, petroleum, and minerals are most dispersed. Crafts and Mulatu (2006) find that industry localization and regional specialization in the United Kingdom remained relatively stable over a surprisingly long period (1841–1911).[15]

Maurel and Sédillot (1999) use a slight variation of the Ellison-Glaeser index to investigate geographic concentration in France in 1993. They find that 27 percent of industries at the four-digit industry level were very localized, 23 percent were moderately localized, and about half displayed a low degree of concentration. The most localized industries were extractive industries (such as iron ore, coal, and shipbuilding) and traditional indus-

---

15 Tirado, Paluzie, and Pons (2002) find that the geographic concentration of industries in Spain rose markedly during its industrial period (1856–93), causing a sharp rise in regional inequality.

tries (such as leather, textiles, and printing and publishing). The least localized industries were motor vehicles, sound recording and reproducing apparatus, farm machinery, electronic components, rubber products, metal work for construction, and nonferrous metals. Surprisingly, Maurel and Sédillot find a correlation between the U.S. and French industry localization of 0.60. The main outliers were furniture and transportation, which were significantly more localized in the United States, and printing and publishing, which were more localized in France.

Midelfart-Knarvik and others (2000) provide a useful summary of the patterns of regional inequality and industry localization for Europe as whole for the period 1970–95. Europe reveals less regional specialization or inequality than the United States, and European industries are generally more dispersed. Surprisingly, however, regional inequality in per capita income is higher in Europe (Puga 2002), for reasons that are not clear.

The trends in European regional industrial inequality seem to differ from those in regional income inequality as well. In most European countries, the industrial structure converged during the 1970s, reversed the trend in the early 1980s, and then diverged significantly in the 1990s. European regional per capita income converged between 1950 and 1980 and then stopped converging between 1980 and 1995. When the regional incomes are decomposed in greater detail, however, the evidence shows that regional inequalities widened significantly between 1980 and 1995 but that the divergence was counterbalanced by a substantial convergence in inequalities across countries (Puga 2002).

Midelfart-Knarvik and others (2000) find that the location of many industries changed significantly between 1970 and 1995. Many slow-growing, labor-intensive industries were initially dispersed but became more concentrated over time in peripheral low-wage regions. About half of the geographically concentrated industries remained concentrated over time, but many medium- to high-tech industries in high-growth sectors became more dispersed across Europe. As in the United States, services were generally more dispersed than manufacturing, so that the shift from manufacturing to services contributed to the general decrease in regional inequality in Europe.

Evidence on Urban Spatial Inequality

One of the most basic measures of urban inequality is the urban–rural wage gap. Because urban wages are typically higher than rural wages, urbanization introduces spatial inequality in wages and incomes between cities and rural areas as well as across cities of different sizes. Summarizing the evidence from numerous studies that estimate the level of urbanization economies, Rosenthal and Strange (2004) conclude that productivity increases about 3–8 percent as a city's size doubles. Glaeser and Maré (2001) find that U.S. workers in cities earn one-third more than those in rural areas. Wheeler (2004) and Kim (2006), among others, also find an urban wage premium.

Given these findings, the recent urban experience in Africa presents a puzzle. Because cities are associated with higher wages and productivity, urbanization is usually correlated with income growth.[16] However, between 1970 and 1995 Africa's per capita GDP fell 0.66 percent a year while its urban population grew 5.3 percent a year (Fay and Opal 2000). Is Africa's urbanization caused by noneconomic factors, such as war, ethnic conflict, or bright lights, rather than by urban agglomeration economies and higher productivity?

Fay and Opal (2000) argue that Africa's level of urbanization is not altogether different from countries with similar levels of income and economic structure. They suggest that because Africa was underurbanized during the colonial period, the recent surge in urbanization without growth may be accounted for by a catching-up hypothesis. Kessides (2005) also argues that urbanization in Africa is not excessive or imbalanced but that urbanization in the region—as well as in Latin America and the Caribbean, the Middle East and North Africa, and South Asia—seems only weakly correlated with industrialization. Urbanization in these regions seems to be fueled by growth in the informal service sector.

Barrios, Bertinelli, and Strobl (2006) find that rural migrants to cities were not pulled by these jobs but rather were pushed out of their rural locations. The lack of rainfall between 1960 and 1990 significantly dampened agricultural productivity in rural Sub-Saharan Africa, pushing farmers into cities. McCormick and Wahba (2003) find that returning international migrants bring greater savings into Egypt's urban areas than to its rural areas, further widening spatial inequalities.

The distribution of city sizes by population provides another important alternative measure for urban spatial inequality.[17] Urban inequality is greater when the urban population is concentrated in a few of the country's largest cities; it is much lower if the population is evenly distributed across cities large and small. While the estimates are often sensitive to the definition of a city, Rosen and Resnick (1980) find that a large majority of countries possess city-size distributions that favor smaller cities; urban inequality seems moderate for a majority of countries. There seems to be some evidence that urban inequality is greater in developing countries, however. Soo (2005) finds that size distribution is significantly skewed toward larger cities in Colombia, Ecuador, Guatemala, Jordan, Kenya, the Republic of Korea, Malaysia, Morocco, Mozambique, and Saudi Arabia; it is skewed toward smaller cities in most developed countries, including Belgium, Canada, Denmark, the United Kingdom, and the United States.

---

16 Henderson (2002) finds that variations in GDP per capita explain 70 percent of the cross-country variation in urbanization (also see Fay and Opal 2000).

17 There are two standard measures of urban spatial inequality: rank-size distribution (or Zipf's Law) and urban primacy. The most common distribution is the Pareto distribution: $R = \alpha C^{-\beta}$, where R is the rank of an urban area or the number of urban areas with population C or more; C is the population of the urban area; and α and β are constants. The distribution is typically estimated in the following log form: $\log(R) = \log(\alpha) - \beta \log(C)$. If β equals 1, city sizes are deemed to be evenly distributed; if β is greater (less) than 1, city sizes are skewed toward smaller (larger) cities. Urban primacy is calculated using the share of the urban population in the largest city or cities or the ratio of the largest city to the sum of the top 5 or top 50 cities.

Urban inequality measured using primacy may also be higher in developing countries, and its relation may not be linear. Using metropolitan areas that account for 70 percent of the total urban population, Wheaton and Shishido (1981) examine urban concentration in 38 countries at varying levels of development, based on two different measures, a Hirfindel index and urban primacy. They find that as per capita GNP initially rose across countries, urban inequality rose until income passed $2,000 per capita, after which it declined. Rosen and Resnick (1980) show that urban inequality can be consistently measured using both the size distribution of cities and a variety of measures of primacy.

Comparisons of Regional and Urban Economic Structures

Considerable evidence supports the view that urban development is fundamentally linked to regional development. Cities are highly specialized in a few identifiable industries that form their export base (Alexandersson 1959; Bergsman, Greenston, and Healy 1975). Based on cluster analysis using 229 U.S. industries in 1970, Henderson (1988) finds evidence for specialized cities in the automobile, textiles, food-processing, aircraft, apparel, steel, leather, industrial machinery, and other industries. Black and Henderson (2003) classify city specialization by two-digit industry in 1992. They find that while about 65 percent of the local labor force is typically engaged in "nontraded" good activity, the remaining labor force is specialized into 55 distinct clusters. Large cities that form market centers are more diverse.

Cities within a region are more likely to be specialized in the same set of industries. All 12 of the automobile cities Henderson (1988) studies were located in the East-North-Central region, and all six of the textile cities were located in the South. Using data for the earlier industrial period in the United States (1880–1920), Kim (2000) finds that industrial cities within a particular region were specialized in the same set of industries, suggesting strong regional geographic ties for cities. In any given region, however, the largest cities were more diversified and seemed to possess a disproportionate share of employment in transaction services, indicating their role as regional (and national) centers of markets for financial services and trade.

Long-Run Trends in Regional and Urban Spatial Inequality

How does the level of spatial inequality evolve over time with economic development? While the information is based on small cross-national samples, there seems to be some evidence of a spatial Kuznets curve: regional and urban spatial inequalities increase as economies develop, then diminish as they grow and mature. Williamson (1965) finds that middle-income countries have higher regional income inequality than low- and high-income countries. Wheaton and Shishido (1981) show that urban concentration peaks at a population of about 20 million as annual per capita income rises to $2,000 (in 1976 dollars) but that urban deconcentration begins as income rises beyond that level. Using a much larger panel data of countries, Henderson (2002) estimates that urban primacy increases up to $5,300, the approximate mean in world per capita GDP for 1990, before declining thereafter.

Studies based on the size distribution of cities seem to suggest that growth and development often occur with little change in urban inequality (Gabaix and Ioannides 2004). Eaton and Eckstein (1997) study the size distribution of cities in France and Japan in the period during which each country experienced its industrial revolution. Despite the great increase in urbanization during industrialization, the rank-size distribution of cities in both countries remained surprisingly stable. Eaton and Eckstein argue that because cities of all sizes seem to grow in parallel, the driving forces of industrialization seem to be present in cities in proportion to their initial populations. Dobkins and Ioannides (2000) report similar findings for the United States for the 1900–90 period (also see Black and Henderson 2003). Similar studies for developing countries do not appear to have been conducted.

Evidence on Trade and Spatial Inequality

The evidence on the impact of foreign trade on domestic regional and urban inequality is mixed. While much more evidence is needed, there seems to be some evidence that trade openness contributes to increasing regional inequality. Kanbur and Zhang (2005) find that the recent sharp increase in inequality in China may partly reflect growth in trade; Rodriquez-Pose and Sanchez-Reaza (2005) find similar evidence for Mexico.

Based on their survey of the evidence for more than 50 developing countries, Kanbur and Venables (2005a, 2005b) argue that the uneven spatial impact of trade and globalization played a major role in the increase in regional and urban spatial inequalities in developing countries in recent years. They argue that in addition to geographic remoteness, backward regions and rural areas suffer from an inequitable distribution of infrastructure, public services, and policies that constrains the free migration of people from backward places.

Numerous scholars believe that development in Africa is significantly held back by geographic remoteness. The fact that many African countries are landlocked and isolated, possess rugged terrain, and face high transportation costs hinders trade and productive activities.[18]

Some evidence seems to suggest that openness to trade reduces urban inequality, at least as measured by urban primacy. Based on a cross-section of 85 countries and 5 case studies, Ades and Glaeser (1995) find that a shift in a nation's workforce away from agriculture to industry increases urban primacy, but openness to trade and development of transportation networks reduces primacy, as Krugman and Livas Elizondo (1996) also claim. Using a panel data of 85 countries for 1960–90, Henderson (2002) also finds that primacy is negatively correlated with openness to trade and to transportation and communication infrastructure networks (waterway, road, and telephone densities).

---

18 Nunn and Puga (2007) suggest an important historical reason why populations may have concentrated in remote and rugged areas in Africa. According to them, such areas provided protection against slave raids. This short-term benefit may have increased the long-term costs of development in Africa by encouraging population concentration in rugged areas.

Evidence on Institutions and Spatial Inequality

The empirical evidence on the importance of institutions for regional and urban inequality is limited but growing. In the United States spatial inequalities, especially between the North and the South, rose between 1840 and 1920 and then declined significantly between 1920 and 2000 (Kim and Margo 2004). While the rise of the North–South core-periphery regions is often seen as a consequence of economic factors (Krugman 1991a, 1991b), many scholars believe that institutional factors played a major role in the divergence and later convergence of the North and the South in the United States (Acemoglu, Johnson, and Robinson 2004). Although the roots of regional divergence date back to the colonial period (Kim 2007b), Mitchener and McLean (2003) find that institutional impediments in states associated with slavery had a persistent pernicious effect on productivity well into the 20th century. The convergence of political institutions following the Civil War and major federal interventions also likely contributed to the economic convergence between the two regions.

Institutions from the colonial era seem to continue to exert considerable influence within regions in developing countries. Banerjee and Iyer (2005) argue that British colonial institutions played a major role in the divergence of agricultural productivity between the historically landlord (*zamindari*) and nonlandlord (*ryotwari*) areas in India between 1960 and 1990.[19] Kapur and Kim (2006) suggest that the British land tax institutions may have contributed to the divergence of India's regional economies during the British colonial period as well. For a sample of eight countries in the Americas, Bruhn and Gallego (2007) find that regions that possessed colonial extractive industries and sugar cultivation have 18 percent lower per capita GDP today as a result.

There is some evidence that decentralized federalism promotes regional and urban equality. Developed countries are more likely than developing countries to have a decentralized federalist system. Henderson (2002) finds that developed countries are more politically decentralized than developing countries. Fiscal decentralization is also positively correlated with population size and land area; it is negatively correlated with the share of the population that is Muslim (Oats 1985; Epple and Nechyba 2004). The nature of the federalist system is likely to depend greatly on the nature of the tax system. Sokoloff and Zolt (2006) show that developing countries are much

---

19 When the British colonized and annexed various parts of India during the eighteenth and nineteenth centuries, they implemented two major land tax systems: *zamindari* (landlord) and *ryotwari* (nonlandlord). In the *zamindari* areas of Bengal, Bihar, Central Province, Orissa, and some parts of Madras, land taxes and property rights were assigned to landlords. In these areas nonresident landlords often owned rights to numerous villages and developed extensive bureaucratic organizations and policing forces to employ and manage local villagers to farm the land under sharecropping or wage contracts. By contrast, in the *ryotwari* areas, land taxes and property rights were assigned to individual villagers in Assam, Bombay, and most of Madras or to an entire village under the *mahalwari* system in parts of the Punjab. In these areas local resident landowners either farmed their own land or employed low-caste village laborers under sharecropping or wage contracts.

more likely than developed countries to impose taxes at the national rather than the state and local level.

In China the strong political power at the provincial level may have contributed to excessive spatial equality. China's politics of localism, strong provincial governments, severe migration restrictions (the *houkou* system), and administrative spatial hierarchy played a major role in determining regional and urban spatial inequality (Henderson 1988; Fujita and others 2004). Because of these political institutions, most economists believe that China's spatial inequality suffers from too little rather than too much inequality. Moreover, policies that restrict urban growth, such as immigration restrictions and national urban planning, have kept cities in China too small. Relative to most developing and developed countries, cities in China are small and are more equally distributed (Fujita and others 2004). A decentralized federalist system may have increased spatial and urban equality in the United States, but it did so to a much lesser extent than such policies did in China (Kim 2008). In Latin America generally strong federal and weak local governments may have contributed to excessive regional and urban inequality.

The empirical evidence on urban primacy suggests that political factors may be the dominant cause of primacy. Ades and Glaeser (1995) find that dictatorships and political instability cause a significant increase in the concentration of population in the primate city. Henderson (2002) finds that primacy is positively correlated with capital city status and central government consumption. He also finds that countries in Asia, Latin America, and Sub-Saharan Africa had significantly higher shares of population in primate cities than countries in other regions, suggesting the important impact of political institutions on urban concentration.

Household Income Inequality and Spatial Inequality

Although income inequality is a major focus of development economics, there is little systematic evidence on the relation between household income inequality and spatial inequality (Ray 1998). Superficially, Kuznets's (1955) inverted-U pattern of household income inequality seems to be related to Williamson's (1965) inverted-U pattern of regional income inequality. However, with the construction of Deininger and Squire's (1996) large cross-country data set on income inequality, the existence of the Kuznets curve has come into question.[20] Indeed, some scholars, such as Persson and Tabellini

---

20 Banerjee and Duflo (2003) present a cautionary critique of the literature on income inequality and development that may also be relevant for research on spatial inequality. While most cross-sectional ordinary least squares (OLS) estimates using cross-country data typically show a negative correlation between household income inequality and growth, those using panel data with fixed-effects show a positive correlation. In addition, most studies on inequality assume a linear structure. Banerjee and Duflo find that the relation between inequality and growth is likely to be nonlinear and that the reason for the variations in the results of OLS, fixed-effects, and random-effects models may be caused by the differing structural explanations of the reduced-form results.

(1994) and Alesina and Rodrik (1994), believe that the causality is reversed: inequality is likely to hamper economic growth as a result of political economy considerations (Ferreira 1999). Further research is needed to clarify the relation between income inequality and spatial inequality.

Policy Lessons

The literature does not provide specific policy recommendations for reducing "excessive" spatial inequality or increasing "beneficial" spatial inequality. It does provide some general guidelines and lessons.

Industry Localization

It may be possible to identify the proximate causes of spatial inequality by studying trends in the regional industrial economy. One of the most consistent empirical findings is the industrial patterns of localization and dispersion, especially in developed countries, where there seems to be a fairly robust and consistent industrial pattern of spatial agglomerations and inequality. Consistent with this finding is the idea that industry localization economies (within-industry spillovers) are generally more important than urbanization economies (across-industry spillovers). Thus at least in principle, policy makers may be able to affect spatial inequality by targeting industry-specific subsidies or infrastructure investments.

From the broad sectoral perspective, the most geographically concentrated industries tend to be extractive industries (agriculture and mining), followed by manufacturing and then services, which tends to be most dispersed. Within the manufacturing sector, studies on industry localization in the European Union, France, the United Kingdom, the United States, and many developing countries suggest that traditional industries, such as textiles and apparel, are much more likely to be spatially localized. In contrast, medium- to high-tech industries are much more likely to be dispersed. Numerous studies also find that localization rather than urbanization economies seem more significant for both developed and developing countries (Henderson 1988, 2003; Wheaton and Lewis 2002; Rosenthal and Strange 2003).[21]

However, as there is little consensus on which source of agglomeration economies is most important (see Rosenthal and Strange 2004; Overman

---

21 Evidence for localization economies is presented by Henderson (1988) for most two-digit industries in Brazil; by Chen (1996) for the machinery and food industries in China; by Henderson and Kuncoro (1996) for the apparel (including textiles), nonmetallic minerals, and machinery industries in Indonesia; by Henderson, Lee, and Lee (2001) for traditional, heavy, transport, and machinery industries in Korea; and by Lee and Zang (1998) for 19 industries in Korea. Evidence of urbanization economies is presented by Mitra (2000) for 11 of 17 industries in India; by Lall and Chakravorty (2005) for the food-processing, textiles, leather, paper, chemical, basic metals, mechanical machinery, and electrical machinery industries in India; and by Henderson, Lee, and Lee (2001) for high-tech industries in Korea. See Rosenthal and Strange (2004) and Overman and Venables (2005) for excellent summaries of the literature.

and Venables 2005), the literature provides no guide to policy makers as to which policies might be most effective in fostering or reducing spatial inequality.[22] If technological spillovers or labor-matching economies are important, policy makers may pursue policies that encourage information exchanges in ideas or jobs. If market size is important, it may be more effective to implement policies that foster the growth of markets.

While the nature of the evidence varies somewhat, there seems to be strong reason to believe that agglomeration economies are temporally persistent and dynamic. If successful, policies may therefore have persistent influences over time. Glaeser and Maré (2001) find that the urban wage premium in the United States is higher for long-time urban residents. Henderson (2003) finds that U.S. high-tech firms benefit from the scale of past activity. Dekle (2002) finds evidence of dynamic externalities measured using total factor productivity growth at the prefecture level for the finance, services, and wholesale and retail trade industries but not for manufacturing in Japan between 1975 and 1995.

Long-Run Perspective

The patterns of spatial inequality are likely to change over time. While not substantial, there is some evidence of an inverted-U pattern of regional and urban inequality: spatial inequality seems to rise and then fall with development. The data on industrial localization suggest a partial explanation. In the early phase of development, countries tend to specialize in extractive and low-skilled industries, such as textiles and apparel, which are geographically concentrated. With development the economy shifts toward high-tech manufacturing and services, which are geographically more dispersed. There is, however, no generally accepted theory of the inverted-U pattern of spatial inequality. The explanations proposed by Kuznets (1955), Williamson (1965), and Kim (1995) are ad hoc. While Krugman and Venable's (1995) theory based on declining transportation costs is elegant, there is no evidence that the long-run trends in spatial inequality are consistent with their model.

---

22 Empirical advances have come at many levels, both intensive and extensive. Numerous studies have moved beyond the analysis of aggregate industry and city-, county-, state-, regional-level data to firm- or plant-level data using finer geographic locations such as zip (postal) codes. At the same time, the number of studies has mushroomed to include an ever-increasing number of countries around the world. Indeed, from studies dominated by U.S. regions and cities, there has been a major shift to studying not only Europe and Japan but also numerous developing countries. Despite these major advances, scholars have not narrowed in on the causes of spatial inequality. Evidence covers natural advantage (Kim 1995, 1999; Ellison and Glaeser 1997); technological spillovers (Jaffe, Trajtenberg, and Henderson 1993); labor-market pooling (Dumais, Ellison, and Glaeser 2002); input linkages (Holmes 1999; Amiti and Cameron 2007); market size (Hanson 1997, 2005); amenities (Tabuchi and Yoshida 2000); and rent seeking (Ades and Glaeser 1995). Because agglomeration economies seem to attenuate rapidly by distance, the influence of policies is likely to be geographically localized (Rosenthal and Strange 2003). In addition, because agglomeration economies seem to vary by firm births and deaths, industry plant sizes, and the level of competition, policy makers also need to consider the industrial organization of industries (Dumais, Ellison, and Glaeser 2002; Rosenthal and Strange 2003).

Globalization and Trade

Globalization and foreign trade can significantly affect domestic regional and urban inequality. However, neither theory nor empirics provides a good guide to the direction of impact. From a theoretical perspective, foreign trade, like domestic trade, can increase or reduce spatial inequality; the empirical evidence presented above finds instances of both. Because openness to trade is likely to be an important component of development for many developing countries, careful analysis of the impact of foreign trade on domestic inequality is necessary.

Institutions

Political institutions can play a significant role in determining regional and urban inequality. Differences in regional institutions may cause divergence in regional economies. Dictatorship, political weakness, and centralized power seem to contribute to a centralized urban population. In general, the distribution of political and fiscal power across federal, state, and local governments can significantly influence regional as well as urban spatial inequality. Different jurisdictions of government have different political incentives and are likely to prefer different levels of public goods, which affect spatial inequality. The empirical evidence suggests that countries with strong state and local governments may have greater spatial equality than countries with relatively strong federal governments.

Infrastructure

Some evidence suggests that investments in transportation and communications infrastructure are associated with a decline in spatial inequality. Several studies find that interregional infrastructure investments may contribute to the reduction of urban concentration. Investments in national navigable waterways (Gallup, Sachs, and Mellinger 1999); railways (Rosen and Resnick 1980); and national roads and highways (Henderson 2002; Baum-Snow 2007) all seem to have contributed to reducing spatial inequality.

Cautionary Tales

Few policy efforts to reduce spatial inequality have been successful. Indeed, efforts to reduce spatial inequality within EU countries—where policies sought to promote the development of lagging regions, support areas facing structural difficulties, and develop systems of education, training, and employment—present a cautionary tale (Puga 2002). To meet these objectives, the European Union devoted €195 billion (in 1999 prices) between 2000 and 2006—more than 30 percent of total EU spending. The Cohesion Fund, designed to reduce economic and social disparities, added another €18 billion. Despite this massive allocation of resources, regional inequalities have not narrowed and by some accounts have even widened.

Korea's policy of deconcentration has been seen as a rare success story in combating the ills of excessive concentration. As Korea began to industrialize in the 1960s, its population became increasingly concentrated in Seoul, which was home to 41 percent of Korea's urban population by 1970. Between 1970 and 1990, the trend reversed, as Seoul's share fell to 33 percent (Lee 1997). The deconcentration of the population in Seoul was caused partly by the massive dispersal of manufacturing industries from Seoul to outlying areas. Henderson, Lee, and Lee (2001) and Henderson (2002) argue that the deconcentration was caused by two major factors: economic liberalization, which reduced the importance of locating in Seoul for access to the political bureaucracy (Kwon 1985), and massive investments in roads and communications, which blanketed Korea and provided important transportation and communications infrastructure. Despite these changes, however, Seoul remains one of the densest cities in the world, denser than Tokyo and twice as dense as New York. Deconcentration to satellite cities was mainly in manufacturing branch plants.

Conclusion

Why do spatial inequalities arise? This survey of the literature highlights two classes of explanations based on first and second natures of geography. The neoclassical model emphasizes the role of the first nature, such as resource endowments and proximity to rivers and ports. The increasing returns model emphasizes the role of the second nature, created by the density of human interactions. Because economic development allows regions to take advantage of the first and second natures of geography, an increase in spatial inequality may be beneficial as productivity is increased. However, because congestion costs may not be internalized by individuals, spatial inequality in the form of excessive urban concentration or urban primacy may be harmful. Theory thus suggests that there is an optimal level of spatial inequality.

Spatial inequality is a concern for policy makers for a variety of reasons. First, from an efficiency standpoint, they want to obtain the optimal level of spatial inequality. Because most of the second-nature explanations imply market imperfections and inefficient levels of agglomeration, policy makers may want to adopt policies to correct these failures. Second, even when spatial inequality is beneficial, they may want to reduce the effects of uneven spatial development for equity reasons. Third, policy makers may be concerned that wide regional divergence in the economic fortunes of different regions may contribute to deep political divisions that may impose significant social costs.

Implementing policies that foster or reduce spatial inequality is likely to be much more challenging than suggested by the standard literature. Economic development often involves major shifts in the economic and social structures of societies. A successful shift from a traditional agricultural-based society to a modern manufacturing- and service-based society is likely to involve a transition from a traditional society based on personal exchanges to a modern society based on impersonal exchanges. Because the developmental transition tears at the fabric of society held together by traditional family and inheritance institutions as well as traditional gender roles, making a successful transition is significantly more challenging than suggested by the models surveyed here.

More important, political elites in many developing countries may not face the incentives to treat problems associated with too little or too much spatial inequality. Local political elites in China have little incentive to remove restrictions on the mobility of workers. Political elites in Asia and Latin America have little incentive to reduce problems associated with urban primacy if they benefit from politics of corruption and patronage. If spatial disparity is fundamentally driven by political institutions, implementing difficult political reforms may be a necessary first step toward addressing problems associated with spatial inequality.

What do researchers need to do? Despite the enormous advances in the understanding of the determinants of economic geography in recent years, knowledge is still inadequate in many respects, especially for understanding the nature of spatial inequality in developing countries.

From an empirical standpoint, more empirical evidence is needed on regional and urban inequalities in developing countries, as Overman and Venables (2005) note. While evidence from developed countries may be useful, the patterns of development of many developing countries seem to differ from those of developed countries. In many developing countries, for example, the informal service sector accounts for a significant share of urban activity, yet there is little evidence on the nature of their agglomeration economies. In addition, while most models predict market failure in cities, it has been extremely difficult to estimate optimal city sizes. The estimates for China obtained by Au and Henderson (2004) are useful, but it remains to be seen whether these estimates can be generalized to other developing countries.

The causes of the long-run inverted-U pattern of spatial inequality, to the extent that it exists, are still not well understood. With the exception of Krugman and Venables (1995), most theories of the inverted-U pattern of spatial inequality are ad hoc, and most models of economic geography are not closely linked to the long-run process of development.

Better understanding is also needed of the link between household income inequality and spatial income inequality and on the interactions among regions and cities. Regions may affect their local urban development because of their resources or the size of their markets; cities may also affect their regional development, because they provide financial and transaction services that reduce regional costs of capital and trade. An understanding of these interactions is likely to provide a more coherent approach to reducing costs associated with spatial inequality.

Better understanding is also needed of the institutional and political histories of developing countries. As Benabou (2000) notes, economic inequality and policies may be jointly determined, suggesting that policy instruments cannot be treated as completely exogenous. If a society chooses an equilibrium path along which high inequality and low redistribution are mutually reinforcing, attempts to introduce policies of equality may be futile. Policy constraints may be even more important in nondemocratic societies. Economic development and growth may depend on some general factors that affect all countries. But every country possesses different geographic, institutional, and political conditions, which may ultimately determine the set of policies available for solving problems associated with spatial inequality.

References

Abdel-Rahman, Hesham M. 1996. "When Do Cities Specialize in Production?" *Regional Science and Urban Economics* 26 (1): 1–22.

Abdel-Rahman, Hesham M., and Masahisa Fujita. 1990. "Product Variety, Marshallian Externalities and City Sizes." *Journal of Regional Science* 30 (2): 165–83.

Acemoglu, Daron, Simon Johnson, and James A. Robinson. 2001. "The Colonial Origins of Comparative Development: An Empirical Investigation." *American Economic Review* 91 (5): 1369–401.

———. 2002. "Reversal of Fortunes: Geography and Institutions in the Making of the Modern World Income Distribution." *Quarterly Journal of Economics* 117 (4): 1231–94.

———. 2004. "Institutions as the Fundamental Cause of Long-Run Growth." Department of Economics, Massachusetts Institute of Technology, Cambridge, MA.

Ades, Alberto F., and Edward L. Glaeser. 1995. "Trade and Circuses: Explaining Urban Giants." *Quarterly Journal of Economics* 110 (1): 195–227.

Alesina, Alberto, and Dani Rodrik. 1994. "Distributive Politics and Economic Growth." *Quarterly Journal of Economics* 109 (2): 465–89.

Alexandersson, Gunnar. 1959. *The Industrial Structure of American Cities.* Lincoln: University of Nebraska Press.

Amiti, Mary, and Lisa Cameron. 2007. "Economic Geography and Wages." *Review of Economics and Statistics* 89 (1): 15–29.

Au, Chung-Chung, and Vernon J. Henderson. 2004. "How Migration Restrictions Limit Agglomeration and Productivity in China." Department of Economics, Brown University, Providence, RI.

Azzoni, Carlos, Naercio Menezes-Filho, and Taitane Menezes. 2005. "Opening the Convergence Black Box: Measurement Problems and Demographic Aspects." In *Spatial Inequality and Development*, ed. Ravi Kanbur and Anthony J. Venables. Oxford: Oxford University Press.

Balisacan, Arsenio M., and Nobuhiko Fuwa. 2006. "Changes in Spatial Income Inequality in the Philippines: An Exploratory Analysis." In *Spatial Disparities in Human Development: Perspectives from Asia*, ed. Ravi Kanbur, Anthony J. Venables, and Guanghua Wan. New York: United Nations.

Banerjee, Abhijit V., and Esther Duflo. 2003. "Inequality and Growth: What Can the Data Say?" *Journal of Economic Growth* 8 (3): 267–99.

Banerjee, Abhijit V., and Lakshmi Iyer. 2005. "History, Institutions and Economic Performance: The Legacy of Colonial Land Tenure Systems in India." *American Economic Review* 95 (4): 1190–213.

Barrios, Salvador, Luisito Bertinelli, and Eric Strobl. 2006. "Climatic Change and Rural-Urban Migration: The Case of Sub-Saharan Africa." *Journal of Urban Economics* 60 (3): 357–71.

Baum-Snow, Nathaniel. 2007. "Did Highways Cause Suburbanization?" *Quarterly Journal of Economics* 122 (2): 775–805.

Benabou, Roland. 2000. "Unequal Societies: Income Distribution and the Social Contract." *American Economic Review* 90 (1): 96–129.

Bergsman, Joel, Peter Greenston, and Robert Healy. 1975. "A Classification of Economic Activities Based on Location Patterns." *Journal of Urban Economics* 2 (1): 1–28.

Berliant, Marcus. 2007. "Prospects for a Unified Urban General Equilibrium Theory." *Regional Science and Urban Economics* 37 (4): 466–71.

Black, Duncan, and J. Vernon Henderson. 2003. "Urban Evolution in the USA." *Journal of Economic Geography* 3 (4): 343–72.

Brülhart, Marius, and Rolf Traeger. 2005. "An Account of Geographic Concentration Patterns in Europe." *Regional Science and Urban Economics* 35 (6): 597–624.

Bruhn, Miriam, and Francisco A. Gallego. 2007. "Good, Bad, and Ugly Colonial Activities: Studying Development across the Americas." Instituto de Economía, Pontificia Universidad Católica de Chile.

Chen, Yimin. 1996. "Impact of Regional Factors on Productivity in China." *Journal of Regional Science* 36 (3): 417–36.

Christaller, Walter. 1933 (reprinted 1966). *Central Places in Southern Germany*. Englewood Cliffs, NJ : Prentice-Hall.

Crafts, Nicholas, and Abay Mulatu. 2006. "How Did the Location of Industry Respond to Falling Transportation Costs in Britain before World War I?" *Journal of Economic History* 66 (3): 575–606.

Cronon, William. 1991. *Nature's Metropolis*. New York: W.W. Norton.

Dekle, Robert. 2002. "Industrial Concentration and Regional Growth: Evidence from Prefectures." *Review of Economics and Statistics* 84 (2): 310–15.

Deininger, Klaus, and Lyn Squire. 1996. "A New Data Set Measuring Income Inequality." *World Bank Economic Review* 10 (3): 565–91.

Dixit, Avinash K., and Joseph E. Stiglitz. 1977. "Monopolistic Competition and Optimum Product Diversity." *American Economic Review* 67 (3): 297–308.

Dobkins, Linda H., and Yannis M. Ioannides. 2000. "Dynamic Evolution of the Size Distribution of U.S. Cities." In *Economics of Cities*, ed. Jean-Marie Juriot and Jacques-François Thisse. New York: Cambridge University Press.

Dumais, Guy, Glenn Ellison, and Edward L. Glaeser. 2002. "Geographic Concentration as a Dynamic Process." *Review of Economics and Statistics* 84 (2): 193–204.

Duranton, Gilles, and Henry G. Overman. 2005. "Testing for Localisation Using Micro-Geographic Data." *Review of Economic Studies* 72 (4): 1077–106.

Duranton, Gilles, and Diego Puga. 2001. "Nursery Cities: Urban Diversity, Process Innovation, and the Life Cycle of Products." *American Economic Review* 91: 1454–77.

———. 2004. "Micro-Foundations of Urban Agglomeration Economies." In *Handbook of Regional and Urban Economics,* vol. 4, ed. J. Vernon Henderson and Jacques-François Thisse, 2063–17. Amsterdam: North-Holland.

Eaton, Jonathan, and Zvi Eckstein. 1997. "Cities and Growth: Theory and Evidence from France and Japan." *Regional Science and Urban Economics* 27 (4–5): 443–74.

Elbers, Chris, Peter Lanjouw, Johan Mistiaen, Berk Özler, and Kenneth R. Simler. 2005. "Are Neighbours Equal? Estimating Local Inequality in Three Developing Countries." In *Spatial Inequality and Development*, ed. Ravi Kanbur and Anthony J. Venables. Oxford: Oxford University Press.

Ellison, Glenn, and Edward Glaeser. 1997. "Geographic Concentration in U.S. Manufacturing Industries: A Dartboard Approach." *Journal of Political Economy* 105 (October): 889–927.

Engerman, Stanley L., and Kenneth L. Sokoloff. 1997. "Factor Endowments, Institutions, and Differential Paths of Growth among New World Economies: A View From Economic Historians of the United States." In *How Latin America Fell Behind: Essays on the Economic Histories of Brazil and Mexico 1800–1914*, ed. Stephen Haber. Stanford, CA: Stanford University Press.

Escobal, Javier, and Maximo Torero. 2005. "Adverse Geography and Differences in Welfare in Peru." In *Spatial Inequality and Development*, ed. R. Kanbur and Anthony J. Venables. Oxford: Oxford University Press.

Epple, Dennis, and Thomas Nechyba. 2004. "Fiscal Decentralization." In *Handbook of Regional and Urban Economics,* vol. 4, ed. J. Vernon Henderson and Jacques-François Thisse. Amsterdam: North-Holland.

Ethier, Wilfred J. 1982. "National and International Returns to Scale in the Modern Theory of International Trade." *American Economic Review* 72 (3): 389–405.

Fay, Marianne, and Charlotte Opal. 2000. "Urbanization without Growth: A Not So Uncommon Phenomenon." Policy Research Working Paper 2412, World Bank, Washington, DC.

Ferreira, Francisco H. G. 1999. "Inequality and Economic Performance." World Bank, Washington, DC.

Forster, Michael, David Jesuit, and Timothy Smeeding. 2005. "Regional Poverty and Income Inequality in Central and Eastern Europe: Evidence from the Luxembourg Income Study." In *Spatial Inequality and Development*, ed. R. Kanbur and Anthony J. Venables. Oxford: Oxford University Press.

Friedman, Jed. 2005. "How Responsive Is Poverty to Growth? A Regional Analysis of Poverty, Inequality, and Growth in Indonesia 1984–99." In *Spatial Inequality and Development*, ed. R. Kanbur and Anthony J. Venables. Oxford: Oxford University Press.

Fujita, Masahisa, Paul Krugman, and Anthony J. Venables. 1999. *The Spatial Economy: Cities, Regions, and International Trade.* Cambridge, MA: MIT Press.

Fujita, Masahisa, Tomoya Mori, J. Vernon Henderson, and Yoshitsugu Kanemoto. 2004. "Spatial Distribution of Economic Activities in Japan and China." In *Handbook of Regional and Urban Economics,* vol. 4, ed. J. Vernon Henderson and Jacques-François Thisse. Amsterdam: North-Holland.

Fujita, Masahisa, and Jacques-François Thisse. 2002. *Economics of Agglomeration: Cities, Industrial Location, and Regional Growth.* Cambridge: Cambridge University Press.

Gabaix, Xavier, and Yannis M. Ioannides. 2004. "The Evolution of City Size Distributions." In *Handbook of Regional and Urban Economics,* vol. 4, ed. J. Vernon Henderson and Jacques-François Thisse. Amsterdam: North-Holland.

Gallup, John L., Jeffrey D. Sachs, and Andrew D. Mellinger. 1999. "Geography and Economic Development." *International Regional Science Review* 22 (2): 179–232.

Glaeser, Edward L., and David C. Maré. 2001. "Cities and Skills." *Journal of Labor Economics* 19 (2): 316–42.

Hanson, Gordon H. 1997. "Increasing Returns, Trade and the Regional Structure of Wages." *Economic Journal* 107 (1): 113–33.

———. 2005. "Market Potential, Increasing Returns, and Geographic Concentration." *Journal of International Economics* 67 (1): 1–24.

———. 2007. "Globalization, Labor Income and Poverty in Mexico." In *Globalization and Poverty,* ed. Ann Harrison. Chicago: University of Chicago Press.

Harris, John R., and Michael P. Todaro. 1970. "Migration, Unemployment and Development: Two-Sector Analysis." *American Economic Review* 60 (1): 126–42.

Head, Keith, and Thierry Mayer. 2004. "The Empirics of Agglomeration and Trade." In *Handbook of Regional and Urban Economics,* vol. 4, ed. J. Vernon Henderson and Jacques-François Thisse. Amsterdam: North-Holland.

Henderson, J. Vernon. 1974. "The Sizes and Types of Cities." *American Economic Review* 64 (4): 640–56.

———. 1988. *Urban Development: Theory, Fact and Illusion.* Oxford: Oxford University Press.

———. 2002. "Urbanization in Developing Countries." *World Bank Research Observer* 17(1): 89–112.

———. 2003. "The Urbanization Process and Economic Growth: The So-What Question." *Journal of Economic Growth* 8 (1): 47–71.

Henderson, J. Vernon, and A. Kuncoro. 1996. "Industrial Centralization in Indonesia." *World Bank Economic Review* 10 (3): 513–40.

Henderson, J. Vernon, and Jacques-François Thisse, eds. 2004. *Handbook of Regional and Urban Economics,* vol. 4. Amsterdam: North-Holland.

Henderson, J. Vernon, Todd Lee, and Yung Joon Lee. 2001. "Scale Externalities in Korea." *Journal of Urban Economics* 49 (3): 479–504.

Hirschman, Albert O. 1958. *Strategies of Economic Development.* New Haven, CT: Yale University Press.

Holmes, Thomas J. 1999. "Localization of Industry and Vertical Disintegration." *Review of Economics and Statistics* 81 (2): 314–25.

Holmes, Thomas J., and John J. Stevens. 2004. "Spatial Distribution of Economic Activities in North America." In *Handbook of Regional and Urban Economics,* vol. 4, ed. J. Vernon Henderson and Jacques-François Thisse. Amsterdam: North-Holland.

Jaffe, Adam B., Manuel Trajtenberg, and Rebecca Henderson. 1993. "Geographic Localization of Knowledge Spillovers as Evidenced by Patent Citations." *Quarterly Journal of Economics* 108 (3): 577–98.

Kanbur, Ravi, and Anthony J. Venables. 2005a. "Spatial Inequality and Development." In *Spatial Inequality and Development*, ed. Ravi Kanbur and Anthony J. Venables. Oxford: Oxford University Press.

———. 2005b. "Spatial Inequality and Development: Overview of UNU-WIDER Project." Department of Economics, Cornell University, Ithaca, NY.

Kanbur, Ravi, Anthony J. Venables, and Guanghua Wan. 2006. *Spatial Disparities in Human Development: Perspectives from Asia.* New York: United Nations.

Kanbur, Ravi, and Xiaobo Zhang. 2005. "Fifty Years of Regional Inequality in China: A Journey through Central Planning, Reform and Openness." *Review of Development Economics* 9 (1): 87–106.

Kapur, Shilpi, and Sukkoo Kim. 2006. "British Colonial Institutions and Economic Development in India." NBER Working Paper 12613, National Bureau of Economic Research, Cambridge, MA.

Kessides, Christine. 2005. "The Urban Transition in Sub-Saharan Africa: Implications for Economic Growth and Poverty Reduction." Working Paper 97, World Bank, Africa Region, Washington, DC.

Kim, Sukkoo. 1995. "Expansion of Markets and the Geographic Distribution of Economic Activities: The Trends in U.S. Regional Manufacturing Structure, 1860–1987." *Quarterly Journal of Economics* 110 (4): 881–908.

———. 1998. "Economic Integration and Convergence: U.S. Regions, 1840–1990." *Journal of Economic History* 58 (2): 659–83.

———. 1999. "Regions, Resources and Economic Geography: The Sources of U.S. Regional Comparative Advantage, 1880–1987." *Regional Science and Urban Economics* 29: 1–32.

———. 2000. "Urban Development in the United States, 1690–1990." *Southern Economic Journal* 66 (4): 855–80.

———. 2006. "Division of Labor and the Rise of Cities: Evidence from U.S. Industrialization, 1850–1880." *Journal of Economic Geography* 6 (4): 469–91.

———. 2007a. "Changes in the Nature of Urban Spatial Structures in the United States, 1890–2000." *Journal of Regional Science* 47 (2): 273–87.

———. 2007b. "Institutions and U.S. Regional Development: A Study of Massachusetts and Virginia." NBER Working Paper 13431, National Bureau of Economic Research, Cambridge, MA.

———. 2008. "Political Institutions, Federalism and U.S. Urban Development: The Case of American Exceptionalism." Washington University, St. Louis, MO.

Kim, Sukkoo, and Robert Margo. 2004. "Historical Perspectives on U.S. Economic Geography." In *Handbook of Regional and Urban Economics,* vol. 4, ed. J. Vernon Henderson and Jacques-François Thisse. Amsterdam: North-Holland.

Knight, John, Li Shi, and Zhao Renwei. 2006. "Divergent Means and Convergent Inequality of Incomes among the Provinces and Cities of Urban China." In *Spatial Disparities in Human Development: Perspectives from Asia*, ed. Ravi Kanbur, Anthony J. Venables, and Guanghua Wan. New York: United Nations.

Krugman, Paul. 1991a. *Geography and Trade*. Cambridge, MA: MIT Press.

———. 1991b. "Increasing Returns and Economic Geography." *Journal of Political Economy* 99 (3): 483–99.

Krugman, Paul, and Raul. E. Livas Elizondo. 1996. "Trade Policy and the Third World Metropolis." *Journal of Development Economics* 49 (1): 137–50.

Krugman, Paul, and Anthony J. Venables. 1995. "Globalization and the Inequality of Income." *Quarterly Journal of Economics* 110 (4): 857–80.

Kuznets, Simon. 1955. "Economic Growth and Income Inequality." *American Economic Review* 45 (1): 1–28.

Kwon, W. G. 1985. "Issues and Problems in Planning and Implementing Industrial Location Policies in Korea." Discussion Paper, World Bank, Washington, DC.

Lall, Somik Vinay, and Sanjoy Chakravorty. 2005. "Industrial Location and Spatial Inequality: Theory and Evidence from India." *Review of Development Economics* 9 (1): 47–68.

Lee, T. C. 1997. "Industry Deconcentration and Regional Specialization in Korean Manufacturing." Ph.D. diss., Department of Economics, Brown University, Providence, RI.

Lee, Yung Joon, and Hyoungsoo Zang. 1998. "Urbanization and Regional Productivity in Korean Manufacturing." *Urban Studies* 35 (11): 2085–99.

Lewis, Arthur. 1954. "Economic Development with Unlimited Supply of Labor." *Manchester School of Economic and Social Studies* 22 (2): 139–91.

Lindert, Peter, and Jeffrey Williamson. 1985. "Growth, Equality and History." *Explorations in Economic History* 22 (October): 341–77.

Losch, August. 1954. *The Economics of Location*. Oxford: Oxford University Press.

Maurel, Françoise, and Bétrice Sédillot. 1999. "A Measure of Geographic Concentration in French Manufacturing Industries." *Regional Science and Urban Economics* 29 (5): 575–604.

McCormick, Barry, and Jacqueline Wahba. 2003. "Return International Migration and Geographical Inequality: The Case of Egypt." *Journal of African Economies* 12 (4): 500–32.

Midelfart-Knarvik, Karen Helene, Henry G. Overman, Stephen J. Redding, and Anthony J. Venables. 2000. "The Location of European Industry." Report prepared for the European Commission, Brussels.

Mitchener, Kris, and Ian McLean. 2003. "The Productivity of U.S. States since 1880." *Journal of Economic Growth* 8 (1): 73–114.

Mitra, Arup. 2000. "Total Factor Productivity Growth and Urbanization Economies: A Case of Indian Industries." *Review of Urban and Regional Development Studies* 12 (2): 97–108.

Murata, Yasusada. 2002. "Rural-Urban Interdependence and Industrialization." *Journal of Development Economics* 68 (1): 1–34.

———. Forthcoming. "Engel's Law, Petty's Law, and Agglomeration." *Journal of Development Economics*.

Naude, Willem, and Waldo Krugell. 2003. "An Inquiry into Cities and Their Role in Subnational Economic Growth in South Africa." *Journal of African Economies* 12 (4): 473–75.

North, Douglass C. 1990. *Institutions, Institutional Change and Economic Performance*. New York: Cambridge University Press.

Nunn, Nathan, and Diego Puga. 2007. "Ruggedness: The Blessing of Bad Geography in Africa." Harvard University, Cambridge, MA.

Oats, Wallace E. 1985. "Searching for Leviathan: An Empirical Study." *American Economic Review* 75 (September): 748–57.

Overman, Henry G., and Anthony J. Venables. 2005. "Cities in the Developing World." Department of Geography, London School of Economics and Political Science.

Persson, Torsten, and Guido Tabellini. 1994. "Is Inequality Harmful for Growth? Theory and Evidence." *American Economic Review* 84 (3): 600–21.

Puga, Diego. 1998. "Urbanization Patterns: European vs. Less Developed Countries." *Journal of Regional Science* 38 (2): 231–52.

———. 1999. "The Rise and Fall of Regional Inequalities." *European Economic Review* 43 (2): 303–34.

———. 2002. "European Regional Policies in Light of Recent Location Theories." *Journal of Economic Geography* 2 (4): 372–406.

Puga, Diego, and Anthony J. Venables. 1999. "Agglomeration and Economic Development: Import Substitution vs. Trade Liberalisation." *Economic Journal* 109 (455): 292–311.

Rauch, James E. 1993. "Economic Development, Urban Underemployment, and Income Inequality." *Canadian Journal of Economics* 26 (4): 901–18.

Ray, Debraj. 1998. *Development Economics*. Princeton, NJ: Princeton University Press. ·

Rodriguez-Pose, Andres, and Javier Sanchez-Reaza. 2005. "Economic Polarization through Trade: Trade Liberalization and Regional Growth in Mexico." In *Spatial Inequality and Development*, ed. Ravi Kanbur and Anthony J. Venables. Oxford: Oxford University Press.

Rosen, Kenneth T., and Mitchell Resnick. 1980. "The Size Distribution of Cities: An Examination of the Pareto Law and Primacy." *Journal of Urban Economics* 8 (2): 165–86.

Rosenthal, Stuart S., and William C. Strange. 2003. "Geography, Industrial Organization, and Agglomeration." *Review of Economics and Statistics* 85 (2): 377–93.

———. 2004. "Evidence on the Nature and Sources of Agglomeration Economies." In *Handbook of Regional and Urban Economics*, vol. 4, ed. J. Vernon Henderson and Jacques-François Thisse. Amsterdam: North-Holland.

Samuelson, Paul. 1952. "The Transfer Problem and Transport Cost: The Terms of Trade When Impediments Are Absent." *Economic Journal* 64 (246): 278–304.

Sokoloff, Kenneth L., and Eric M. Zolt. 2006. "Inequality and the Evolution of Institution of Taxation: Evidence from the Economic History of the Americas." University of California, Los Angeles..

Soo, Kwok Tong. 2005. "Zipf's Law for Cities: A Cross-Country Investigation." *Regional Science and Urban Economics* 35 (3): 239–63.

Spence, Michael. 1976. "Product Selection, Fixed Costs, and Monopolistic Competition." *Review of Economic Studies* 43 (2): 217–35.

Starrett, David. 1974. "Principles of Optimal Location in a Large Homogenous Area." *Journal of Economic Theory* 9 (4): 418–48.

Tabuchi, Takatoshi, and Atsushi Yoshida. 2000. "Separating Urban Agglomeration Economies in Consumption and Production." *Journal of Urban Economics* 48 (1): 70–84.

Tirado, Daniel A., Elisenda Paluzie, and Jordi Pons. 2002. "Economic Integration and Industrial Location: The Case of Spain before World War I." *Journal of Economic Geography* 2 (3): 343–63.

Venables, Anthony J. 1996. "Equilibrium Locations of Vertically Linked Industries." *International Economic Review* 37 (2): 341–59.

Wheaton, William C., and Hisanobu Shishido. 1981. "Urban Concentration, Agglomeration Economies and the Level of Economic Development." *Economic Development and Cultural Change* 30 (1): 17–30.

Wheaton, William C., and Mark J. Lewis. 2002. "Urban Wages and Labor Market Agglomeration." *Journal of Urban Economics* 51 (3): 542–62.

Wheeler, Christopher. 2004. "Wage Inequality and Urban Density." *Journal of Economic Geography* 4 (4): 421–37.

Williamson, Jeffrey. 1965. "Regional Inequality and the Process of National Development: A Description of the Patterns." *Economic Development and Cultural Change* 13 (4): 3–84.

CHAPTER 6
Housing Policy in Developing Countries: The Importance of the Informal Economy

Richard Arnott

Introduction

In the foreword to *The Challenge of Slums* (2003), published by UN-HABITAT, Kofi Annan wrote:

> Almost 1 billion, or 32 percent of the world's urban population, live in slums, the majority of them in the developing world. Moreover, the locus of global poverty is moving to the cities, a process now recognized as the 'urbanization of poverty.' Without concerted action on the part of municipal authorities, national governments, civil society actors and the international community, the number of slum dwellers is likely to increase in most developing countries. And if no serious action is taken, the number of slum dwellers worldwide is projected to rise over the next 30 years to 2 billion.

While one may dispute the numbers and question the use of the word *slum*, with its sociopathological connotations, there is no doubt of the magnitude of the housing problems in developing countries. The ideal would be massive redistribution from the overconsuming haves to the have-nots, eliminating poverty. But that is not about to happen. Given their scarce resources, what policies should developing countries employ

I would like to thank Patricia Annez for detailed comments on earlier drafts of the paper, and Santiago Pinto for a useful discussion.

to best deal with their housing problems, and, ruling out massive redistribution from rich to poor countries, what can the international community do to help?

Though the pace of economic research on housing in developing countries has increased rapidly in recent years,[1] there is still very little empirical work analyzing housing policy in developing countries that is persuasive by modern standards in applied econometrics. Either the data are unreliable or insufficiently rich, or the empirical analysis suffers from obvious pitfalls. Case studies are suggestive but not conclusive. The housing policy experience of developed countries is considerably better documented and analyzed. Apart from adjustments that need to be made to reflect the income differences between the two classes of countries, can the received wisdom in developed countries on what constitutes good housing policy be applied to developing countries? Would housing policies that have been successful in developed countries necessarily be successful when applied to developing countries?

This chapter will argue that the large size of the informal sector[2] relative to the economy in developing countries, as well as the high proportion of housing that is informal, substantially alter the housing policy design problem, so that policies that have succeeded in developing countries may not work well in developing countries.

Table 6.1, which reproduces part of table 6.1 of UN-HABITAT (2003), presents data on the extent of informal employment[3] by City Development Index (CDI) quintile. In the two lowest quintiles about 50 percent of workers are informally employed, which is more than double that for the two highest quintiles. In developing countries, the bulk of the poor work in the informal sector.

Informal employment is one aspect of the informal economy. Informal housing is another. Angel (2000) defines *unauthorized housing* to be hous-

Table 6.1 GNP Per Capita and Informal Employment by City Development Index, 1998

CDI quintile	1	2	3	4	5
GNP per capita, US$	606	1,571	2,087	3230	11,822
Informal employment, %	49	51	40	26	19

---

1 See Buckley and Kalarickal (2005) for an enlightening and informed review.

2 Guha-Khasnobis, Kanbur, and Ostrom (2006) contains essays that focus on different aspects of the informal-formal sector dichotomy. Some discuss alternative definitions, others the changing character of the informal sector and perceptions of it.

3 "Informal employment" is not precisely defined. The imprecise definition is that an informal employee is "an employee in an unregistered enterprise." A note to table 6.1 states: "There is no clear distinction between informally employed and unemployed, which relates to actively seeking work in the formal sector. Quite often, officially unemployed people will work in the informal sector."

   The data were collected by the Housing Indicators Program, which was initiated by Stephen Mayo and Shlomo Angel at the World Bank, and has been continued by the World Bank and UN-HABITAT. The data were collected for one of the largest cities in each of the 57 countries in the sample.

Table 6.2 Rates of Owner-Occupancy, Unauthorized Housing, and Squatter Housing by Country Income Group, 1990

Country type	Low income	Lower middle income	Upper middle income	High income
Owner occupancy, %	33	59	57	59
Unauthorized housing, %	64	27	9	0
Squatter housing, %	17	16	4	0

ing that is not in compliance with current regulations concerning land ownership, land use and zoning, or construction, and *squatter housing* to be housing that is currently occupying land illegally.[4] This chapter will use the term *informal housing* as synonymous with Angel's definition of unauthorized housing.

Table 6.2, which reproduces part of table 23.2 of Angel (2000), presents data related to housing tenure type for four sets of countries, grouped by income. The most striking result in the table is that in 1990 about two-thirds of housing units in low-income countries were unauthorized, while essentially none in high-income countries was.

The main theme of this chapter is that the larger relative size of the informal economy in developing countries imposes important constraints on government policy that are not present in developed countries. These constraints significantly influence the form of sound housing policy in developing countries and undermine the effectiveness of many housing policies that have been successful in developed countries. The gist of the argument runs as follows:

1. Since the bulk of the poor in developing countries work in the informal sector, government cannot accurately measure their incomes. This severely compromises the effectiveness of broad income-related transfer programs and more generally limits the scope for redistribution.
2. At least in low-income countries, most households, and probably therefore the bulk of the most needy households, live in unauthorized housing. Since governments are reluctant to subsidize unauthorized housing, their housing programs, with the exception of public housing and slum upgrading projects, are biased towards authorized housing and therefore against the neediest households. Furthermore, the inability to measure household incomes accurately effectively precludes broad housing assistance programs that are geared to income.
3. Holding constant the real income of an economy, the larger is the informal sector, the lower is its fiscal capacity—the maximum amount its governments can collect in tax revenue on a sustained basis. To meet the demand for public services in the face of reduced fiscal capacity, governments in

---

4   To this definition of squatter housing, Angel adds the following footnote: "This definition fail[s] to include structures occupied illegally by squatters. Squatter settlements that are recognized by authorities as permanent settlements and that are provided with documentation to this effect have been excluded from the definition."

developing countries impose high tax rates on formal-sector income and turn to other revenue sources that are inherently inefficient, resulting in highly distortionary fiscal systems. This diminished revenue-raising capability relative to the size of the economy restricts the scale and scope of expenditure programs that governments can and should undertake, and encourages the use of regulation, both to direct the economy and to collect fee revenue.

4. The consensus is that redistribution in developed countries is best undertaken by the central government since doing so reduces welfare-induced migration. In developing countries, however, local governments and community organizations are better able than the central government to identify the truly needy, which argues for more decentralized redistribution.

The above line of argument is static and takes the degree of informality as exogenous. Over the medium and long term, however, the size of the informal economy relative to the formal economy, as well as the proportion of housing that is informal, are endogenous. Both firms and individuals decide whether to participate in the informal or the formal economy on the basis of perceived self-interest. All else equal, the government would like to increase the proportions of the economy and of the housing market that are formal, since doing provides them with greater control and expands fiscal capacity. Increasing the degree of formality, either by making formal participation more attractive or informal participation less, may entail some sacrifice of short-run efficiency. For example, in the short run the government would like to regularize informal housing not only to collect more in tax revenue and to extend its control over housing delivery, but also to facilitate public service provision to the poor. Doing so however would encourage new unauthorized settlements, which conflicts with its goal of increasing the housing sector's degree of formality. One can pose this tradeoff as a conflict between short-run and long-run objectives. But probably a more useful way of framing the problem is to enquire into the optimal transition path from the status quo to a more formal economy—that is, to treat the policy design problem as dynamic rather than static.

The chapter distinguishes between developed and developing countries. When we speak of developing countries as a group, we have in mind the poorer developing countries. Some of our arguments need to be qualified when applied to emerging developed countries such as Mexico, Brazil, and China, or to countries that were formerly in the Soviet Bloc.

The remainder of the chapter is organized as follows. The next section discusses the welfare economics of housing policy in developed countries, and the third section that for developing countries. The fourth section gives a thumbnail history of the housing policy experience in developed countries. The fifth section briefly reviews the housing policy experience of developing countries, and relates differences in the policy experiences between developed and developing countries to informality. The final section draws together the discussion and provides concluding comments.

The main theme is that in developing countries the primary role of the central government in the housing sector should be to act as a facilitator, both enabling housing markets to work and taking a leadership role with respect to policy. In assisting low-income households to acquire adequate housing, governments should avoid expensive and broad-based housing programs and should instead assist local governments and community organizations to provide housing assistance to the neediest households. A subsidiary theme is that loans from the international community to help developing countries finance urban infrastructure would go a long way towards easing the strains deriving from their rapid urbanization.

The Welfare Economics of Housing Policy in Developed Countries

In almost all housing policy debates, economists argue for less government intervention in the housing sector than other groups of experts. Most economists have at least qualified faith in the efficiency of markets and argue for government intervention to oil the wheels of the market mechanism. They hold this view of the housing sector as well, arguing that the principal roles of government with respect to housing should be to enable housing markets to work and to ensure the adequate provision of infrastructure—a public goods problem. Much of housing policy in developed countries is redistributive in nature, having the ideal of providing "decent and affordable" housing for all. Economists tend to respect consumer sovereignty—that households know best how to spend their incomes—and therefore tend to favor income redistribution (which Tobin [1970] referred to as general egalitarianism) over redistribution in kind (specific egalitarianism), though many believe that social justice entails ensuring that all households enjoy at least basic levels of "merit goods"—decent housing, adequate nutrition, clothing, sanitation and health services, a safe and healthy environment, and access to at least a decent basic education for children. One may question whether homelessness is consistent with human dignity, even in the poorest countries, and reasonably maintain that the government should bear responsibility as the landlord of last resort.

The foundation on which economists have built their belief in the efficiency of markets is The Invisible Hand, as formalized in the theory of competitive general equilibrium. The First Theorem of Welfare Economics states that, under conditions of perfect competition, a market economy is efficient in the sense that it is impossible to make one person better off without making another worse off. Since the conditions of perfect competition are unrealistically strict, the Theorem provides a benchmark. Government intervention to improve the efficiency of markets may be justified because the real world economy deviates from the assumptions of perfect competition.

For many years, the dominant view among economists concerning the role of government was based on the classic theory of market failure (see, for example, Bator 1958). There are two central elements of the theory. The first is that there are three principal sources of market failure—natural monopoly (increasing returns to scale), externalities, and public goods. Government intervention may be justified on efficiency grounds to deal with each. The second is that equity and social justice should be achieved through the lump-sum redistribution of income. Since natural monopoly and public goods are unimportant in the housing sector per se, and since housing-related externalities can be dealt with on a piecemeal basis (for example, land use externalities are dealt with via zoning, and social capital externalities partially through the subsidization of home ownership), adherents of the classic market failure view of the role of government argue for limited government intervention in the housing market to improve efficiency, and income transfers rather than housing assistance to improve equity.[5] According to this perspective, government does, however. have an important role to play in the provision of urban infrastructure, including urban residential infrastructure, since it has public goods elements and some natural monopoly characteristics.

While many housing economists continue to base their policy arguments on the classic theory of market failure, over the last few decades new perspectives have emerged. On the one hand, public choice theorists emphasize that there are government failures as well as market failures. Politicians may be more concerned with getting reelected than with efficiency or equity; bureaucrats have an incentive to increase the size of their bureaus, whatever the social value of the services they provide; governments are power hungry; and so on. When account is taken of government failure, there is no presumption that market failure justifies government intervention—it may or it may not, depending on the economic and political circumstances. On the other hand, developments in economic theory, particularly the theory of optimal economic policy under asymmetric information, point to a potentially expanded role of government.

The theory of optimal economic policy under asymmetric information is now presented since it is central to this chapter's argument. In the theory of market failure, efficiency is achieved by correcting market failures, equity via lump-sum redistribution. Lump-sum redistribution would be feasible if the government could observe need directly, but it cannot, and instead must imperfectly infer need on the basis of what it can observe. Suppose, for the sake of argument, that individuals differ only in ability, so that a needier individual is simply a less able individual, and that there is a single generic consumption good. Suppose, too, that the government can observe an individual's income, but not his ability nor how many hours nor how hard he works (since the individual knows his ability, hours worked, and work

---

5 Most economics principles textbooks contain a section "proving" that income redistribution is more efficient than income-related housing allowances. They do this by assuming that income redistribution is lump sum and that the housing market is perfectly competitive.

effort better than the government, this is where asymmetric information enters the problem). Then the government must redistribute on the basis of income, which it does through income taxation. Faced with a positive marginal tax rate, an individual has an incentive to work fewer hours and less hard,[6] which leads to inefficiency. Thus, perfectly efficient redistribution is impossible. The (second-best)[7] optimal income tax system has the property that the marginal social benefit of a dollar transferred from a richer to a poorer individual equals the marginal social cost, the efficiency loss caused by the transfer.[8]

Now expand the model to include two consumption goods, one of which is more complementary to leisure than the other. The good that is more complementary to leisure should be taxed since this reduces the labor-leisure distortion due to the income tax. Now expand the model to include another dimension of need, such as health status. The government cannot observe an individual's health status directly but it can observe her expenditures on medical care. Second-best redistribution then entails an income tax that adjusts the tax payable or the transfer made on the basis of health expenditures, plus commodity taxes and subsidies. The general point is that when account is taken of the limited information the government has relevant to redistribution, the form of second-best redistribution may be complicated, entailing not only an income tax with many deductions, exemptions, and credits, but also the taxation of some commodities, the subsidization of others, and the rationed provision of yet others. The model can be extended further to treat public services. In deciding on the level of various public services, the government should take into account the implicit redistribution they entail. A second-best tax/expenditure package might entail the free provision of clean and safe drinking water, for example.

Since the menu of second-best redistributive policies might include housing subsidy programs, consideration of asymmetric information provides a potential basis for an expanded role of government in the housing sector, beyond correcting for the classic market failures. But this argument is too broad. Is there good reason to believe that housing is an efficient commodity on the basis of which to redistribute? After controlling for other signals of need such as low-income and high health expenditures, is housing consumption strongly positively correlated with need? And how strong are the adverse incentives associated with providing housing assistance? Many developed countries attempt to come to terms with these issues in the design of their housing allowance programs. Housing need is typically measured

---

6   Inefficiencies are associated with substitution effects. Income taxation generates substitution effects away from labor and towards leisure, and towards less effort.

7   The term "second best" is employed when there is some unalterable constraint that precludes attainment of the first best. Here the constraint is the government's inability to observe individuals' ability, work hours, and effort.

8   The optimal income tax problem was first formulated by Vickrey (1945) and later reformulated and solved by Mirrlees (1971). Their shared perception of asymmetric information as an essential feature in the formulation of optimal policy was the principal reason they were co-recipients of the Nobel Prize in economics in 1996.

by housing expenditure in excess of a certain fraction of income, and the possible adverse incentive effects of housing allowances on housing consumption are typically dealt with by relating the housing subsidy for a particular demographic group to the market rent of a basic housing unit for that group.

Most of the study of welfare economics does not deal specifically with children, but it should. Adults may bear some responsibility for their condition of poverty, but children do not. Every social system that purports to be just should provide children with minimal conditions needed for good health, security, and educational opportunity. Since almost all social systems around the world are family based, covering the basic needs of children entails covering some of the basic needs of other household members as well.

What priority should be accorded to providing decent and affordable housing compared to providing clean water, healthy sanitary and sewage conditions, educational opportunity, and adequate nutrition and clothing? A common response is that these other needs should be accorded higher priority, since they are what matter most for the well-being of children. One rejoinder is that decent and affordable housing is necessary for healthy living conditions and for childhood development,[9] another that respecting consumer sovereignty entails allowing households to make the tradeoff between these other desiderata and better housing themselves.

Although the theory of optimal economic policy under asymmetric information has not generated clear policy prescriptions concerning redistributive policy, it has strongly influenced public policy in another way. It has highlighted how large the efficiency losses generated by distortionary taxation can be. Public policy makers are now quite conscious that the social cost of raising an extra dollar of revenue—the marginal cost of public funds—may considerably exceed one dollar,[10] and that this argues

---

9   There is a body of literature that examines the effects of overcrowding in housing on the health status of adults and children and on childhood educational achievement, and finds that overcrowding is correlated with adverse outcomes. Generally speaking, the literature fails to establish causality since it does not adequately control for other factors, such as past poverty that may cause both overcrowding and the adverse outcomes.

A notable exception is Cattaneo et al. (2007), which analyzes the effects of a Mexican housing program, *Piso Firme*. Under the program, the government covered the dirt floors of participating households with concrete, without charge. Households within a well-defined geographic area whose housing units had dirt floors were eligible to participate. The study found "significant decreases in the incidence of parasitic infestations, diarrhea, and the prevalence of anemia, and a significant improvement in children's cognitive development" and in household happiness after the floors were installed (p. 2). The study also found that the program is significantly more cost-effective than Mexico's well-known, anti-poverty, conditional cash transfer program called OPORTUNIDADES and previously called PROGRESA. The success of *Piso Firme* indicates the potential value of specific, well-targeted housing programs but not of general housing assistance to the poor.

10   When the government extracts as much tax revenue as it can from the economy, given its limited information, the marginal cost of public funds is infinite. If the government raises tax rates beyond this point, the economy is "on the wrong side of the Laffer curve"—distortion increases and tax revenue declines.

for less revenue-intensive policy intervention. This has been a major impetus in the regulated privatization and contracting out of public services, in the establishment of public-private partnerships, and more generally in the push to enable markets to work and in the withering away of the welfare state.[11]

Another issue related to the welfare economics of housing policy is the level of government that should undertake it. The standard argument, deriving from the literature on fiscal federalism, is that the central government should undertake broad-based redistributive policy because its doing so generates less welfare-induced migration and, according to some standards, is fairer. Contrary to this is the argument that local governments are better informed about local conditions and are better able to judge which households are the most needy. In the United States, broad-based housing programs are set up and funded by the central government but are administered at the local level.

Much of the literature on housing policy overlooks spatial aspects. Where a household lives determines its access to public services, including education and jobs, as well as neighborhood quality.[12] A housing program that is otherwise well designed may lead to its beneficiaries being socially isolated and having poor access to job opportunities. More generally, housing policy can have long-term effects on the spatial structure of cities,[13] influencing especially the social composition of neighborhoods.

The discussion thus far in this section has tended to treat housing policy in the abstract. But most actual housing policies are targeted towards either renters or homeowners, and are directed at either the supply-side or the demand-side of the market. Governments almost everywhere favor home ownership, perceiving it to foster social stability, even though home ownership for the poor is highly risky, as the recent rapid rise in U.S. subprime foreclosures has shown. Since the bulk of poor households are—and should be—renters, redistributive housing policies should be directed primarily at the rental housing market. Whether redistributive housing policy should be

---

11 Consciousness of asymmetric information has impacted government policy in many other ways as well. For example, it is now well recognized that the asymmetric information faced by banks in mortgage markets, and more generally financial institutions in primary and secondary credit markets, gives rise to market failures that may justify extensive credit market regulation.

12 This theme is taken up by the essays in De Souza Briggs (2005).

13 Under perfect competition, markets provide the right signals for efficient spatial development. Market failures, such as unpriced traffic congestion and distortionary policy, can lead to inefficient spatial development, whose social costs can be considerable. Squatter settlements can occur at locations that are better suited for other land uses and are efficiently developed at different densities; they may, for example, be in prime locations that are better suited to office buildings or in locations that have poor transportation access to job opportunities. But ill-advised zoning can lead to such inefficient outcomes too. In both cases, the market provides signals for the correction of mistakes. Property owners in centrally located squatter settlements respond to high rents by increasing density; informal firms have an incentive to relocate to squatter settlements with poor job access; and if land is zoned for an inefficient land use, the market makes it profitable for it to be rezoned in its highest and best use. Since informal sector developers are likely to be more responsive to market pressures than planners, the spatial pattern of urban development may well improve with increased informality.

targeted on the demand-side or the supply-side of the housing market will be touched on later.

Informality and the Welfare Economics of Housing Policy in Developing Countries

In the theory of optimal economic policy, the benevolent government chooses policies so as to maximize social welfare, subject to a variety of constraints. These constraints reflect not only the scarcity of resources but also how the government's lack of information restricts its policy choices.

The Informal Economy

The larger the informal sector, the less well informed is the government about the economy, which constrains its policy choices. In the optimal income tax problem reviewed in the previous section, it was assumed that the government cannot observe an individual's ability, effort, or work hours, but can observe her income. Those informational assumptions are reasonable for a developed country with only a small informal sector. But in developing countries, where the informal economy is more important, the optimal policy problem needs to take into account that the government cannot observe *informal* wage and capital income. The government can apply the income tax only to formal wage and capital income, which is both inefficient and unfair—inefficient since it encourages individuals and firms to operate in the informal sector, and unfair since a low civil servant pays more in income tax than does a wealthy, informal sector entrepreneur. The presence of a large informal sector also sharply diminishes the effectiveness of income-contingent, in-kind transfer programs, such as food stamps and housing allowances, as redistributive devices.

A large informal sector affects optimal policy in other ways as well. First, since income taxes are collected from only a fraction of the population, the government must turn to other sources of revenue. The tax bases of many other revenue sources too will be eroded by the unobservability of transactions in the informal sector. All else equal, the government should raise revenue from those sources that are the least subject to evasion. Import and export taxes are effective since the bulk of goods that are imported and exported are done so legally. So too is value-added taxation applied to registered and government enterprises, including multinationals, since it encourages them to purchase their inputs from other registered enterprises. Gordon and Li (2005) argue along these lines in explaining the "puzzling" fiscal structures that developing countries employ.

Second, since the effectiveness of income taxation and income-contingent, in-kind transfer programs as redistributive tools is severely compromised by a large informal sector, other tax policy instruments, as well as other types of government expenditure programs, need to be used to achieve distributional goals. The theory of optimal taxation investigates the optimal tax rates on commodities when there is no income taxation.[14] As intuition would suggest, necessities should be subsidized and luxuries taxed, and in order to reduce distortion, the rates of taxation and subsidization should be higher the less elastically are the goods supplied and demanded.[15] In developing countries, these rules must be adapted to take into account the tax evasion that occurs in the informal sector. An obvious but important point is that taxes are evaded but subsidies are not. These considerations explain why many developing countries heavily subsidize the basic staple. The basic staple is an inelastically demanded necessity and subsidizing it generates no evasive activity. The theory of optimal commodity taxation has also been extended to treat public services. The government can improve the lot of the poor by changing the composition of public services to their benefit by, for example, providing free health clinics, and by charging for services that disproportionately benefit the rich, such as tolling urban freeways.[16]

Third, informality reduces fiscal capacity. Consider the following conceptual exercise. Increase the size of a country's informal sector, while simultaneously reducing the size of the formal sector. Because the informal sector evades taxes, the country's fiscal capacity falls. Holding fixed the set of taxes employed, raising a given amount of revenue requires higher tax rates. Taxation should be carried to the point where the marginal benefit of an extra dollar of revenue raised equals the marginal cost. Since the marginal cost curve is higher when fiscal capacity is diminished, the optimal amount of revenue to collect, and therefore the size of the government budget, falls. Furthermore, since the marginal cost is higher at the optimum, the optimum tax system entails higher tax rates and is more distortionary. In the face of a larger informal sector, the government should not only apply higher tax rates to conventional tax bases, but should also collect revenue from sources that developed countries avoid because they entail intrinsically high distortion. An important example is setting permit fees above processing costs and requiring permits where they are unnecessary, even though doing so discourages entrepreneurship (see, for example, De Soto 2000) and encourages informality.

One can think of the optimal tax structure design problem facing governments in developing countries at different levels of conceptual sophistication. In the simplest model, the proportion of various types of economic transactions that are informal is taken as exogenous, and the government has to raise a given amount of revenue in an optimal manner. In a more sophisticated model, the government budget is endogenous. The government

---

14 Important contributions to the theory of optimal commodity taxation include Ramsey (1927), Corlett and Hague (1953), Diamond and Mirrlees (1971), and Diamond (1975).

15 These simple results are derived from partial equilibrium analysis, which ignores income and cross-price effects. Taking these effects into account in a general equilibrium analysis considerably complicates the optimal commodity tax results.

16 Pinto (2004) argues that the redistributive target efficiency of public expenditure programs can be improved by geographical targeting and by "self-targeting"—taking advantage of differences in participation costs (such as crowding and delay in service) across households.

decides simultaneously on the tax structure and the level and composition of government expenditures. As noted above, an increase in the level of informality reduces the (second-best) optimal size of the government budget and hence government expenditures, raises the optimal tax rates applied to formal-sector tax bases, and encourages higher permitting fees. In an even more sophisticated model, the degree of informality as well is treated as endogenous.[17] Each economic agent decides whether to participate in the formal or informal sector, or perhaps how to divide his time between the two, keeping in mind the tax rates applied to formal sector activity and the size of permit fees. If the government changes the composition of public expenditures so as to favor the formal sector, some agents will switch from informal-sector to formal-sector participation, reducing the tax base erosion due to informality.

Excessive and dysfunctional regulation by government is a pervasive theme in the development economics literature. There is a ubiquitous tendency among civil servants to overregulate. Yet there seem to be no well-articulated explanations of why developing country governments regulate more excessively. Perhaps one reason is civil servants' wishful thinking in the face of an informal sector over which they have little control—irrationally hoping that regulating an outcome will make it happen. Impose minimum quality standards for housing and magically all housing will be built according to those standards. Another, more rational, reason is that bureaucrats see regulation as a way of increasing revenue for their cash-strapped bureaus through fees and fines. If the government were a single decision-making entity, it would not be rational for it to set fees and fines so high that compliance shrinks to the point where fee and fine revenue less enforcement costs is on the wrong side of the Laffer curve. But a dysfunctional outcome is likely if there are many levels of government, or many bureaus within a level of government, each competing for a slice of the pie. Thus, excessive regulation can be rational at the level of the individual bureau, and at the same time be dysfunctional from the perspective of the government as a whole.

---

17 There are several papers that model the determinants of informality. Lucas (1978) assumed that managerial ability differs across agents in the economy, with high-ability agents becoming managers and those with low ability workers. Rauch (1991) adapted Lucas's model to investigate the determinants of informality, by assuming that agents with the highest managerial ability become formal managers, those with intermediate ability run informal firms, whose size is limited by assumption, and those with the lowest ability become workers. De Paula and Scheinkman (2007) in turn adapted Rauch's model, giving formal firms access to cheaper credit.

Bosch, Goni, and Maloney (2007) document the changing character of the informal labor market in Brazil. The standard view, formalized in the Harris-Todaro model (Harris and Todaro 1970), is that workers in the informal sector queue for better jobs in the formal sector. However, the recent pattern in Brazil of worker transitions between formal and informal employment is similar to the job-to-job dynamics in the United States. This is consistent with the view taken in this chapter that enterprises and workers choose between formal- and informal-sector participation based on perceived profitability.

McKenzie and Sakho (2007) empirically compare the profitability of registered and unregistered firms in Bolivia by firm size.

It was argued above that the high cost of public funds encourages governments in developing countries to collect revenue from sources that developed countries would not employ because they are too distortionary. One can carry this line of reasoning further, and more controversially, to provide an explanation for why many developing countries have such high degrees of public corruption. Civil servants have information on the basis of which "tax and fee discrimination" can be exercised. Pay a civil servant a low salary and implicitly allow him to supplement his salary with bribes. The bribe may be paid to avoid being audited, to speed up the processing of a permit application, or to prevent prosecution for illegal activity. Based on his experience, the civil servant can vary the bribe he demands according to his perception of the briber's willingness to pay. This amounts to fee discrimination. From the perspective of the government, turning a blind eye to public corruption has pros and cons. On the one hand, the cash-strapped government can pay low civil service salaries and, through tax and fee discrimination, the public sector (including the civil servants) is able to extract more revenue from the private sector. On the other hand, corruption undermines the ability of the government to control the economy, sours the climate for foreign investment, and probably discourages entrepreneurship.

One could say that the government is caught in a Pareto inferior equilibrium. If all economic activity were magically formalized, everyone could be made better off. The expansion of tax bases would allow tax rates and fees to be reduced and the revenue collected by the government to rise at the same time. This would allow the government to upgrade the public services it provides and also to redistribute on the basis of income. Poor households would benefit from improved public services and redistribution through the income tax system. Rich households would benefit too from reduced tax rates and an improved business environment. But this way of looking at the problem is misleading. With the exception of the former Communist Bloc countries, today's developing countries had economies that used to be even more informal. Globalization, and the increase in trade that has come with it, has encouraged some informal enterprises to formalize their activities so as to gain access to international markets, and other informal enterprises that supply services to exporting companies to follow suit. Also, urbanization weakens the bonds of trust and the discipline of reputation in economic relationships, increasing the benefits from formal contracts. It is therefore more appropriate to view developing country economies as on a transition path to increased formality. Government can encourage private-sector agents to participate in the formal economy by lowering tax rates on formal-sector income, concentrating expenditures on services that benefit formal enterprises, facilitating formal-sector investment by easing permiting requirements and reducing fees, providing formal-sector firms with even more preferential access to credit, and by harassing informal activity. Unfortunately, this policy strategy likely helps the rich at the expense of the poor, and big business at the expense of small business. The design of the optimal time path of policy is evidently delicate.

Housing

It will be useful to begin with a discussion of some salient features of informal housing markets.

In many respects the distinction between formal and informal housing is analogous to the more familiar distinction between formal and informal labor and product markets. Land and property owners are analogous to the owners of informal enterprises, and renters to workers. Owners decide whether to develop their properties formally. The advantages of formal development include access to formal credit markets, preferential provision of public services, and reduced uncertainty. The disadvantages include payment of property-related taxes and compliance with onerous and profit-reducing regulation. Renters too decide whether to participate in the formal or informal market; informal housing has lower rents and more flexible lease arrangements but reduced security of tenure and probably lower-quality public services. But there are also important differences. Squatter housing entails the illegal occupation of land, which is more serious than tax evasion and noncompliance with regulation. Also, in many developing countries, the bulk of households cannot afford to live in formal housing, so that informal housing is to a larger extent housing for the poor than informal employment is employment for the poor. Thus, issues related to poverty loom larger in policy debates about informal housing than they do in debates about informal labor and product markets.

In most developing countries formal housing markets are overregulated. This is argued forcefully in De Soto (2000) and is also widely acknowledged (see, for example, World Bank 1993; Angel 2000). The construction permitting process is expensive and may take several years, and building and zoning standards are unrealistic given the country's state of development. One reason is that cash-strapped local governments use permitting to generate revenue, another that many planners strive in vain to enforce their vision of the City Beautiful against the power of market forces. Whatever the reasons, the overregulation makes formal housing unaffordable for the poor and much of the middle class too. It is also dysfunctional, since by encouraging the construction of noncompliant housing, it reduces the power of planners to influence the spatial development of the city.

Even with limited contract enforceability, informal housing markets function in much the same way as do formal housing markets.[18] Units are bought and sold and rental markets are active. Informal housing markets do differ from formal housing markets in one important respect, however. In formal housing markets, a durable structure meeting building codes is constructed on a titled plot of land. Over the years, densification may occur

---

18 World Bank (1993) and Angel (2000) report on the results of a long-term empirical research program at the World Bank comparing the operation of housing markets across countries, and make a persuasive empirical case that housing markets in developing countries respond in the way textbook models predict. They argue on this basis that "housing policy matters" in developing countries, and that developing country governments should employ policies that enable housing markets to work, which includes easing regulation of land, housing, and housing financial markets. Malpezzi (1999) argues along the same lines.

through legal add-ons and in-fills, as well as demolition and reconstruction at higher density. In areas of informal housing, this process is more continuous and incremental. The initial structure on a site is often no more than a shack. As the owner of the shack accumulates savings, he replaces the shack with the first floor of a durable structure, and then adds rooms and floors as he can afford to do so, often financing the expansion by renting out part of the structure. Squatter housing differs from other informal housing in being built on illegally occupied land. In the past, many governments in developing countries were hostile to squatter settlements and undertook slum clearance programs. One reason was to discourage rural-urban migration, which used to be widely viewed as excessive, another was to deter the illegal settlement of land, and yet another to discourage unauthorized housing. The tide has been changing. The ideological pendulum has been swinging away from the state attempting to micromanage the economy to its harnessing and channeling market forces by enabling markets to work. Also, cities are now widely viewed as engines of economic growth.[19] Accordingly, most governments in developing countries today view squatter settlements, and more generally informal housing, as an inevitable albeit unwelcome byproduct of the economic growth they wish to foster. As experience with them has developed, squatter settlements are being increasingly viewed more benignly as nascent communities.[20]

The previous subsection discussed how a large informal sector constrains government policy. A large informal housing sector further restricts the ability of the government to deal with urban housing and related problems.

Governments have little information about their informal housing communities since they are largely undocumented. Not having a clear idea of

---

19 In his essay for the Commission, Duranton (2008) provides a masterful overview of the empirical and theoretical literatures on the subject.

20 To Western observers, squatter settlements remain a puzzling phenomenon. Why do governments in many developing countries tolerate the "theft" of land by squatter groups when they do not tolerate what appear to be more minor infractions of the law? Does not doing so undermine respect for private property and the law, and pose a serious threat to the wealthy? Economic models of squatting do not provide fully satisfactory answers. The current orthodoxy, originally articulated in Hoy and Jimenez (1991) and recently elaborated by Turnbull (2008), is that landowners tolerate squatting only as a *temporary* land use. They tolerate it only because the cost of opposing the temporary occupation exceeds the benefit, and only until their land becomes ripe for development, at which time they will evict the squatters. According to this view, squatter settlements are akin to downtown surface parking lots—strictly a transitional land use. This may have been an accurate view when eviction and slum clearance were the norm, but today most squatter settlements are permanent.

In many cities in developing countries, governments have large tracts of land in central areas that remain undeveloped (Buckley and Kalarickal 2006, give the example of Dhaka). Perhaps the government is simply allowing "the market"—as represented by squatters—to determine how this land will be used. Even if sound, this line of reasoning fails to explain squatting on private land. Brueckner and Selod (2008) model a game between a private landowner and a squatter leader, in which the squatter leader chooses the amount of land to occupy and the amount of defensive expenditures necessary just to make it unprofitable for the landowner to evict the squatters.

I conjecture that the degree of tolerance of squatting is the outcome of class conflict, as mediated through the political process, with populist and democratic governments being more tolerant than governments that are autocratic or represent the interests of elites.

the size and income-demographic composition of a settlement's population, or the characteristics of its housing stock, including the degree of overcrowding and sanitary conditions, makes diagnosing housing needs and prescribing effective housing policy more difficult. Governments' lack of information also reduces the target efficiency of policies. While local governments likely have a good idea about the relative poverty and housing conditions of different neighborhoods, they do not have information on which households are the most in need, and must therefore tailor policies to neighborhoods rather than to specific households.

The defining characteristics of informal housing are that it is in violation of landownership laws, zoning regulations, and/or building codes, and evades property-related taxes. Thus, almost by definition, local authorities have limited influence on informal housing through taxation and regulation. Furthermore, just as informal productive activity erodes the income tax, commodity tax, and value-added tax bases, so too does informal housing erode the bases of property-related taxes. In many countries, the central government takes the plum taxes, leaving local governments to collect fees and property taxes that are best administered at the local level. While local governments are better able to assess local housing needs than the central government, and therefore better informed to administer redistributive housing policies, their fiscal ability to implement such policies is limited.

The limited fiscal capacity of developing country governments makes the provision of urban infrastructure, including transportation, water, electricity, solid waste disposal, sewage, fire and police protection, schools, and medical facilities, more difficult. In informal settlements, these problems are compounded by the government's poor knowledge of their current state and inability to control their future development. Furthermore, even a benign government faces a policy dilemma in deciding on the quality of infrastructure to provide informal settlements. On the one hand, if it turns a blind eye to violation of regulations and provides the same level of services to informal as to formal settlements, it encourages the development of more informal settlements in the future. This problem is particularly acute for squatter settlements, since the government is naturally loath to implicitly endorse settlements that were established through the expropriation of government or private property. On the other hand, informal settlements contain the bulk of poor households, who would benefit considerably from the provision of at least basic public services. Also, not providing informal settlements with basic services encourages crime and contagion, externalities that hurt all residents, and produces neighborhoods that will remain blighted for years to come.

In the countries of Western Europe, over the last 50 years the pressure on city center infrastructure has diminished. Their levels of urbanization have leveled off, their demographic transitions have been completed, and rising automobile ownership rates have resulted in decentralization of both residence and employment. The same can be expected to happen in due course in developing countries, but over the next 50 years the inadequacy of their city center infrastructure will become critical. The urban population in developing countries has been growing at rates that have no historical precedent (Williamson 1990, table 1.1). Since developing countries have not yet passed through their demographic transition, since their rural-urban migrations are still under way, since per capita incomes are likely to continue to grow steadily, and since only a fraction of the population currently owns cars, there is every reason to believe that the pressure on urban infrastructure in the city cores will continue to grow rapidly over the next 50 years. Most cities in developing countries are already nasty—ugly, choked with traffic, and foul with pollution—and many are disease ridden as well. Unless there is a radical change in infrastructure policy, the poor quality of life they provide will deteriorate even further. Why does such misery need to be endured along the transition path to a likely prosperous and pleasant future?

The growth rate of the urban population in developing countries is similar to that experienced by Western European countries during their industrial revolutions, and is indeed somewhat higher. How did the countries in Western Europe cope with the infrastructure needs of their rapidly growing cities during their industrial revolutions, and do their historical experiences provide any insights for today's developing countries? Britain's experience has been well documented. In *Coping with City Growth during the British Industrial Revolution* (1990), Jeffrey Williamson documents the low level of social capital investment during the British Industrial Revolution,[21] then estimates the social rate of return on investment in city social overhead in the 1830s and 1840s, and finding it to be considerably higher than the rate of return on private investment during the period, asks why investment was so low when social returns were so high. He supports an hypothesis developed by Wohl (1983) that "the public failure lay with an inefficient and unjust tax system" (p. 295), and argues that a turnaround occurred in the 1860s when the central government offered municipalities loans at below-market interest rates. The situation in developing countries today is different in many respects from that in Britain during its industrial revolution: in developing countries, on average, cities despite all their problems are healthier places to live than the countryside; also, the capital intensity of urbanization has been higher. But the main insight from

---

21 "Investment requirements during the late eighteenth century were kept modest by allowing the stock of social overhead [residential housing plus public works and public buildings] to fall, contributing, presumably, to a deterioration in the quality of life. . . . This growth strategy continued for the first three decades of the nineteenth century, although not with the same intensity. Per capita stocks in public works continued to decline, but dwelling stocks per capita began to rise. The latter did not rise enough to regain the levels of 1760.

By 1830, therefore, Britain had accumulated an enormous deficit in her social overhead stocks by pursuing seventy years of industrialization on the cheap. It cost her dearly, as the social reformers were about to point out. Between 1830 and 1860, there is some evidence of catching up in public works, but the gap in growth rates between dwelling stocks and all other fixed capital per capita increased." (p. 273)

the British experience, that an inefficient tax system failed to raise enough revenue to finance much-needed urban infrastructure but subsidized loans succeeded, is most germane. From the perspective of intergenerational equity, it makes no sense for the entire infrastructure costs associated with the present rapid urbanization in developing countries to be borne by the current generation, when future generations that will benefit from the investment will be considerably wealthier. To ensure a reasonable quality of life over the next half century, cities in developing countries will need to increase their rates of investment in urban public infrastructure, and a strong case can be made that this investment should be debt financed. But who is to provide the loans? In contrast to the British experience in the 1860s, the public finances of central governments in developing countries are not much healthier than local governments', largely due to the extent of tax evasion arising from informality. The desirability of loans from the international community seems clear cut. Yet, as shall be commented on in the next section, which deals with the housing policy experience in developing countries, recent donor aid to support urban infrastructure has been niggardly. This needs to change.

The provision of basic urban infrastructure to a neighborhood in which most housing is informal "regularizes" it (gives it quasi-legal status). By strengthening property rights, regularization stimulates investment in the neighborhood's housing. Regularization of a neighborhood in which housing is simply in violation of code may encourage the development of more housing that is in violation of code, and may well be unsightly and poorly planned, but surely this is better than the status quo. Regularizing squatter settlements on vacant government land that is poorly used seems sensible too. Appropriate policy with respect to squatter settlements on government land that has been left vacant for good reason or on private land is more problematical.

We conclude this section by summarizing the major constraints informality imposes on the design of housing policy in developing countries, which provides a backdrop for a broad-brush review of these countries' housing policy experience in the section that follows.

Recent housing policy experience in developed countries, which will be reviewed in the next section, indicates that demand-side, income-related housing subsidy programs are generally more effective in getting decent and affordable housing to the needy than public housing and other supply-side programs (Olsen, 2003). Unfortunately, in most developing countries, because of the large informal sector, household income cannot be measured at all accurately, which effectively precludes broad-based, income-related, demand-side housing programs, such as housing allowances and housing vouchers, being employed. This consideration by itself suggests that supply-side housing subsidy programs might be relatively more effective in developing countries than developed countries. Examples of such programs include public housing in poor neighborhoods and the subsidization of the basic building materials used in self-help housing.

But other considerations call into question the effectiveness of broad, supply-side housing policy generally as a redistributive tool in developing countries. Research in developed countries suggests that the target efficiency of such policies is low (Olsen 2003). Also, as explained above, the fiscal constraints on governments in developing countries are more severe than those in developed countries, which limits the scope for redistribution. The poor might be better helped by stimulating economic growth through channeling market forces—a rising tide lifts all boats—than by undertaking ambitious redistributive expenditure programs. And other redistributive expenditure programs, such as subsidizing basic staples, and upgrading the infrastructure in poor neighborhoods to ensure adequate basic education, health, and sanitation, are likely more cost-effective redistributive tools. However, geographically targeted slum upgrading projects that combine infrastructure provision with subsidies for housing upgrading have proved to be effective.

Housing Policy Experience in Developed Countries

Olsen (2003) and Green and Malpezzi (2003) provide expert reviews of the current state of housing policy in the United States, as well as some of its history. The federal government plays a dominant role in low-income housing policy, though in recent years local governments have been playing a larger role. There are three types of federal rental housing assistance programs, none of which is an entitlement program. The first is public housing, housing projects that are owned and operated by local public housing authorities established by local governments but funded primarily by the federal government. The second involves projects that are owned privately, either by nonprofits or for-profit firms, and receive subsidies from the government. The third is tenant-based assistance in private housing—housing allowance and housing voucher programs. All the programs have exhibited considerable, indeed rather bewildering, variation over time, in terms of the form and magnitude of the subsidies provided to building owners, as well as tenant eligibility criteria and tenant rent formulae. Less than half of the 14 million renter households that satisfy the eligibility criteria actually receive rental assistance. Over the past four decades, there has been a steady movement away from public housing and towards housing allowances calculated according to tenant household income, so that now only about 30 percent of federally subsidized housing units are in public housing. The current majority view, based on numerous empirical studies, many of which are reviewed in Olsen (2003), is that demand-side, income-related, rental assistance policies are more efficient than supply-side rental assistance policies, according to a variety of criteria. As well, the bad experience with public housing has led policy makers to favor the "deconcentration of poverty populations" and broader housing choice for rent-assisted tenants. Most owner-occupied housing assistance comes via the income tax system, in particular the deductibility of homeowner mortgage interest payments for households that choose itemized deductions. Since most poor households pay less income tax by not itemizing, the income tax provides little encouragement to poor households for homeownership.

There seem to be no overall reviews of housing policy in Europe comparable to Olsen's and Green and Malpezzi's for the United States. Several differences from the U.S. experience during the post–World War II era are, however, evident, as well as similarities to it. First, especially in Northern Europe in the 40 years after World War II, government involvement in the housing sector was far more extensive than in the United States, to the extent that in some countries most housing units were built and allocated by the state. In some countries, this was due to different social philosophies; the Nordic countries especially were more socialistic and less market-oriented, placing more emphasis on equity and less on efficiency. In other countries, housing institutions set up to respond to the critical housing situation after the war were only slowly dismantled. The application of first-generation rent control programs to private rental housing was ubiquitous. Second, in response to both the inefficiencies created by overregulation and the heavy fiscal burden of government-provided housing, over the last 20 years all European countries have been gradually withdrawing from the housing sector, by deregulating and moving towards greater reliance on markets in the provision of housing, with rental housing assistance being increasingly geared to income. Third, there has been the same trend as in the United States towards demand-side, tenant-based housing allowances, and away from supply-side, construction-based subsidies. And fourth, while European countries have moved to greater reliance on the market in the provision of housing, the sentiment lingers that it is the responsibility of government in a civil society to ensure decent and affordable housing for all its citizens.

Housing Policy Experience in Developing Countries

Since housing policy in developing countries is poorly documented, this section will review the World Bank's experience with housing policy assistance to developing countries, which is generally well documented. The World Bank has supported a series of housing policy initiatives. Public housing projects were dominant during the 1960s and are now widely acknowledged to have been a failure. Funds were often made available for construction but not for maintenance, and most rents fell sharply in real terms due to rent control, leading to rapid deterioration of housing units. The evolution of the Bank's housing policy from 1970 to 1992 is expertly documented in "Housing: Enabling Markets to Work" (World Bank 1993, pp. 51–69). Quotes from those pages follow:

> The evolution of the World Bank's housing policy through two decades can be divided into three stages. The first decade of Bank housing policy focused mainly on "sites and services" and slum-upgrading projects; the second gradu-

ally shifted the emphasis to housing finance development; and recently there has been a gradual shift to "housing policy development" loans.

Sites-and-services and slum upgrading projects, initiated in Senegal in 1972, signaled the first fundamental shift in housing policy in the postwar years—from total public housing provision to public assistance in private housing construction. The shift was based on the realization that in most developing countries legal housing produced by the private sector was not affordable for most urban residents; the mass production of enough high-standard housing to meet urban needs required massive subsidies that most governments in market-oriented economies were either unwilling or unable to afford; that low-income countries were building affordable housing through an evolutionary process, with self-help and self-management of the building process; and that providing secure land tenure and basic infrastructure services increased the incentives of households themselves to invest their savings, labor, and management skills in housing.

Sites-and-services and slum upgrading projects sought to translate these observations into practical solutions by implementing more affordable building standards and providing basic infrastructure services or core-housing units instead of finished units. In this manner, the serviced sites, with secure titles and long-term leases, would provide households with an affordable foothold in the housing sector without requiring subsidies. These projects, although in some cases relatively large, were conceived as experimental demonstration projects seeking to meet three primary objectives: the provision of affordable adequate housing for low-income families; cost recovery from beneficiaries resulting in the elimination of public subsidies; and replicability of such projects by the private sector, demonstrating that it could move down-market to produce affordable housing in large numbers.

The first objective of these projects, physical provision of low-cost housing units, was broadly achieved. Unfortunately, the large majority of projects met neither the second nor the third objectives. A detailed 1987 Bank study [Mayo and Gross 1987] on subsidies in sites-and-services projects observed substantial interest rate subsidies in [most] of the projects carried out. A detailed study of subsidies in Bank-assisted projects . . . yielded estimates of subsidies ranging from 50 to 75 percent of the true economic cost . . . for five of the seven projects. . . .

The third, objective, replicability . . . was generally not met because key features were not replicable [by the private sector] on a large scale. The waiver of zoning, land use, and building regulations, availability of foreign and domestic expertise, access to government land at below-market prices, and interest rate subsidies were important aspects of such projects that either were not or could not be replicated.

Slum upgrading projects . . . were, conversely, able to satisfy the replicability criterion, and to distribute subsidies more widely to the poor. . . . Although loans for such projects were smaller and more difficult to administer than housing finance loans, they will remain a critical component of Bank lending for years to come.

A significant shift in housing policy and practice within the Bank took place during the 1980s. Lending gradually moved away from sites-and-services toward lending to housing finance institutions. The shift was motivated by two broad objectives. First, there was a perceived opportunity for the Bank to address broader economic issues in the borrowing countries. A well-functioning housing finance system was seen as contributing to financial sector objectives through improved domestic resource mobilization, and to fiscal objectives by making subsidies more transparent and better targeted.

The second, and perhaps more immediate, objective was to affect overall policies and performance of the housing sector through the broad instrument of housing finance system development.

The monograph goes on to say that the main lessons learned at the Bank during the two decades were as follows: the macroeconomic and regulatory environments are important; the informal housing sector has significant contributions to make; projects have limited impacts; attention should continue to shift to the housing sector as a whole; and emphasis should shift from projects to institutional reform.

Thirty Years of World Bank Shelter Lending (Buckley and Kalarickal 2006) provides an updated history of World Bank shelter lending, presents current thinking at the Bank about which housing policies are effective and which are not, and discusses promising directions for future shelter lending. The monograph reports on significant improvement in the policy environment in most developing countries since the 1993 monograph was written; housing financial markets have been significantly liberalized. At the same time, reflecting the reaction against the "Washington consensus," it argues that that the withdrawal of governments and the World Bank from housing assistance to low-income households has been excessive. Also, reflecting the policy debate surrounding Hernando De Soto's (2000) book, *The Mystery of Capital*, Buckley and Kalarickal place more emphasis on the importance of improving the functioning of urban land markets in developing countries while being skeptical of the value of expanding titling. Finally, reflecting the profession's shift in policy analysis, there is more discussion of the political economy of housing and land market policy.

Housing finance system development is ongoing and is already widely credited with stimulating investment in formal, owner-occupied housing at the top end of the housing market in many developing countries, which has likely had a beneficial, trickle-down effect on the informal housing sector. But it has not directly stimulated informal housing sector production; banks have not been interested in getting involved, because informality is inconsistent with prudential management and because serving the poor is unprofitable. There is also widespread recognition that government plays two important roles in housing finance liberalization: (i) deregulating and fostering financial innovation but (ii) at the same time providing prudential regulation and macroeconomic management to avoid housing financial crises.

Most developing countries have substantial housing subsidy programs. For reasons discussed in the section above, the bulk of these programs are aimed at middle-income owner-occupiers and so score poorly in terms of redistributive impact. The two exceptions are public housing and rent control,[22] which have been widely condemned for their inefficiency. The rationale for most of these programs seems to be political rather than economic. The Bank has been active in assisting several middle-income coun-

---

22 Rent control, in the form applied in most developing countries, can be regarded as a way of requiring landlords to subsidize their tenants' housing.

tries (Brazil, Iran, Mexico, Morocco, and Russia) improve the economic efficiency of their subsidy systems. Buckley and Kalarickal's discussion of housing subsidy programs is consistent with the argument made in the section above that in countries with a large informal sector the scope for redistributive housing subsidy programs is limited.

Buckley and Kalarickal's discussion of land market issues is enlightening. De Soto (2000) argued that investment in housing in developing countries has been severely impeded by regulation, that investment in informal housing has been further impeded by ambiguous property rights, and that titling land with ambiguous property rights will sharply stimulate investment in low- and middle-income housing. On the first point he was right, as evidenced by the inelasticity of formal housing sector supply and the high price of titled land in most cities in developing countries. On the second point, he may or may not have been right, but on the third point he was largely wrong. Titling by itself appears to do little to solve land market problems. The titling process is costly and time consuming; titling land that is illegally occupied raises legal and compensation problems; titling may conflict with traditional property rights; and titling a property is not enough to obtain a mortgage. Nevertheless, De Soto succeeded in underscoring the need for deep reform to make the land supplied for development more responsive to price signals,[23] Such reform would, however, encounter strong political opposition from landed elites.

Between 1972 and 1981, about 90 percent of World Bank shelter lending went to slum upgrading and sites and services projects. For the period 1992 to 2005, this figure fell to only slightly over 10 percent. The Bank has been reconsidering its withdrawal from direct involvement with low-cost housing, and is now advocating the expansion of lending for such projects but on a larger scale than before, under the principle of subsidiarity, and with extensive community participation. Most of these projects involve infrastructure construction or upgrading with self-help housing subsidies.

Over the past 15 years, there have been other initiatives in World Bank lending that do not involve housing policy per se but are intimately tied to housing. The first is "private participation in infrastructure" (PPI), which includes both privatization in the construction and provision of urban infrastructure services and private-public partnerships. Annez (2006) provides a thorough and thoughtful review of the policy experience with PPIs. Her conclusions are cautionary:

> The private financing for urban PPI has been quite limited and undeniably disappointing in relation to the high expectations prevailing in the 1990s. . . . PPI appears to be a[n] unreliable source of finance. . . . Those local governments strapped for funding and keen to expand their investments would be wise to recognize [the] limitations [of PPI] . . . and [central] governments encouraging local governments to use PPI to support their investment programs need to recognize that PPI entails important fiscal risks as well. . . . PPI is inherently

---

23 The Bank's Articles of Agreement have recently been amended to allow it to provide loans for the purchase of land. This may open up a new avenue for Bank policy.

limited in scope for financing urban infrastructure for the wide array of non-commercial infrastructure services cities need. Even for commercial services like water supply, subsidies are prevalent all over the world, and in many of the poorest, most rapidly urbanizing countries, it will be difficult to attract private finance for necessary expansions of the water network while restructuring subsidies to make them financially sustainable and socially acceptable.

The assessment of the United Nations Human Settlements Programme (UN-HABITAT) (2005, pp. 47–49) points as well to the adverse distributional effects of PPI in developing countries. As economic theory would suggest, privatization is often profitable only when providers have effective monopoly power and exploit it.[24]

The second such initiative in recent years is well known: microfinance. Chapters 6 and 7 of UN-HABITAT (2005) provide a well-informed discussion of recent developments. The chapters contrast four forms of loans: mortgage finance by banks, microenterprise finance, shelter microfinance, and community funds. Microenterprise finance is targeted to small entrepreneurs, shelter microfinance to households with land wishing to improve their structures, and community funds to those without secure tenure for the construction of basic housing and infrastructure. A dominant theme is that shelter microfinance agencies and community organizations need links to the state to provide funding on the required scale but that establishing these links carries with it the dangers of bureaucratization.

The Bank has also experimented with making its housing-related loans conditional on the recipient country's streamlining its housing regulatory régime. And recently the Bank has been researching the effects of decentralized poverty alleviation programs (Galasso and Ravallion 2005), whereby the central government allocates poverty alleviation funds to community organizations, which in turn decide on the allocation of funding across households. The tentative finding is that the community organizations do a better job of targeting funding to the neediest households than central governments do in allocating funding to the neediest communities.

It is noteworthy that, after public housing, the World Bank has provided little loan support to programs that give direct assistance to renters, even though the poorest households must be predominantly renters.

Funding is, of course, central to housing policy. In most developing countries, the central government collects taxes from the more attractive tax bases, leaving the less attractive tax bases to local governments. In recent years there has been a worldwide trend towards the decentralization of government expenditure functions. In developed countries, this has been accompanied by an increase in formula-based intergovernmental grants. In many developing countries, local governments have simply been left to do more with little or no increase in funding from the central government.[25]

---

24 The privatization of water supply in a poor country seems a particularly dangerous ideological excess because of the extreme harm its faulty execution may cause.

25 Theory suggests that land taxation is an efficient revenue source for local governments. Even when account is taken of ambiguities in property rights for land and tax evasion in the informal sector, it is disappointing that local governments in developing countries do not generate more revenue from this source.

While cursory, this review of the housing policy experience of developing countries, from the perspective of the World Bank and UN-HABITAT, reinforces points made in the earlier section on the welfare economics of housing policy in developing countries, particularly how severely the presence of a large informal economy constrains housing policy.

1. In discussions of housing policy in developing countries, there is little if any mention of income-related housing assistance programs, simply because the bulk of income received by poor households is derived from informal economic activity and is therefore undocumented. Whatever redistribution occurs via housing policy is done without being explicitly tied to household income. Furthermore, with the exception of public housing, direct assistance to renters is rare.

2. The lack of available funds to conduct housing programs at a national scale is of central concern in almost all developing country housing policy discussions. One might think that this simply reflects the relative poverty of developing countries. But cross-country studies (see, for example, Malpezzi and Mayo 1987), as well as casual intuition, indicate that households in developing countries do not spend a larger proportion of their incomes on housing than households in developed countries. Thus, the greater difficulty developing countries have had in mounting national housing programs than developed countries can be ascribed to the greater difficulty they have had in raising revenue, *relative to the size of their economies*, which derives from tax evasion in the informal economy eroding their tax bases.

3. Another common theme is the dysfunctionality of housing policy in developing countries. Not only do central governments fail to establish national housing programs but also governments at all levels set up numerous impediments to private housing development, primarily excessive and burdensome housing and land use regulation and excessive fees (Angel 2000). It was argued earlier that this dysfunctional behavior is, at least to some extent, a rational response by government agents to low fiscal capacity relative to the size of the economy, deriving from the large relative size of the informal economy.

4. From the mid-1980s until very recently, the literature on housing policy in developing countries emphasized the importance of removing the impediments to the smooth operation of housing markets but contained little discussion of housing policy as a redistributive tool. Even UN-HABITAT, whose rhetoric concerning slums is decidedly left wing, said little about large-scale housing programs directed specifically at the neediest households. It seemed that the community concerned with housing policy in developing countries had resigned itself to the inability of government to provide "decent and affordable housing for all." But the tide now seems to be changing.

Even though governments in developing countries face more severe constraints in the design of effective housing policy than do developed countries, the picture is not altogether bleak. The research consensus is that both formal and informal housing markets in developing countries respond to market and policy stimuli as textbook models suggest. Thus, housing policy can be effective. The poor information central governments have about household incomes precludes broad-based redistributive housing policy, and the high cost of public funds means that governments must choose their housing policies with care. But there is still scope for ameliorating housing policy. The central government should take the lead in enabling markets to work, which it can do by liberalizing but at the same time prudentially regulating housing finance markets and by instituting land market reform, and by reducing the regulatory burden it imposes and providing incentives for lower levels of governments to reduce theirs, and more generally by promoting policies that increase participation in the formal housing sector. It also has an important role to play in redistributive housing policy, albeit an indirect one, by accepting responsibility for ensuring that all households, especially those with children, are housed according to realistic minimum standards and receive basic infrastructure services, and by providing matching grants to local governments that institute policies to meet these standards. The tasks of local governments are to work with neighborhood and community associations to come up with policies that target neighborhoods with the greatest housing need, and to provide the tax revenues needed to partially fund the policies.

The international community can help in myriad ways, but one policy initiative stands out: Help national governments borrow to finance their urban infrastructure needs during their periods of rapid urbanization, so that the costs are not completely borne by the current generation. Doing so would not only relieve much misery today but would result in more pleasant cities for future generations.

Conclusions

Developing countries differ from developed countries not only in per capita income but also in having a relatively large informal sector. In the major cities of poor countries, defined here as the bottom two quintiles of countries classified by per capita income, about half of the labor force works in the informal sector, and a considerably larger proportion of the poorest households does so. As well, in the lowest income countries, almost two thirds of the urban population lives in informal housing, and again an even larger proportion of the poorest households does so. This chapter has argued that the relatively large informal sector along with the relatively large proportion of informal housing in these countries substantially affects what housing policies will work and what will not, so that much of the housing policy experience of developed countries is not transferable to developing countries.

In developed countries there has been a major reorientation in low-income, rental housing policy over the last three decades, away from public housing and subsidized construction of private housing units for the poor and toward housing allowances based on household income. Since governments in developing countries cannot observe informal-sector incomes with any accuracy, any income-related housing assistance would have to be based on formal-sector income. But since those with zero or very low formal income include not only the destitute but also wealthy, informal-sector entrepreneurs, conditioning housing assistance on formal income would have very low target efficiency. Thus, a large informal sector effectively precludes income-related housing assistance.

A large informal sector affects housing policy in another important way. The larger is the relative size of the informal sector, the smaller is the proportion of economic activity that is taxed. Thus, holding constant the level of "real" per capita income—which includes both formal- and informal-sector income—in a country, the larger is the informal sector, the smaller is fiscal capacity. In turn, the smaller is fiscal capacity, the higher are the tax rates needed to raise a given amount of government revenue, the more distortionary is the tax system, and the lower is the optimal size of the government budget. If the same is true of the equilibrium as for the optimum, then one should observe governments in developing countries being hard pressed to finance even the basic level of public services commensurate with the average standard of living, and that is indeed what one observes. To some extent, one can also attribute some other characteristics of developing countries to their governments being strapped for cash: excessive regulation, excessive fees for permits, low-paid civil servants, and bureaucratic corruption.

Unauthorized housing is housing that violates regulations concerning land ownership, land use and zoning, and building construction. Squatter housing is housing that occupies land illegally. The large proportion of housing that is unauthorized has impacts on government housing policy too. If the government were to simply regularize unauthorized housing, developers would have little incentive to conform to regulations. Thus, the government must strike a balance between discouraging unauthorized housing and disrupting the informal housing market and hurting the needy.

Economists make a fundamental distinction between efficiency and equity. Most economists who are experts on housing in developing countries argue that housing policy can best achieve efficiency by enabling housing markets to work. There is abundant evidence that informal housing markets operate in essentially the same way as formal housing markets. Thus, enabling housing markets to work entails not only correcting market failures and reducing the excessive amount of government land use and housing regulation, but also tolerating and facilitating informal housing markets. Assisting community organizations in setting up microfinance for informal housing and infrastructure investment is a promising new line of policy.

Achieving equity is more difficult. In developed countries, the primary tools for achieving equity have been redistribution via the income tax and the free or heavily subsidized provision of basic services—health, primary education, sewerage, sanitation, and police. Providing subsidized housing for low-income households has also played an important role, especially in Europe. In developing countries, the scope for redistribution is considerably more circumscribed. Formal-sector incomes can be taxed, but since the government cannot observe informal-sector incomes, and since the bulk of the poor earn their living in the informal sector, redistribution through the income tax system would be ineffective. Redistribution via the subsidized provision of basic services to poor neighborhoods is potentially effective, but governments in developing countries are so strapped for cash that even the most benevolent would be hard pressed to provide adequate services for the poor.

What role should housing policy in developing countries play in achieving equity? Income-related housing assistance cannot be implemented effectively. One may reasonably argue that the poor need adequate food, clothing, and health care, and a clean and secure environment, more than they need more spacious housing. Even if this argument is correct (some recent evidence suggests that a minimal level of housing is important for both health and happiness), the issue remains of how best to provide housing to the very needy—the homeless, the destitute, and poor families with children receiving inadequate services. Since most very needy urban households are renters, and since income-related rental housing assistance is unworkable, perhaps the best that can be done for them is to ensure that the neighborhoods in which they reside receive adequate basic services.

Developing countries are urbanizing at an unprecedented rate and their cities are showing the strains. Enabling formal and informal markets to work will go a considerable way to relieving the strains, but active government intervention is also needed to ensure that adequate infrastructure for this period of rapid urbanization is provided and that the poor lead lives consistent with dignity. Unfortunately, the high proportion of economic activity that takes place in the informal sector and the high proportion of housing that is informal severely restrict the scope for redistribution and redistributive housing policy by government. The most promising avenue to achieving some degree of economic justice would appear to be the provision of a minimal level of public services—health, sanitation, sewage, primary education, and water—and this in turn will require the infrastructure needed to provide such services. Because infrastructure is durable, its costs should be shared across generations, but this is not an option for most developing countries without assistance from the international community.

References

Angel, S. 2000. *Housing Policy Matters*. Oxford: Oxford University Press.

Annez, P. 2006. "Urban Infrastructure from Private Operators: What Have We Learned from Recent Experience?" Policy Research Paper 4045, World Bank, Washington, DC.

Bator, F. 1958. "The Anatomy of Market Failure." *Quarterly Journal of Economics* 72: 351–79.

Bosch, M., E. Goni, and W. Maloney. 2007. "The Determinants of Rising Informality in Brazil: Evidence from Gross Worker Flows." Policy Research Working Paper 4375, World Bank, Washington, DC.

Brueckner, J., and H. Selod. 2008. "A Theory of Urban Squatting and Land-Tenure Formalization in Developing Countries." Unpublished paper, Commission on Growth and Development, Washington, DC.

Buckley, R., and J. Kalarickal. 2005. "Housing Policy in Developing Countries: Conjectures and Refutations." *The World Bank Research Observer* 20: 233–57.

Buckley, R., and J. Kalarikcal, eds. 2006. *Thirty Years of World Bank Shelter Lending: What Have We Learned?* Washington, DC: World Bank.

Cattaneo, M., S. Galiani, P. Gertler, S. Martinez, and R. Titunik. 2007. "Housing, Health, and Happiness." Policy Research Working Paper 4214, World Bank, Washington, DC.

Corlett, W., and D. Hague. 1953. "Complementarity and the Excess Burden of Taxation." *Review of Economic Studies* 21: 21–30.

De Paula, A., and J. Scheinkman. 2007. "The Informal Sector." Working Paper 13486, National Bureau of Economic Research, Cambridge, MA.

De Souza Briggs, X. ed. 2005. *The Geography of Opportunity.* Washington, DC: Brookings.

De Soto, H. 2000. *The Mystery of Capital.* New York: Basic Books.

Diamond, P. 1975. "A Many-Person Ramsey Tax Rule." *Journal of Public Economics* 4: 335–42.

Diamond, P., and J. Mirrlees. 1971. "Optimal Taxation and Public Production." *American Economic Review* 61: 8–27, 261–78.

Duranton, G. 2008. "Cities: Engines of Growth and Prosperity for Developing Countries." Working Paper No. 12, Commission on Growth and Development, Washington, DC.

Galasso, E., and M. Ravallion. 2005. "Decentralized Targeting of an Anti-Poverty Program." *Journal of Public Economics* 89: 705–27.

Gordon, R., and W. Li. 2005. "Puzzling Tax Structures in Developing Countries: A Comparison of Two Alternative Explanations." Working Paper 11661, National Bureau of Economic Research, Cambridge, MA.

Green, R., and S. Malpezzi. 2003. *A Primer on U.S. Housing Markets and Housing Policy.* Washington, DC: Urban Institute Press.

Guha-Khasnobis, B., R. Kanbur, and E. Ostrom. 2006. *Linking the Formal and Informal Economy: Concepts and Policies.* Oxford: Oxford University Press.

Harris, J., and M. Todaro. 1970. "Migration, Unemployment, and Development: A Two-Sector Analysis." *American Economic Review* 60: 126–42.

Hoy, M., and E. Jimenez. 1991. "Squatters' Rights and Urban Development: An Economic Perspective." *Economica* 58: 79–92.

Lucas, R. 1978. "On the Size Distribution of Firms." *Bell Journal of Economics* 9: 508–23.

Malpezzi, S. 1999. "Economic Analysis of Housing Markets in Developing and Transition Economies." In chapter 44 of *Handbook of Regional and Urban Economics*, ed. E. Mills and P. Nijkamp. Amsterdam: Elsevier.

Malpezzi, S., and S. Mayo. 1987. "The Demand for Housing in Developing Countries." *Economic Development and Cultural Change* 35: 687–721.

Mayo, S., and D. Gross. 1987. "Sites and Services—and Subsidies: The Economics of Low-Cost Housing in Developing Countries." *World Bank Economic Review* 1: 301–35.

McKenzie, D., and Y. Sakho. 2007. "Does It Pay Firms to Register for Taxes? The Impact of Formality on Firm Productivity." Policy Research Working Paper 4449, World Bank, Washington, DC.

Mirrlees, J. 1971. "An Exploration in the Theory of Optimal Income Taxation." *Review of Economic Studies* 38: 175–208.

Olsen, E. 2003. "Housing Programs for Low-Income Households." In *Tested Transfer Programs in the United States*, ed. R. Moffitt. Chicago: University of Chicago Press.

Pinto, S. 2004. "Assistance to Poor Households When Income Is Not Observed: Targeted In-Kind and In-Cash Transfers." *Journal of Urban Economics* 56: 536–53.

Ramsey, F. 1927. "A Contribution to the Theory of Taxation." *Economic Journal* 37: 41–61.

Rauch, J. 1991. "Modeling the Informal Sector Formally." *Journal of Development Economics* 35: 33–47.

Tobin, J. 1970. "On Limiting the Domain of Inequality." *Journal of Law and Economics* 13: 263–67.

Turnbull, G. 2008. "Squatting, Eviction, and Development." *Regional Science and Urban Economics*, in press.

UN-HABITAT. 2003. *The Challenge of Slums: Global Report on Human Settlement 2003*. London: Earthscan and UN-HABITAT.

———. 2005. *Financing Urban Shelter: Global Report on Human Settlement 2005*. London: Earthscan and UN-HABITAT.

———. 2006. *State of the World's Cities 2006*. London: Earthscan and UN-HABITAT.

Vickrey, W. 1945. "Measuring Marginal Utility by Reactions to Risk." *Econometrica* 13: 319–33.

Williamson, J. 1990. *Coping with City Growth during the British Industrial Revolution*. Cambridge: Cambridge University Press.

Wohl, A. 1983. *Endangered Lives: Public Health in Victorian Britain*. Cambridge, MA: Harvard University Press.

World Bank. 1993. "Housing: Enabling Markets to Work." World Bank Policy Paper, World Bank, Washington, DC.

CHAPTER 7
The U.S. Subprime Mortgage Crisis: Issues Raised and Lessons Learned

Dwight M. Jaffee

Introduction

The subprime mortgage crisis ranks among the most serious economic events affecting the United States since the Great Depression of the 1930s. This study analyzes the key issues raised by the crisis. These issues are fundamental to risk bearing, sharing, and transfer in financial markets and institutions around the world. The hope is that the analysis in this chapter will facilitate the design of new and efficient policies to mitigate the costs of the current crisis and to reduce the likelihood and costs of similar future events.

The chapter has been prepared for the Commission on Growth and Development, which was initiated in 2006 to explore the most effective approaches to stimulate growth in developing countries, and is sponsored by various governments, foundations, and the World Bank. Many of the

An earlier version of this chapter was presented at the April 11, 2008 Workshop on Fiscal and Monetary Policies and Growth, sponsored by the Commission on Growth and Development, the World Bank, and the Brookings Institution. I would like to thank discussants Alice Rivlin, Kevin Villani, Loic Chiquier, and all the Workshop participants for very helpful comments. For data help, I thank Jay Brinkman of the Mortgage Bankers Association and Mark Carrington of First American CoreLogic/LoanPerformance. Finally, I thank Patricia Annez, Robert Buckley, Michael Fratantoni, Richard Green, Alex Pollock, Bertrand Renaud, Peter Wallison, and John Weicher, all of whom offered helpful comments. None of the above is responsible for the opinions expressed or any errors that remain.

Editor's note: This chapter was completed after the Bear Stearns bailout of March 2008, but before the subsequent bailouts and multiple government interventions during the Fall of 2008.

issues raised by the U.S. subprime crisis also apply to high-risk loan markets in developing countries. The lessons learned from the crisis can thus play an important role in the growth and development of emerging economies.

Because the causes, propagation mechanisms, and results of the subprime mortgage crisis are themselves highly complex, an analytic framework is essential if the discussion is to proceed in a cohesive fashion. The framework applied in this chapter analyzes subprime mortgage lending as a major financial market innovation. The next section briefly describes the innovation process and its connection to the subprime mortgage crisis. The third section provides an annotated list of issues raised and lessons learned, in effect an executive summary. The fourth through sixth sections provide the more detailed analyses that underlie the listed issues and lessons. The final section provides brief concluding comments.

Subprime Mortgage Lending as a Financial Innovation

Financial market innovations generally occur in the context of three fundamental conditions, all of which are highly relevant to the origins of subprime mortgage lending:

- **The existence of previously underserved borrowers and investors.** Subprime borrowers were eager to use mortgage loans to finance home purchases, while a worldwide savings glut created large numbers of investors eager to earn the relatively high interest rates promised on U.S. subprime mortgage securities.[1]
- **The catalyst of advances in technology and know-how.** Subprime mortgage securitization applied state-of-the-art tools of security design and financial risk management, expanding on the successful implementation of similar tools to earlier classes of high-risk securitizations ranging from credit card loans to natural disaster catastrophe bonds.[2]
- **A benign and even encouraging regulatory environment.**[3] Although U.S. mortgage lenders face a complex network of state and federal regulations, few of these regulations impeded the origination of subprime loans.[4] Furthermore, the existing system of commercial bank capital

---

1 See Bernanke (2005) for just one of many discussions of the worldwide savings glut. See Bardhan and Jaffee (2007) for a discussion of how the demand for U.S. mortgage securities was significantly expanded by the enormous pools of foreign-held, but dollar-based, investment funds created by the U.S. trade deficits.

2 As part of an extensive literature on financial innovation, Allen and Gale (1994) and Molyneux and Shamroukh (1999) are two books that emphasize innovations in contract design and risk-sharing techniques, making them highly relevant to the innovation of subprime lending. Duffie (1995) provides a survey that includes a focus on the role of incomplete markets as a motivation for financial market innovation and security design. Silber (1975) provides a more institutional approach, including a chapter on mortgage market innovations by Jaffee (1975).

3 The regulatory environment should be interpreted broadly, certainly to include tax inducements for innovation. Papers that focus on the various forces creating innovation include Frame and White (2002), White (2000), Tufano (1995), Merton (1992), and Miller (1986, 1992).

4 U.S. Treasury (2008), Bernanke (2007), and Angell and Rowley (2006) highlight the earlier regulatory changes that provided an accommodating setting for the innovation of subprime lending.

requirements provided banks with strong incentives to securitize many of the subprime mortgage loans they originated.

Financial innovations are risky undertakings, all the more so when they create new classes of risky loans and securities. For example, the innovation of synthetic "portfolio insurance," introduced during the 1980s based on the then newly developed concept of dynamic portfolio replication, came asunder during the stock market crash of 1987. Similarly, the new market for trading "junk" bonds broke down as a result of the Michael Milken scandals of the early 1980s.[5] Most recently in the mid-1990s, Long-Term Capital Management (LTCM) was among the first hedge funds applying an innovative arbitrage strategy, but it had to be liquidated in the aftermath of the 1998 Russian financial crisis. Although each of these innovations was associated with a crisis, modified forms of the innovations still provide significant benefits today. It is hoped that the subprime mortgage innovation can be similarly reformed and refined, in order to provide future subprime borrowers with a continuing opportunity for homeownership.

Issues Raised and Lessons Learned

This section summarizes the study's conclusions in the form of an annotated list of issues and lessons. The complex issues require the analysis to be separated into three broad categories:

- Issues directly and specifically relating to subprime mortgage lending
- Issues relating to the securitization of subprime mortgages
- Issues affecting financial markets and institutions

The section will conclude with a discussion of how these issues are linked to financial markets in developing countries.

Issues Arising Directly from Subprime Mortgage Lending[6]

The Benefits of Subprime Mortgage Lending
Subprime mortgage lending is estimated to have funded more than 5 million home purchases, including access to first-time homeownership for more than an estimated 1 million households. Young and minority households have been among the primary beneficiaries. These are key benefits in view of the long-standing U.S. policy goals for increased homeownership. The increased homeownership has also stimulated a corresponding amount of new home construction.

---

5 The U.S. Savings and Loan crisis of the 1980s is not included because it was not the result of a failed innovation. Instead, it was the result of a misguided investment policy, in which the thrifts maintained a severe maturity mismatch, funding a portfolio of fixed rate mortgages with variable rate deposits. It is noted below that the portfolio losses afflicting certain subprime mortgage investors are the result of strikingly similar investment strategies.

6 Background material on the issues listed here is provided in the fourth section below.

Predatory Lending

Competitive market forces generally protect uninformed consumers from predatory forces, but subprime lending has revealed market failures in this regard. The substantial existing consumer protection regulations not withstanding, regulatory improvements are needed. Care must be taken, however, not to create destructive regulations that effectively end all subprime lending.

Loan Modifications for Defaulting Borrowers

Home mortgage lenders and servicers have traditionally been reluctant to modify loan terms, lest all their borrowers (current and future) request such changes; servicers also face contractual limitations. Nevertheless, lenders and servicers have been amenable to current governmental plans, perhaps because the resulting loan modifications can be characterized as one-time emergency transactions. Unfortunately, it is also the case that many defaulting subprime borrowers are beyond such help, and the default rate on once-modified loans is itself quite high.

Limiting Borrower Costs from Subprime Mortgage Default and Foreclosure

The costs imposed by subprime loan foreclosures are limited because mortgage borrowers simply give up their home in lieu of making the mortgage payments. Although a borrower's (already subprime) credit rating will fall further and access to a new mortgage is unlikely for several years, steps can be taken to minimize even these costs; see http://youwalkaway.com/.

Issues Relating to the Securitization of Subprime Loans[7]

The Securitization Process Was Not a Substantial Source of the Subprime Mortgage Crisis

The recent report of the President's Working Group on Financial Markets (2008), among others, suggests that incomplete disclosures and the securitization process caused investors to be duped into purchasing high-risk subprime mortgage securities. The purchasers of these securities, however, almost uniformly include only the most sophisticated institutional investors worldwide. The name "subprime" also seems clear enough, and data documenting the extremely high foreclosure rates on subprime loans have been publicly available at least since 2002. In short, the securitization process per se was not a fundamental source of the subprime mortgage crisis.

Mortgage Lending and Real Estate Price Cycles

Boom and bust cycles in real estate prices are a recurring phenomena, in large part based on the reinforcing process in which expected rising real estate prices expand mortgage lending, while expanded mortgage lending drives prices higher. Of course, fundamentals eventually take hold, and a crash inevitably ensues. If there has been a "moral hazard" in subprime mortgage lending and securitization, it lies with the failure of lenders, inves-

---

7 Background material on the issues listed here is provided in the fifth section below.

tors, the credit rating agencies, and the monetary authority to recognize that mortgage lending booms almost inevitably end in crashes.[8]

The Credit Rating Agencies Underestimated Correlated Risks and House Price Declines

The credit rating agencies (CRAs) systematically underestimated the risk on subprime mortgage pools, attributing too much weight to FICO scores and too little weight to the likelihood of falling house prices and its powerful effect in creating mortgage defaults.[9] For similar reasons, the CRAs also underestimated the risk on collateralized debt obligations (CDOs) that were backed by subprime securitization tranches. The major CRAs have now all announced plans to modify their rating methodologies for subprime mortgages pools and CDOs.

Investor Strategies Concentrated Investor Losses

The intensity of the losses suffered by many subprime mortgage investors is primarily the result of their having concentrated the risks by leveraging their positions with borrowed funds. The use of 10 to 1 leverage, for example, can transform a 10 percent realized loss into a 100 percent loss for a given initial capital. Furthermore, many of the positions were funded with very short-term loans. This strategy remarkably parallels that of the Savings and Loan Associations of the 1980s, who also used maturity mismatched and leveraged portfolios, and with similarly dire results.

Issues Regarding Regulatory Policies for Financial Markets and Institutions[10]

The Federal Reserve Loan to Expedite the Bear Stearns Merger

The Fed's emergency loan to expedite the Bear Stearns merger deviated from its standard rules by allowing the borrower both to post low-quality collateral and to deny the Fed the right of recourse to other assets if the loan were not repaid. The unique circumstances of the Bear Stearns crisis include (i) the very large dollar amounts, (ii) the generally weakened condition of most investment banks, and (iii) the need to avoid a formal Bear Stearns bankruptcy in view of that firm's very large positions as a derivative counterparty; see also issue (10).

Interlinking Counterparty Risks Require Regulatory Action

The Federal Reserve's direct participation in the Bear Stearns merger formally recognized, for the first time, the fundamental risks posed for the financial system by interlinking counterparty risks among the largest commercial

---

8 An extensive literature, extending across many countries and time, documents how expanded mortgage lending creates a boom in real estate prices, invariably followed by a crash. See, for example, Reinhart and Rogoff (2008), Gramlich (2007b), Brunnermeier and Julliard (2008), Jaffee (1994), and Litan (1992). Mian and Sufi (2008) specifically show that mortgage lending and house prices rose rapidly between 2001 and 2005 in precisely those zip codes with previously high rates of loan denial (based on Home Mortgage Disclosure Act [HMDA] data). And after 2005, these zip codes faced slowing price appreciation and rapidly rising mortgage default rates.

9 FICO is an abbreviation of Fair Isaac Company, which standardized the concept of individual credit scores.

10 Background material on the issues listed here is provided in the sixth section below.

and investment banks. The Fed feared that the failure of one central counterparty could topple the entire system. The implication is that the derivative counterparty system now parallels the payments system as a fundamental component of the financial system's infrastructure. Expanded federal regulation of the primary derivative market counterparties is now required, to parallel the regulations long imposed on depository institutions to safeguard the payments system.[11]

Market Illiquidity and Opaque Subprime Securities

A major factor in extending the subprime crisis has been a breakdown in financial market trading and liquidity, which has allowed the market prices for many subprime securities to fall well below what many would consider their "fundamental value." The unwillingness of investors to purchase these apparently undervalued subprime securities and CDOs can be attributed in part to the complex, opaque nature of the instruments. Investment banks are also generally required to report declines in the market value of their investment portfolios, which then reinforces the illiquidity problem. The Federal Reserve has responded appropriately by offering huge volumes of liquidity, but to date it has not succeeded in reviving the effective demand for the subprime and CDO securities.

Applying the Lessons of Subprime Mortgage Lending to Emerging Economies

Financial markets in general, and mortgage markets in particular, provide great potential benefits for economic growth and development in emerging economies.[12] The defining feature of mortgage loans, of course, is that land and structures can serve as collateral, allowing lenders to make loans in amounts that far exceed what they would otherwise be willing to extend to most consumer borrowers. Most developing countries have a comparatively rich endowment of land and structure collateral, giving the market a feasible starting point. A mortgage market will also encourage new home construction, since mortgage borrowing creates an expedited path to homeownership. A mortgage market will also increase the market liquidity for existing home sales, which has the key benefit of promoting a more mobile labor force.

Mortgage Market Innovations in Emerging Economies. The earlier discussion highlighted three key factors associated with mortgage market innovation in developed economies, namely (i) an effective demand and supply, (ii) access to expanding technology and know-how, and (iii) an accommodating regulatory structure. These three factors are equally critical for emerging economies. A strong demand for mortgage credit can be assumed in emerging economies, since financial services are generally underprovided.

---

11 More detailed proposals are offered in Jaffee and Perlow (2008), as well in the discussion in the sixth section below.

12 See Levine (1997) and (2003) for surveys on the benefits financial development provides for economic growth in emerging economies. See also Warnock and Warnock (2007), Renaud and Kim (2007), Buckley, Chiquier, and Lea (2006), and Jaffee and Renaud (1997) for the specific benefits of mortgage markets in emerging economies.

Figure 7.1 shows the mortgage debt to GDP ratios of a range of countries, developed and emerging, illustrating that the mortgage debt ratios tend to be very low in most emerging economies. Various methods of technology transfer also now allow mortgage technology and know-how to be readily available to emerging economies from any number of international firms and organizations (including the World Bank).

The dominant bottleneck for mortgage market innovations in emerging economies is an accommodating regulatory and legal system; governments must recognize that the benefits of a mortgage finance system will only be realized if property rights are reliably protected by the state. A sufficient supply of loanable funds is a second critical bottleneck. The banking system normally takes the lead in innovating mortgage lending, but there is a limited supply of deposit funds and many competing loan demands. Therefore, as the mortgage market expands, the banking system inevitably outruns its own capacity to hold all the originated mortgage loans.

Solutions for augmenting bank resources for holding mortgages can include the following:

- A bank may issue special "covered mortgage bonds" secured by pools of mortgages owned by the bank. The bonds would be sold in local or foreign capital markets.
- The banking system or the government may set up a "mortgage bank" that purchases mortgages, funding the portfolio with debt issued in local or foreign capital markets.
- Securitization can expedite the sale of mortgages to capital market investors, either locally or abroad.

Figure 7.1 Ratio of Mortgage Debt Outstanding to GDP

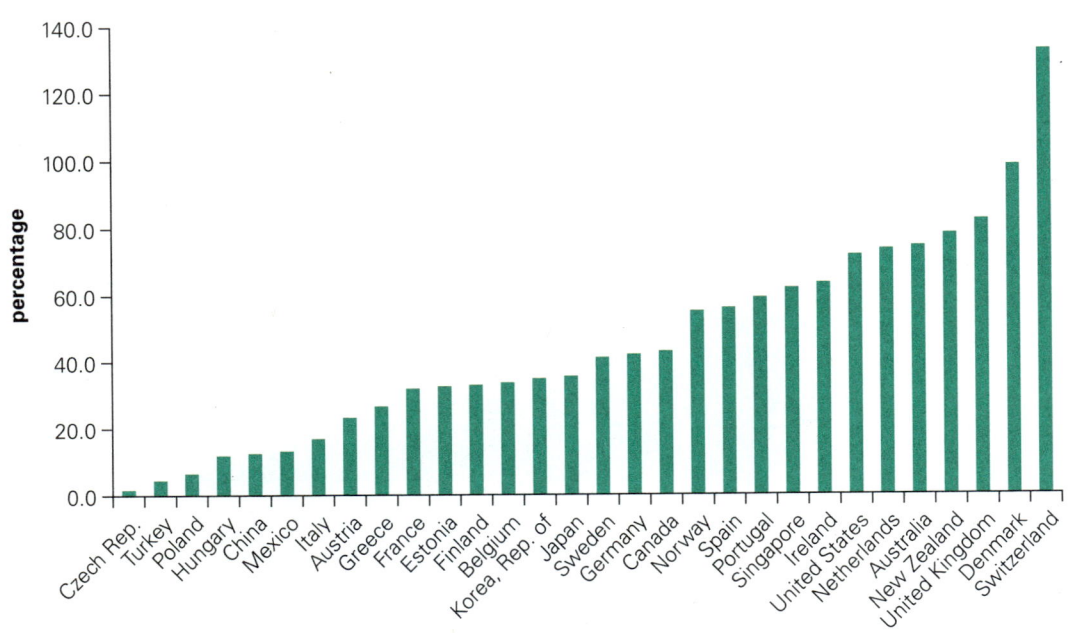

Source: Renaud and Kim (2007).

It is worth stressing that securitization provides a unique mechanism for accessing capital market funding for mortgage loans.[13] The key advantage of securitization is that a structured vehicle distributes the overall risk across the various tranches, thus creating a range of risk levels from the very high quality senior tranche to the riskiest equity tranche. Securitization thus allows the risks to be allocated to different investors, matching each investor's risk tolerance with the appropriate tranche. None of the events of the U.S. subprime mortgage crisis has changed this fundamental benefit of securitization.

The Pitfalls of Subprime Mortgage Lending Must Also Be Recognized. The subprime mortgage crisis also demonstrates that mortgage markets, and especially subprime mortgage markets, come with a potential cost. The following summarizes the lessons learned that may be considered particularly relevant for mortgage markets in emerging economies:[14]

- Starting with the "real" fundamentals, a legal infrastructure is critical to document ownership and to allow eviction in case of default. Co-signers are common on emerging economy loans, creating a form of recourse that goes beyond the real estate collateral. Local bank lenders may consider co-signers an adequate substitute for clear ownership and eviction powers. Investors in securitized mortgage pools, however, will consider strong title and eviction powers to be essential.
- Incomplete income records are common in emerging economies, especially where the grey-market economy may dominate the organized economy in size and importance. Lenders in emerging economies, however, can develop the equivalent of FICO scores, based on the borrower's credit card payment record. The concept is simple: a borrower must have a source of income if (s)he stays current on large credit card expenditures.
- Within the mortgage market, a regulatory and institutional infrastructure is needed to moderate the costs associated with the borrower defaults that are sure to occur. This should include a mechanism for providing loan modifications to avert loan defaults and a legal structure that minimizes the costs imposed on those borrowers who do default.
- Consumer protection legislation will become essential as the mortgage market expands and loans are made to relatively inexperienced and uninformed consumer borrowers. A review of the many existing U.S. programs is a good starting point.[15] The creation of standardized mortgage contract designs and forms may be particularly valuable.

---

13 Jaffee and Renaud (1997) stress the importance of capital market funding for mortgage markets in emerging and transition markets, and they provide a comparison of the different methods for accessing the capital market funding.

14 An extensive literature exists, of course, analyzing the benefits and pitfalls of creating mortgage markets in developing countries. See, for example, Buckley, Chiquier, and Lea (2006) and Renaud (2008) and the literature they cite. Buckley, Hendershott, and Villani (1995) discuss the privatization of the housing sector in transition economies.

15 See the discussion in the next section.

- Mortgage loans are unavoidably risky, raising the possibility of large-scale loan losses. It is thus essential that the banking regulations and regulators create suitable capital requirements and develop plans to deal with distressed institutions.
- The same forces of mortgage market innovation and increased mortgage lending that created the boom-bust real estate cycle as a component of the U.S. subprime crisis are an evident risk in an emerging economy; see Renaud and Kim (2007) for an excellent discussion of the U.S. housing price boom with comments on the comparable risk in emerging economies.

Subprime Mortgage Lending in the United States

This section provides more detailed background on the development of subprime mortgage lending in the United States. Figure 7.2 shows the growth in subprime lending, starting with the first available data in 1994 and continuing through 2007, based on data from the *Inside Mortgage Finance* (IMF) newsletter (http://www.imfpubs.com/issues/imfpubs_imf/).

Figure 7.2 Subprime Mortgage Originations, Annual Volume and Percent of Total

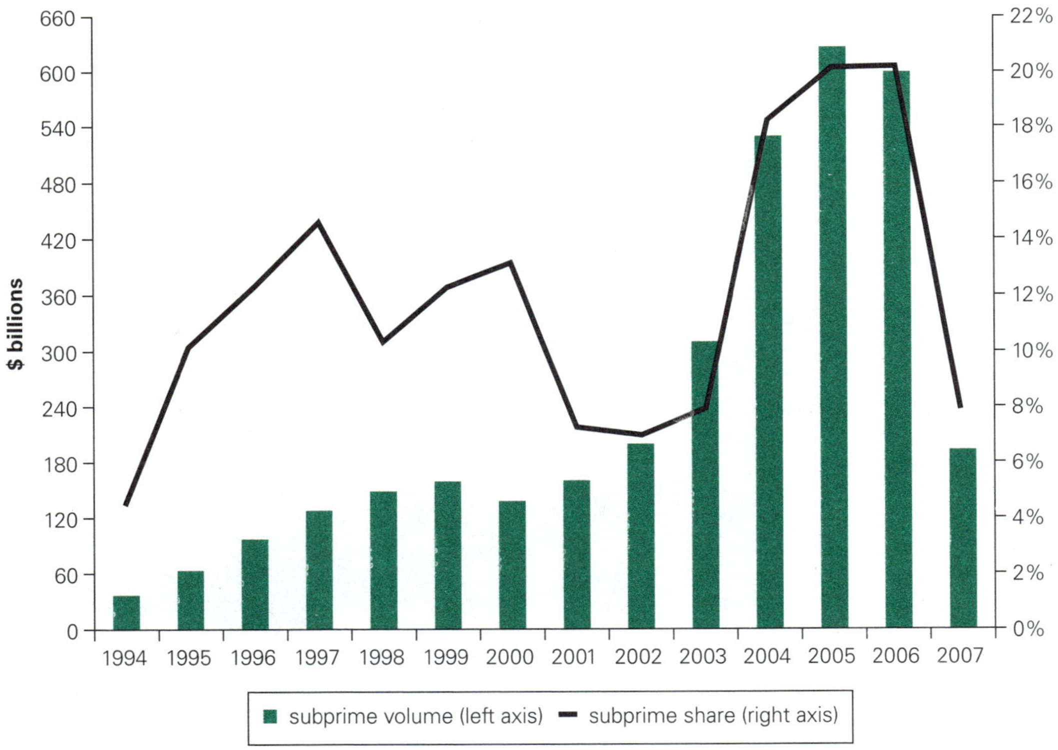

Source: Inside Mortgage Finance.

The figure shows two distinct periods of expansion in subprime lending. The first expansion occurred during the late 1990s, with subprime lending reaching an annual volume of US$150 billion and as much as 13 percent of the total annual mortgage originations. That expansion ended with the dot-com bust in 2000–01. The second expansion started in 2002, reaching annual loan volumes of over US$600 billion in 2005 and 2006 and representing over 20 percent of the total annual mortgage originations in those years.

Subprime Mortgage Lending: Benefits

The benefit of subprime mortgage lending can be measured by the number of households who purchased homes and achieved homeownership as the direct result of subprime mortgages. Table 7.1 shows the number of subprime loans originated, including the percentage that represented loans for home purchase, from 2000 to 2006 using the LoanPerformance (LP) data from First American CoreLogic (http://www.facorelogic.com/). While the LP data indicate almost 9 million first-lien subprime loans were made between 2000 and 2006, just over one-third—that is 3.28 million subprime loans—were made with the stated purpose of home purchase.[16] On the other hand, the LP data cover only approximately 70 percent of all subprime loans. Adjusting the LP home purchase number to be consistent

Table 7.1 Subprime Loans Originated for Home Purchase

Year	1 Total number of subprime loans (thousands)	2 Loans for home purchase (percent)	3 Number of homes purchased (thousands)	4 Adjusted number of homes purchased* (thousands)
2000	422	32.4	137	433
2001	508	30.3	154	385
2002	768	29.0	223	400
2003	1,273	29.9	381	567
2004	1,932	35.8	692	1,059
2005	2,274	41.3	940	1,296
2006	1,777	42.4	753	1,201
Total (2000–06)	8,954	36.6	3,280	5,340

Source: LoanPerformance (LP) data from First American CoreLogic.
*Adjusted to subprime dollar volume universe from Inside Mortgage Finance (see figure 2) versus sample total for the LP data.

---

16 Gerardi, Shapiro, and Willen (2007) also stress the importance of recognizing that almost two-thirds of subprime mortgages refinanced already existing mortgages. One result is that the aggregate number of subprime loan originations involves substantial double counting and thereby exaggerates their risk. This motivates our focus on home purchase subprime loans.

with the universe of all subprime mortgages (column 4 of table 7.1), we find approximately 5.34 million home purchases were funded with subprime mortgages.

An alternative measure of subprime homeownership benefits is based on the number of existing home and new home sales that used subprime lending. In table 7.2, the third column shows the total number of home sales, the sum of new and existing home sales. The fourth column shows subprime mortgage loans as the percentage of total mortgage originations, as graphed in figure 7.2. The estimate of the number of home sales that can be attributed to subprime lending is then derived as the product of the total number of home sales and the subprime share of total mortgage originations. Summing the years 2000 to 2006, we obtain an estimate of 6.2 million home sales, which, given the coarseness of the two methods, is reasonably close to the estimate of 5.3 million subprime home purchase mortgage loans shown in table 7.1.

The two estimates indicate that somewhat more than 5 million home purchases can be attributed to subprime mortgage lending. It should be understood, however, that this estimate will exceed, and probably far exceed, the number of first-time home purchases that can be attributed to subprime mortgages. Three key factors are as follows:

- Some subprime borrowers had already owned homes purchased with prime mortgages.
- Some subprime borrowers bought and sold several homes.
- Some subprime borrowers were investors, and possibly purchased multiple homes.

A third method of measuring subprime homeowner benefits is based on the number of new homeowners tabulated in the American Community

Table 7.2 Home Sales, Total and Attributable to Subprime Loans

Year	1 Existing home sales (thousands)	2 New home sales (thousands)	3 Total home sales (thousands)	4 Subprime originations (percent)	5 Subprime home sales (thousands)
2000	4,603	877	5,480	13.2	722
2001	4,734	908	5,642	7.2	408
2002	4,975	973	5,948	6.9	412
2003	5,443	1,086	6,529	7.9	513
2004	5,959	1,203	7,162	18.2	1,300
2005	6,180	1,283	7,463	20.0	1,495
2006	5,677	1,051	6,728	20.1	1,355
Total (2000–06)	37,571	7,381	44,952		6,204

Source: National Association of Realtors, Bureau of the Census, figure 2.

Survey of the U.S. Bureau of the Census. Table 7.3 shows the basic structure of the computation. Table 7.3A shows the homeownership rates, defined as the percentage of households that own the unit in which they live. The data are tabulated by the age of the head of the household. It can be seen that the ownership rates were generally rising between 2000 and 2006, although most of the age groups reached their peak ownership rate before 2006.

Table 7.3B tabulates the number of new homeowners during the 2000 to 2006 time period controlling for the "compositional" increase in home-ownership that would arise simply due to population aging and other changes in the demographic structure of households.[17]

The first column in table 7.3B shows that 6.59 million net homeowners were added between 2000 and 2006. This value includes the natural increase due to population aging, which is quantitatively dominant because older households have distinctly higher ownership rates (as shown in table 7.3A) and because the very large postwar baby boom cohort is just reaching the age of maximum homeownership. We control for this compositional increase in ownership by multiplying the number of households in 2000 for each age group (column 2) by the maximum increase in the homeownership rate observed for that age group between 2000 and 2006 (column 3). The resulting estimate is an increase of 1.38 million new homeowners between 2000 and 2006. We interpret this number as a first rough estimate of the

Table 7.3A Owner Occupancy Rates

Age of household head	Owner occupancy rates						
	2000	2001	2002	2003	2004	2005	2006
15 to 24 years	0.170	0.174	0.184	0.179	0.177	0.177	0.178
25 to 34 years	0.446	0.451	0.459	0.467	0.470	0.466	0.467
35 to 44 years	0.657	0.661	0.666	0.668	0.671	0.664	0.663
45 to 54 years	0.746	0.748	0.752	0.751	0.752	0.747	0.745
55 to 59 years	0.788	0.790	0.794	0.798	0.800	0.789	0.788
60 to 64 years	0.806	0.805	0.813	0.812	0.804	0.810	0.807
65 to 74 years	0.812	0.811	0.814	0.820	0.822	0.816	0.813
75 to 84 years	0.770	0.774	0.783	0.786	0.786	0.785	0.789
85 years and over	0.670	0.666	0.677	0.673	0.681	0.683	0.680
Total for all ages	0.653	0.657	0.664	0.668	0.671	0.669	0.673

Source: American Community Survey, U.S. Bureau of the Census.

17 Haurin and Rosenthal (2004) provide a careful empirical analysis of the factors inducing changes in U.S. homeownership rates between 1970 and 2000. Eggers (2005) provides a detailed analysis of the evolution of homeownership rates during the 1990s. Eggers, in particular, decomposes the increase in homeownership into a *rate effect*—reflecting changes in homeownership that arise due to changes in the homeownership rates within specific age and racial categories—and a *composition effect*—arising as the result of changes in the demographic structure of households (ownership rates remaining constant). The paper shows that of the aggregate increase in the homeownership rate during the 1990s of 1.96 percentage points, the rate effect accounted for 1.54 percentage points and the composition effect for 0.54 percentage points. We employ a similar method in table 3B to control for the composition effect during the 2000s.

Table 7.3B Computing Home Purchases

Age of household head	Total change in ownership 2000–06 (millions)	Number of households, 2000 census (millions)	Maximum change ownership rate (percent)	Subprime-induced new ownership (millions)
15 to 24 years	_0.07	6.0	0.014	0.08
25 to 34 years	0.15	18.5	0.024	0.44
35 to 44 years	_0.43	23.9	0.014	0.33
45 to 54 years	2.31	21.0	0.006	0.13
55 to 59 years	2.20	7.6	0.011	0.08
60 to 64 years	1.37	6.2	0.003	0.02
65 to 74 years	0.17	11.3	0.010	0.11
75 to 84 years	0.50	7.9	0.019	0.15
85 years and over	0.39	2.3	0.013	0.03
Total	**6.59**	104.8		**1.38**

Source: American Community Survey, U.S. Bureau of the Census.

number of first-time homeowners that might be attributed to subprime lending.[18]

Subprime Mortgage Loan Design

Mortgage contract design has played an essential role in the subprime innovation process.[19] Numerous subprime mortgages have been created, including:[20]

- standard, long-term, fixed-rate mortgages
- "option" mortgages, which allow borrowers to defer some of their payments
- converting ARMs, which start with fixed rates, then convert to adjustable rates
- low document loans, for borrowers that cannot provide complete documentation

---

18 The finding of a significant number of first-time homebuyers among subprime borrowers is consistent with the results of Mian and Sufi (2008). They use the HMDA data to determine the specific set of zip codes that faced exceptionally high rates of loan application denials prior to 2001. They then show that it is precisely these zip codes that benefited from a large increase in mortgage lending during the subprime boom period from 2001 to 2005. The analyses of Gerardi, Shapiro, and Willen (2007) and Demyanyk and Van Hemert (2008) also focus on home purchase decisions.

19 The design of U.S. mortgage contracts has an interesting history. The now standard, long-term, fixed-rate mortgage was developed by the Federal Housing Administration in the depths of the Great Depression to provide a functional instrument for homebuyers. The wave of soaring inflation and interest rates during the late 1970s and early 1980s created another wave of innovation; see Modigliani and Lessard (1975) and Jaffee (1984). Green and Wachter (2005) provide a recent overall survey of the history of mortgage lending in the United States.

20 Piskorski and Tchistyi (2007, 2008) describe the security design of subprime mortgages and Mayer and Piskorski (2008) provide a corresponding empirical analysis. Cutts and Van Order (2005) provide a general introduction to the economics of subprime lending.

These mortgages were all designed to meet specific needs: option mortgages for borrowers with widely fluctuating incomes, converting ARMs for borrowers who expect a rising income profile, and so on. Many subprime loans were also originated with the expectation that the borrowers would soon refinance into higher-quality loans, assuming the borrower's credit rating would improve and/or the borrower's equity in the house would rise as the result of rising home prices; see Pennington-Cross and Chomsisengphet (2007).

The credit quality of subprime mortgages also covers a wide spectrum.[21] For example, at the higher quality levels, subprime mortgages were purchased by the GSEs. The subprime lenders also succeeded in attracting a significant number of borrowers who would otherwise have been among the higher-quality FHA borrowers.[22]

Subprime Mortgage Loan Performance

Figures 7.3 to 7.5 show the available delinquency and foreclosure data from the Mortgage Bankers Association, with clear evidence that subprime loans included a significant number of low-quality credits. Figure 7.3 shows the

Figure 7.3 All Loans Past Due as Percentage of Category Total Outstanding

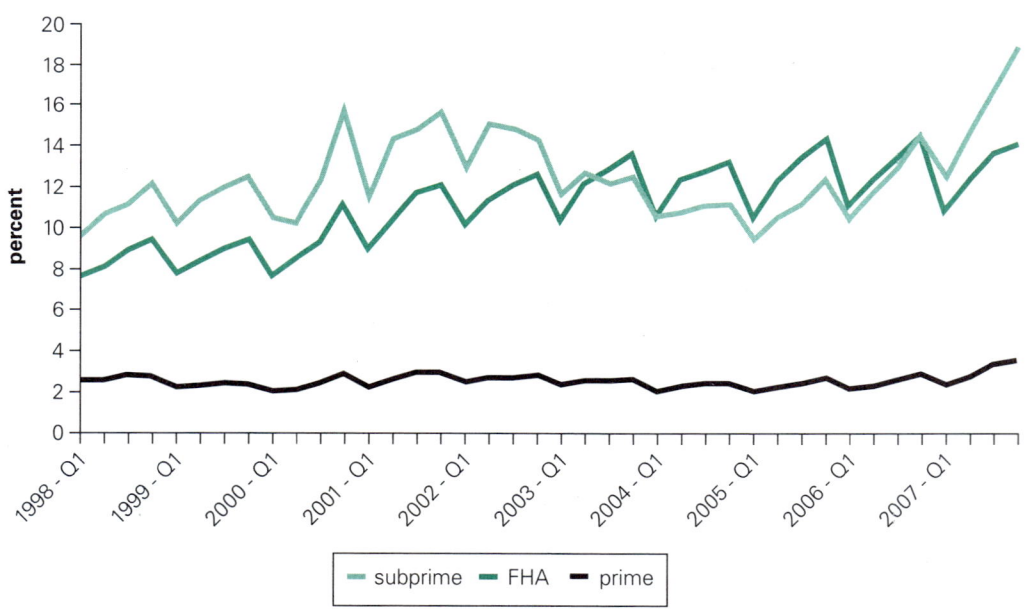

Source: Mortgage Bankers Association.

---

21 Chomsisengphet and Pennington-Cross (2006) provide an informative discussion of the evolution of subprime loans and the various terms on them. Their data, for example, show FICO scores that range from prime values approaching 700 to the very low, distinctly subprime levels below 550.

22 See Jaffee and Quigley (2007b) for a more complete analysis of the decline in FHA lending volume created by the expansion of subprime mortgage lending and a discussion of possible policy solutions.

past due loans in each category as a percentage of the total outstanding loans in that category. The lower line shows that past due prime loans have ranged from 2 to 4 percent of total prime loans since 1998, while past due FHA mortgages ranged from 8 to 14 percent of the FHA total, and past due subprime mortgages ranged from 10 to 19 percent of the subprime total.

Figure 7.4 shows the foreclosures started quarterly as a percent of the total loans outstanding in each category. Here the distinction between subprime and FHA loans is more dramatic, with many more subprime loans reaching the stage of foreclosure. This is likely the result of at least three factors: (i) FHA loans may require larger downpayment ratios, (ii) the average FHA loan has been outstanding much longer, allowing a greater buildup of borrower equity, and (iii) FHA loans are generally fixed-rate loans. It is also plausible that the underwriting standards applied on FHA loans were generally higher than the standards applied on subprime loans. The percentage of subprime loans starting foreclosure is now at its all-time high, but there was a previous cycle during the 2000 to 2002 period, at the time of the dot-com bust. Mortgage Bankers data showing the high delinquency and foreclosure rates on subprime loans during the 2000 to 2002 period were first publicly released in the fall of 2002, and have been updated quarterly ever since. Thus, since the fall of 2002, investors in subprime mortgage securities would have been aware of the relatively severe foreclosure behavior of subprime mortgages during the earlier cycle.

Figure 7.4 Foreclosures Started during Quarter as Percent of Category Total Outstanding

Source: Mortgage Bankers Association.

Figure 7.5 Loans in Foreclosure as Percent of Category Total Outstanding

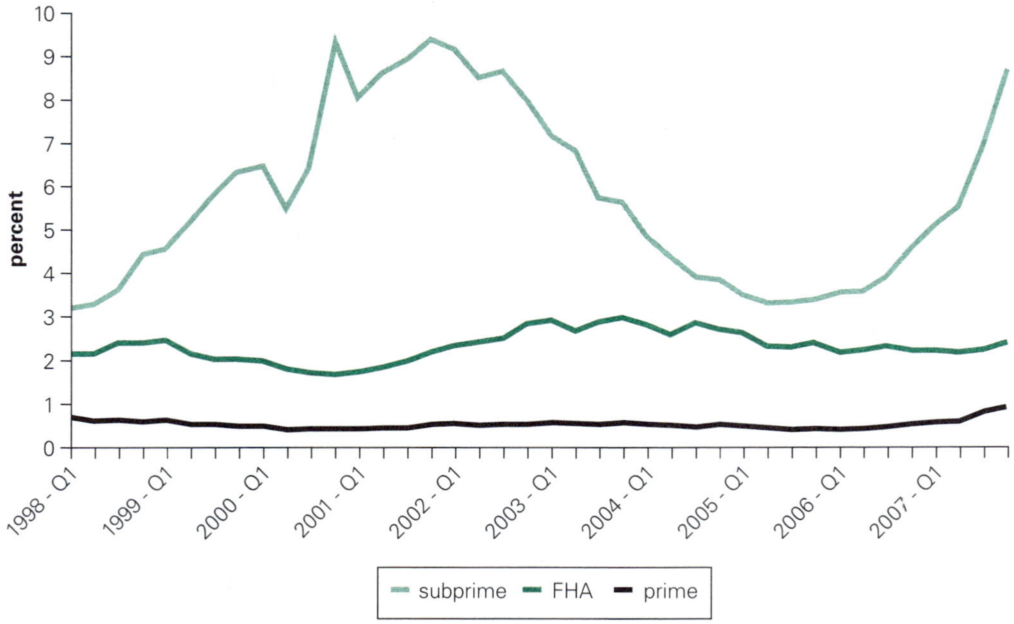

Source: Mortgage Bankers Association.

Figure 7.5 shows the inventory of loans in foreclosure as a percent of each category total. The foreclosure inventory percentages for prime and FHA loans have fluctuated within relatively narrow bands over time. In contrast, the percent of subprime loans in the process of foreclosure has fluctuated widely, with a baseline of about 3 percent, but reaching a peak in excess of 9 percent in the 2000 to 2002 period; the most recent observation at year-end 2007 is 8.65 percent. It is worth stressing that the data showing the earlier peak during the 2000 to 2002 period have been available to investors since 2002. This would belie the suggestion of the President's Working Group (2008) that investors had not received adequate disclosures concerning the riskiness of subprime loans.

Changing Credit Standards on Subprime Mortgage Originations

While figures 7.3 to 7.5 show the aggregate delinquency and foreclosure rates on subprime mortgages, they do not provide information on how the credit quality on subprime mortgages may have varied based on the year of origination. In particular, it has been suggested that the standards imposed by lenders may have deteriorated over time, such that the loans made in, for example, 2006 and 2007 were of substantially lower quality than the loans made in 2000 and 2001. Figure 7.6 sheds light on the issue, showing the delinquency rates (60 days or more) on subprime loans based on months since origination and the year of origination. The figure shows that the default rates on the 2006 and 2007 vintages far exceed the rates observed on the earlier vintages. Beyond these two vintages, however, the pattern is much

Figure 7.6 Subprime Delinquency Rate 60+ Days, by Age and Year of Origination

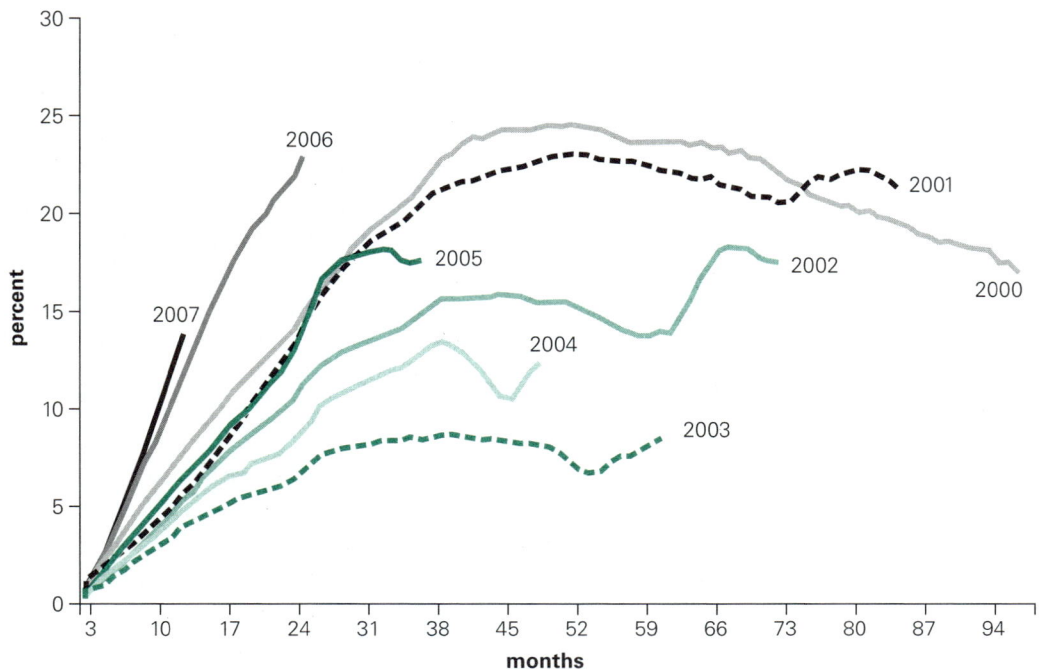

Source: LoanPerformance (LP) data from First American CoreLogic.

less clear, since the 2000 and 2001 vintages appear to be worse than 2005, while the 2003 vintage has the lowest delinquency rates of all the vintages.

An obvious issue in interpreting this evidence is whether changes in other factors over time might also be affecting the observed delinquency and foreclosure rates. At least the following three sets of potential determinants of delinquency and foreclosure rates could be relevant.

Measurable Loan and Borrower Characteristics. Both the types of subprime loans made and the objective borrower characteristics have changed over time. Table 7.4 provides a summary of some of the more important of these characteristics. FICO scores have actually been systematically improving from 2001 to 2006. The debt service to income ratio, in contrast, shows a progressively heavier payment burden over time. Similarly, the rising combined loan to value ratios (which include both first- and second-lien mort-

Table 7.4 Subprime Borrower and Subprime Loan Observable Factors

	2001	2002	2003	2004	2005	2006
FICO score	620	631	641	646	654	655
Debt service to income (%)	37.8	38.1	38.2	38.5	39.1	39.8
Combined loan to value ratio (%)	80.0	79.9	80.6	82.8	83.5	84.4
Fixed rate mortgages (%)	41.4	39.9	43.3	28.2	25.1	26.1

Source: Table 1, Demyanyk and Van Hemert (2008).

gages) and the falling share of fixed-rate mortgages are both further signs of riskier loans.

House Price Inflation. Whatever the objective loan and borrower characteristics, rising home prices will discourage mortgage defaults—borrowers can just sell their homes if need be—whereas falling home prices will dramatically increase the default rates. Figure 7.7 shows that as recently as 2005, house prices were rising at 9 percent annual rates, clearly counteracting any other tendencies toward rising mortgage defaults. House price appreciation, however, suddenly slowed starting in mid-2006, and signficant house price declines have been the norm since mid-2007. The recent studies by Demyanyk and Van Hemert (2008) and Gerardi, Shapiro, and Willen (2007), among others, document the critical role that declining house prices have played in subprime mortgage defaults.

Implicit Underwriting Standards. Beyond the objective factors of borrower and loan characteristics and the observed house price inflation, lenders may have access to other borrower information that is not objectively available to investors. For example, loan officers may enforce either weaker or stronger standards at differerent times with respect to factors that are not objectively included on loan applications. Fraudulent misstatements, such as inflating the borrower's income or the house appraisal, are more extreme examples. By their very nature, these factors are not objectively measurable.

Figure 7.7 The OFHEO House Price Index, Quarterly Changes at Annual Rates

Source: Office of Federal Housing Enterprise Oversight (OFHEO).

The recent study by Demyanyk and Van Hemert (2008) attempts to measure changes in the implicit underwriting standards from the actual delinquency and foreclosure data. They first estimate equations explaining the observed delinquency and foreclosure rates on the basis of the actual data on borrower and loan characteristics and house price inflation. Interpreting the residuals from these equations as the implicit underwriting standards, they then determine the role the three factors played over time in determining the delinquency and foreclosure rates. Their key result is that a significant and systematic decline in the implicit credit standards remains after controlling for the measured effects of changes in loan and borrower characteristics and of actual house price inflation.

Predatory Subprime Lending and Loan Modifications

As the subprime mortgage crisis has unfolded, the two most pressing issues from the consumer standpoint have been predatory lending and loan modifications.

Predatory Lending. Predatory lending arises when borrowers are induced to take out mortgage loans that are not in their best interest. The borrowers would presumably not have taken out such loans had they had full disclosure and understanding of the actual loan terms. A well-functioning and competitive market should protect uninformed borrowers from such predatory tactics, since it would be in the best interest of a competitor to inform the borrowers of a better alternative in order to obtain their business.

The evidence is clear, however, that certain parts of the subprime mortgage market have failed in this regard. One part of the problem is that the mortgages can be quite complex, with options both to defer payments and to refinance, as well as offering choices that include fixed and adjustable rates, and switching from fixed to floating rates over time. A second problem is that mortgage brokers obtain their fees as soon as the mortgage is originated, and some brokers have clearly acted without regard to their future reputation. A third problem is that fraud has appeared within the origination process, such as intentionally overstating borrower income or house values. The investors in the mortgage securities and the borrowers who ultimately default are both harmed by such activity.

Predatory lending has occurred even in the presence of a significant array of mortgage borrower protection legislation and regulations. Major existing programs include the following:

- The Truth in Lending Act (TILA) is part of Regulation Z of the Federal Reserve Act and is administered by the Federal Reserve. It requires clear and accurate information on loan terms and conditions, including disclosure of the annual percentage rate (APR), which informs the borrower of the effective interest rate including the effects of fees and points.

- The Homeowners Equity Protection Act (HOEPA) was passed in 1994 to augment the TILA, in order to provide further protections for consumers on mortgages with exceptionally high contract rates or fees. HOEPA requires a variety of additional disclosures as well prohibiting a variety of practices. The Federal Trade Commission handles HOEPA complaints.
- The Real Estate Settlement and Procedures Act (RESPA) is a third consumer protection act, passed in 1974, and administered by the Department of Housing and Urban Development (HUD). It sets detailed rules and procedures for the mortgage origination transaction, including the requirement of various disclosures at the closing.
- The general U.S. legal prohibitions on fraud and deceptive practices apply to mortgage lending, and are enforced by the Federal Trade Commission.

Given the breadth and depth of the existing mortgage borrower protection legislation, the open issues are not matters of principle, but rather how to make the existing protections generally more effective and how to improve certain specific components. For example, the President's Working Group on Financial Markets (2008), among others, has proposed licensing requirements for mortgage brokers, while the newly issued Blueprint from the U.S. Treasury (2008) proposes the creation of a new federal commission, the Mortgage Origination Commission (MOC). Although the existing protections can surely be improved, it must be recognized that destructive legislation would simply end all subprime lending.[23]

Jaffee and Quigley (2007b) also offer two innovative proposals for dealing with the predatory lending problem. The first is to use a specifically designed FHA mortgage as a standard alternative loan, and to require that all subprime lenders bring this alternative to the notice of their borrowers. The second is to create a new suitability standard, which would require that subprime lenders affirm that the borrowers to whom they are lending meet the standard. Stockbrokers, for example, have long been required to apply a suitability standard that ensures investors' goals and expertise are matched with the type of securities they are allowed to trade. The result is that only the more knowledgeable investors are allowed to trade in futures and options contracts. A potential drawback to suitability standards, however, is that the financial service providers may become overly cautious. This problem might be avoided if there were administrative remedies through which a consumer could petition to obtain the services, thus providing the service provider with a safe harbor against future complaints.

---

23 For example, the city of Oakland, CA, among others, passed an ordinance in 2002 that imposed punitive damages and unlimited assignee liability on all investors and securitizers, if a mortgage loan in which they were involved was later judged to be predatory. Not surprisingly, all securitization of Oakland mortgages abruptly ceased, as did most Oakland mortgage lending, until the ordinance was rescinded; see Fitch Ratings (2003) for further details.

Loan Modifications.[24] Loan default and foreclosure create deadweight costs, meaning that the process is costly to both the borrower and the lender, in effect a "lose-lose" outcome. It thus may be beneficial to both the borrower and the lender to avoid a mortgage default by modifying the loan terms to a level the borrower can afford. Lenders, however, are reluctant to gain a reputation for modifying loans, lest all their borrowers (current and future) apply for such modifications. The servicers on securitizations face similar reputational dilemmas, as well as contractual limitations on their powers.

It is noteworthy that loan modifications, or workouts as they are called, are common on commercial real estate loans. A key factor is that loan payments on commercial mortgages derive primarily from the rental income the landlord receives. If the rental income falls below the debt service required on the loan, then a default will be imminent. Since the rental income receipts are generally objective and verifiable, lenders do not face significant reputational costs when offering loan modifications to such commercial borrowers. On home mortgages, in contrast, borrowers may substitute consumption for the mortgage payments, and it will be difficult for lenders to objectively identify those consumers for whom the loan payments are truly impossible.

The outcome has been that relatively few home loan foreclosures have been avoided through the use of loan modifications. Facing rising pressure, the government has intervened to create a number of voluntary programs, and the FHA has set up a specific program, FHA Secure, through which it could refinance modified loans. Lenders and servicers have been generally amenable to these government programs, perhaps because the resulting loan modifications can be characterized as one-time emergency transactions. To date, however, the programs have achieved only limited success. In particular, it appears that many defaulting subprime borrowers are beyond such help, a point in evidence being that the default rates on once-modified loans are themselves very high.

There are also pending proposals for the government to intervene more directly with explicit subsidies to purchase or modify subprime loans. These proposals face three fundamental pitfalls:

- Prudent mortgage borrowers who have managed their budget and are making their loan payments object strenuously to using taxpayer dollars to bail out their less prudent brethren.
- Current mortgage borrowers will have incentive to stop making their payments in order to benefit from government bailout programs. It is implausible that government programs can be designed to subsidize only the intended beneficiaries of such programs.
- A current government bailout program provides future borrowers and lenders with an incentive to take on risky mortgages on the presumption that a future government bailout program will be available as needed.

---

24 Two recent studies, Brinkman (2008) and Cutts and Merrill (2008), provide extensive data and analytic discussions of the issues and experience relating to subprime loan modifications.

The Securitization of Subprime Mortgages

The securitization of subprime mortgages represents just the most recent step in a series of mortgage securitization innovations dating back 40 years. The Government National Mortgage Association (Ginnie Mae; GNMA) passthrough security, created in 1968, may be considered the starting point for the evolution of modern mortgage-backed securities (MBS). The GNMA innovation created, for the first time, a standardized format for pooling mortgages, which greatly expedited the sale of mortgage pools by lenders to final investors. The innovation was immediately accepted in the marketplace because the underlying mortgages and the MBS were directly guaranteed by the U.S. government.[25] Related innovations soon followed, such as the first organized futures market for trading long-term debt securities, which in turn helped to create a wide range of derivative instruments for hedging interest rate risk. Based on the GNMA innovation, Fannie Mae and Freddie Mac, the two large U.S. government-sponsored enterprises (GSEs), soon created their own MBS programs. Although the mortgages underlying the GSE programs are generally not government guaranteed, the two firms guarantee the interest and principal payments on their MBS, a guarantee that investors generally treat as tantamount to a government guarantee.

"Private Label" Mortgage-Backed Securities

The first fully private-market MBS programs—started during the mid-1980s—created mortgage securities that for the first time presented investors with a very real risk of default, since neither the mortgages nor the issuers had any actual or presumed links to government guarantees. The key innovation was a subordination structure—hence the term "structured finance"—in which the principal payments from the underlying mortgages were directed first to the most senior tranche, then to the second most senior tranche, and continuing downward, as in a waterfall, to each junior tranche, ending with the residual equity tranche. Nevertheless, unlike the GNMA and GSE MBS, these so-called "private label" MBS programs contained an undeniable default risk, which in principle could reach even the most senior tranche. It was thus critical that there be objective measures of these risks, so they could be disclosed to investors and priced appropriately. Solutions for the measurement problem included FICO scores for borrower creditworthiness and rating agency methodologies to evaluate each securitization tranche.

In addition to the basic senior and junior tranche structure, most private MBS used a variety of additional credit enhancements to raise their credit

---

25 GNMA was, and is, an agency within the U.S. Department of Housing and Urban Development. The underlying mortgages must be either FHA or VA government guaranteed mortgages. GNMA provides a further guarantee for payment of all interest and principal on the overall pool. The securities have equal standing with Treasury bonds.

ratings. The most economically interesting is an "excess spread" account. Excess spread refers to the excess of the weighted average coupon on the underlying mortgages over the weighted average coupons promised on the securitization tranches. This spread can be interpreted as compensation for the annual losses due to default that are expected to occur on the underlying mortgages annually. Most securitizations, therefore, accumulate their excess spreads in a reserve account to cover future losses. As long as the actual losses do not exceed the excess spread, investors receive their promised payments.[26]

Starting in the 1990s and continuing to the present, similar securitization methods were successfully applied to an ever-expanding range of risky loan classes, including auto, credit card, commercial mortgage, student, and business loans. Even catastrophe risks from natural disasters were covered through insurance-linked securitizations. Figure 7.8 shows the growth in the outstanding amount of the major categories, which totaled almost US$2.5 trillion at year-end 2007. The "other" category includes CDOs, among other items. The introduction of each new asset class required specific methods to

Figure 7.8 Non-Mortgage, Asset-Backed Securities Outstanding

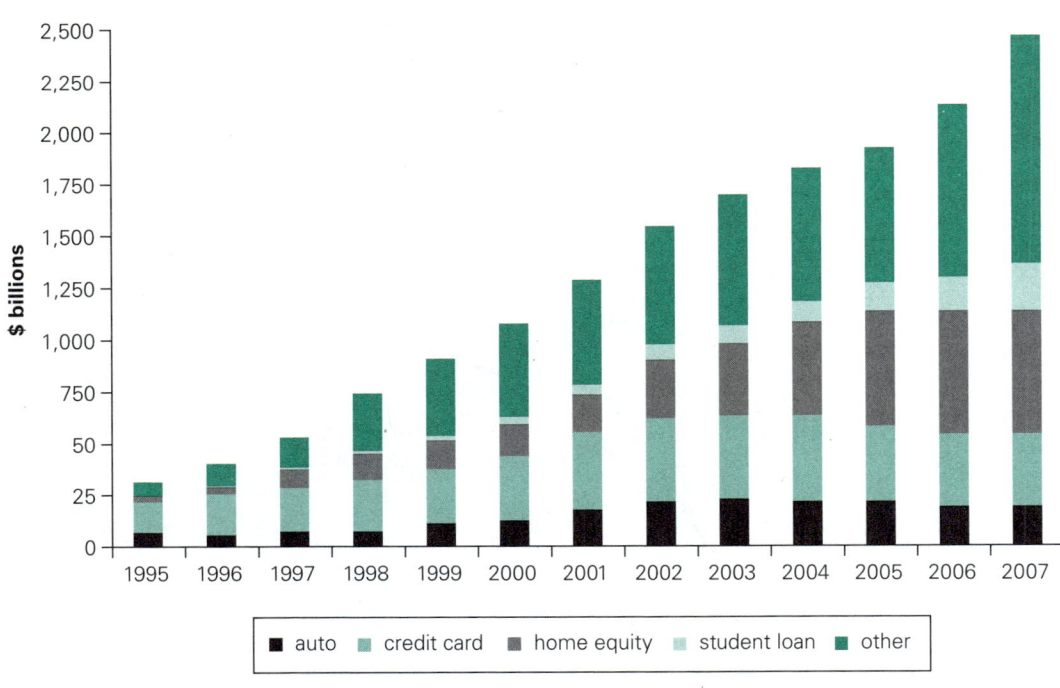

Source: Securities Industry and Financial Markets Association.

---

26 Unfortunately, in some subprime mortgage securitizations, the excess spread reserve account was distributed as a cash payout after a period of good performance. Then, when major defaults suddenly arose, the accumulated excess spread earnings were no longer accessible to protect the tranche investors.

measure the risk and to rate the new securities. To date, there have been no crises among these loan classes.

Subprime Mortgage Securitization

The securitization of subprime mortgages started in the 1990s, and it has steadily accelerated since then. Figure 7.9 shows the annual securitization rates—the percentage of the originated loans that were securitized—for the available mortgage categories since 2001. The securitization rates for FHA and VA mortgages—which are the mortgages used to create GNMA MBS—have always been close to 100 percent. The securitization rates for conforming mortgages—which are the mortgages eligible for the Fannie Mae and Freddie Mac MBS programs—have grown from 70 percent to now over 90 percent. The securitization rates for Prime Jumbo mortgages—which are prime mortgages that are not eligible for GSE securitization—have been much lower, now just reaching 50 percent. The relatively high securitization rates for the FHA/VA and GSE-conforming mortgages reflect the fact that investors recognize that the risk of loss due to mortgage default is virtually zero on these MBS. In comparison to these categories, the securitization rates on subprime and Alt A mortgages have

Figure 7.9 Securitization Rates for Mortgage Categories

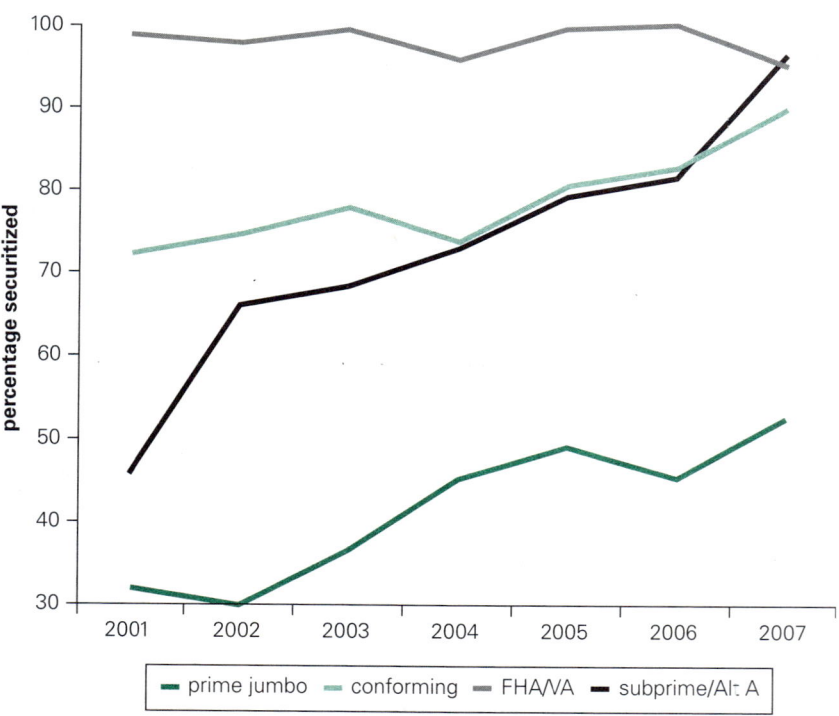

Source: Securities Industry and Financial Markets Association.

grown steadily, from under 50 percent to almost 100 percent in 2007.[27] It is important to note that the securitization rates for subprime and Alt A mortgages far exceed the corresponding rates for Prime Jumbo loans, even though the expected default rates on the subprime and Alt A category are far higher.

In most respects, subprime mortgage securitization represented a natural progression in the trend of the previous 20 years toward the securitization of increasingly risky loan classes. Subprime loans, however, represented the first time that securitization was applied to an entirely new loan class; previously, securitization was applied only to loan classes with an already well-documented record of satisfactory performance. The absence of a subprime loan track record limited the information that could be disclosed to investors and complicated the task of the rating agencies. Investors, however, received promised returns that exceeded the returns available on other classes of comparably rated securities. These excess returns appear to have been particularly effective in attracting investors to purchase the highest rated AA and AAA tranche. Given that the purchasers were only institutional investors, representing the largest and most sophisticated funds and banks, it is reasonable to assume that they understood that the excess spreads they were receiving were compensation for the "excess" risks they were bearing.

A less positive evaluation of the process used to securitize subprime mortgage loans is developed in the March 2008 *Policy Statement on Financial Market Developments* from the President's Working Group on Financial Markets (2008, p. 2, italics in original):

> Originators, underwriters, asset managers, credit rating agencies, and investors failed to obtain sufficient information or to conduct comprehensive risk assessments on instruments that often were quite complex. Investors relied excessively on credit ratings, which contributed to their complacency about the risks they were assuming in pursuit of higher returns. *Although market participants had economic incentives to conduct due diligence and evaluate risk-adjusted returns, the steps they took were insufficient, resulting in a significant erosion of market discipline.*

The President's Working Group statement raises two points, also raised in other discussions, namely that (i) securitization contributed to a decline in subprime lending standards by allowing the risks to be inappropriately transferred from the originating lenders to the final investors; and (ii) the rating agency methodologies failed to alert investors to the risks. We discuss these issues in turn.

---

27 Alt A mortgages are mortgages with incomplete documentation and possibly other attributes that make them less than prime. Alt A mortgages could also be interpreted as A–, compared with the B or C ratings of subprime loans. Unfortunately, the available data on subprime securitization rates do not separate Alt A and subprime mortgages.

Risk Transfer within the Securitization Process. The President's Working Group and others have suggested that the securitization process has created a "moral hazard," allowing subprime lending risks to be passed in a sequence starting with mortgage brokers, then to lenders, then to securitizers, and ending as risks in investor portfolios. Although it is understandable that each of these transactors might participate in the chain as long as they were confident they could transfer the risk to the next stage, it is perplexing why the final investors would accept the risks knowing that they were the end of the line. Had the final investors been unwilling to hold the risks, then, of course, the whole process would unravel.

So the key question is why the final investors purchased and held these highly risky securities. It has already been noted that the investors included only the most sophisticated institutional investors, in the form of hedge, pension, and foreign sovereign funds, and commercial and investment banks.[28] Thus, the President's Working Group and others must be suggesting that either the institutional investors were duped by inaccurate or incomplete disclosures, or that they had been negligent in their risk evaluations. To date, however, there is no direct evidence of either factor, and it does appear prima facie implausible that the largest, wealthiest, and most sophisticated institutional investors were systematically either duped or negligent. It also worth recalling that subprime lending was a new loan class with a limited historical record, so there had to be a large band of uncertainty around any estimate of expected loss.

The outcomes from risky lending are, of course, probabilistic. Thus, there is always the possibility of a disaster, and the newer the loan class, the less information there is to rule that out. Two sources of publicly available evidence also confirmed that subprime loans were highly risky:

- The Mortgage Bankers Association data shown in figures 3 to 5 were already being publicly released and publicized by 2002, showing that very large percentages of subprime loans had ended in foreclosure. In fact, the current percentage of loans in foreclosure (figure 5) has not yet reached the peak foreclosure rate from that earlier episode.
- Subprime mortgage loans with annual interest rates of, say, 3 percentage points above prime mortgage rates directly imply expected annual excess default rates on the order of perhaps 10 percent.[29] Furthermore, it appears that many of the hedge fund and investment bank investors were holding highly leveraged positions, which could readily create an effective 100 percent default rate. Consider, for example, an investor purchasing a $100 portfolio with $10 of equity and $90 of loans. A 10

---

28 The good news is that consumer investors were considered unqualified to purchase these securities directly, and that there were few, if any, attempts to create retail entities to sell the securities.

29 The derivation is straightforward. Assume, for the argument, that lenders lose 30 percent of the loan value on foreclosed loans. Then, if 10 percent of the loans default each year, the resulting loss rate will equal 3 percent (0.30 * 10 percent). Thus a 3 percent excess annual loan interest rate can compensate for a 10 percent expected annual excess default rate.

percent loss rate wipes out 100 percent of the investor's capital. These investors surely understood the ramifications of using high leverage. In summary, it is not plausible that the securitization process itself led to a systematic misrepresentation of the riskiness of subprime loans.[30]

There is a real problem, but it is caused by the intense concentration of securitized risks in certain investor portfolios. The concentration of securitized risks is ironic because a key benefit of securitization is to provide a flexible mechanism for disbursing risks across a wide class of diversified investors. The obvious explanation for why investors, such as Bear Stearns, concentrated subprime mortgage risks in their portfolios is that they expected to earn excess returns. This is also the obvious reason for why such investors also maintained a severe maturity mismatch, using very short-term borrowings to leverage a portfolio of long-term MBS.

The bottom line is that the massive losses associated with the subprime loan crisis are not due to the process of securitization, but to the investors who concentrated the risks from subprime MBS by adding leverage and a maturity mismatch, and both in extreme proportions. The basic value of securitization as a means for distributing and allocating risky securities to a wide range of diversified investors remains intact. It is investors, not securitization, which propagated the crisis.

Rating Agency Methodologies for Subprime MBS and CDO. The President's Working Group on Financial Markets (2008) and many others have attributed a key role in the subprime crisis to the significant underestimation by the major credit rating agencies (CRAs) of the risks associated with subprime MBS. Indeed, the major CRAs have all now acknowledged the underestimation and they all have programs in process to rectify the methodological failings. Nevertheless, it is useful in this part (i) to describe the primary basis for the methodological failings and (ii) to connect these failings with the comparable failings in the CRA ratings of CDOs.

---

30 Two recent empirical papers, however, argue that the securitization of subprime loans did create lax lending standards. Mian and Sufi (2008), also discussed in footnote (8), rely on the fact that loans in zip codes with intensive subprime lending were also intensively securitized. However, most classes of risky consumer loans, including credit card and auto loans, are also highly securitized. Thus, it would appear that the primary causation is that risky loans are securitized, not that securitization makes loans risky.

In another study, Keys, Mukherjee, Seru, and Vig (2008) rely on the fact that securitized subprime loans with FICO scores just above 620 (say 620+) have higher delinquency rates than securitized subprime loans with FICO scores just below 620 (say 620−), leading to their claim that lenders provided lax screening on their 620+ loans. The paper focuses on the 620 FICO score because it has been considered the standard minimum for Fannie Mae and Freddie Mac to securitize mortgages; the paper argues that lenders were lax on the 620+ loans because they anticipated these loans would be securitized. However, the 620− loans in the sample were also securitized, so it is not clear why the lenders would have had different incentives on these loans. Furthermore, given that there is no baseline standard for loan screening, it is unclear what is the meaning of "lax standards." It could just as well be said that the lenders provided superlative screening on their 620− loans. Most important, there is no evidence to suggest that the institutional investors in subprime securities were systematically unaware of the standards that were being applied.

The Failure in Rating Subprime Loan Securitizations

If they were individually rated, most subprime mortgages would receive a letter rating of B or C, depending on the quality of the specific mortgage.[31] Investors in subprime mortgage securities, however, purchase tranches of securitized pools of subprime mortgages. Thus, the ratings provided by the CRAs are determined tranche by tranche. The basic method employed to determine these ratings is easily summarized:

- A distribution for the annual default rates is estimated for each mortgage in the pool, based on historical data and the objective features of the loans and the borrowers in the specific pool (such as FICO scores, loan to value ratios, and so forth).[32]
- An estimate is made of the correlation coefficient that is expected to hold pairwise among all the loans in the pool. It is usually assumed that a single common correlation coefficient applies to all the pairs.
- Based on (1) and (2), the probability distribution of possible outcomes is computed.
- Based on the subordination structure proposed by the issuer and the distribution in (3), the probability of default and the associated letter rating are assigned to each tranche.
- The issuer may propose revised subordination structures and will receive revised ratings per (4), until the final subordination structure and ratings are determined.

Errors in this rating process arise primarily from errors in estimating the distribution in (1) or the correlation coefficient in (2). In understating the default probabilities of subprime mortgages (step 1), it appears the primary mistake of the CRAs was to understate the importance of house price declines in two regards: (i) house price declines were given insufficient weight as a determinant of mortgage default, and (ii) the likelihood of a significant decline in those prices was understated. This led to optimistic ratings, especially for the more junior tranches. At the same time, house price declines are a key systematic factor creating correlated mortgage defaults. Thus, by underestimating the importance of possible house price declines, the CRAs also underestimated the correlation of mortgage defaults (step 2). Higher correlation coefficients significantly raise the probability of a major crisis that may even reach the senior tranches. The bottom line is

---

31 For example, a primary newsletter covering the subprime market is called *Inside B and C Lending*; see http://www.imfpubs.com/imfpubs_ibcl/about.html. Also, LoanPerformance, the source of a primary database of subprime loans, refers to subprime loans as "BC loans."

32 The CRAs vary (individually, over time, and by loan class) whether their ratings are to be interpreted in terms of expected annual default rates or expected annual loss rates, the difference being whether expected recoveries are themselves modeled as part of the process. Once an average default or loss rate is determined for the pool, the simplifying assumption is commonly made that the average rate applies to each individual loan as well.

that by underestimating the importance of house price declines in the default process, the CRAs systematically underestimated the risks, and thereby overstated the ratings, across all tranches.

The Failure in Rating Collateralized Debt Obligations

CDOs represent a "resecuritization" in which a pool is created from the tranches of already issued securitizations, and a new structured vehicle is then issued on the basis of this new pool. As a common example, a CDO could be created by combing the already issued B tranches from, say, 20 existing subprime MBS. The goal for the issuer is to create a new securitization that provides additional highly rated (that is, above B) tranches. This is possible because the CRAs give CDOs credit for the diversification benefits they provide compared to individual MBS. In effect, a CDO is a "fund of funds" and there will be diversification benefits, assuming that the individual MBS tranches from which it is formed are not themselves too highly correlated.[33] Unfortunately, the CRAs underestimated the impact that house price declines would have in creating correlated losses on the subprime MBS tranches that formed the subprime CDOs. The result was a serious underestimation of CDO losses across all tranches.

Subprime Mortgage Securitization: Conclusions

The primary factor creating the subprime mortgage crisis was the boom and bust cycle in house prices. In the boom phase, rising prices motivated lenders and investors to put ever more money at risk. The CRAs reinforced these investment decisions by posting ratings that underestimated the impact that falling house prices could have on subprime mortgage defaults. The error, however, is properly shared among all the market participants—lenders, investors, CRAs, and even the monetary authority—since they all failed to recognize that their actions were creating a house price boom that would almost surely end in a crisis.

A second factor that significantly broadened the impact of the subprime crisis was the action of institutional investors to concentrate the riskiness of their subprime MBS portfolios by using extremely high leverage and by creating extreme maturity mismatches in their funding. This investment

---

33 Issuing a CDO can also be analyzed as an arbitrage transaction, in which a new pool is created by purchasing tranches from existing securitizations, then creating a new structure and selling the new tranche components. This raises the question why arbitrage did not extinguish any profit: that is, the very process of purchasing the existing tranche and selling the new tranche could be expected to drive the profits to zero. A possible answer is that the glut of world savings created an almost insatiable demand for highly rated debt instruments, and while individual investors potentially could have created their own diversified portfolios, transaction costs and perhaps asymmetric information induced these investors to accept a slightly lower yield on market-created CDOs. In this sense, the underlying markets are incomplete, and the CDOs provide an economic benefit in helping to span them.

strategy will always be crisis-prone independent of the underlying securities, as two examples confirm:

- The U.S. Savings and Loan crisis of the 1980s arose from leveraged and maturity mismatched portfolios, although the underlying securities were prime mortgages with minor default risk.
- The Long Term Capital Management crisis also arose from a leveraged and maturity mismatched portfolio, even though U.S. Treasury bonds were a primary instrument.

Subprime mortgage securitization has been intrinsic to both the over-expansion of subprime mortgage lending and the concentration of subprime risks in investor portfolios, so it must be considered an accessory to the crime. However, the fundamental economic benefit of securitization is that it allows risks to be widely distributed across diversified portfolios, while also matching each investor's risk tolerance with the appropriate tranche. This basic economic rationale for securitizing subprime mortgages has not been challenged by the subprime mortgage crisis.

The Subprime Mortgage Crisis and Financial System Regulation

The most dramatic ramifications of the subprime mortgage crisis have occurred at the level of the overall financial system, including the Federal Reserve's role in the recent merger of Bear Stearns. The discussion in this section reviews the major events of the subprime mortgage crisis that have had systemwide impacts on financial markets and financial institutions. The most important lesson learned at this level is the need to expand government regulation of the major investment banks.

The Systemic Risks Revealed by the Bear Stearns Crisis[34]

The Federal Reserve's actions to provide emergency funding to expedite the Bear Stearns merger reveals a fundamental weakness in the U.S. financial system that requires swift regulatory action. Two key facts were revealed by the Fed's actions:

- The Bear Stearns portfolio of subprime MBS and CDOs was sufficiently leveraged to create serious concerns that the firm's investment losses could exceed its capital resources. Furthermore, the portfolio had been funded with short-term loans, in effect a major maturity mismatch. By Friday, March 14, 2008, Bear Stearns feared it could no longer roll over its debt, and if actions were not taken before markets opened on Monday, March 17, Bear Stearns expected to fail on its obligations and therefore would require bankruptcy protection.

---

34 This manuscript was finalized before the subsequent bailouts of Fannie Mae, Freddie Mac, and AIG. It appears, however, that the comments made in the text remain valid for these later bailouts as well as for Bear Stearns.

- Bear Stearns was a principal counterparty in the over-the-counter (OTC) markets for interest rate, foreign exchange, and credit default derivatives. The worldwide outstanding notional amount of OTC derivative positions as of June 2007 was US$516 trillion, with credit default swaps alone accounting for US$43 trillion.[35] Bear Stearns was a central counterparty in all of these markets. It was thus plausible, even likely, that were Bear Stearns to take bankruptcy protection, there would be a cascade of failures, as Bear Stearns' creditors, upon not receiving their payments from Bear Stearns, would fail on their own obligations, and so on.

The Fed's emergency loan to expedite the Bear Stearns merger deviated from its standard rules by allowing the borrower both to post low-quality collateral and to deny the Fed the right of recourse to other assets if the loan were not repaid. The unique circumstances of the Bear Stearns crisis include (i) the very large dollar amounts, (ii) the generally weakened condition of most investment banks, and (iii) the need to avoid a formal Bear Stearns bankruptcy in view of that firm's very large positions as a derivative counterparty. Facing this situation, the Federal Reserve took the emergency action of providing the loan.[36] A key component of the agreement was that JP Morgan Chase took over all the counterparty obligations of Bear Stearns.

The Bear Stearns event has revealed that the derivative counterparty system now parallels the payments system as a fundamental component of the financial system's infrastructure. The implication is that the combination of risky investment strategies by investment banks and their central role as counterparties in the OTC derivative markets requires regulatory controls. Otherwise, as long as the investment banks continue to carry out risky investment strategies in combination with a counterparty business, the system is at high risk for another crisis.

The United States has a long-established and effective regulatory structure for the payments system as administered by the country's commercial banks. The explicit core elements are (i) a set of risk-based capital requirements, and (ii) a requirement for "prompt corrective action" (PCA). The latter requires that the commercial bank regulators take prompt action to require a troubled bank to obtain additional capital or to merge. Otherwise, the bank is promptly closed. Bank managers, of course, anticipate this regulatory action and thus take ex ante actions to avoid them. As a result, the number of U.S. commercial bank failures since 1995 has been minimal.

The proposal offered here is that those investment banks that choose to participate as counterparties in the OTC derivative markets must satisfy

---

35 The Bank for International Settlements (BIS) maintains an extensive database of the notional value of derivative positions outstanding by instrument, currency, maturity, contract form, and so forth.

36 In comparison, the Fed had no financial participation in the 1998 Long Term Capital Management liquidation.

expanded regulatory requirements that would make a replay of the Bear Stearns experience highly unlikely. One possible format for such regulation is to allow the investment banks to separate the capital that underlies their counterparty activities from the capital that underlies their investment activities. If this format were in force, losses suffered by the investment division, or even market fears of such losses, would not endanger the counterparty division, and therefore would not require Federal Reserve action. In brief, an expansion of federally mandated regulatory requirements should be required of the primary derivative market counterparties, in a manner that would parallel the requirements imposed on depository institutions to safeguard the payments system.

As it happens, the U.S. Treasury just issued (March 2008) a major policy proposal for the U.S. financial system, "The Department of the Treasury Blueprint for a Modernized Financial Regulatory Structure," hereafter referred to as the Blueprint. The Blueprint proposes a new regulatory framework based on three primary functions—market stability, prudential regulation, and business conduct regulation—to replace the current system, which is a complex mixture of functional and charter-based regulations. The Blueprint also proposes to rationalize the chartering of financial institutions, to merge the U.S. Securities and Exchange Commission (SEC) and the U.S. Commodity Futures Trading Commission (CFTC), and to create, for the first time, federal regulation of insurance activities.

The Blueprint, however, does not discuss the special problems relating to investment banks and their counterparty activities as they were revealed through the Bear Stearns merger. Presumably, it is intended that the SEC would continue to regulate investment banks as it does currently. Furthermore, under the market stability function, the Federal Reserve would continue to supervise the payments and settlement systems, but this activity would be distinct from prudential regulation, which is to be carried out by a new and separate entity.

In contrast, the Bear Stearns crisis would appear to require that the market stability and prudential regulation functions be highly integrated in order to ensure that the losses from a firm's investment activities not endanger its role as a central counterparty in the OTC derivatives system. It would seem that a core principle in this regard would be to expand the regulatory requirements imposed on OTC counterparties, a topic that the Blueprint does not raise.[37]

Market Illiquidity and Opaque Subprime Securities

A second major factor in extending the subprime crisis has been a breakdown in financial market trading and liquidity, which has allowed the market prices for many subprime securities to fall well below what many would consider their "fundamental value." In part, this reflects a "flight to safety"

---

37 Jaffee and Perlow (2008) provide more detailed proposals for the expanded regulation of the counterparty activities of the major investment banks.

in which investors attempt to acquire additional liquidity when facing a suddenly uncertain financial situation; this regularly occurs in financial panics. The unwillingness of investors specifically to purchase the apparently undervalued subprime securities and CDOs must also be attributed to the complex, opaque nature of these instruments.

The illiquidity problem is reinforced by "mark to market" accounting rules that generally require investment banks to report the declines in the market value of their investment portfolios. While mark to market accounting has the obvious benefit of providing investors with current information based on market prices, more complex questions arise when the informational content of the market prices themselves is itself limited due to illiquid markets and disrupted trading. It is unclear how the situation can be improved, but it has been an evident factor in propagating the effects of the subprime mortgage crisis across the financial markets. The Federal Reserve has responded appropriately to this situation by offering huge volumes of liquidity, including its new Term Auction Facility. However, to date it has not succeeded in reviving the effective demand for the subprime MBS and CDO instruments.

The subprime mortgage crisis has also revealed a comparable and fundamental weakness in the U.S. financial markets concerning structured investment vehicles (SIVs). U.S. commercial banks have long faced the dilemma that it is difficult, if not impossible, for an A-rated commercial bank to lend money to an AAA-rated operating corporation. In principle, the corporation has access to loanable funds in the commercial paper market at a lower cost than the bank could provide. As this issue developed in the 1980s, the banks acted to maintain their relationships with their AAA clients by creating SIVs, through which they could lend funds to AAA corporations at AAA interest rates. The SIV was an off-balance-sheet entity that would hold only AAA loans, and therefore could fund itself in the commercial paper (CP) markets at AAA interest rates. The CP markets, however, are subject to potential liquidity crises, and thus to ensure continuity in the SIV funding, the commercial banks provided their SIVs with an emergency backup line of credit.

The SIV mechanism worked well for many years, but it has been challenged as a result of the subprime mortgage crisis. The primary new issue is that some SIVs have invested in longer-term and riskier securities, including subprime MBS and CDO, while continuing to use short-term CP funding. It was thus only a matter of time before the CP lenders would become concerned with the quality of the SIV portfolios they were funding. The problem has further expanded because the underlying MBS and CDO securities are themselves complex and opaque, reinforcing the fears of the CP investors. The result has been a funding crisis for many of the SIVs, including a number of cases where the parent bank's backup facility has been used. The primary issue here lies with the investment and funding strategies applied by the SIVs, which is the same issue described above for subprime MBS and constant proportion debt obligation (CDPO) investors more generally.

Concluding Comments

The subprime mortgage crisis raises issues at three distinct levels: the subprime mortgage markets themselves, the securitization of subprime mortgages, and the mortgages' systemwide impacts on financial markets and institutions. The same issues are also relevant to the operation of mortgage markets in emerging economies. The following summarizes the major conclusions in each category.

Subprime Mortgage Lending

Subprime mortgage lending has provided funding to more than an estimated 5 million home purchasers, including more than 1 million first-time home purchasers. This benefit, however, is offset by the costs created by predatory lending practices, the difficulty of modifying loans, and the ramifications of borrower default. Various solutions have been proposed and some are already in action. Predatory lending practices should be controlled through additional regulatory actions. Programs have already been enacted to facilitate loan modifications for defaulting borrowers, but many of these borrowers are beyond help. The costs imposed on defaulting borrowers are actually limited, and useful information is already available to help these borrowers minimize the costs they face.

Subprime Mortgage Securitization

The recent report by the President's Working Group on Financial Markets (2008) and other studies have focused on securitization as a primary source of the subprime crisis. In contrast, the argument in this chapter is that information regarding the high risk of subprime mortgage securities has been readily available, and that it is implausible that the large and sophisticated institutional investors that purchased subprime mortgages were either duped or were negligent.

Responsibility for the subprime mortgage crisis is more properly shared among the market participants—lenders, investors, and the credit rating agencies—since they all failed to recognize that their actions relating to subprime mortgage lending were creating a house price boom that almost surely would end in a crisis. The subprime mortgage crisis, in fact, is only the most recent in a worldwide series of real estate boom and bust cycles. It is at least fitting, therefore, that the major direct costs of the crisis have been imposed precisely on these market participants. It can also be hoped that future market participants will better anticipate these developments, and it is possible that monetary policy should also take a more active role in dampening the boom phase.

Systemwide Effects on Financial Markets and Institutions

The subprime mortgage crisis has had major effects on both the financial markets and financial institutions. As a result of their highly leveraged and maturity-mismatched investments in subprime MBS and CDOs, many investment banks have suffered enormous losses. In particular, Bear Stearns had to be merged in order to avoid an imminent bankruptcy, and rumors continue to circulate concerning serious financial distress at other investment banks.

The near-bankruptcy of Bear Stearns and the clearly weakened condition of other investment banks has also had impacts on the financial markets. One serious problem is that the major investment banks are all central counterparties in the enormous OTC derivative markets. The actual failure of a major investment bank could thus create a chain reaction of failures and a financial market catastrophe. The Federal Reserve took its unique actions to facilitate the Bear Stearns merger precisely to avoid such a disaster. To avoid future reoccurrences, it is essential that the major investment banks face expanded prudential regulation.

A second serious financial market problem has been the lack of trading and liquidity for many of the subprime MBS and CDO instruments. This is a common symptom of a "flight to safety," but it has been magnified in the current crisis by the particularly opaque and complex nature of the subprime MBS and CDO instruments. Eventually, of course, the actions of opportune investors will drive market prices to their fair fundamental value and the trading volume and liquidity will return. In the meantime, the Federal Reserve has responded appropriately by dousing the system with liquidity, but with limited success to date.

References

Allen, Franklin, and Douglas Gale. 1994. *Financial Innovation and Risk Sharing.* Cambridge MA: MIT Press.

Angell, Cynthia, and Clare Rowley. 2006. "Breaking New Ground in U.S. Mortgage Lending." *FDIC Outlook*, Summer 2006.

Bardhan, Ashok, and Dwight Jaffee. 2007. "Impact of Global Capital Flows and Foreign Financing on U.S. Interest Rates," Research Institute for Housing America, September 2007, available at: http://housingamerica.org/default.html.

Bernanke, Ben. 2007. "Housing, Housing Finance, and Monetary Policy (2007)." Speech on August, 31, 2007.

———. 2005. "The Global Saving Glut and the U.S. Current Account Deficit." Speech on April 14, 2005.

Brinkman, Jay. 2008. "An Examination of Mortgage Foreclosures, Modifications, Repayment Plans and Other Loss Mitigation Activities." Mortgage Bankers Association Working Paper.

Brunnermeier, Markus, and Christian Julliard. 2008. "Money Illusion and Housing Frenzies." *Review of Financial Studies* 21(1):135–180.

Buckley, Robert, Patrick Hendershott, and Kevin Villani. 1995. "Rapid Housing Privatization in Reforming Economies: Pay the Special Dividend Now." *Journal of Real Estate Finance and Economics* 10: 63–80.

Buckley, Robert, Loic Chiquier, and Michael Lea. 2006. "Housing Finance and the Economy." Forthcoming in *Housing Finance in Emerging Economies*. World Bank, Washington, DC.

Chomsisengphet, Soiuphala, and Anthony Pennington-Cross. 2006. "The Evolution of the Subprime Mortgage Market." *Federal Reserve Bank of St. Louis Review* (January/February).

Cutts, Amy Crews, and Robert Van Order. 2005. "On the Economics of Subprime Lending." *Journal of Real Estate Finance and Economics* 30(2): 167–96.

Cutts, Amy Crews, and William Merrill. 2008. "Interventions in Mortgage Default: Policies and Practices to Prevent Home Loss and Lower Costs." Working Paper #08-01, March. Freddie Mac, Washington, DC.

Demyanyk, Yulia, and Otto Van Hemert. 2008. "Understanding the Subprime Mortgage Crisis." Supervisory Policy Analysis Working Paper 2007-05, Federal Reserve Bank of St. Louis. Available at: http://papers.ssrn.com/ sol3/papers .cfm?abstract_id=1020396.

Downing, Chris, Dwight Jaffee, and Nancy Wallace. 2008. "Are Mortgage Backed Securities a Market for Lemons?" Forthcoming in *Review of Financial Studies*.

Duffie, Darrell. 1995. "Financial Market Innovation and Security Design: An Introduction." *Journal of Economic Theory* 65: 1–42.

Eggers, Frederick. 2005. "Homeownership Gains during the 1990s: Composition Effects and Rate Effects." January. Office of Policy Development and Research, U.S. Department of Housing and Urban Development, Washington, DC.

Fitch Ratings. 2003. "Fitch Addresses Predatory Lending Legislation of Oakland, CA." Release of October 24, 2003. http://www.fitchratings.com.

Frame, Scott, and Lawrence White. 2002. "Empirical Studies of Financial Innovation: Lots of Talk, Little Action?" Working Paper Series 2002–12. Federal Reserve Bank of Atlanta.

Gerardi, Kristopher, Adam Hale Shapiro, and Paul Willen. 2007. "Subprime Outcomes: Risky Mortgages, Homeownership Experiences, and Foreclosures." Paper No. 07-15. Federal Reserve Bank of Boston.

Gramlich, Edward. 2007a. "America's Second Housing Boom." February. The Urban Institute, Washington, DC.

———. 2007b. "Booms and Busts: The Case of Subprime Mortgages." Economic Review, Federal Reserve Bank of Kansas City, 4th Quarter 2007.

Gennotte, Gerard, and Hayne Leland. 1990. "Market Liquidity, Hedging, and Crashes." *American Economic Review* 80: 999–1021.

Green, Richard, and Susan Wachter. 2005. "The American Mortgage in Historical and International Context." *Journal of Economic Perspectives* 19(4).

———. 2007. "The Housing Finance Revolution." Paper presented at the Housing, Housing Finance, and Monetary Policy symposium, Jackson Hole, Wyoming, August 31.

Grossman, Sanford. 1988. "An Analysis of the Implications for Stock and Futures Price Volatility of Program Trading and Dynamic Hedging Strategies." *Journal of Business* 61: 275–98.

Haurin, Donald, and Stuart Rosenthal. 2004. "The Influence of Household Information on Homeownership Rates across Time and Race. Abt Associates,

Office of Policy Development and Research, U.S. Department of Housing and Urban Development, Washington, DC.

International Monetary Fund. 2007. "Financial Market Update." July. IMF, Washington, DC.

———. 2008. "Global Financial Stability Report." January 29. IMF, Washington, DC.

Jaffee, Dwight. 1975. "Innovations in the Mortgage Market." In *Financial Innovation*, William Silver, ed. Lexington Books.

———. 1984. "Creative Finance: Measures, Sources, and Tests." *Housing Finance Review* 3(1) (January): 1–18.

———. 1994. *The Swedish Real Estate Crisis*. Stockholm: Studieförbundet Näringsliv och Samhälle (SNS, Center for Business and Policy Studies).

Jaffee, Dwight, and Bertrand Renaud. 1997. "Strategies to Develop Mortgage Markets in Transition Economies." In *Financial Sector Reform and Privatisation in Transition Economies*, ed. J. Doukas, V. Murinde, and C. Wihlborg. Amsterdam: Elsevier. Also published in Polish by Poznan University Press; also available as World Bank Policy Research Working Paper No. 1697, available at http://papers.ssrn.com/sol3/ papers.cfm?abstract_id=623883.

Jaffee, Dwight, and John Quigley. 2007a. "Housing Subsidies and Homeowners: What Role for Government-Sponsored Enterprises?" *Brookings-Wharton Papers on Urban Affairs: 2007*. Washington, DC: Brookings Institution Press.

———. 2007b. "Housing Policy, Mortgage Policy, and the Federal Housing Administration." Program on Housing and Urban Policy Working Paper No. W07-04, at http://urbanpolicy.berkeley.edu/publist.htm#Working%20Papers. University of California at Berkeley.

Jaffee, Dwight, and Mark Perlow. 2008. "Investment Bank Regulation after the Bear Rescue." Forthcoming in *Central Banking Journal*.

Keys, Benjamin, Tanmoy Mukherjee, Amit Seru, and Vikrant Vig. 2008. "Did Securitization Lead to Lax Screening: Evidence from SubPrime Loans 2001-2006." Available at SSRN: http://ssrn.com/abstract=1093137.

Kiff, John, and Paul Mills. 2007. "Money for Nothing and Checks for Free: Recent Developments in U.S. Subprime Mortgage Markets." IMF WPO/07/188, July. IMF, Washington, DC.

Levine, Ross. 1997. "Financial Development and Economic Growth: Views and Agenda." *Journal of Economic Literature* 35(2): 688–726.

———. 2003. "Finance and Growth: Theory, Evidence and Mechanisms." In *Handbook of Economic Growth,* ed. Philippe Aghion and Steven Durlauf. Amsterdam: Elsevier.

Litan, Robert. 1992. "Banks and Real Estate: Regulating the Unholy Alliance." *Conference Series No. 36, Real Estate and the Credit Crunch*. Federal Reserve Bank of Boston.

Mason, Joseph, and Joshua Rosner. 2007. "How Resilient Are Mortgage Backed Securities to Collateralized Debt Obligation Market Disruptions." February. Available at SSRN: http://ssrn.com/ abstract=1027472.

Mayer, Chris, and Tomasz Piskorski. 2008. "The Inefficiency of Refinancing: Why Prepayment Penalties Are Good for Risky Borrowers." February. Available at http://isites.harvard.edu/fs/docs/icb.topic185988.files/04_07_Piskorski.pdf.

Merton, Robert. 1992. "Financial Innovation and Economic Performance." *Journal of Applied Corporate Finance* 4(4) (Winter).

Mian, Atif, and Amir Sufi. 2008. "The Consequences of Mortgage Credit Expansion: Evidence from the 2007 Mortgage Default Crisis." January. Available at SSRN: http://ssrn.com/abstract=1072304.

Miller, Merton. 1986. "Financial Innovation: The Last Twenty Five Years and the Next." *Journal of Financial and Quantitative Analysis* 21(4), December.

———. 1992. "Financial Innovation: Achievements and Prospects." *Journal of Applied Corporate Finance* 4(4), Winter.

Modigliani, Franco, and Donald Lessard. 1975. "New Mortgage Designs for Stable Housing in an Inflationary Environment." Conference Series No. 14, Federal Reserve Bank of Boston.

Molyneux, Philip, and Nidal Shamroukh. 1999. *Financial Innovation.* New York: John Wiley & Sons.

Pennington-Cross, Anthony, and Soiuphala Chomsisengphet. 2007. "Subprime Refinancing: Equity Extraction and Mortgage Termination." *Real Estate Economics* 35(2): 233–63.

Piskorski, Tomasz, and Alexei Tchistyi. 2007. "Optimal Mortgage Design." Working paper. University of California, Berkeley. Available at http://www.haas.berkeley.edu/finance/shp18.pdf.

———. 2008. "Stochastic House Appreciation and Optimal Subprime Lending." Working paper, February.

President's Working Group on Financial Markets. 2008. "Policy Statement on Financial Market Developments." March 13. Washington, DC.

Reinhart, Carmen, and Kenneth Rogoff. 2008. "Is the 2007 U.S. Sub-Prime Financial Crisis so Different: An Historical Comparison." (January). NBER Working Paper No. W13761 Available at SSRN: http://ssrn.com/abstract=1088675.

Rosengren, Eric. 2007. "Subprime Mortgage Problems: Research, Opportunities, and Policy Considerations." Federal Reserve Bank of Boston.

Renaud, Bertrand. 2008. "Mortgage Markets in Emerging Markets: Constraints and Feasible Development Paths." Chapter 11, pp. 253–288. In Danny Ben-Shahar, et al., eds., *Mortgage Markets Worldwide.* London: Blackwell Publishing.

Renaud, Bertrand, and Kyung-Hwan Kim. 2007. "The Global Housing Price Boom and Its Aftermath." Forthcoming, *Housing Finance International* 21.

Silber, William. 1975. "Towards a Theory of Financial Innovations." In *Financial Innovation*, William Silber, ed. Lexington Books.

Tufano, Peter. 1989. "Financial Innovation and First-Mover Advantages." *Journal of Financial Economics* 25: 213–40.

———. 1995. "Securities Innovations: A Historical and Functional Perspective." *Journal of Applied Corporate Finance* 7(4), Winter.

U.S. Treasury. 2008. "The Department of the Treasury Blueprint for a Modernized Financial Regulatory Structure." March. Washington, DC.

Vickrey, James. 2007. "How Do Financial Frictions Share the Product Market: Evidence from Mortgage Originations." Federal Reserve Bank of New York, October.

Warnock, Veronica, and Francis Warnock. 2007. "Markets and Housing Finance." NBER Working Paper No. W13081, May. National Bureau of Economic Research, Cambridge, MA.

White, Lawrence. 2000. "Technological Change, Financial Innovation, and Financial Regulation in the U.S.: The Challenges for Public Policy." In *Performance of Financial Institutions: Efficiency, Innovation, Regulation,* ed. Patrick Harker and Stavros Zenios. Cambridge, UK: Cambridge University Press.

Wray, L. Randall. 2007. "Lesson from the Subprime Meltdown." Working Paper No. 522. December. The Levy Economics Institute, Bard College, Annandale-on-Hudson, NY.

Index

Boxes, figures, notes, and tables are indicated by *b*, *f*, *n*, and *t*, respectively.

A

Abdel-Raman, Hesham M., 139, 140
Accra (Ghana), 56
Acemoglu, Daron, 14, 142, 152
Ades, Alberto F., 85, 127, 142, 151, 153, 155*n*22
Africa. *See* Middle East and North Africa; Sub-Saharan Africa; and specific countries by name
African Growth and Opportunity Act (AGOA), 60
Agarwala, R., 25
agglomeration and agglomeration effects, xx, 115–28
   advantages of, 14–19
   in developing countries, 81–83
   externalities, 117–19
   knowledge sharing and spillovers, 118–19, 122
   law of large numbers, 119
   productivity gains, 116–17, 121–25
   reasons for location in cities, 116–17
   size of cities
      efficient or optimal, 125–28
      limits on, 119–21

specialization, 117–18
transaction costs and complementarities, 118
AGOA (African Growth and Opportunity Act), 60
Agrawal, Ajay, 105
agriculture, economic growth and shift away from, 8–12, 12*f*, 151
Alcalá, Francisco, 106
Alesina, Alberto, 154
Alexandersson, Gunnar, 150
Allen, Franklin, 198*n*2
Almeida, Paul, 105
Amiti, Mary, 49, 90, 155*n*22
Angel, Shlomo, 168–69, 180, 191
Angell, Cynthia, 198*n*4
Annan, Kofi, 167
Annez, Patricia Clarke, xix, xxiii, 1, 67, 115, 133, 167, 189, 197
Argentina, 26, 31, 85
arguments against urbanization, 19–26, 115–16
   developing countries' desire to limit rural-urban migration, 67, 68, 91–92
   governmental views, 3, 33–36*t*, 115–16
   Harris-Todaro model of counterproductivity of rural-urban migration, 22–24, 91–93, 92*f*, 121, 140

W

Wachter, Susan, 209n19

Wacziarg, Romain, 55n3, 106

wage curve, framework for urbanization and economic growth in developing countries, 71–72, 71f

wage/income gradients in global market, 53–54, 53f

Wahba, Jacqueline, 149

Wang, Hyoung Gun, 84

Warnock, Veronica and Francis, 202n12

Washington consensus, 188

water and sewage systems
in developing countries, 22
"killer cities" in UK, role of finance in cleaning up, 10–11b

Weeks, John, 6n2, 23, 25, 26

Welch, Karen Horn, 106

welfare economics
framework for urbanization and economic growth in developing countries, 75–79, 76f
of housing policy
in developed countries, 171–76
in developing countries, 180–85

Western Europe. *See* Europe and Central Asia; European Union; specific countries

Wheaton, William C., 122, 150, 154

Wheaton, William C. and Lewis, Mark J., 122, 154

Wheeler, Christopher H., 102, 148

White, Lawrence, 198n3

Willen, Paul, 206n16, 209n18, 214

Williamson, Jeffrey A., 2

Williamson, Jeffrey G., 10–11b, 20, 22n10, 23, 24, 143, 150, 153, 155, 183

Wodon, Quentin, 83

Wohl, Anthony S., 11b, 183

women and urbanization, xiv

workforce. *See* employment/unemployment

workouts (modification of loans) for defaulting borrowers, 200, 217

World Bank
housing policy initiatives supported by, 186–91
mortgage technology transfer via, 203

World Development Report (World Bank), 8

World Population Policies (UN), 33

Wright, Mark L. J., 75n7, 99

Wu, Weiping, 13

Y

Yepes, Tito, 82, 90

Yoshida, Atsushi, 155n22

Yusuf, Shahid, 13

Z

Zang, Hyoungsoo, 124, 154n21

Zenou, Yves, 93n25

Zhang, Xiaobo, 145, 151

Zhou, Quanhou, 28

Zipf's law, 149n17

Zlotnik, H., 24

Zolt, Eric M., 142, 152